W9-AGB-858

The Middle East Military Balance 2001–2002

The BCSIA Studies in International Security book series is edited at the Belfer Center for Science and International Affairs at Harvard University's John F. Kennedy School of Government and published by The MIT Press. The series publishes books on contemporary issues in international security policy, as well as their conceptual and historical foundations. Topics of particular interest to the series include the spread of weapons of mass destruction, internal conflict, the international effects of democracy and democratization, and U.S. defense policy.

A complete list of BCSIA Studies appears at the back of this volume.

The Middle East Military Balance 2001–2002

Shlomo Brom and Yiftah Shapir
Editors

BCSIA Studies in International Security

Jaffee Center for Strategic Studies
Tel Aviv University

The MIT Press
Cambridge, Massachusetts
London, England

John F. Kennedy School of Government, Harvard University
Cambridge, Massachusetts 02138
(617) 495-1400

Library of Congress Control Number: 2002109408
ISBN: 0-262-06231-3

The Middle East Military Balance is published with the generous assistance of the Dr. I. B. Burnett Research Fund for Quantitative Analysis of the Arab Israeli Conflict.

Jaffee Center for Strategic Studies
The purpose of the Jaffee Center is, first, to conduct basic research that meets the highest academic standards on matters related to Israel's national security as well as Middle East regional and international security affairs. The Center also aims to contribute to the public debate and governmental deliberation of issues that are--or should be--at the top of Israel's national security agenda. The Center seeks to address the strategic community in Israel and abroad, Israeli policymakers and opinion makers, and the general public. The Center relates to the concept of strategy in its broadest meaning, namely the complex of processes involved in the identification, mobilization, and application of resources in peace and in war, in order to solidify and strengthen national and international security.

This book was typeset in Israel by Kedem Ltd., Tel Aviv, and was printed and bound in the United States of America.

Cover photo: Development Options for Cooperation: The Middle East/East Mediterranean Region 1996. Government of Israel, Jerusalem: August 1995.

Contents

Contents *(continued)*

Contents *(continued)*

Preface

The violence that broke out between Israel and the Palestinians in late September 2000 has demonstrated that overall, the forces favoring stability and the status quo continue to predominate in the Middle East. These forces, despite coming under strain in the wake of the El-Aqsa Intifada, have prevented the collapse of Israeli-Palestinian negotiations from turning into a wider regional conflict in 2001 and early 2002. This does not mean, however, that the ongoing Israeli-Palestinian violence has been free of severe negative effects. Israeli-Palestinian violence has dragged on, fostering negative reactions in the Arab world, and spreading pessimism in its wake. It has also demonstrated, once again, the folly of underestimating those forces that could undermine future stability.

Moreover, the sheer scale of the attacks that took place in the United States on September 11, 2001 has had far-reaching consequences throughout the Middle East. While it is not clear how long these consequences will continue to be felt, there can be no doubt that they will not be limited to Afghanistan or al-Qa'ida. The effects of September 11 have already had an impact on the violent conflict raging between Israel and the Palestinians, and on the prospects for the resumption of the negotiations process. Regardless of how these effects play out, there is no denying that the Middle East, with its overwhelming Muslim majority, is at the center of the storm. The repercussions from the bombing could well be profound, on both the social and the political levels.

The first part of this volume is divided into five chapters, dealing with the strategic developments in the Middle East. The first chapter analyzes the main factors that have led to changing moods in the region. It will argue that these factors threaten to narrow the 'window of opportunity' that has existed since the Gulf War for a peaceful resolution of the Arab-Israeli conflict. The second chapter describes the violent confrontation that has developed between the Israelis and the Palestinians, as well as its regional consequences. The third chapter analyzes developments in the Persian Gulf region, while the fourth discusses the roles and influence of extra-regional actors in the Middle Eastern arena. Finally, the fifth chapter will explore various developments in the region's strategic balance.

The second part of this volume, compiled by Yiftah Shapir, provides the most detailed data available in open literature regarding the composition of the region's military forces. It is updated until early 2002. Since changes in the region's military balance rarely develop overnight, we expect the balance to remain accurate for most of 2003.

The Jaffee Center launched its study of military forces in the Middle East in the early 1980s. The first volume analyzing these forces was published in 1983 and, beginning in 1985, the volume was produced on an annual basis.

The *Middle East Military Balance 2001–2002* is the third to be published by MIT Press in the framework of the BCSIA Studies in International Security. Previously they had been published in conjunction with the Jerusalem Post and Columbia University Press. The publication is yet another facet of the growing relationship between Tel Aviv University's Jaffee Center for Strategic Studies and the Belfer Center for Science and International Affairs at Harvard University's John F. Kennedy School of Government. JCSS is grateful to Graham Allison, Director of the Belfer Center, and to Steven Miller, Director of the International Security Program at the Center, for having initiated the relationship that resulted in the production of this volume.

Finally, I would like to express my gratitude to those who made the preparation of this volume possible. Moshe Grundman, assistant to the Head of the JCSS, coordinated every aspect of completing this volume and bringing it to press; Daniel Levine made an invaluable contribution in translating and editing the text. Yoel Kozak and Tamir Magal performed the difficult task of compiling, updating and setting the data on the region's military forces; helpful assistance and comments were provided by JCSS researchers, research assistants and documentation managers, especially Orna Zeltzer, Tamar Malz, Shahar Koren and Avi Mor.

I am also deeply indebted to Karen Motley, Executive Editor at the Belfer Center, for the time and energy she invested in supervising the entire production process and for the extreme care and patience she demonstrated during the months that resulted in the publication of this volume.

Shlomo Brom
Senior Research Associate, JCSS

Tel Aviv
May 2002

Note on Usage and Style

Several different schools of usage exist for the transliteration of Hebrew and Arabic names and places, all of which are extremely complex and tend to the esoteric. In general, this volume employs spellings and usages as they most commonly appear in English, with an eye to what is most likely to be familiar to the well-informed (but not multi-lingual) English-language reader. Hence, Hosni Mubarak appears rather than Husni Mubarak, Ehud Barak rather than Ehud Baraq, etc. Similarly, place-names reflect English usage: Cairo, Jerusalem, and Gaza, are used rather than Al-Qahira, Yerushalayim/Il-Quds, or 'Azza. The spelling for Al-Jazeera, the Arabic-language satellite news network, reflects the English spelling that appears on that organization's English-language web-site.

Particular difficulty relates to rules governing Arabic nouns that take the article *al/el* ('the') and Hebrew rules of *beged-kefet*. These have also been rendered according to most common usage. Hence, Muhammad a-Durra is used instead of Muhammad al-Durra, but the Arabic name for the El-Aqsa Mosque complex is given as the Haram el-Sharif, rather than al-Haram ash-Sharif, despite the fact that these usages reflect inconsistent application of the aforementioned rules. With regard to *beged-kefet*, this volume follows modern Israeli usage rather than classical usage, hence the Israeli Parliament is the Knesset, rather than the Knesseth.

State names are given according to familiar forms used in English, even if these contradict the official (Latin alphabet) spelling. Hence Turkey appears, rather than Türkiye. States are usually given by their commonly used name, hence Egypt, Jordan, Russia, and Libya, rather than the ARE (Arab Republic of Egypt), The Hashemite Kingdom of Jordan, The Russian Federation, or The Great Libyan Socialist Arab Jamahariya. The Palestinian National Authority is referred to by its shortened name, the Palestinian Authority (or as the PA).

By contrast, titles are generally given formally, hence, German Federal Minister for Foreign Affairs Joschka Fischer, rather than German Foreign Minister Joschka Fischer. However, this is not done when the formal title tends to obscure the function, as in the case of George Tenet, who is called here CIA Director rather than DCI (i.e., Director of Central Intelligence). When referring to royalty, the *court titre* is used – hence, King Abdullah II rather than HM Abdullah II, King of the Hashemite Kingdom of Jordan.

There is a degree of political disagreement over the correct nomenclature regarding political-geographic realities that developed in the wake of the 1967 Arab-Israeli War. Choices in this nomenclature were made with an eye to common English usage and are not an attempt to impose a specific political interpretation on these events. Israeli communities inside the green line are referred to as towns or cities. Israeli communities outside of the green line are referred to as settlements. The territory immediately to the west of the Jordan River that has been held by Israel since 1967 is referred to as the West Bank or the Occupied Territories, rather than Judea and Samaria or the Administered Territories.

PART I

MIDDLE EAST STRATEGIC ASSESSMENT

Shlomo Brom

Chapter One

Major Developments in the Middle East

Despite various ups and downs, the Middle East at the close of the twentieth century seemed charged with an atmosphere of optimism, at least among key decision-makers and ruling elites. The fuel that fed this sense of optimism – a vision of which was set out by Shimon Peres in a book aptly titled *The New Middle East* – was continuous progress in the Middle East peace process. However, that mood changed entirely following the outbreak of violence between Israel and the Palestinians in late September 2000. The sense of optimism and progress was replaced with tension, violence, and an abiding pessimism regarding the future of the peace process, which seemed to be moving backwards. Despite the fact that changes had been in the offing for some time, the intensity of the shift still surprised many observers. As of late 2001, it was still too early to determine whether the terrorist attacks of September 11, 2001 would cause a real shift in the direction of developments, but they certainly added to the atmosphere of gloom.

The factors that contributed to this growing pessimism were as follows:

- *Oslo at a standstill.* Despite the expectations of its progenitors, the Oslo process had not created an environment conducive to reaching a permanent settlement of the Israeli-Palestinian conflict. The conflict's complex layers proved too great for the process to overcome. Different explanations were given for this: first, the gaps between the two sides' positions might have been so great that they could not possibly have been overcome. Alternatively, it is possible that an otherwise workable process was doomed by the miscalculations of both sides. Indeed, these two explanations are not mutually exclusive.
- *The United States eclipsed.* Despite U.S. pre-eminence as the world's "sole remaining superpower," and despite unprecedented standing following the Gulf War, the United States did not enjoy unlimited influence in the region. A number of regional actors retained a surprising degree of maneuvering

room, even when their actions threatened U.S. interests.

- *Iraq ascendant.* Saddam Hussein's regime survived. It put an end to monitoring and inspections carried out by the United Nations Special Commission on Iraq (UNSCOM), succeeded in weakening the effects of the sanctions, and rejuvenated its international standing to some degree.
- *Reform setbacks in Iran.* Conservative forces in Iran stymied the agenda of pro-reform leaders, though candidates representing the latter continued to perform strongly at the polls.
- *Weapons of mass destruction.* There was some success in slowing Iranian and Iraqi efforts to develop surface-to-surface missiles and weapons of mass destruction. With that, neither state had abandoned its intentions in this field, and both were continuing their efforts at development and acquisition.
- *Socioeconomic issues.* Most of the Arab world remained stuck in the throes of economic recession and stagnation. Arab states had not succeeded in positioning themselves as players in the new global economy, and many came to view globalization as more of a risk than an opportunity. Moreover, states that had expected a 'peace dividend' were bitterly disappointed: the fruits of peace yielded only a slim harvest. This disappointment reduced the overall openness of the Arab world to globalization, since the peace process and entry into the global economy were perceived as part of the same process. For many states, entry into the peace process was an attempt to open up to the West, since the risks entailed were similar (angering Islamic elements, increasing economic inequality, etc.). The failure of states like Jordan to derive prosperity from the peace process has served to discredit openness to the West in general.
- *New leaders at the helm.* The inter-generational transfer of power that took place in many Arab regimes created a leadership vacuum at a time when strong leadership was needed. Though most of the regimes in the Arab world were stable and did not face serious internal challenges over the course of 2000–2001, the new leaders themselves suffer from a sense of insecurity, and the crisis atmosphere weighed heavily on their actions.

Given these developments – some major changes, and others merely hopes or expectations of positive developments that failed to materialize – there were fears that the crisis between Israel and the Palestinians would seriously undermine the regional status quo. These fears persisted, despite the essential stability of the underlying strategic balance in the region. Indeed, the factors underpinning the regional status quo not only remained constant in 2001, but have in some ways become even more salient.

The persistence of these fears served to demonstrate that the strategic balance in the Middle East was by no means the only factor at work in the region. Other factors were important as well, such as the degree of motivation among various non–status quo actors to effect fundamental changes in the political make-up of the region. In addition, ideological, psychological, and emotional factors also played a role. To these were added the possibility of finding modes of action that bypassed the constraints imposed by the overall strategic balance of the region. For example, some anti-Israel elements, recognizing that Arab armies could not compete with the battlefield superiority of the Israel Defense Forces (IDF), successfully shifted their emphasis to low-intensity tactics, such as terrorism, guerilla warfare, and civil uprisings. By their nature, these tactics rendered the IDF's advantages in traditional warfare largely irrelevant. Israel's withdrawal from Southern Lebanon in mid–2000 drove home the idea that such tactics could prove effective, and showed once again that Israeli deterrence, while strong in many areas, was not effective in this particular type of confrontation.

In these sorts of conflicts, different parameters came into play. Traditional military thinking had to give way to considerations of popular mood and the public's willingness to sustain losses. In addition, each side exploited the international media, as well as the media of the other side. Finally, the leaders directing the conflict needed to display a high degree of political acumen, balancing military and political moves in order to attain victory.

The overall strategic balance still clearly favored Israel in 2001, and the IDF retained a clear-cut military superiority over its potential enemies. Its military strength (in traditional terms) continued to increase, as did its mastery over the elements of modern (or perhaps, post-modern) warfare. By contrast, the Arab states, with the exception of Egypt and the oil-rich states of the Gulf, were presiding over aging forces that were rapidly falling into obsolescence. The increase in the price of oil recorded over 2000–2001 did not significantly alter this reality: Israel continued to enjoy the patronage of the world's sole remaining superpower, while by and large its rivals did not.

Internal political divisions also hampered the strategic potential of the Arab world. Pan-Arabism has long given way to territorial nationalism, with each country focused primarily on its own affairs and interests. Consequently, the Arab world remained politically divided. This was seen in the lukewarm reactions of the Arab world to the El-Aqsa Intifada: for most Arab regimes, Israeli-Palestinian violence remained little more than an irritant, one which they would have liked to push to the sidelines. Until early 2002, they involved themselves in the crisis only to the extent that public opinion, which was hostile to Israel and supportive of the Palestinians, obligated them to do so. Most would have preferred to make the Palestinian issue disappear from the regional agenda altogether.

Many observers have likened the confluence of interests that made the Israeli-Arab peace process possible to a 'window of opportunity.' It was this window of opportunity that enabled the signing of a Jordanian-Israeli peace deal. It also allowed a series of interim agreements to be reached between Israel and the Palestinians, and made possible serious negotiations between Israel and the Syrians. Had this confluence of interests disappeared over the course of 2001? Was the Middle East entering a new era in which progress in the peace process would give way to violent conflict? Had the proverbial window of opportunity closed?

As of early 2002, the answer to this question seemed to be a qualified "no." On the face of things, the strategic balance remained constant: Israel retained its military edge, the Arab states were divided and focused on internal problems, and U.S. hegemony remained unchallenged. Most Arab regimes – which successfully met the challenge posed to their stability by radical Islamic movements – would have liked to see a renewal of the peace process, as would have Israel. Thus, while developments such as the ongoing Israeli-Palestinian violence may have narrowed the window of opportunity to some extent, it would be an exaggeration to say that it has closed entirely.

The difficulty is that, in order to return to a state in which this window of opportunity could be exploited, several difficult obstacles need to be met first:

- The cycle of violence and counter-violence between Israel and the Palestinians has to be brought under control. Each side feels victimized by the other – forced against its will to defend itself. The dominant desire was to respond to acts of violence by exacting revenge. These developments, moreover, took place against a backdrop of near-total mistrust between the two sides, which made the complete cessation of violence – a pre-condition for any effective negotiation – extremely difficult to achieve.
- The events of 2000–2001 negatively affected public opinion on both sides. Both became increasingly disenchanted with, and mistrustful of the peace process. Both societies, moreover, began to demonize the other.
- Hatred and opposition of Israel were on the increase in various parts of the Arab Middle East. Images of Israeli soldiers facing unarmed Palestinian civilians, brought into Arab homes by the media, had a powerful effect on public opinion. While the region's various regimes might have wished to curtail the influence of the Israeli-Palestinian conflict and to return to their regular agendas, the public mood made it difficult for them to do so. Their ability to contain, limit, and channel this mood was further circumscribed by new, independent sources of news and information that enjoyed a higher level of editorial freedom than did traditional, state-run media services. Most

notable among these were satellite television stations like Al-Jazeera and the Arab News Network.

- In Israel, there was disappointment from the Palestinians' violent response to what Israelis perceived as a brave attempt to reach a final status agreement by former Prime Minister Ehud Barak. This had a profound effect on the internal political discourse, as reflected in the elections that brought Ariel Sharon into power in February 2001 and in public opinion polls and surveys. There was great mistrust of Palestinians in general and particularly of their leadership, in the person of Palestinian Authority Chairman Yasser Arafat. Little credence was now being given to the view that an agreement with the Palestinians was feasible, or that the Palestinians would have upheld their part of such an agreement, had one been reached.
- In Israel, the shifts in public opinion noted above led to major changes in the political map. The political camp that favored moderation, and was willing to make significant concessions in order to reach a settlement with the Palestinians, suffered a mortal blow. In the February 2000 elections, right-wing leader Ariel Sharon beat Ehud Barak in a landslide victory. Even if the violence had ended – or merely declined considerably – these shifts would have nonetheless made it difficult to reach an agreement. The right wing held a clear majority within the Sharon-led National Unity Government and would certainly have approached negotiations with less flexibility than did Barak. On the Palestinian side, internal divisions increased, and voices willing to take a stand independent of Arafat's leadership were gaining strength. In particular, the opposition to Arafat from within his own political camp grew, as shown by the rising influence of the Tanzim, the armed militia of Arafat's Fatah movement. This reduced Arafat's freedom of action. With less political capital than before, Arafat found it difficult to take the dramatic step of moving from the present violence into meaningful negotiations with Israel and preferred to side with the militants in his camp who were orchestrating terror activities.
- Prior to September 11, the Bush administration had not been willing to invest significantly in influencing the two sides toward a cessation of violence and a renewal of negotiations. America's newfound reticence reflected its own disappointment in the process and a new skepticism regarding its potential. All of this had led the administration to adopt a position that projected both weakness and a lack of dedication to the entire undertaking. In the aftermath of the Bin Laden attacks on the United States, the Bush administration was forced to recognize the risks of abstention from active involvement in this turbulent area.

- There was a need to neutralize the influence of actors that opposed a renewal of the process, and which viewed the renewed violence as an opportunity to foster a long-term Israeli-Palestinian impasse. These actors included Iran, the Iraqi leadership, the Hizballah in Lebanon, and other radical Islamic organizations.

In June 2001, both Israelis and Palestinians agreed to a cease-fire based on a plan set forth by U.S. CIA Director George Tenet to implement the recommendations of the Mitchell commission. The Tenet plan provided an opportunity to test the abilities of all sides to overcome the difficulties inherent in moving from violence to political engagement. It pitted the desire that existed on both sides for a renewal of the peace process against the difficulties involved in reducing the level of violence needed for such a renewal to succeed. In the months following the formulation of the Tenet-Mitchell plans, no progress was made in achieving a complete cessation of violence, and on the eve of September 11 it seemed as if they were headed for a complete collapse. Following the attacks of September 11, and the U.S. decision to lead an international coalition against terrorism, significant changes could be observed in the behavior of both the Palestinian and the Israeli leadership. However, these changes proved insufficient for the implementation of the Tenet-Mitchell package.

Both crises, moreover, have pointed out the complex web of interrelationships that connect different sub-regions in the Middle East. Here it is useful to recall how the peace process began, in the wake of the Gulf War. The consequences of that war influenced the strategic balance of the entire region. It weakened the power of radical regimes that opposed reconciliation with Israel, strengthened divisions among Arab states, and increased U.S. dominance over the region as a whole. This in turn created confluent interests between Israel and a number of Arab regimes. It is not by coincidence that the Madrid Conference, which opened the door for the negotiations that have taken place over the last decade, convened in the wake of that war.

Ten years later, it seemed that the relationship between the Gulf and the Arab-Israeli arena was having the opposite effect. Saddam Hussein's power was growing – he even used the events of September 11 to further provoke the United States – and the Bush administration seemed unable to stop him. This served to embolden those forces that opposed U.S. hegemony in the Middle East. Iraq showed that it was possible to pursue a policy that displeased the United States, without having been forced to pay an unbearable price for doing so. This could not have escaped the awareness of Palestinian Authority (PA) Chairman Arafat, who had himself opted on various occasions to provoke the United States. In parallel, growing anti-American sentiments in the Arab public, fed by ongoing Israeli-Palestinian violence, made it difficult for the United States to re-form its Gulf War coalition. This in turn made it harder to ensure the level of Arab cooperation that was deemed essential for pursuing an effective policy of containing Iraq, let alone for changing its regime.

The moderate majority in the Arab world remained interested in preventing the Israeli-Palestinian violence from sliding into a regional confrontation, and as of early 2002, it had succeeded in doing so. Some states managed to avoid any role at all in the violence. Others, which were closer to it (especially Egypt and Jordan), adopted policies intended to contain its dimensions, though not always successfully. The leaders of this latter group of states found that they were unable to influence the Palestinians effectively when their own domestic audiences so clearly favored Palestinian positions.

By contrast, Syria's policies at the opening phases of the violence sought to fan the flames of a regional conflagration. Under the leadership of its new President, Bashar al-Assad, Syria supported and encouraged Hizballah actions against Israel, risking another cycle of violence. Syrian actions were ultimately restrained by a combination of political and military factors. Heavy pressure was brought to bear on Syria by the United States, the European Union (EU), and moderate states in the region. At the same time, Israel responded to Hizballah actions by targeting Syrian army positions in Lebanon, demonstrating the degree to which Syria was unprepared to face Israel militarily. Taken together, these factors moved Syria to rein in the Hizballah (though the organization did not completely cease its activities), which reduced the likelihood of armed confrontations along the Israeli-Lebanese border. By early 2002, Hizballah reactions to further escalation in the Israeli-Palestinian sphere raised doubts whether this delicate equilibrium could be maintained.

Iran is particularly relevant concerning this danger of escalation. It continued to play a destabilizing role in the context of the Israeli-Arab conflict, supporting extremists in both Lebanon and the PA. The U.S.-led war on terrorism gave Iran an opportunity to improve its relations with the United States. However, this potential for positive change was blocked by Iran's conservative religious leaders.

Chapter Two

The Israeli-Arab Sphere: Crisis and Consequences

Israel and the Palestinians

As of early 2002, Israel and the Palestinians remained locked in the throes of the violent confrontation that broke out in September 2000, following unsuccessful attempts by Israeli Prime Minister Barak and PA Chairman Arafat to reach a final status agreement. Moreover, the deep political divisions underlying this conflict have led a number of observers to predict that it will not fade quickly or easily. The El-Aqsa Intifada, the name chosen by the Palestinians for this struggle, set in motion a series of internal changes within both the Israeli and Palestinian camps. These changes hampered efforts to end the violence and threatened to turn it into a chronic state of affairs – a development that would make resolving the crisis progressively more difficult, barring substantial political developments.

The Israeli Domestic Scene

On the Israeli side, there was a major domestic-political shift. From the Israeli public's perspective, the Palestinian leadership made a conscious choice not to take advantage of the peace offer made by the Barak government and to adopt violence instead. This perception, in turn, had a deep effect on Israeli voters. For some years, a nearly equal balance – one might even say a deadlock – had existed between those on the left and center of Israeli politics and those on the right. The former had voiced varying degrees of support for reconciliation with the Palestinians and had been willing to make difficult concessions in order to reach peace with them. The latter continued to harbor deep suspicions regarding the ultimate goals of the Palestinians and showed either limited or total unwillingness for concessions.

The positions presented by the Palestinians in the final phases of the negotiations, and what Israelis perceived as their considered decision to resort to violence, effectively broke this deadlock in favor of the right. Palestinian insistence that the right of return applied to refugees that wished to return to Israel, and not only to a Palestinian state, raised considerable doubts among Israelis about the Palestinian commitment to a two-state solution. These doubts, when coupled with the Palestinian decision to resort to violence, effectively destroyed the alliance between the Israeli center and the Israeli left. Palestinian violence convinced a critical mass of Israelis that the existential fears voiced by the right, which had been discredited after the initial advances of the negotiations, had actually been valid all along. It now appeared to the Israeli center that the Palestinians were not truly interested in peace, and their 'real' goal was to use the peace process as a stepping stone to effect the phased destruction of Israel.

Events in the Arab world at large further reinforced this perception among Israelis. Declarations made by Arab states during the Camp David II negotiations, which rejected Arafat's right to make concessions on Jerusalem, stripped him of pan-Arab support for any kind of flexibility. Following the outbreak of violence, the Arab states expressed what seemed to Israel like monolithic support for Palestinian positions. Diplomatic sanctions by Jordan and Egypt undermined the Israeli public's faith in the durability of its existing peace agreements. In early elections held on February 6, 2000, this shift in attitudes led a stampede of voters away from the center and the left, giving Likud candidate Ariel Sharon a landslide victory. Even among those who continued to support Ehud Barak, many adopted more hawkish views and advocated a tougher stance *vis-à-vis* the Palestinians.

With these developments as a canvas, Prime Minister-elect Sharon was able to form a government of national unity between his own party, the Likud, and the Labor party. However, this government, unlike the Labor-Likud unity governments of the 1980s, was not formed based on the principle of equality between its two largest participants, and its right-wing flank had a clear majority. A government so composed could effectively tackle the violent confrontation with the Palestinians, for a number of reasons: first, it had the assured support of the Israeli public, necessary in a struggle where the popular support and social unity were a *sine qua non*. Second, the presence of both right and center-left elements gave it resilience: Labor's presence provided credibility for harsh measures, should the government decide to take them, while also providing structural limitations that would hold the extreme right in check. Labor's presence also lent the government a greater degree of international credibility and legitimacy than a narrow right-wing government could have been expected to enjoy. This move seemed to pay off, at least initially: following its formation, the new government took a number of harsh military steps that went beyond what the Barak government had done, without incurring overly harsh international condemnation.

However, this resilience came at a price. The very assets which give the government its resilience in the face of violence could have paralyzed it, had the time come to formulate policies geared toward reducing violence, or effecting a resumption of negotiations. Given the government's right-wing orientation, any attempt to formulate conciliatory policies would necessarily have become an issue of contention. Here it is necessary to recall that the peace process is based on the principle of land-for-peace – a principle that has never been wholly accepted by the Israeli right. To that extent, Palestinian violence and the suspension of negotiations removed the dilemma with which they had been forced to grapple since the start of the Oslo process. Given that any proposal for negotiations would have been intended to reinstate a process based on territorial concessions, it is clear that the government's right wing would have had no choice but to reject them. In other words, any offer with even the slightest chance of attracting the Palestinians would have placed the right and left flanks of the government at loggerheads, and would likely lead to the breakup of the unity coalition.

Following its formation, the government stated that it would not agree to a resumption of political negotiations as long as Palestinian violence continued. The continuation of the violence at a constant level, therefore, ensured the survival of the unity government, since it effectively silenced the differences of opinion regarding the peace process. However, even if Labor had left the government, Prime Minister Sharon would still have been able to form a narrow right-wing government that would have ensured his majority in the Knesset. Such a government, though, would have had clear limitations. The Prime Minister would have been more vulnerable to right-wing pressures calling for a more aggressive policy regarding the Palestinian issue, which would have drawn increased fire from the international community. Even if such a process were to have led to early elections, it seems certain that the shift in public opinion since the outbreak of violence would have brought the right back into power with a substantial margin.

Immediately following the elections there were voices, both in Israel and abroad, that suggested that Sharon would behave differently as Prime Minister than he had in the past—that despite his political track record, there was a possibility that he would pursue a conciliatory policy with the Palestinians and seek some sort of agreement. Supporters of this position pointed to another Prime Minister, Menachem Begin, who rose from the right and ultimately signed a peace agreement with Egypt. However, Sharon's performance in 2001 and early 2002 did not support this supposition. While Sharon did show a degree of moderation, refraining from drastic or irreversible military steps, there has been no indication that his core positions have changed. Moreover, an analysis of his political situation seemed to preclude such a possibility: Sharon needed the right in order to remain in power over the long term. Moreover, statements that he had made after taking office did not show any changes in his traditional positions: minimal territorial concessions to the Palestinians and keeping – at the very least – a majority of the settlements in place. Indeed, when compared to the Barak government, even his ability to maintain a posture of relative restraint seemed limited. There were two reasons for this: first, as noted, his core political-strategic outlook seemed to preclude this. Second, the voters that gave him their support expected him to make good on his promise to deliver personal security. As long as this promise remained unfulfilled, the public pressure on him to make a show of force could only have increased.

Despite the strong hawkish swing in Israeli public opinion since the outbreak of the El-Aqsa Intifada, a number of trends took place that would likely make it easier to reach a future agreement with the Palestinians. The first of these was a consensus that formed among Israeli voters regarding the creation of a Palestinian state, albeit within the framework of an agreement. This consensus received official license in a speech delivered by Foreign Minister Shimon Peres before the United Nations General Assembly in early November 2001, with Prime Minister Sharon's consent. The second was a growing acceptance of the position that a final-status agreement would require the evacuation of a considerable number of settlements. The third was a rising desire on the part of Israelis to disengage from the Palestinians. This could be discerned in polls that showed a general acceptance of the transfer of Arab neighborhoods within Jerusalem to Palestinian sovereignty. In the eyes of much of the Israeli Jewish population, the question of the demographic balance between Jews and Arabs in the country had grown in prominence. The need to ensure a Jewish majority in Israel fostered a willingness to concede lands that might in the past have been seen as bearing strategic, religious, or symbolic importance, in order to achieve separation from the Palestinians. However, as public opinion polls conducted in early 2002 demonstrate, the escalation of violence resulted in a general hardening of positions regarding these issues.

The Palestinian Domestic Scene

Among the Palestinians, there was a parallel distancing from the peace process. At the beginning of the violence, there was evidence that some circles within the Palestinian Authority did not see the purpose of encouraging a state of confrontation. Despite identifying with the goals of the PA *vis-à-vis* Israel, they questioned the decision by Chairman Arafat in terms of timing and tactics.

However, rising numbers of casualties and ongoing anti-Israeli incitement in mosques and in the Palestinian media drowned these voices out. Polls taken among the Palestinians showed that support for the present violence was on the rise. While Israeli responses to the El-Aqsa Intifada caused considerable hardship for the Palestinian populace, the PA's leadership had managed to deflect resentment away from itself and onto Israel. Indeed, the PA may have had more to risk by an end to violence than by its continuation: if the violence had been brought to an end without any visible achievements, it would likely have resulted in a backlash directed squarely at the Palestinian leadership. The Palestinian public would have wondered what good had come from the hardships that it had been forced to bear. Moreover, Arafat seemed to have realized this.

The violence also had a direct influence on Chairman Arafat's political standing, which had suffered both because the peace process was deemed a failure and because the PA, under his leadership, had become a corrupt and inefficient political machine. The renewed violence changed all of this, returning him to undisputed leadership of the Palestinian people's historic struggle for national liberation. In the longer term, however, the ongoing violence set substantial changes in motion within Palestinian society, in the form of increased standing for local leaders who were involved personally in the violence, which could threaten Arafat's leadership. These leaders were able to use their prominence in the armed struggle to enhance their personal authority and prestige, allowing them to undermine decisions made by the PA Chairman. This, in turn, accelerated a process of fragmentation that threatened to turn the PA from a national body into a collection of loosely connected city-states.

Some of Israel's countermeasures, particularly the cordoning of the West Bank and Gaza into districts among which there was no movement of goods or persons, contributed to this process of fragmentation. Combined with the endemic violence of the Intifada, this process threatened to bring about a collapse of Palestinian civil institutions. In terms of prestige, the civil authorities could not compete with the various focal points of Palestinian violence. At the same time, the Palestinian security services reached a kind of alliance with various opposition groups, among them radical Islamic movements like the Hamas and the Islamic Jihad. This decision greatly curtailed Arafat's freedom of action.

Throughout 2001, there were varying estimates regarding the degree to which Arafat had lost control over the situation. Many indicators of Arafat's control over the PA were often mixed with disinformation that was meant to serve the political interests of either side, which made this question even more difficult to answer definitively. Both the Palestinians and their regional allies were interested in achieving a resumption of negotiations without making a prior commitment to halt the violence. To that end, the PA clearly stood to benefit from the impression that Chairman Arafat would have *liked* to bring about a cessation of violence, but was *unable* to do so. For only, this line continued, if negotiations were renewed and yielded positive results would Arafat have been able to reassert control and effect a reduction of violence. Similarly, it was convenient for some Israeli political circles to portray Arafat as having total control of the situation, describing him as a master manipulator who had hoodwinked both Israel and the international community. The logical conclusion for such a line of thinking was that Arafat was seeking to renew negotiations while retaining the use of violence as a pressure tactic at the negotiating table. Though this claim could very well have been true, it is easy to see how such a reading of events would have served Israel's interests.

While the situation in question was extremely dynamic, it nonetheless appears that the truth was somewhere between these two positions. While Arafat still had effective control over most of the important positions in the Palestinian Authority, cracks did appear in his authority, which could have degenerated into a total loss of control. This was seen to explain why Arafat could achieve short-term drops in the overall level of violence in order to serve specific political or diplomatic goals, but was less successful in enforcing longer-term decisions. Drops in violence were registered for short periods, such as during U.S. Secretary of State Colin Powell's visit, or following the declaration of a cease-fire after the deadly suicide attack on a Tel Aviv dance club in June 2001. At the same time, attempts to effect a permanent cessation of certain kinds of attacks were less successful. For example, bans on shooting on Israeli targets from within Palestinian population centers or on the use of mortar fire against targets within the green line were only imperfectly observed. In any case, it seemed clear that as long as the violence were to continue, the cracks in Arafat's authority would only increase, even if the process was a gradual one.

Developments in the Confrontation

The Palestinians had a number of interests that were served by the outbreak of violence, while Israel had few or none. Hence, it should not be surprising in retrospect that the Palestinians tried to perpetuate and harness the violence to score diplomatic achievements. Since Israel was primarily interested in a return to the *status quo ante*, its use of force was intended to effect an end to the violence and to deny the Palestinians the objectives they sought.

Consequently, the Palestinians had generally been those that initiated escalatory moves. Israel's moves, though at times certainly feeding the cycle of escalation, were largely responsive. Such was the case when the Intifada began.

The Palestinians initiated the use of violence through violent civil uprisings and shootings from territories under their control into Israeli-controlled areas in the West Bank and Gaza. This was followed by shooting attacks on vehicles, roadside bombs, and suicide attacks, and later, by the use of mortar and rocket fire against Israeli settlements. An escalatory pattern could also be discerned from the choices of targets made by the Palestinians: attacks on isolated settlements gave way to shootings on Israeli neighborhoods in East Jerusalem, and to terrorist attacks within the green line. Those organizations that were under the authority of Chairman Arafat at first limited most of their activity to areas within the West Bank and Gaza, though they did not entirely refrain from bombing attacks within Israel proper. The Hamas and the Islamic Jihad, which have traditionally acted independently of – and at times directly at odds with – organizations subordinate to Chairman Arafat, also resumed terrorist activities. This resumption followed the Authority's decision to end restrictions on the activities of these organizations and to release their activists from PA custody. Their activities followed traditional patterns, focusing primarily on suicide bomb attacks and car bombs within Israel. However, with the general escalation of the conflict in early 2002, the difference in *modus operandi* among these organizations became increasingly blurred.

As the fighting continued, cooperation between radical Islamic organizations and forces under the control of the PA Chairman – including the Authority's various security services – increased. In the case of the various PA security services, the different preferences of the commanders of these bodies largely dictated the degree and form of their involvement. Some were greatly involved in the fighting, even taking outright part in terrorist operations, while others had little involvement, or none at all.

Since 1996, following the violence that broke out in the wake of the opening of the Hasmonean tunnel in Jerusalem, both Israel and the PA had been aware of the possibility that a violent confrontation could erupt between them. However, the IDF was better able to translate that time into preparations on the ground, developing operational responses and training its forces accordingly. Among the Palestinians, preparations for such an eventuality primarily took the form of efforts to amass weapons beyond the limits set forth in the interim agreements through smuggling and illicit purchases from criminal elements within Israel.

The gap in preparations and operational capabilities between the two sides came into clear relief in the opening phases of the military confrontation, during which the Palestinians sustained much heavier losses than did the IDF. With that, as the violence continued, the Palestinian 'learning curve' swung upward; their forces effectively made a transition to guerilla and terrorist tactics, against which standing armies generally have difficulty formulating a response. The result was increased numbers of Israeli casualties, though Palestinian losses remained higher. The Palestinians also attempted to acquire capabilities that would counterbalance Israel's superiority in means and *materiel*. These attempts included relatively large-scale Palestinian smuggling operations, including underground tunnels from Egypt, which served as conduits for smuggling weapons into Gaza. Israel's efforts at interdiction turned up anti-armor and anti-aircraft missiles, including Strela missiles. The Palestinians were also interested in acquiring weapons that would have improved their ability to fire on civilian targets from greater distances, such as mortars and rockets. In addition, the Palestinians developed the means to manufacture their own arms. Using a decentralized network of small workshops, the PA successfully manufactured both mortars and mortar shells without being detected by the IDF. However, these efforts did not increase overall Palestinian capabilities significantly. Hence, suicide bombings remained their most effective weapon.

As a response to Palestinian escalation in both means and methods, the IDF pursued escalatory policies of its own. IDF responses, which were undertaken largely following the formation of the Sharon-led government, were based on three major patterns:

- IDF-initiated actions against Palestinian operatives and commanders who were involved in the fighting against Israel, by a variety of means (the policy of 'focused prevention');
- The use of precision-guided munitions against targets associated with the Palestinian security services, both from the ground and by means of helicopter gunships;
- The dispatching of Israeli forces into 'A' areas (areas defined by the interim agreements as being under full Palestinian civil and military control) in order to stop attacks emanating from those areas or to destroy Palestinian emplacements within them.

At first, leaders in both the IDF and the Israeli government believed that the IDF would be able to take over and hold small swatches of 'A' areas for extended periods of time, both to put pressure on the PA and to improve the IDF's tactical positions in some locations. However, international reactions to such moves were sharper than expected, and so it was decided that incursions into 'A' areas would be of short duration. Nevertheless, an exception to this decision was observable in late March 2002, when the IDF launched a large-scale ground attack against what it termed Palestinian terrorist infrastructures in 'A' areas in the West Bank, in response to a particularly deadly series of suicide bombings.

Additional escalatory responses undertaken by Israel included increasing the number of actions taken at the IDF's initiative (i.e., which were not necessarily in direct response to concrete acts by the PA), especially against the PA's security services. The final phase of escalation was the use of fighter planes against pinpoint targets, also associated with the PA security services, in Palestinian-controlled cities and towns. Such escalations were not without risk: as IDF responses grew in severity, the risk of a mistake or miscalculation also rose, as did the potential for inadvertently inflicting large-scale civilian casualties. Beyond the obvious humanitarian tragedy that would have resulted from such a mistake, the consequences would have been disastrous for Israel, unleashing a firestorm in media and diplomatic circles.

In addition to outright military actions against the Palestinians, Israel took other steps, which were intended to restrict the Palestinians' freedom of movement and create domestic pressure on the PA. The most obvious of these was the closure, which prevented Palestinians from entering Israel, with the exception of a very small number of workers. Additional measures included the division of the Palestinian areas into 'cantons' by denying the free movement of people among the different regions of the West Bank that were under PA control. Finally, Israel stopped transferring import and value-added-taxes collected by it for the PA, as obligated under the interim agreements. The Israeli administration also sought ways to bring the fight directly to the Palestinian leadership in a way that would have spared undue suffering to rank-and-file civilians; however such ways were not found.

Despite the risk of spiraling violence, there were a number of constraints on both sides which moderated and slowed the pace of escalation. Israel understood that restraint was in its interest. From its perspective, the Palestinian use of violence was meant to score coups in diplomatic-media circles, and in this framework, the Palestinians had a particular interest in goading Israel into brutal reactions, especially against civilians. An incident in which massive numbers of civilians were killed (like the one that occurred in Lebanon, when an Israeli artillery shell mistakenly hit the UN headquarters at Kafr Kana in 1996) would likely have conferred significant benefit upon the Palestinian leadership in the political-diplomatic arena. Israel clearly wished to avoid this. In addition, despite considerable frustration directed at Arafat by much of the present Israeli administration, most Israeli leaders still believed that the only alternative to him was anarchy. From Israel's perspective, chaos would have been worse than Arafat's continued rule, though contrasting opinions on this point did make themselves heard in Israeli governing circles. Therefore, the primary efforts were directed at conducting an effective military campaign against Palestinian violence, without bringing about a collapse in Arafat's rule. Beyond this, the presence of the Labor party in the Israeli ruling coalition also ensured a measure of restraint.

On the Palestinian side, there was evidence of some favoring a more rapid escalation of violence, arguing that mounting provocations would eventually result in harsh Israeli reactions that would serve the Palestinian cause. However, the Palestinian leadership was aware of the dangers involved in over-escalation. These dangers were twofold: first, escalation against Israel would have provided the IDF with an opening to revert to more conventional military operations where it had an advantage. Second, the PA leadership realized that such provocations would have subjected Palestinian civilians to increasing suffering and misery. The PA leadership knew that it could not take the support of the Palestinian people for granted, and it showed sensitivity to fatigue or unwillingness among the civil populace. A typical example of this was seen in the Palestinian shooting attacks on Gilo, a Jewish neighborhood in East Jerusalem, from the nearby Palestinian town of Beit Jallah. These attacks exposed Beit Jallah to harsh Israeli reactions, while the international community viewed them as a needless provocation. In the meantime, the attacks led to an anti-PA backlash among its residents. Upon realizing this, Chairman Arafat moved vigorously to stop the shooting from Beit Jallah, which was relatively successful. Events were expected to reach a kind of equilibrium, punctuated with occasional ups and downs, with each side periodically changing its tactics and choice of weapons. With that, the potential for particularly horrific events – whether committed by accident or by intent – brought an element of randomness into the equation. Episodes such as the suicide bombing of the Tel Aviv Dolphinarium in June 2001, which killed twenty-one Israeli youths, could have forced the sides into a spiral of violence, despite a common desire to prevent escalation. Such dangers are the primary difficulty in this form of confrontation: events often overtake both sides, forcing a loss of control, even if both sides clearly wish to avoid such an eventuality. This proved to be the case in late March and early April, 2002.

The aftermath of the attacks that took place in the United States on September 11, 2001 also had an inhibiting effect on both sides. Israeli leaders were at first under the mistaken impression that the "war on terrorism" declared by the United States would endow them with more freedom of action in their war against Palestinian violence. However, they soon learned that the United States looked upon any escalation in the Israeli-Palestinian conflict as a potential stumbling block along their path to forming an international anti-terror coalition. Since the United States felt that such a coalition needed a number of Arab and Muslim states, the need to restrain Israel and to reduce the violence of the Israeli-Palestinian conflict became particularly acute. For its part, the Palestinian leadership was terrified from the very beginning that the attacks on the United

States could 'pull the rug out from under them,' and concluded that they had to avoid being identified with the terrorists.

If escalation were nonetheless to have taken place, it would likely have taken the form of more ambitious or far-reaching actions against the other side. The PA was believed to have yet-untapped means at its disposal, such as rockets with greater ranges than those used to date, as well as infantry-fired anti-tank missiles. The Palestinians could have attempted to broaden their military activities by invading and conquering an Israeli settlement, by widespread shooting attacks on Israeli communities adjacent to the green line, or by attacks on main transportation arteries within Israel.

On the Israeli side the possibilities were greater still, comprising the full spectrum of options and weapons available to a well-equipped standing army. Israel could have considerably expanded its use of air and ground attacks against the PA with heavy weapons, or could have taken over PA-controlled areas for extended periods in order to purge them of suspected terrorists. From Israel's point of view, the turning point would have come if it had changed its position regarding the value of the PA. Had Israel decided it no longer had an interest in preserving the Authority, its military operations would likely have increased in both pace and scope. Such a decision would likely have led to actions intended to destroy the PA and expel Chairman Arafat and his ruling circle from the West Bank and Gaza. Israel was close to adopting such a strategic move in April 2002.

There were some on the Israeli right who claimed that Palestinian violence would be checked by the controlled use of massive force. However, this option was not acceptable to the Israeli left, and circles on both the left and the right apparently did not believe that the Intifada could be stopped entirely without some sort of diplomatic or political breakthrough. The most Israel could have hoped for through the use of increased force and pressure was a reduced level of violence and casualties. Experience from the first Intifada, which began in 1987 and only came to a complete end after the beginning of the Oslo process, reinforced this perception, having demonstrated that the Palestinian population has considerable staying power, even after extended periods of material distress.

This should not be taken to mean that the Palestinians had endless reserves for continuing the conflict at the same level of intensity – there were signs of fatigue and attrition. Popular participation in the conflict with Israel, which in any case had been limited compared to the first Intifada, declined considerably. For this reason, as the violence wore on, the nature of the confrontations moved in favor of guerilla and terrorist tactics.

Attempts to Renew Negotiations

Ariel Sharon's victory at the polls, and the formation of a Likud-led government under his leadership, made renewal of final status negotiations based on what was reached at Camp David nearly impossible. The parties on the right were unequivocal in their rejection of the concessions that Prime Minister Barak had either made or seemed willing to make. Within Labor, several of Barak's fellow party members came to believe that the Palestinians were not negotiating in good faith. Barak's political needs, they claimed, had obligated him to reach an agreement with the Palestinians, regardless of cost. However, this line of thinking continues, the PA had never intended to reach agreement in the last round of negotiations. Rather, the PA's goal had been to exploit Barak's weakness to extract concessions, which would then become the starting point for future negotiations. This, in turn, would allow them to achieve still more concessions later on.

Little wonder, then, that when the new government was formed, Labor and Likud agreed on coalition guidelines that called for the pursuit of long-term partial or interim agreements, rather than a renewal of final-status negotiations. Sharon's worldview ruled out the attainment of a final status agreement as a realistic goal. Since such an agreement did not seem possible, both sides had to make do with some sort of long-term interim agreement. In this framework, Sharon was willing to make tactical concessions to the Palestinians, and was even willing to conduct simultaneous negotiations on both interim and final-status issues, but without determining a binding timetable for progress on the latter. It must also have been clear to all concerned that in the course of such negotiations, Sharon would adopt much tougher positions than did Barak.

In addition, the guidelines of the new government specified that there were to be no negotiations with the Palestinians while the violence continued – not even negotiations geared toward partial agreements. While these guidelines were binding on the government as a whole, its left and right flanks disagreed regarding their exact meaning. The right-wing parties to the government took it essentially at face value. That is, from their point of view, no meaningful negotiations could take place until all violence came to a halt, and while the violence continued the government's sole mandate was to negotiate ways to bring about its cessation. However, the government's Labor members had a more moderate interpretation of this condition. According to their view, two main elements constituted a cessation of violence by the PA. First, an unequivocal directive from the PA Chairman to his subordinates to end violence and incitement directed against Israel, accompanied by steps to enforce such a directive. Second, a renewal of efforts intended to curb the activities of opposition groups, including the arrest of members of the Hamas and the Islamic Jihad, who were released by the PA at the beginning of the confrontation. Labor ministers understood that an unequivocal demand for a total and absolute cessation of violence could not possibly have been met. Given that this was the case, they claimed that blindly insisting on such a demand would be tantamount to consigning any chance for meaningful political negotiations to failure. Laborites thus stated that they would be satisfied by a '100 percent effort' to put an end to the violence, even if the results of these efforts fell short in the initial period. Had the Palestinians actually undertaken such an effort, or had they offered to do so on the condition that negotiations be renewed, a rift would likely have formed in the Labor-Likud unity government. Sharon would likely have insisted on adopting the right-wing interpretation of a cessation of violence, and the onus would then have been on the Labor party to leave the government.

Israel adopted a similarly results-oriented approach to removing the sanctions that it had placed on rank-and-file Palestinians. Its leaders stated that measures to return Palestinian life in the territories to normal would be taken only in parallel to a significant drop in the level of violence. Such measures included the lifting of the closures that limited Palestinian movement both within the West Bank and Gaza and from there into Israel proper, and the withdrawal of IDF forces from their forward deployments.

For his part, Arafat was unwilling to seek a cessation of violence, even by the more accommodating standards of the Labor party. The most he had done in this regard was to make verbal declarations to Israel, the United States and the European states, in which he stated that he *desired* a reduction of violence and a renewal of negotiations. These declarations, when they were made, were not accompanied by vigorous activity to ensure their implementation and did not lead to an extended reduction in the level of violence. The Palestinians claimed that they could not reduce the violence, since the actions in question were executed without central planning. The only way to reduce the violence was to give the Palestinian leadership the tools to change the political atmosphere. This, the PA claimed, could only be done by renewing negotiations in a manner that would lead quickly to tangible achievements that Arafat could show to his electorate. Hence, from the Palestinian perspective, both the renewal of negotiations and making significant progress within them were pre-conditions for PA action toward reducing the violence. The Palestinian position differed from Israel's also regarding the content of the negotiations. The PA insisted that negotiations on a final status agreement must continue from the point at which they left off in Taba, just prior to the Israeli elections. The Palestinians also demanded that the steps required of Israel in order to ensure the normalization of Palestinian life (removal of roadblocks and closures, etc.) be taken prior to any efforts at reducing violence.

Though gaps between the two sides seemed unbridgeable, pressure was applied to both sides in order to effect a reduction of violence and a return to negotiations. On the Israeli side, there was wide recognition that it would be difficult to achieve a significant reduction in the level of violence without presenting some positive vision to the Palestinians. Such was the position taken by the Labor party, a senior coalition partner, and the Prime Minister presumably had to consider it. Sharon also showed sensitivity to public opinion. In that regard, he likely took note of opinion polls that showed strong popular support for a renewal of the peace process, despite also supporting the positions of his government. Moreover, Israelis seemed willing to pay a price for renewing talks: polls showed general willingness to freeze settlement activity in order to bring about a renewal of negotiations. At the same time, external actors, among them Jordan, Egypt, the United States, and the EU all pressured both sides to make concessions and renew talks. These actors were motivated primarily by a concern that, if the situation were to continue unchanged, it would deal a deadly blow to greater regional stability.

The main efforts for bringing the two sides to an understanding revolved around the Jordanian-Egyptian initiative of April–May 2001, and the report of the Mitchell commission, which was published on April 30, 2001. In the initial formulation of their initiative, Egypt's President Mubarak and Jordan's King Abdullah did not waver in their rhetorical support of the Palestinians. The demands made of the Palestinians to put a stop to violence were unspecific, lacking either a list of required actions or a firm timetable. By contrast, Israel was expected to agree to a list of concrete, detailed demands, among them steps required to return Palestinian life to normal, and a complete cessation of settlement activity. On this basis, it was suggested that existing agreements be implemented in full, and that negotiations for a final-status agreement resume, to be completed within one year. The negotiations would resume from the point at which the two sides had left off in their previous negotiations.

In deference to Foreign Minister Shimon Peres, the Government of Israel did not entirely reject the plan and agreed to a series of meetings to discuss changes that would make it more acceptable to Israel. While the Egyptians and the Jordanians were willing to make relatively far-reaching changes to the plan, they were unwilling to concede the demand that Israel freeze all settlement activity immediately with the initiative's entry into force. Ultimately, the Sharon government rejected the initiative on this basis. Even so, the initiative proved a useful and constructive exercise. It served as a convenient joint basis upon which the different parties were able to continue discussing the conditions that would make a renewal of talks possible, even if it ultimately became apparent that the initiative itself could not serve as a basis for future agreement.

Another potential platform for the cessation of violence and a renewal of talks was the publication of the report of the Mitchell commission. The report was drawn up by the fact-finding mission set up by President Bill Clinton in November 2000, following the summit in Sharm el-Sheikh. It described the process by which relations between the sides had degenerated into conflict and made a series of recommendations as to how the ongoing violence could be overcome. The report envisioned a three-phase process: first, a cessation of violence; second, a period of confidence-building measures; and third, a renewal of negotiations. It also gave detailed recommendations regarding the first two phases, the main points of which were as follows:

Phase 1: *Cessation of Violence*

- An unequivocal demand that both sides take steps to show that they were fully committed to ending violence. In this context, the two sides were also to reaffirm their commitment to all existing signed agreements.
- Israel and the PA were to immediately resume security cooperation.
- The Palestinians were to refrain from firing from highly populated areas and into highly populated areas.

Phase 2: *Confidence-Building Measures*

- The PA was to clarify both to Israel and to the Palestinian public that acts of terrorism were unacceptable, and that it condemned them. The PA was also to undertake a '100 percent effort' to counter such acts, and to punish those who perpetrate them. In this context, it was also to take immediate steps to incarcerate terrorists operating from areas under its control.
- Israel was to completely freeze all building activity in the settlements.
- Israel was to take measures to implement the use of non-lethal weapons against unarmed protesters.
- Israel was to reverse all measures which harmed the Palestinian economy. It was to resume the transfer of taxes and duties to the PA, permit the entry of Palestinian workers into Israel, cease the destruction of houses and roads, and stop uprooting trees in Palestinian orchards, olive groves, and the like.
- The PA was to resume security coordination with Israel, to ensure that entry permits into Israel would not be used improperly.
- Both sides were to undertake joint measures to ensure the sanctity of holy places.
- Both sides were to lend their support to nongovernmental organizations dedicated to encouraging good relations between their respective peoples.

The report's authors believed that if both sides implemented its recommendations, the path to a renewal of negotiations would be clear of all obstacles. To that end, the committee members seemed to be balancing a cessation of Palestinian violence and incitement against an Israeli freeze on settlement building. They recommended that the first phase of talks focus on reaffirming the commitment of both sides to all agreements or understandings already in force, and that steps be taken to implement all measures that remained outstanding, such as the third further redeployment (FRD), as set out in the Oslo accords.

The two sides' initial reactions did not raise hopes that the report's recommendations would be implemented in good faith. While both sides announced that they accepted the report in its entirety, they did so with a number of stipulations. The Palestinians went so far as to call for another conference in Sharm el-Sheikh, for the purpose of discussing how the report was to be implemented. However, they did so while ignoring the demands made of them in the report, and in an attempt to create leverage on Israel for a freeze on settlements, without displaying any willingness to take substantive measures to quell the violence. For its part, Israel also accepted the report, but registered a number of stipulations of its own. The government was unwilling to accept the unequivocal recommendation that settlements be entirely frozen – the government, Israel said, cannot be prevented from construction in built-up areas, for the purpose of what it termed "natural growth."

Beyond the dispute over whether the settlements were or were not the main obstacle to progress, there was an additional disagreement that developed over the sequencing of events. Israel claimed that following the PA's moves to end violence, a "cooling-off" period of several months must ensue, during which it would be possible to determine if a real cessation of violence had taken place. Only in such a case, the government of Israel noted, would it be willing to implement its confidence-building measures as set out in the Mitchell report, including the third FRD.

Israel demanded such a period for two reasons. The first was the need to ensure that the Palestinians were living up to their commitments. Previous experiences by Israel had proved bitter: Palestinian commitments to curb violence were often not implemented over the long term. In cases where Israeli concessions were linked to Palestinian efforts to control violence (such as in the timetable attached to the Wye River Memorandum), Israel had discovered that the PA's commitment to such efforts would wane once Israel had carried out its part of the agreement. Since many Israeli commitments, such as territorial redeployments, were effectively irreversible, Israel came away from these experiences with a sense of having been deceived. There was no way to retroactively "take back" steps that had been taken on the basis of Israeli-Palestinian *quid pro quos* that had failed to materialize over the long term. The second reason was political. Israel wanted to defer for as long as possible the execution of commitments that would limit its freedom of action regarding settlement building – commitments which would be hard for Sharon to live with, given the composition of his government. For their part, the Palestinians objected to any cooling off period of more than a week, the period they deemed necessary for taking the required steps to rein in violence.

Regardless of the difficulties, the United States tried to make the best of the opportunity that the Mitchell report offered. To that end, the Bush administration departed from its original decision not to become too deeply involved in the activities of the Israeli-Palestinian track. President Bush appointed a team, headed by William Burns—Assistant Secretary of State for Middle Eastern Affairs—to serve as "point men" for implementing the report. Its goal was to conduct contacts between the two parties in order to enable the implementation of the Mitchell report and to bring a measure of stability back to the region. The Burns-led team also included two additional experienced Middle East "hands": outgoing U.S. Ambassador to Israel Martin Indyk, and U.S. Consul General to Jerusalem Ronald Schlicher. However, the team was unable to soften Palestinian positions regarding a cease-fire.

Simultaneously, Israel decided at the end of May 2001 to initiate a unilateral cease-fire, ordering its forces not to undertake unprovoked military actions against the Palestinians and to limit themselves to defensive actions. The PA responded negatively to the Israeli announcement, and violence only escalated in the following period. This violence further escalated when a Palestinian suicide bomber blew himself up in the midst of a group of Israeli youths outside the Pacha dance club in Tel Aviv (the so-called "Dolphinarium attack"). This action led Israel to implement tough measures against the PA. These were to include a declaration that the Authority itself was involved in planning and executing acts of terror, and a decision to limit Chairman Arafat's personal freedom of movement. To this were added harsh economic sanctions. Arafat, for his part, tried to limit the damage by announcing that he was willing to enter into negotiations that would lead to a real effort to stop the violence. Israel ultimately refrained from implementing some of these decisions, out of a desire to determine if the shockwave that followed the attack could serve to pressure the PA into a serious and sustained effort to limit the violence.

At the time, it seemed possible that the terrible toll of the Dolphinarium attack might prove to be the high water mark in the ongoing violence, since in its wake massive international pressure mounted on both sides to reach a cease-fire. In addition to efforts by the United States, pressure came from a number of other quarters. This included German Federal Minister for Foreign Affairs Joschka Fischer, who was at the time on a visit to Israel, EU High Representative for the Common Foreign and Security Policy Javier Solana, and UN Secretary-General Kofi Annan. In this context, CIA Director George Tenet also came to the region, and through his mediation the two sides accepted a plan to implement a cease-fire. The plan obligated the Palestinian leadership to take steps that were difficult in light of their domestic political needs.

Indeed, prior to the events of September 11, 2001, it seemed that all external attempts to quell the violence and push the sides into implementation of the Mitchell-Tenet package were destined to collapse. The Palestinian leadership seemed either unwilling or unable to achieve a real reduction in the level of violence. Without such a reduction, Israel would not be able to scale back its retaliatory strikes over the long term, and the cycle of violence would continue. At the time, the shock of the attacks staged in the United States, and the attendant changes in U.S. policy – putting the war on terrorism center-stage – were expected to improve the prospects for putting these plans back on track. In the aftermath of these events, the United States demonstrated a willingness to put more pressure on both sides to implement their respective obligations. In this framework, former U.S. Marines General Anthony Zinni was appointed to mediate security arrangements that would enable implementation of the Tenet-Mitchell plans. Moreover, both sides became interested in finding ways to exploit the new, post–September 11 environment to advance their own agendas and thus developed an interest in helping the United States calm the situation, as long as they did not have to place their core interests at risk. However, by early 2002 these developments were reversed under the pressure of escalating violence.

Even if the United States and its allies had been successful in reducing the gaps in the positions of the two sides regarding the implementation of the Mitchell report, there was still some doubt as to whether the report could actually have been implemented. Both sides have appeared to be on the verge of a cease-fire agreement several times since the outbreak of the violence. Such was the case at both the Paris Summit and the Sharm el-Sheikh conference in October 2000. In each of these cases, the agreements fell through because of the PA Chairman's apparent unwillingness to take the necessary tough measures needed to quell Palestinian violence. It was difficult to imagine how things could be any different in subsequent talks. Moreover, even if there were a sustained reduction in violence, the talks would likely run aground over the deep differences in the positions of the two sides.

Should Israel and the Palestinians agree to renew peace negotiations, the following issues would then have to be discussed:

- *Negotiations on the implementation of existing agreements.* The Palestinians believe that they can garner significant achievements through such negotiations, primarily the enlargement of the territory under their control, the release of prisoners, and the opening of the safe passage routes between

Gaza and the West Bank. Moreover, such achievements could be reached without having to make concessions on their core positions on final-status issues. The Israeli interest in these negotiations results from their potential to reduce tensions on the Palestinian "street" without requiring significant concessions. The difficulty is that large gaps exist between Israeli and Palestinian interpretations of the unimplemented aspects of the interim agreements. For example, according to Sharon's reading of the interim agreements, Israel is not obligated to transfer to Palestinian control any more than one percent of the West Bank in the third FRD. The Palestinians, however, interpret the agreement to mean that nearly all territory currently under Israeli control must be transferred to them. Talks on this point are liable to reveal deep differences of opinion, which could quickly lead to an impasse.

- *Negotiations on additional partial agreements.* The Palestinians have historically resisted negotiations on partial agreements, insisting that negotiations must focus on a final status agreement. With that, there is a possibility that they may in the future agree to such negotiations, which could take place in parallel to final-status agreements. Here, too, many difficulties may be expected. First, the Palestinians would want an interim agreement that is limited in duration, so as not to harm their chances for reaching a final settlement, while Israel will want a long-term agreement. Second, the negotiations at and following Camp David II progressed to such a point that it is doubtful if the Palestinians would want – or could accept – an interim agreement that did not include elements on which they had already obtained concessions, especially in the territorial sphere. Israel, on the other hand, would have difficulty making large territorial concessions in the course of an interim agreement. Its leadership would fear that, should final status agreements not proceed in accordance with Palestinian expectations, the PA might resume the use of violence. Were the Palestinians to do so, the territorial concessions gained in a partial agreement would presumably improve their tactical positions on the ground. In addition, any partial agreement would likely be based on the assumption that no solutions could be found over refugees or Jerusalem. It is hard to imagine how the two sides might reach a durable partial agreement without finding resolutions for these two very important issues.
- *Negotiations on final status.* The political picture on both sides points to an impasse. It does not seem likely that progress could be achieved through negotiations on these issues, given the positions of the Sharon government on the one hand, and those of the PA leadership on the other.

For the sake of conjecture, one could imagine a situation in which the Palestinians had agreed to Israel's demand that renewed negotiations not resume from the point at which they left off following Camp David II. However, both sides would still keenly have felt the effects of the previous talks, and this would doubtless have affected their positions. Of particular significance would have been the bridging proposals made by U.S. President Clinton and presented to both sides on December 23, 2000. According to this offer, all of the Gaza Strip and some 94–96 percent of the West Bank were to be transferred to Palestinian sovereignty for the creation of a state. The remainder of the territory, which would have included large settlement blocs, was to be annexed to Israel, with the Palestinians receiving compensation in the form of alternative territories from inside Israel. Israeli security would have been guaranteed by a limited-term Israeli military presence in the Jordan Valley, early-warning stations, and limitations on Palestinian armaments, while the security of both sides would have been shored up by the presence of an international force. Jewish neighborhoods in Jerusalem would have been placed under Israeli rule, and Arab ones under the rule of the State of Palestine. The Palestinians would have controlled the Temple Mount, while Israel would have controlled the Western Wall. Arrangements would have been made regarding the area underneath the Temple Mount, to safeguard antiquities of historical importance to Judaism. Palestinian refugees would have been able to return to the Palestinian State or to settle in other countries (including Israel), subject to the policies of those states. The refugees would have received compensation, and the two sides would have declared that the conflict had formally ended.

Beyond the bilateral difficulties inherent in a renewal of negotiations, the changeover in Washington also took its toll. The Bush administration entered office with a firm decision not to be drawn into micro-managing the Israeli-Palestinian relationship, as they claimed the Clinton administration had. Rather, the new administration felt that the two sides must solve their problems by themselves. Accordingly, outgoing U.S. Special Envoy to the Middle East Dennis Ross was not replaced.

As the violence continued, it became clear to officials in the new administration that the Israeli-Palestinian facedown threatened vital U.S. interests in the Middle East, and that it would not be resolved without U.S. intervention. It was in this framework that the CIA again became involved in trying to foster Israeli-Palestinian security coordination, and that the team of U.S. diplomats noted above was set up to mediate between the two sides.

In the aftermath of September 11, the Bush administration had to put the Middle East back in the center of its political agenda. In that context, the United States apparently also realized that there would be a need for more active involvement in the Israeli-Palestinian conflict.

Unilateral Approaches

The continuing violence and the inability to return to a constructive negotiating process have spurred each side to explore unilateral approaches. In Israel, this has fed a public debate surrounding what is variously termed either "unilateral disengagement" or "unilateral separation" from the Palestinians. While specific approaches vary, all envision some form of physical separation between Israelis and Palestinians, which would enable Israel to more effectively protect its citizens from terrorist violence. From there, however, disagreements begin to appear among the various plans, mirroring pre-existing domestic ideological fault lines. Left-wing advocates of separation seek to accomplish this goal by unilaterally 'relocating' (i.e., removing) settlements in order to create a more defensible separation line, while right-wing advocates favor physical separation based on the existing settlement map.

By contrast, the Palestinian leadership has grown increasingly disenchanted with the unilateral option at its disposal. Over the course of 1999–2000, the Palestinians had actively considered a unilateral declaration of independence (UDI). UDI was again examined by Chairman Arafat after the failure of Camp David II, as a possible means for breaking out of the diplomatic *cul-de-sac* into which he had been maneuvered. However, by early 2002, there were no signs that the Palestinians continued to consider this option seriously. From the outside, it appears that PA leaders realized that doing so would play into Israel's hands. Israel would likely have taken steps intended to perpetuate the present situation, especially in terms of control over territory. Moreover, declaring independence would have robbed the PA of its ambiguous position under international law. This was especially true with regard to responsibility for acts taken by parties, or from territories, which were nominally under Palestinian control.

The Role of an International Force

Another issue on the agenda in the context of the violence related to a possible role for an international force in helping to bring calm. The Palestinian leadership had played for some time with the idea of using the present violence to leverage deeper international intervention in the conflict, using events in the Balkans as a model. Such an involvement, it was supposed, might lead to the creation of an international tribunal, which in turn would impose a settlement favorable to the Palestinians. This imposed solution would then be enforced by an international force sent to the region, and would ensure, from the Palestinian perspective, their security in the face of Israel's military superiority. Israel opposed this idea in the strongest possible terms, seeing it as a ploy to avoid direct, bilateral negotiations. Without such negotiations, Israeli leaders believed, there would be nothing to obligate the Palestinians to recognize Israel's essential security needs in the framework of a final-status agreement.

The Palestinians tried to bring about such intervention by moving along two channels. First, they used violence against Israelis, in the hopes of goading Israel into a harsh reaction that would encourage international involvement. In this, the Palestinians sought to emulate the precedent provided by international intervention in Bosnia, which was spurred forward by the scores of casualties caused by Serbian shelling of Bosnian cities and marketplaces. To that end, Palestinian snipers began a series of shooting attacks on the Jewish neighborhood of Gilo, in East Jerusalem. These attacks originated from Beit Jallah, a nearby town populated largely by Palestinian Christians. The attacks were apparently motivated by hopes that Israel would respond harshly against a Christian population, leading to international condemnation. Israeli responses to these attacks, however, appear to have been more controlled in character than the PA had expected, and in any case did not trigger international intervention.

In addition, the Palestinians invested considerable diplomatic effort toward obtaining international support for a peacekeeping force to be sent to the region. These attempts focused on a variety of international forums, chief among them the UN Security Council. The attempts failed for two basic reasons. First, there was firm U.S. opposition to such a move. Second, it became clear to the international community that such a decision would not be feasible under existing circumstances. Even some Palestinians came to believe that posting an international force under the present circumstances would likely have increased Israel's standing in the areas under its control. At the behest of the Palestinian Authority, the Mitchell report discussed this possibility, and effectively ruled it out by making it conditional on the agreement of both sides.

Discussions of an international force did raise awareness among some Israelis and Palestinians that such a force could play a role in the context of monitoring and guaranteeing the implementation of a signed Israeli-Palestinian agreement. Indeed, both sides began to realize that breaking out of the cycle of violence and returning to negotiations would be difficult without deeper international involvement. In that context, an international presence could assist the two sides in narrowing the gaps in their respective positions. One outspoken advocate of this position was Prof. Shlomo Ben-Ami, who had served as Foreign Minister in the Barak government.

The Media and the Israeli-Palestinian Confrontation

The mass media play a central role in any low-intensity conflict, and the Israeli-Palestinian conflict proves no exception. However, in the complex environment of the Israeli-Palestinian conflict, the function of the media has been subtly different than in most other low-intensity conflicts. Usually, the weaker side of the conflict attempts to manipulate the media of the stronger side, in order to influence public opinion there. The goal of such attempts is to create public pressure on the government of the stronger side, in order to convince it to accept the weaker side's demands. At the same time, the weaker side may also use its own domestic media to shore up support at home. For its part, the stronger side usually seeks to prevent this scenario from taking place, while relying on its greater military power to resolve the conflict before domestic support begins to erode.

The struggle for capturing media attention has existed in the Israeli-Palestinian conflict as well, though the role of the media in this case was rather different. The two sides quickly realized that the conflict would be won neither on the ground nor in the hearts and minds of their rivals. Both Israelis and Palestinians were trying to manipulate the international media to win third-party support for their respective policies and goals. In that context, the present conflict has had a number of special characteristics:

- For the first time, the Arab-language mass media could broadcast throughout the Middle East. Previously, the only Arab broadcast media services were state-run television and radio stations. These services were subject to the direct control of the government of each state; news items could be altered or presented in a fashion that suited each government's particular interests. However, the appearance of satellite broadcast networks, such as Al-Jazeera, changed all of this. Individual Arab regimes could no longer control the media messages that reached their respective audiences. This forced them to be more sensitive to public opinion when forming policy.
- Another development was the appearance of a number of Palestinian-run television stations. Following the establishment of the Palestinian Authority, a large number of television and radio stations had been set up by both the PA and by independent operators. On the one hand, this gave the PA and other organizations in Palestinian society the ability to reach the Palestinian public and rouse them to action. At the same time, their large number made it difficult for the PA to reign in incitement when it wished to do so.
- Foreign media services have had to maneuver between two entities, Israel and the PA. Foreign journalists and media professionals have also been subjected to tremendous pressure and even threats of violence, especially by the PA.

From the initial phases of the conflict, television images have proved central. An outstanding example of this was the media uproar that took place after the death of Muhammad a-Durra. A-Durra, a child, was caught with his father in the crossfire of a shootout between Israelis and Palestinians in Gaza. During the course of the firefight, he was wounded by gunfire while he and his father were trapped at the scene of the battle. Eventually, he died in his father's arms. All of this was captured on tape by France-2 Television and broadcast that day.

The pictures from the scene of the shootout caused an uproar, both in the Arab world and to a lesser degree in the West. This, in turn, translated into political capital for the PA. Both sides were aware of the great influence of the media, and this awareness has influenced their actions. In an attempt to play off the media, Chairman Arafat worked assiduously to blur his role in the ongoing violence. By having created a situation that fostered violence, while relying on organizations whose links to him were unclear, he created a measure of plausible deniability around himself. The result was that he gave those who looked to him for leadership the impression that violent acts would be welcomed by the regime, without creating a direct chain linking the PA to violence when it actually took place. For this reason, the PA preferred to keep the majority of its official quasi-military forces out of the fighting. While members of the Palestinian security services did participate in violence on a large scale, often using the PA's munitions and *materiel*, this was done on a supposedly informal and 'personal' basis. Moreover, those involved in the violence were generally from one of the PA's various small and highly compartmentalized intelligence services, or from the Tanzim, an informal militia tied to Arafat's Fatah movement.

Israel and its Arab-Palestinian Minority

In early October 2000, there were violent clashes between police and Arab-Israelis. While there was some concern that such confrontations might prove ongoing, there has been no further violence. In and of itself, this is a matter of some note: various memorial days for Arab-Israelis – among them Land Day, *Yawm il-Nakba* (i.e., the day commemorating the Palestinian catastrophe of 1948), and the one-year anniversary of the clashes themselves – have since come and gone without major incident, despite fears to the contrary.

In the aftermath of the October 2000 riots, Arab-Israelis, the government of Israel, and Israeli Jews all underwent a period of introspection, with each side trying to draw conclusions from the awful events that had taken place. All realized that they were standing at the brink of an abyss and were now trying figure out what had been gained and lost. Moreover, they needed to determine how they could best realize their respective social and national goals while preventing further escalation, from which there might be no turning back.

The Israeli government understood that it had to take a series of steps to prevent future escalations. In the short term, the Israeli police tried to learn from the events, changing their operating procedures to reduce the likelihood of violent confrontations with the Arab populace. The police have since authorized large-scale protests, without hurrying into confrontation with the demonstrators. In parallel, a long-term approach has been adopted toward identifying problems facing the Arab minority in Israel, and a dialogue has been initiated to search for ways to deal with their claims. It was clear to the government that the ferocity of the clashes stemmed from a combination of nationalist and religious motivations, on the one hand, and socioeconomic ones on the other. The former motivations stemmed from both the El-Aqsa Intifada and an abiding sense that Arab-Israelis had no appropriate venue for expression within Israel as a national group. The latter were related to ongoing discrimination against Arabs in Israeli society. This was expressed, for example, in unemployment rates within the Arab-Israeli sector, which have been consistently higher than those in the Jewish sector. This was but one of a long list of other indicators that showed a consistent pattern of neglect or discrimination against Arab-Israelis.

The government was also concerned that in giving expression to the nationalist desires of the Arabs, it would endanger Israel's existence as a state that sought to combine Jewish, democratic, and Zionist elements into its national character. Given the difficulty of trying to co-opt these diverse, and sometimes contradictory, elements into a cohesive whole, there was concern that recognizing Arab collective aspirations could set into motion a process that would threaten this character over the long term. Because of these fears, most Jews opposed granting Arabs in Israel the status of a national minority. However, there was considerable willingness on the part of the government – be it left-wing or right-wing – to try to deal with socioeconomic hardships within the community. To that end, there was a consensus on the need to invest considerable funds and attention. In any event, even if the necessary funds were invested, there would still be a need to overcome bureaucratic hurdles. Improving the socioeconomic situation of the Arab community in Israel would be a long, slow process.

The Jewish public in Israel reacted sharply to the uprisings. A minority of Jews concluded that there was a need for an intensive Jewish-Arab dialogue in Israel, and demonstrated willingness to take part in such a process. However, the majority of Israeli Jews responded more harshly. The apparent ease with which Arab-Israeli citizens had taken part in violence against the institutions of the state, and against individual Jews, as well as the expressions of hate that accompanied them, filled many Jewish Israelis with both fear and loathing. This reaction was reinforced by fiery statements from Arab political leaders and members of Knesset; for many Israeli Jews, the events at home seemed eerily reminiscent of what was happening in the West Bank and Gaza Strip.

The knee-jerk reaction of the Jewish majority in Israel was to sever its ties with the Arab public. Jews stopped entering Arab towns, and scaled back commercial activities with Arabs. This in turn intensified the already severe economic crisis in the Arab sector, which only reinforced the sense of discrimination among them. It also showed the Arab public and its leadership that violent confrontation and uncontrolled behavior would carry a price. This realization led in part to the aforementioned introspection within the Arab-Israeli community.

The short-term lesson for Arab-Israelis was to avoid violent mass outbursts that would likely bring more fatalities in confrontations with the police. However, in the longer term, the events of late 2000 served only to intensify and accelerate processes that were already underway. Those Arabs in Israel that stressed acceptance of the existence of Israel as a Jewish-Democratic-Zionist state, and who were willing to confine the common struggle to issues of personal discrimination and socioeconomic welfare, suffered a setback. In their place, more radical leaders have grown in stature. This newer thinking demanded a change in the nature of the State of Israel – from a Jewish state to what is called "a state for all its citizens." In the past, this political current was characterized by a small group of intellectuals, whose most outspoken leader was MK Azmi Bishara, head of the National-Democratic Coalition (Balad). However, over the last decade, this approach has gained new supporters from broad sectors of the Israeli-Arab community.

A complex link has also developed between the often-problematic Israeli-Palestinian relationship across the Green Line, and relations between Jews and Arabs in Israel proper. Clearly, the events on the Temple Mount/Haram el-Sharif and the violence between Israelis and Palestinians provided the catalyst for the conflagration between Arab-Israelis and the police in October. However, the connection runs deeper still. Since the Oslo process began in 1993, frustration among Arabs in Israel has deepened. The reason for this was a growing sense that the problems of the Palestinians in the West Bank and Gaza were being addressed while they – citizens of the state – were being left to their own devices, with no redress for their needs. If they wished to be heard, they had no choice but to increase the intensity of their demands.

In addition, there was a growing suspicion among Arab-Israelis that the Palestinian problem was going to be solved at their expense. The evacuation of settlers from the West Bank and Gaza would require the establishment of new towns in Israel proper, leading to the confiscation of additional village lands. These suspicions seemed to be confirmed in 1998, when large swathes of land in Wadi 'Ara, an area with a high concentration of Arab-Israelis, were expropriated for the IDF to use as training grounds, resulting in a violent clash with police in September of that year. Particularly unsettling for many Arab-Israelis was the fact that the training grounds were meant to replace similar areas in the West Bank that had been given over to Palestinian control. The act of expropriating lands near Israeli-Arab population centers to replace lands transferred to the PA was seen as a harbinger of things to come.

From the other direction, the events within Israel also affected the Israeli-Palestinian dynamic. The October riots demonstrated to many Israelis that the "Arab demographic threat" was something not to be taken lightly. Many Israeli Jews came to believe that, in the state's dealings with the Palestinians over the creation of a permanent settlement, there was a need to give priority to demographic considerations. This in turn fostered a certain degree of moderation when considering a final settlement. For example, when discussing a possible solution for Jerusalem, increased numbers of Israeli Jews now saw the benefit in transferring heavily populated Arab neighborhoods to Palestinian sovereignty. Some even began to consider the transfer of other areas populated heavily by Arab-Israelis – such as Wadi 'Ara – to Palestinian sovereignty, as part of a swap in exchange for settlement blocs, an idea vehemently opposed by Arab-Israelis. Such changes in Israeli outlook could eventually ease the reaching of a final-status agreement, should negotiations resume. On the other hand, these same events reduced the willingness of the Jewish public in Israel to agree to any return of Palestinian refugees into Israel proper, even in small, symbolic numbers. This development would no doubt make reaching an agreement harder.

Concluding Thoughts on the Israeli-Palestinian Confrontation

Attempting to analyze the complex balance of events that have taken place in 2001 is not a straightforward task. Given that the Palestinians were the ones who set off the violence, and are those that stand to derive the most benefit from it, it seems appropriate to begin discussing questions of gain and loss from their perspective:

- PA Chairman Arafat successfully extricated himself and his leadership from the diplomatic deadlock that followed the failure of the Camp David II talks, revamping his image both at home and abroad. The Palestinian public once again stood united in support of his policies. However, the continuation of violence threatened to undermine his control over territories under PA rule in the short to medium term. In the longer term, his standing personally could be threatened.
- The Palestinians revamped their international image as underdog. In doing so, they restored much of their ability to mobilize international support,

especially from Europe.

- On the other hand, the standing enjoyed by the Palestinians in the United States suffered a major setback. The Clinton and Bush administrations, Congress, and much of the American press blamed the Palestinians for the failure of the final-status talks, and for the continuation of the violence. Arafat lost his close relations with the White House, one of his most noteworthy achievements from the days of the Clinton administration.
- Palestinian expectations that a violent confrontation would foment dissension between the Israeli left and right proved false. Instead, the Israeli public *en masse* moved sharply rightward, while dealing with the violence helped foster a common agenda among different parts of the electorate. The Palestinians, in effect, gave rise to a shift in Israeli politics that worked against their presumed interest in a negotiated settlement.
- The violence strengthened Israeli popular support for separation from the Palestinians. The positive aspect of this, from the Palestinian perspective, was that it solidified Israeli acceptance of a Palestinian state, and enlarged Israeli willingness for territorial concessions in the framework of a permanent status agreement. However, there was a negative side to this as well, since unilateral separation from the Palestinians would have entailed cutting the PA off from the Israeli economy, on which it was largely dependent. In addition, it would also have meant that the delineation of Palestinian and Israeli-controlled areas would have been made unilaterally by the Israelis.
- Palestinian hopes that they would successfully goad Israel into harsh reactions against them, and in so doing force international intervention, have proven empty. While international involvement was on the rise, it was focused primarily on a cessation of the violence, and much of the resulting pressure was directed largely against the Palestinians themselves.
- The Palestinians did not succeed in turning the confrontation with the Israelis into a regional confrontation. Reactions from Arab states, and the aid that the Palestinians received from them, were far below what had been expected.
- The Palestinians paid a heavy price, both in casualties and in economic losses.

For Israel, there were never any gains to be made by the continuation of violence. Israel's major goal has been to end the confrontation and return to the *status quo ante*. However, here too the balance of gain and loss is a problematic one:

- Israel was unable to reduce violence to acceptable levels, or to provide its citizens with a sense of personal security.
- The Palestinians again demonstrated their ability to affect political processes within Israel, and to cause both the fall of one government and the election of another. This, from the standpoint of any sovereign state, is unacceptable.

- Israel succeeded in heading off unwanted international intervention in the conflict.
- While the rate of Israeli casualties was markedly lower than that of those suffered by the Palestinians, it was still higher than most Israelis were willing to accept. However, the violence did not erode the country's willingness to stand firm in the face of confrontation with the Palestinians.
- Israel paid a significant economic price for the conflict, especially in terms of lost tourist revenues, but its economy seemed able to withstand this.

From this analysis, it is clear that the Israeli-Palestinian confrontation is not a zero-sum game. Indeed, by early 2002, both sides seemed the poorer for it.

Syria, Lebanon, and Israel

Israeli-Syrian negotiations fell into an impasse following President Clinton's unsuccessful meeting with the late President Hafez al-Assad of Syria in March 2000, and as of mid–2002, had not been renewed. With the fall of the Barak government and Sharon's rise to power, there were some indications that Israeli leaders had considered a renewal of talks with Syria. At first glance this might seem odd: the negotiations that fell apart in March 2000 were over territorial disagreements between the two sides. Syria's late president had reportedly demanded that Israel commit to a full withdrawal to the June 6, 1967 lines, up to the very edge of the Sea of Galilee—a move Barak was not willing to make. Considering that the Sharon government was composed primarily of parties whose platforms rejected the idea of *any* sizeable withdrawal from the Golan Heights, there would have seemed to be little common ground for talks. However, this was not entirely the case – unlike the territorial issues on the Israeli-Palestinian front, the territorial issues surrounding the Golan Heights are not charged with the same ideological-emotional importance as are those relating to the West Bank. Consequently, there was some latitude for a right-wing government to explore the idea of putting the Palestinian track on hold in favor of a renewal of the Syrian track.

However, it was not clear how realistic such ideas were in light of the ongoing Israeli-Palestinian violence, and considering the changes of government that had taken place in both Israel and Syria. The intensity of the Israeli-Palestinian confrontation raised doubts about the possibility of downgrading negotiations on that track and settling into a purely military confrontation with the Palestinians. Concerning changes in the governments of Syria and Israel, it eventually became clear that, despite some Israeli and Western expectations, the change of power in Syria had reduced the prospects of a settlement.

While Syria's new president, Bashar Assad, remained something of an enigma in 2001, his performance in office did not give cause for optimism regarding either his desire or his ability to propel Syria into peace with Israel. In addition, Israel's withdrawal from southern Lebanon removed the question of the 'Lebanese ulcer' from the Israeli national agenda, and with it much of the motive for painful concessions along the Syrian front. Finally, disappointments from both the Palestinian and Syrian tracks had taken a toll on the Israeli national mood. Levels of confidence and trust among Israelis for "the Arabs" had declined, and with it belief in the value of peace agreements as a tool for resolving conflict. This in turn reduced willingness for concessions on the Golan in exchange for a treaty with Syria.

When Bashar Assad came to power, there had been hope that as a young leader, he would espouse liberal-democratic values, such as those to which he had been exposed during his schooling in Britain. There was also an expectation that he would try to modernize Syria and integrate it into the global economy. However, his actions since taking power have not lived up to these hopes. Bashar rose to power on the basis of support that he received from the country's old guard. His mincing efforts toward any kind of openness in the Syrian domestic sphere were cut short as soon as the country's old leadership explained the dangers that they entailed. In this context, Assad the son adopted the same tough stances that characterized Assad the father in matters relating to an accord with Israel.

On top of this, statements made by Bashar resonated negatively on an emotional level as well. Declarations made by him – especially at the Arab League Summit meetings that followed the outbreak of the Israeli-Palestinian violence – revealed an old-school Arab nationalist, replete with fiery anti-Israeli rhetoric that bore distinctly anti-Semitic overtones. He also expressed admiration for the Hizballah, ostensibly the only Arab organization that had confronted Israel and successfully forced it into submission. This contrasted sharply with the late president Assad, who had taken care to be more circumspect, handling the Hizballah with a mixture of trust and suspicion. On top of all of this, Bashar simply seemed rash. While this was interpreted more as a sign of inexperience than as a basic element of his character, it did not bode well for improvements in Israeli-Syrian relations.

Upon taking office, Bashar made a series of decisions that reduced the prospects for renewed negotiations between Syria and Israel, and increased the likelihood of military confrontation. The first such decision was to create an absolute linkage between the Palestinian and Syrian tracks of the peace process. He declared that negotiations and agreement with Israel would be possible only if they took place in parallel to negotiations with the Palestinians. In doing so, he distanced himself from the very logic of the Madrid process – the separation of the negotiations into distinct bilateral tracks. This also significantly diminished the possibility that there could be political contacts between Damascus and Jerusalem for as long as the Israeli-Palestinian crisis wore on. An additional decision was to give his full support for the Hizballah, even providing the organization with incentives to broaden its fight against Israel.

Israel's unilateral withdrawal from Lebanon put many assumptions to the test. The first of these was that a full withdrawal from southern Lebanon, if done in coordination with the UN, would lead to a cessation of the conflict between the IDF and the Hizballah. This belief was predicated on the assumption that the main goal of that organization was the liberation of Lebanese soil; once that was achieved, there would be no reason for the Hizballah to fight Israel. The second assumption was that even if the Hizballah did continue to fight Israel, it would be easier for Israel to respond. This assumption was based on two propositions: the first was that the withdrawal would deprive Hizballah of easy targets, such as were provided by the IDF's static deployment in the Security Zone. In addition, it was felt that, since Israel's withdrawal would garner international support and recognition of its compliance with UN resolutions, military responses to cross-border attacks would receive full international support. Hence, it was believed that a withdrawal would strengthen Israeli deterrence. An analysis of the events of 2001 and early 2002 shows that these assumptions were only partially correct.

The Israeli withdrawal did in fact trigger widespread opposition in Lebanon to further actions against Israel, and this did curtail the actions of the Hizballah. The leadership of the Hizballah quickly surmised that it could act only in those limited spheres where it enjoyed legitimacy in the eyes of the Lebanese public at large. However, within the ranks of the Hizballah, there remained considerable motivation for continuing the fight, both for ideological and domestic-political reasons. The leadership of the organization was apparently concerned that, without the backdrop that the struggle against Israeli occupation provided, Hizballah domestic standing was liable to decline. Fighting Israel had become a way to distinguish the organization from a host of other ethnic-political movements in Lebanon, and there was as yet nothing to replace it.

The Hizballah solved this quandary by continuing the fight, but within a limited territorial arena – the area known as Shaba farms – while maintaining quiet along the rest of the border. Shaba's convenience as a staging ground for Hizballah actions stemmed from a complex combination of factors. Lebanon claimed the territory as its own, despite a UN decision prior to the IDF withdrawal that it was not in fact Lebanese territory. Here it must be explained that the area in question was not located within Israeli territory *per se*. From the standpoint of international law, Shaba was considered part of the Golan Heights and hence rightfully belonged to Syria; Israel's sovereignty there has not been internationally recognized. Thus the Hizballah was able to claim before the Lebanese public that operations taken against Israel there were legitimate in the framework of liberating occupied Arab lands.

In light of the Hizballah claim, some Israelis suggested that the government simply withdraw unilaterally from the area, as it did in Lebanon, arguing that such a step would negate the legitimacy for continued Hizballah activity. Others have opposed this move, claiming that the organization would simply find another pretext for continuing low-level operations against Israel, such as Lebanese civilians held in Israeli captivity, or other potential points of disagreement along the Israeli-Lebanese border. While both positions were based on some degree of speculation, the latter was judged more credible. If Hizballah, it was reasoned, was bent on continuing the fight with Israel, there was surely no shortage of pretexts upon which it could continue to do so.

Another influential factor in this question was the link between Israeli-Palestinian violence and the activities of the Hizballah. In Israel, some have claimed that the unilateral withdrawal from Lebanon did harm to its deterrent posture, since it demonstrated to Israel's Arab rivals that concessions could be wrung from it by force. By withdrawing in the face of Hizballah attacks, Israel supposedly showed the Arab world that the long and arduous process of negotiating with Israel and making concessions was unnecessary. Why bother, when a campaign based on terror and guerilla warfare is an effective means to bring Israel to its knees? Such tactics effectively neutralized Israel's conventional military superiority, which could not be brought to bear in low-intensity conflicts. Moreover, the Israeli public was highly sensitive to casualties, which undermined public support for any stance taken by the government – a weakness that was magnified by the already raucous nature of Israeli politics. Finally, the freewheeling, commercially driven nature of the Israeli media meant that actions taken against IDF soldiers, or propaganda released by its rivals, would be repeatedly broadcast in sensationalist tones, further splitting public opinion on controversial issues.

So marked were Israel's shortcomings in this kind of conflict that there was some debate within Palestinian circles as to whether the 'Hizballah model' could not be adapted to serve their needs. Ultimately, this debate did not lead to a major shift in Palestinian tactics. Palestinian leaders realized that their own circumstances were entirely different from those of the Hizballah. Consequently, it was difficult to draw comparisons between Lebanon and the Israeli-Palestinian sphere. With that, there could be little doubt that the Hizballah set an example for Palestinians in the lower command echelons, as was evidenced by the appearance of Hizballah flags at Palestinian demonstrations. While the violence between Israel and the Palestinians would surely have broken out even without the unilateral withdrawal, Hizballah's apparent victory over Israel provided encouragement, giving the Palestinians greater resilience in the face of Israeli might. In this sense, it may have added to the overall duration of the Israeli-Palestinian conflict.

The El-Aqsa Intifada, however, also influenced the Hizballah. Resurgent anti-Israeli sentiments in the Arab world made it easier for the organization to justify its activities and to win support; it was surely no coincidence that the organization renewed its activities following the outbreak of the El-Aqsa Intifada. There was evidence to suggest that the Hizballah had begun preparations for activities in the Shaba farms area, and for the kidnapping of Israeli soldiers, before the outbreak of Israeli-Palestinian violence. At the same time, the Intifada clearly eased the decision that the Hizballah leadership had to make. In addition, the organization was able to use the Intifada to expand its base of support in PA-controlled areas, and has begun recruiting Palestinians to carry out attacks against Israel. Indeed, there have already been attacks from PA-controlled areas by cells connected to the Hizballah. By offering to undertake weapons deliveries to the PA, the organization also managed to form a relationship with the Palestinian leadership in early 2002; in this context, two ships carrying weapons supplied by Iran and Hizballah were intercepted by Israel.

Israel has also discovered that the international legitimacy it earned by withdrawing from Lebanon did not necessarily translate into an ability to take the fight directly to the Hizballah. Part of this difficulty was related to timing: the Israeli-Palestinian conflict introduced a new complexity into the regional equation. Had the El-Aqsa Intifada not broken out in October 2000, it might have been easier for Israel to respond to Hizballah attacks, because there would have been no risk of a two-front conflict, or of a regional conflagration. However, even setting this consideration aside, the withdrawal from Southern Lebanon created a fragile situation, and Israel had to take extreme care in weighing its options *vis-à-vis* attacks coming from Lebanon. On the one hand, international legitimacy for Israeli responses grew. On the other, the withdrawal made Israel more vulnerable, increasing the exposure of its northern towns and cities to extended-range Katyusha rocket attacks. For this reason, Israel had no interest in trading blows with the Hizballah. With this in mind, the more reasonable options that remained at Israel's disposal were as follows:

- Limiting the fighting to the Shaba farms region. The disadvantage of this choice was that it meant playing into the hands of the Hizballah. The organization maintained no permanent presence in the region; its forces entered only to carry out specific operations, and then withdrew immediately after these were concluded. This left the IDF with few targets against which it could respond.

- Bypassing the entire dilemma by holding Syria, as Hizballah's patron, responsible for attacks which it undertakes against Israel. Syria encouraged Hizballah attacks against Israel, provided it with freedom of action in the parts of Lebanon occupied by its armed forces, and maintained the organization's supply lines from Iran. Given these ties, a case was made for attacking Syrian assets in response to Hizballah attacks.

Upon taking power, the Sharon government implemented this latter path of action. In April 2001, after an Israeli soldier was killed in the Shaba region from a missile fired by a Hizballah force, Israel's Air Force destroyed a Syrian radar station near Dahar el-Bahar in Lebanon. The attack effectively resolved Israel's dilemma over how to respond to Hizballah attacks, by holding Syria accountable for them. Syria then faced a quandary: on the one hand, it could not confront Israel directly, given the latter's military advantage. At the same time, it could not choose to encourage revenge attacks by Hizballah, since Israel would continue to attack its assets in Lebanon, and possibly even in Syria itself, where again it would have no response. In May 2001 there was an additional Hizballah attack in the same area. While there were no IDF casualties, the attack demonstrated that the Hizballah did intend to continue low-level fighting in this sector. The next month, a number of IDF soldiers were wounded from still another Hizballah attack, and Israel responded by destroying an additional Syrian radar station in southern Lebanon. While this low level of tit-for-tat violence had leveled out by late 2001, the situation remained prone to flare-ups. Continuation or escalation in the Israeli-Palestinian arena would certainly have encouraged the Hizballah to take a risk and expand its actions.

The Lebanese government, especially following the election of Prime Minister Rafik Hariri, clearly expressed its reservations regarding continued attacks by the Hizballah, fearing that such attacks could unleash a firestorm of Israeli counterattacks. Such counterattacks would have harmed the country's attempts to rehabilitate its economy and infrastructure, both shattered after decades of war. Despite this, however, the government proved unable to rein in the Hizballah without Syrian approval throughout 2001. Hence, it refrained from deploying its army in the south over the period in question, leaving the entire border with Israel under Hizballah's control and effectively refraining from reasserting its sovereignty there. Hizballah, for its part, used this opportunity to increase its state of military readiness along the border, preparing for possible broader fighting with Israel. This changed somewhat in April 2002, when the Lebanese government decided on a limited military deployment in the south.

Lebanon has expressed an interest in retaining the UN buffer force (UNIFIL) on its territory, apparently on the assumption that its presence there would prevent the region from again turning into a battleground between Hizballah and Israel. However, tensions have formed between Lebanon and the UN General Secretariat, which has expressed its dissatisfaction with the actions of the Lebanese government. From its standpoint, UNIFIL had essentially served out its mandate once Israel withdrew from the Security Zone. The UN did not want to be drawn into the Lebanese government's decision not to reassert its sovereignty over the southern part of the country. For this reason, the Secretariat has announced its intention to reduce the size of the UNIFIL force, from about 4,000 troops to about 2,000 by mid–2002.

In the meantime, the Israeli withdrawal from southern Lebanon removed a major issue from the Lebanese national agenda. This has led to further developments in the Lebanese domestic sphere, which could threaten the Syrian presence there. At first, the Christian population in the country – including the Maronite Patriarch – called for the removal of Syrian forces from Lebanon under the terms of the Taif Agreement of 1989. Gradually, other groups in Lebanon, among them the Druse, began to take up this call as well, and a number of anti-Syrian demonstrations were held. Moreover, the election of Rafik Hariri to the leadership of Lebanon did not ease Syria's position. While the Hariri government did not display an openly anti-Syrian orientation, it has shown a certain tendency toward independence, which could prove to be a thorn in Syria's side. It is also possible that the death of President Hafez Assad made the task of anti-Syrian forces in Lebanon easier. Young President Bashar was likely perceived as an untried leader, who could be openly challenged more easily than his father was.

Syria also had to consider the price of escalation with Israel in terms of its presence in Lebanon. If tensions were to rise between itself and Hizballah on the one side and Israel on the other, such tensions would likely have been fought out on Lebanese soil. This, in turn, might have fed public calls in Lebanon for Syria's departure. The Syrian leadership was no doubt aware that the destruction of its radar posts in Lebanon could not have overly saddened many Lebanese. For all of these reasons, the anti-Syrian sentiment in Lebanon needed to be brought under control. In August 2001, Bashar decided to take a tougher posture against anti-Syrian groups in Lebanon, pressuring the President of Lebanon to arrest the most vocal critics of its presence there.

The developments in Lebanon again pointed to the impossibility of detaching Syria from the Lebanese-Israeli sphere. Even after the Israeli withdrawal, it was apparent that events on the Israeli-Syrian channel had a direct and immediate impact on Lebanese-Israeli relations, and vice-versa. Moreover, it was assumed that Syria's long-term goal remained returning the Golan to its control. If this was so, then Syria clearly had an interest in perpetuating this connection – Lebanon remained the only arena in which it could continue to pressure Israel by proxy. As long as there was no agreement between Israel and Syria, the latter had no interest in working for calm in Southern Lebanon. However, to successfully implement a long-term policy of brinkmanship along the Lebanese-Israeli border, Syria needed to learn how to finely calibrate the flames in southern Lebanon to a level that would prevent escalation. If it were to provoke Israel into direct confrontation, its clear military inferiority would make it extremely vulnerable. All of this made for a very sensitive situation, which was highly prone to miscalculations and unintended escalation. If the preceding analysis accurately reflects Syrian motives and interests, its leaders will have to walk an extremely narrow tightrope in the future as well.

Paradoxically, the very difficulty of successfully implementing such a policy could have motivated Bashar Assad to soften his stance regarding a renewal of talks with Israel, by removing any linkage between it and events in the Israeli-Palestinian arena. However, as of early 2002 there was no sign that Bashar had indeed considered such a move. Rather, rhetorical declarations notwithstanding, Syria's president seemed to be focusing mainly on internal matters. A new leader, he needed to shore up his standing, and there were high expectations of him to reform Syria's shaky economy. It was therefore hard to imagine that he would undertake a major peace initiative with Israel. Such talks would have obligated him to make difficult decisions and face down opposition forces within his leadership, at a time when his own political future remained uncertain. In any case, Israeli attacks on Syrian assets in Lebanon seem to have impressed upon him the extent of his country's military inferiority, and the risks inherent in a direct confrontation with Israel.

Following September 11, the United States began to consider Syria a potential candidate for its international anti-terror coalition. While Bashar did not want to be seen by the West as having sided with the terrorists, he was also unenthusiastic about leading Syria into a Western-led coalition against terrorism. Accordingly, Syrian leaders have insisted that organizations under their patronage which employ terrorist tactics be considered "national liberation groups" and not "terrorist organizations." The U.S. decision to place Hizballah, Hamas, and the Islamic Jihad among the organizations with which it will deal in the framework of the war on terrorism has placed Syria in a difficult position in light of its support for these and other groups. This has limited Syria's freedom to maneuver, and has had something of a moderating effect on it. This may have contributed to the Bush administration's decision not to include Syria in its so-called "axis of evil."

Lebanon is also facing a problem. Initially the Lebanese government voiced support for the United States, seeing the war on terrorism as an opportunity to crush radical Sunni Islamic groups that threatened it. However, the United States soon added Hizballah to its list of terrorist groups, and demanded Lebanese action against it. This placed the Lebanese government in an awkward position, for several reasons. First, Hizballah was a major player in the Lebanese political establishment. In addition, the organization enjoyed the support of Syria, the major power broker in the country. Finally, Hizballah was the major representative of Lebanon's sizeable Shi'ite community. So far, Lebanon has refused to comply with U.S. demands, and this may yet lead to a clash between the two.

Regional Effects of the Israeli-Palestinian Violence

The El-Aqsa Intifada has affected Arab public opinion much more powerfully than observers of the previous Intifada (1987–1993) might have expected. There are a number of possible explanations for this. For one, Arab anger with Israel may have reflected disappointment in the peace process generally, which had raised hopes throughout the region and then failed to live up to them. Another possible explanation relates to the intensity of the present violence: fighting between Israelis and Palestinians was fiercer than it had been in the first Intifada, and casualties mounted more quickly. Here it must be recalled that, despite the use of shared nomenclature, there were major differences between the first Intifada and the present violence. The former was a civil uprising in the conventional sense, involving only limited use of firearms on both sides. By contrast, the latter has been characterized by more intense combat, and wider use of gunfire. This has resulted in much larger numbers of Palestinian casualties over a shorter period. Notwithstanding these explanations, the changes noted above in the Arab mass media have played a significant role in this context as well, helping to galvanize Arab public opinion.

In the late 1980s and 1990s, the Arab press was still largely local, confined to the territorial boundaries of each state and subject to tight censorship and control by their respective governments. However, as noted above, this situation has changed: the spread of Arabic-language satellite stations, outside of the control of any one government, has proved to be a major development in the Arab world. These stations, which have garnered a wide viewership throughout the Arabic-speaking Middle East, have had a major effect on how the Arab public receives information on world events, and how it relates to that information. Moreover, these stations functioned according to commercial broadcasting interests and standards, seeking to increase ratings by use of sensationalism.

Broadcasts related the harsh realities of the Israeli-Palestinian conflict – such as the killing of twelve-year-old Muhammad a-Durra – into Arab homes with great immediacy and impact. These images, coupled with hyped-up voiceovers, deepened anti-Israeli sentiments throughout the Middle East. While many governments in the region had wanted to see the conflict "blow over," they were unable to control public opinion in light of this kind of coverage.

In many countries, the most affected sectors of society were those already deeply dissatisfied with their regimes. These circles included disaffected intellectuals, frustrated by the decline of socialism and Arab unity, and economically disadvantaged groups drawn to radical Islamic ideologies. This raised concerns among various moderate Arab regimes that the violence might "spill over" into their territories, leading to anti-government uprisings or demonstrations. These concerns were especially evident in Jordan and Egypt. Though it now appears that such fears were largely exaggerated, the crisis atmosphere was palpable at the time. Ultimately, the ability of these regimes to take control of the "street" demonstrated that they were both stronger and more effective than either they themselves, or many outside analysts, had previously believed.

The Jordanians, in particular, felt that they had been caught in an extremely delicate situation. For the Hashemite leadership, the Israeli-Palestinian confrontation loomed to near-existential proportions, due in part to the country's demographic composition. Most of the Jordanian population is of Palestinian ancestry, and the dominant East Bank elites feared a firestorm among Jordanians of Palestinian origin. Their concern was that events on the West Bank could easily and quickly spread to Jordan, igniting a backlash against the government. Jordan also feared that a worsening of the confrontation could drive large numbers of refugees across the Jordan River into its territory. This would adversely affect the Kingdom's already shaky economy, which has had to invest considerable resources in the absorption of Palestinian refugees in the past. A large influx of refugees would also shift the demographic balance in Jordan, which would in turn adversely affect the stability of the regime.

Jordan's solution was to express identification with the Palestinian cause in public statements, which it backed up by a series of diplomatic sanctions against Israel. Jordan downgraded the level of its diplomatic mission to Israel by failing to replace its outgoing ambassador to Tel Aviv. The government reduced high-profile joint activities with Israel, and expressed its support for Palestinian positions in a variety of international forums. Among these forums were two Arab League summit conferences (the first in Cairo, on October 21–22, 2000, and the second in Amman, on March 27–28, 2001) that met following the outbreak of the violence. However, Jordan took care to ensure that its peace treaty with Israel remained intact. It also took a series of steps intended to prevent the situation from deteriorating further, or from developing into a regional conflict:

- The Jordanian regime allowed demonstrations against Israel to take place at the beginning of the violence, as a way of venting frustration. However, it placed limits on both their location and duration, to prevent them from turning into mass uprisings.
- Jordan cooperated with other moderate forces in the Arab world, particularly Egypt, to restrain radical elements in the Arab world. In doing so, it was able to block the Arab summits from making decisions that would endanger existing peace treaties with Israel. A decision during the Arab Summit in Amman that would have called on Egypt and Jordan to violate the obligations set out in their peace agreements was also averted.
- Jordan, together with Egypt, undertook a joint initiative (the aforementioned 'Jordanian-Egyptian Initiative') to end violence between Israel and the Palestinians.
- Beyond the decision to not post a new ambassador to Tel Aviv, Jordan made an effort not to harm the real content of its bilateral relations with Israel, especially in the fields of economics and security. In fact, Israeli-Jordanian bilateral trade actually grew in 2001.

Prime Ministers Barak and Sharon were both aware of Jordan's sensitive position, and tried to adopt policies intended to assist in easing its pressures and constraints. Unfortunately, many of these policies continued to languor under the weight of Israeli red tape. Not unusual was the case of a planned joint Israeli-Jordanian airport, intended to serve the Red Sea resorts of Eilat (in Israel) and Aqaba (in Jordan) from a single, shared facility. In the end, the airport was never constructed.

Egypt continued to sway between the two extremes that have traditionally characterized its foreign policy *vis-à-vis* Israel. On the one hand, it has exploited the collapse of Israeli-Palestinian relations to advance its traditional goal of "reducing Israel to its natural proportions." That is, Egypt sought to use the violence to block the normalization of Israel's ties with third-party Arab states, in keeping with its longtime goal of preventing Israel from forming meaningful ties in the Arab world independent of Cairo. This fit into Egypt's larger Israel policy: preventing Israeli influence from threatening Cairo's claim to regional leadership. For this reason, Egypt supported and even encouraged Arab Summit decisions against normalization with Israel, and against relations between Israel and additional Arab countries, though it did so without resorting to harsh rhetoric. On the other hand, peace with Israel continued to be a cornerstone of

Egypt's strategic policy. President Mubarak recalled the Egyptian Ambassador to Israel, Muhammad Bassiouni, in the waning days of the Barak government because of what he considered excessive Israeli military actions. By doing so, he may have unwittingly contributed to Barak's failure at the polls. Egypt's perceived lack of sensitivity to Israeli concerns during the initial weeks of the violence deepened suspicions among many Israelis regarding overall Arab implacability toward Israel, further undermining confidence in the stability of peace treaties.

However, Mubarak has also made a number of efforts to prevent the Israeli-Palestinian violence from "going regional." He stood at the head of the moderate Arab camp, stemming the anti-Israeli tide that was prevalent at the Arab League summits in Cairo and Amman. Particularly significant were a series of statements made by President Mubarak to a number of Arab leaders as well as to the Arab public at large. In these statements, Mubarak came out sharply opposed to calls for a joint military effort against Israel. He made it unequivocally clear that war was not an option, and that Egypt was not even considering it. The wording of these statements held the rhetoric of more radical leaders like Saddam Hussein and Muammar al-Qaddafi to ridicule. When Hussein and Qaddafi called for war with Israel, Mubarak reminded them that Egypt was the leading Arab military power, and that they ought not be quite so generous in offering to fight Israel "to the last Egyptian soldier." Beyond the need to restrain radical Arab leaders, these statements seemed to reflect awareness of Israeli concerns that had grown in the wake of the violence. Jerusalem needed reassuring that Egypt's harsh rhetoric did not mean that the country was actively preparing to take up arms. Were Israelis to receive this impression, they might have been led to lobby against Egypt in the U.S. Congress, and perhaps move for a reduction in the military aid that Cairo receives from Washington. Later, statements made by senior figures in the Egyptian security establishment were added to those of Mubarak, emphasizing that Egypt's rearmament program was for defensive purposes only.

In contrast to Jordan, Egypt did seek to reduce the substance of its bilateral relations with Israel, although as of early 2002 it had scrupulously avoided any steps that might be construed as not in keeping with its treaty obligations. Egyptian authorities presided over an unprecedented decline in economic ties between the two countries, and vetoed any cultural activity. The isolation surrounding the Israeli embassy in Cairo grew even greater. The results of the Israeli elections worsened relations between the two countries still further; Egypt was concerned by the "radical" policies of Prime Minister Sharon, in whom its leaders had little confidence. President Mubarak has refrained from inviting Sharon to Egypt; there were to be no more televised images of Israeli and

Egyptian leaders together, as had been common during the Barak's tenure in office. Relations between the governments of Israel and Egypt have been conducted primarily via Foreign Minister Shimon Peres, but even his stature has suffered in Egyptian eyes because of his decision to serve in the Sharon government.

Unlike Egypt and Jordan, Saddam Hussein and Muammar al-Qaddafi saw the violence as an opportunity to rehabilitate their standing in the Arab world and to weaken support for the international sanctions against them. While Qaddafi confined himself to rhetoric, Saddam Hussein demonstratively sent large military forces west of Baghdad toward the Jordanian border on two separate occasions. Though taking care not to send them too far west, he sought to demonstrate his willingness to join an Arab war-coalition against Israel. The manner in which these forces were deployed demonstrated that this was largely a "show" gesture, rather than the deployment of forces with a real military potential. Israel and the United States responded to Saddam's actions with restraint – and in large part, simply by ignoring them – and in so doing prevented him from exploiting this military redeployment for the purpose of achieving tangible political or military benefits.

Notwithstanding the pressures of public opinion and the desire to punish Israel for what they considered an excessive use of force, many moderate Arab leaders were extremely angry with the leadership of the PA. While never daring to say so publicly, Arafat came across as irresponsible, having placed the entire region on a crisis footing.

These feelings came to the fore in the decisions made at the close of the Arab League summits in Cairo and Amman. On a rhetorical level, nothing seemed amiss: the second summit in Amman gave its full support to the Palestinians, the Syrians and the Lebanese in their struggle against Israel, and harshly condemned both Israel and the United States. It also called on international forums to take steps against Israel, and for the UN Security Council to station an international force in the area to defend the Palestinians. However, when it came to concrete, operative steps that would actually obligate the Arab states themselves, the statements released by the two summits were more circumspect. Care was taken not to demand measures beyond those that most of the states had already implemented. The summits called for a cessation of normalization, for the renewal of activities by the Arab Boycott Office, and for a refrain from the formation of new relations between Arab states and Israel. All of this was carefully worded to leave existing peace treaties with Israel intact.

Regarding financial support for the Palestinians, the summits set aside a total of U.S. $180 million for six months, a relatively small sum compared to the enormous economic damage suffered by the Palestinian economy. Moreover, experience from the earlier summit in Cairo left room for doubt about whether anything more than a small fraction of this sum would ever be transferred to the Palestinians. Mechanisms were also set up to oversee the transfer of these monies, a step that implied a certain degree of mistrust. The goal of these mechanisms was to prevent Arafat from using aid money as a personal slush fund and to ensure that funds went to specific projects that would benefit the Palestinian population.

Collective Arab behavior since the beginning of the violence seemed to indicate that most Arab leaders wanted the Palestinian "nuisance" to be dealt with at a minimum of cost and bother. Most states wanted to return as quickly as possible to the main issues that were on their local agendas and realized that both the global and regional balances of power had not changed. Israel remained a firm U.S. ally, and a strong military and economic power in its own right. This reality dictated a continued pursuance of moderate, careful policies, with an eye toward returning to the peace process. The majority of the Arab states was still mired in economic stagnation, and there was no alternative superpower sponsor whose patronage might be enlisted in support of an attempt to resolve the Arab-Israeli conflict by force. Moreover, most Arab states still believed that their long-term strategic interests could be served under U.S. auspices. This helps to explain why Israeli-Palestinian violence failed to spread to other states in 2001, despite the increasing intensity of the confrontation between the two sides. It also explains the general desire that existed in the region for a renewal of the peace process.

However, this behavior also reflected a change in the atmosphere in the Middle East. Despite U.S. influence in the region, there were definite limits to its power. The confidence that moderate regimes had placed in U.S. support has atrophied, while at the same time radical regimes not only held their own, but surged back onto the regional scene, like the mythical phoenix. This atmosphere, combined with the domestic concerns of many Arab regimes, made it difficult for them to swim against the current. The prevailing winds blew in favor of extremist responses to ongoing Israeli-Palestinian violence, even if specific leaders might have wished to do otherwise.

Developments in the region since the violence began also pointed to the effects of the inter-generational "passing of the torch." Leaders possessed with experience and power have increasingly been replaced by younger, less experienced ones who were, in comparison to their predecessors, relatively weak and lacking in prestige. This phenomenon characterized monarchical and non-monarchical regimes alike. In Morocco, Muhammad VI replaced the late King Hassan II. In Jordan, King Abdullah II replaced King Hussein, and in Syria, which is in theory governed as a republic, Bashar Assad replaced his father, Hafez Assad.

In Jordan, the changeover reduced the regime's self-confidence, affecting its ability to cope with the effects of the Israeli-Palestinian conflict. In Syria, Bashar Assad was having difficulty in dealing both with the effects of violence in southern Lebanon and with the rising opposition to Syria's presence there. Hopes for accelerated reforms in both of these countries did not bear fruit. In the meantime, the risks stemming from internal instability, and from ill-considered decisions being made by inexperienced leaders, grew.

Chapter Three

The Gulf: Back to the Future

Upon taking office, the Bush administration made the Persian Gulf the central focus of its Middle East policy. In this, President George W. Bush demonstrated continuity with past Republican administrations, which have seen the Arab-Israeli peace process as an extension of its need to ensure stability in the Persian Gulf. That is, by fostering an Arab-Israeli peace, one brings greater stability to the Middle East, which in turn reduces the potential of destabilization in the Gulf. According to this perception, the Clinton administration's focus on the Israeli-Palestinian and Israeli-Syrian tracks served to blur U.S. priorities somewhat. Indeed, had the Israeli-Palestinian violence not broken out, the Bush administration's re-focusing of U.S. priorities to the Gulf would likely have been even more rapid.

Iraq Rattles its Cage, Again

Over the course of 2001, Saddam Hussein enhanced Iraq's regional standing, despite the fact that there were no actual changes in its military capabilities. Sanctions against the country remained in place. There was no evidence that Iraq had succeeded in acquiring significant amounts of military equipment over the period in question, and in any case, it had certainly not acquired any major new weapons systems. With that, the country's oil exports rose – both through UN-controlled channels, and via smuggling that went on outside of the UN's control – and this increased the financial resources at the government's disposal.

As a result of restrictions placed on Iraq through the UN sanctions program, Saddam Hussein has not been able to acquire sophisticated new weapons systems since 1991. While the country's leadership may have succeeded in smuggling in spare parts for existing weapons systems, these were in any case rapidly becoming obsolete. At the same time, other states in the Gulf region with ties to Western arms suppliers have been on a steady course of military procurement, a process that has accelerated since the Gulf War. Iran also strengthened its armed forces over this period. From a purely military standpoint, Saudi Arabia and the smaller Gulf states have continued to improve their ability to cope with an Iraqi threat. Moreover, the U.S. military presence in the region provided an additional deterrent.

Despite the fact that in practice, Iraq's military capabilities remained unchanged, perceptions regarding its power have altered. As in the stock market, where the value of a company is determined in part by estimating its future profitability, Iraq's neighbors were keenly aware of its future military potential. Regional actors believed they were witnessing the beginning of Iraq's slow but inevitable climb out from under the limitations imposed by the UN sanctions regime, and have been preparing themselves against such an eventuality.

Since expelling the UN Special Commission (UNSCOM) from its territory in August 1998, there has been no monitoring of Iraqi non-conventional weapons development and production facilities from inside the country. It was thus assumed by many observers in 2001 that Saddam had tried to exploit this lack of oversight by renewing attempts to acquire such weapons. This assumption was predicated on two observations. First, there was no evidence to indicate that Saddam had decided to abandon his country's efforts to develop non-conventional weapons. Second, his confrontational behavior toward UNSCOM would seem to have indicated exactly the opposite: that Iraq did intend to preserve and rebuild its non-conventional weapons programs.

Notwithstanding the measure of latitude afforded him by the lack of international monitoring, Iraq was still very heavily constrained in terms of what it could do to renew its non-conventional weapons programs. These constraints were of three sorts:

- *UN spending controls.* UN oversight controls limited the spending of most of the country's oil export revenues. Consequently, Saddam was able only to use those funds that became available through smuggling for his rearmament program.
- *Trade sanctions.* There was an oversight mechanism in place to control and limit Iraqi imports. However, this mechanism did suffer from a number of obvious blind spots. For example, Jordan stopped allowing oversight efforts to take place from its territory.
- *Intelligence-gathering resources.* Long-range observation of Iraq took place on a continual basis by means of U.S.-based national-technical intelligence-gathering means.

Saddam therefore would have had to be careful; had the United States obtained unequivocal information regarding Iraqi activity in the non-conventional realm, it would not have hesitated to use military force to put an end to them.

Iraq's political standing was also on an upward course in 2001. The United States found it difficult to mobilize continued international support in favor of sanctions as they had been implemented since the Gulf War. The Arab Summit Meeting in Amman, for example, called in March 2001 for sanctions against Iraq to be fully removed. Given that Arab League decisions can only be made by consensus, it is clear that the U.S. position on sanctions had taken a beating in the Arab world. The decision of the League meant that even the primary victim of Saddam's aggression in 1991, Kuwait, felt unable to vote against such a decision, given the prevailing regional atmosphere. In Europe, only the United Kingdom continued to support the U.S. position on sanctions. Russia and France were openly calling for their removal, perhaps in the hopes of winning lucrative export deals when the Iraqi economy eventually opened up to the world. The economic potential of post-sanction relations with Iraq also led regional actors, such as Turkey and Jordan, to seek a removal of sanctions, despite their awareness of the dangers inherent in Saddam's regime.

All of this created a sense that the end of sanctions was a none-too-distant inevitability. In a post-sanctions environment, it would be easier for Iraq to rebuild its forces, both conventional and non-conventional. This possibility, and the sense of its impending inevitability, exercised an important influence on the behavior of Iraq's neighbors. These states assumed that, at some time in the future, they would have to deal with a militarily resurgent Iraqi regime, without any corresponding guarantee of U.S. protection. The increasing number of states that were seeking to establish direct air links with Baghdad, in defiance of the UN ban on them, clearly demonstrated Iraq's political comeback.

Saddam Hussein was also confident about the security of his regime. While his military capabilities were not sufficient for him to pose a threat to his neighbors, they were certainly sufficient for maintaining domestic stability. He would have had little difficulty in dealing with the Kurdish and Shi'ite opposition movements, and could have brought them both to their knees with relative ease if U.S. patrols over the northern and southern no-fly zones had been removed. With the help of his well-oiled internal security services, Saddam also proved that he was able to handle – with the same ease and brutality that the world had come to expect – any threat that might develop from within the ranks of the regime itself.

For all of these reasons, the Bush administration needed to come to terms with an Iraq whose self-confidence was on the rise and in whose eyes the credibility of the U.S. deterrent was on the decline. All of this was made even more difficult because international support for containing Iraq – through sanctions, UN monitors, no-fly zones, and so forth – was drying up, as was support for the U.S.-led alliance that had been set up for this purpose.

Before the U.S. elections, foreign-policy circles close to Bush had attacked the Clinton policy on Iraq, claiming that it suffered from indecisiveness, and that it had failed to bring results. The Bush team's main criticisms of the Clinton policy were as follows:

- Since the cessation of UNSCOM activities in Iraq, there has been no effective monitoring effort there.
- The existing sanctions had been eroded, and in their then-present form, they would soon have become unenforceable.
- Operations Northern and Southern Watch had been ineffective. The no-fly rules had not effectively limited Saddam's ability to undertake actions against opposition groups. Moreover, the sporadic air attacks on Iraqi targets had not served any purpose and had needlessly exposed U.S. planes to the risk of being shot down. Should that have happened, the crews of those planes would either have been killed or taken prisoner by Iraq.
- No real effort had been made to topple Saddam Hussein. Even when Congress set aside considerable funds for this purpose, they were never used.

The Bush administration has since taken office, and prior to September 11, there had been no significant change in U.S. policy on Iraq. With real-world responsibility firmly on their shoulders, the foreign policy team of the new administration seemed chastened by real-world constraints, having recognized that their ability to produce change was limited. It became clear that they would have to make a choice: there was no possibility of maintaining both sanctions and in-country international monitoring at the same time. That is, there was little chance that Saddam would have accepted the United Nations Monitoring, Verification and Inspection Commission (UNMOVIC), the proposed UN monitoring group intended to replace UNSCOM, without a removal of sanctions. The Iraqi leadership seemed to be betting that, even if it agreed to the presence of UNMOVIC inspectors, it would have been able to continue covertly developing weapons of mass destruction. Therefore, the U.S. administration had to make a decision between pressing for the continuation of sanctions without an agreed-upon mechanism for reinstating UN monitors within Iraq, or for UN monitoring but without the sanctions regime in place.

By late 2001, the Bush administration seemed to have chosen the former. Nevertheless, in doing so, they have recognized that the U.S. must head off international opposition to the humanitarian costs of sanctions, which were perceived as doing more harm to the Iraqi people than to the regime. To that end, the administration formulated a concept called "smart sanctions." The goal of smart sanctions was to apply more focused limits on Iraq, denying it only those goods that might be used for military applications (whether conventional or non-conventional), including dual-use items. However, the U.S. proposal failed to pass when it was brought to the UN Security Council.

In 2001, the Bush administration was yet to formulate a policy regarding the question of military action or the effort to topple Saddam. Any policy in that regard would have had to find a way through a number of difficult constraints. First, there was no regional consensus for such a move, nor was there willingness among the American people to suffer losses to bring down Saddam. The United States would therefore have had to find a low-risk option that did not involve massing large forces in the region or require a strong set of regional allies. Under these constraints, the United States will have found it difficult to develop a military option that could both contain Iraq and produce a change in its regime.

No less difficult was finding a way to change the regime from within: opposition groups outside of Iraq lacked any foothold within the country, while inside Iraq there simply were no effective opposition groups. Moreover, U.S. allies on the border with Iraq had been 'burned' in past efforts to assist the United States in attempts to undermine the Iraqi regime and were not about to hurry to do so again. An example of this was the cooperation between the United States and Jordan following the defection of Hussein Kamel to Amman. Jordanian leaders believed that its cooperation with the United States had gone completely unrewarded and ultimately only served to create enmity between Saddam and Jordanian leaders.

The war on terrorism added another layer of uncertainty regarding future developments in the U.S.-Iraqi relationship and its implications for the Middle East. Some Bush administration officials pushed for a strike against Iraq in the framework of the war on terrorism, though there was at the time no real evidence that Iraq was involved in the September 11, 2001 attacks. Should this idea be adopted, such an attack would likely be wider in scope than the piecemeal attacks that took place in the framework of Operations Northern and Southern Watch. This, in turn, could lead to a backlash: should Saddam feel that his survival was under serious threat, he could react by attacking Israel or Saudi Arabia, as he did in 1991.

Iran: Reform in Retreat

Over 2001, the conservatives scored additional successes in their efforts to trim the wings of the reformists. Despite the fact that popular support for reformist president Muhammad Khatami remained intact, conservatives used their control over the country's most powerful institutions to block the reform agenda. Anti-reform efforts included arrests, trials and the closing of pro-reform newspapers.

In addition, Iran's particular form of government allowed the Council of the Guardians of the Constitution, led by the country's supreme religious leader, Ali Khamenei, to block any legislation it considered unacceptable. As a result, Khatami was unable to make good on much of his reformist agenda, especially in the domestic sphere. This led to great frustration, both for him personally and for his supporters.

The Khatami government did manage some successes in the economic sphere, though this was not entirely due to its specific policies. The rise in petroleum prices had considerably enlarged Iran's oil revenues, and left it with a budget that was larger than projected. The atmosphere of reform and openness that Khatami projected also eased relations with Europe, making the country more open to economic relations and investment.

No change was observed, however, in Iran's foreign and defense policies. The bodies responsible for formulating these policies remained firmly in the control of the conservatives, under the leadership of Khamenei. Iran's involvement in Lebanon, for example, continued unabated; its material and ideological support of the Hizballah remained as firm as ever. Iran also continued to support Palestinian organizations that opposed peace with Israel, and found fertile ground for its activities with the outbreak of the El-Aqsa Intifada. Finally, attempts to hold a dialogue with the United States, which might have led to some sort of U.S.-Iranian thaw, did not go well. Iran was unwilling change policies that were sticking points in its relations with the United States. Nonetheless, reformist elements within Iran have maintained informal dialogues with various bodies in the West, perhaps with the hope that in the future it would be possible for them to expand their influence into Iranian foreign policy. The Iranians that took part in these dialogues demonstrated both openness and a willingness to consider policies that both the United States and Israel could live with. These included refraining from support of terrorism and from activities intended to undermine the Middle East peace process.

Khatami ran for re-election in June 2001. While the difficulties he experienced in implementing his policy agenda caused him to hesitate over whether to run again, he was re-elected by a large majority of the voters. This was not unexpected: all indicators of Iranian public opinion had pointed to the large majority enjoyed by the reformists. In every round of elections that has taken place since coming to power – whether national, parliamentary, or local – the reformists have enjoyed large majorities. The question was whether the disappointment and frustration of many reformists, given the lack of tangible successes by Khatami and his parliament, might have led eventually to despair and indifference among his popular supporters. Some degree of voter disenchantment may have been apparent in the lower rates of participation in the June elections. In any event, the elections again demonstrated that, from a certain perspective, Khatami was *good* for the conservative regime, serving as an outlet for public dissatisfaction. From the conservative viewpoint, Khatami was less dangerous than other alternatives: experience showed that he could be sidelined if necessary, while his presence channeled such dissatisfaction away from other, potentially more dangerous, outlets.

The events following September 11 gave Khatami an opportunity to advance an important item in his foreign policy agenda: improving Iranian relations with the United States. Moreover, in the wake of the attacks, it seemed that the Iranian leader was poised to do so. In that vein, the Iranian government issued a remarkable statement, noting that Iran stood ready to help rescue U.S. air crews shot down over Afghanistan. However, the conservatives overruled Khatami's efforts in this area, as they had done in the past. The United States' frustration with Iran's policy led President Bush, in January 2002, to define it as a member of the "axis of evil."

Iran continued to develop capabilities for the manufacture of weapons of mass destruction, though there were no signs over the course of 2000–2001 that any particular breakthroughs had been achieved. No further tests of the Shahab-3 missile, whose long range would give Iran the ability to strike Israel from its territory, were noted, and it did not yet appear to be operational. In the nuclear field, there was no evidence that Iran had acquired either a uranium-enrichment facility or a plutonium separation plant, essential for the production of weapons-grade fissile materials. Though Iran's nuclear program continued to progress, it did so slowly. This seemed to indicate that the regime wished to create the infrastructure for a future nuclear capability, but in a manner that would not bring down a storm of international condemnation, should it be caught doing so before its achievements could be considered a *fait accompli.*

Iran's behavior regarding chemical weapons could provide future indications regarding its nuclear policy. Iran signed the Chemical Weapons Convention (CWC), ratified it, and even submitted a report to the Organization for the Prohibition of Chemical Weapons (OPCW), as required. In its report, Iran admitted that it had possessed various chemical agents in the past. Since joining the CWC, it has actively participated in the organization's various institutions. Nevertheless, during 2000–2001 western intelligence organizations reported that Iran had continued to manufacture chemical weapons, in stark violation of the treaty. It was not known if there had been specific sightings of violations by the organization's monitoring agency, which was still only partially functional.

The growth in oil revenues from 1997 to 2001 gave Iran increased funds for military procurement, and a parallel increase was observed in expenditures for new weapons systems. In addition, Russian President Vladimir Putin's decision to set aside a 1995 agreement with the United States not to supply Iran with advanced munitions was expected to open new vistas for Iranian conventional rearmament based on Russian-made weapons systems. Negotiations between Russia and Iran were held in this context, and a large-scale framework agreement was signed (though estimates regarding the extent of this agreement in dollar terms varied between U.S. $2–7 billion). Iran was reportedly seeking to acquire Russian-made air-defense systems, such as S-300 missiles and SA-16 shoulder-launched anti-aircraft missiles. In addition, it expressed interest in acquiring large numbers of T-72 tanks, BMP-2 Armored Fighting Vehicles, Mi-17 helicopters, and a small number of Su-25 aircraft. As of late 2001, it was not known which elements of this deal had actually been finalized, beyond the purchase of the SA-16s.

Chapter Four

The Role of Extra-Regional Actors

The outbreak of violence on the Israeli-Palestinian front in September 2000 obligated a number of non-regional actors to reorient their policies concerning the Middle East in 2001. Such a reorientation was also necessary given the results of the elections in the United States, the dominant extra-regional power. In addition, the Russian administration, under the leadership of President Vladimir Putin, had been reconsidering its goals in the region during the period in question. Prior to 2001, the new Russian leadership had been largely preoccupied with affairs in Chechnya, and was unable to undertake a formal and comprehensive review of its foreign policy.

In the meantime, the September 11, 2001 terror attacks on the United States affected U.S.-Russian relations deeply. Both sides now had an interest in resolving a number of outstanding foreign policy disagreements, among them the United States' national missile defense (NMD) program. A similar convergence took place with regard to both states' agendas for the Middle East.

The same cannot be said, however, for relations between the United States and the EU, which continued to be characterized by disagreements on issues of Middle Eastern policy. Indeed, here the war on terrorism only deepened divisions, as disagreements over a possible attack on Iraq come to the fore.

U.S. Policy: At the Crossroads

When President Bush took office in January 2001, there was a definite sense that U.S. foreign policy was about to undergo a major re-evaluation. This could be heard in the rhetoric at the time, which reflected the dim view taken by the Bush team of nearly every aspect of the Clinton administration's policies. Clinton's foreign policy – and specifically, his administration's Middle East policy – was no exception: the new administration was harshly critical of the old. The Bush foreign policy team's criticism of U.S. policy in the Middle East centered on the following points:

- *Incorrect emphases.* Too much energy and attention was being given to Israeli-Palestinian issues and too little to dealing with issues of greater strategic importance to the United States, such as stability in the Persian Gulf.
- *Iraq.* The four elements of the Clinton administration's Iraq policy (monitoring, sanctions, the no-fly zones, and support for opposition groups) were judged ineffective. UN monitoring in Iraq had ceased following Saddam's expulsion of UNSCOM in 1998. The sanctions were too broad in their application, and were taking the majority of their toll on the lives of the Iraqi people. Beyond whatever moral questions might be raised by this, it tended to undermine international support for sanctions and provided ammunition for Iraq's fight to have them revoked. The northern and southern no-fly zones were having no effect on goings-on in the country. Finally, attempts to destabilize the Ba'athist regime had been completely ineffective.
- *Peace Process.* The Clinton administration had allowed itself to get overly involved in the Middle East peace process, micro-managing decisions which should have been left to the parties themselves.

Beyond this, Bush staffers were critical on related issues that, though perhaps not truly Middle Eastern by definition, had a definite effect on events there. Central in this regard were U.S. NMD policy, and relations between the United States and the People's Republic of China.

Like its predecessor, the new administration devoted its initial efforts to domestic issues, such as taxation. While some foreign policy issues were also addressed, these were issues of exceptional scope or urgency, such as NMD or the Sino-American spy-plane crisis. These factors all contributed to a sense that it might prove expedient for the President to detach himself from day-to-day events in the Israeli-Palestinian conflict and not to hasten in the reformulation of U.S. Gulf policy.

Political and strategic considerations notwithstanding, considerable time is required for a new administration to install itself fully in the White House. Presidential transitions are immensely complex affairs. The process of nominating officials to key posts in the State and Defense Departments require Senate approval hearings. All of this takes time, and only after it has been concluded can a coherent process of policy formation take place. The delays inherent as this process got underway may have led some observers to conclude prematurely that the administration had no clear policy on central issues relating to the Middle East.

A major question in 2001 related to what the results of such a policy-formation process would be, once it was completed. Many observers noted that U.S.

foreign policy would likely be more deeply influenced by real-world constraints than presidential campaign rhetoric might have initially indicated. These observers noted that policies advocated from the election trail were all well and good, but that once in the White House things often appeared somewhat different.

Another factor that guided observers of Washington were the different schools of thought that characterized the various senior aides in the Bush administration. These could be roughly divided into three major groups:

- *Neo-Conservatives.* Old school Reaganites ("neo-cons") who favored hard and fast ideological positions that recalled the conservatism of the Reagan administration. Among these were Vice-President Dick Cheney, Defense Secretary Donald Rumsfeld, and Paul Wolfowitz. In the early days of the administration, this group seemed to be the most successful in gaining the ear of the President.
- *Legacies from Bush, Sr.* Holdovers from the previous Bush administration: a group with a generally pragmatic and realist (in international relations terms) outlook. Aides with this general outlook were expected to seek pragmatic ways to advance U.S. goals at the lowest possible cost. Advisers of this bent included Secretary of State Colin Powell and National Security Advisor Condoleezza Rice.
- *Professionals from State.* The third and final group was the professional staff of the State Department. In general, the professional foreign service has in the past acted as a stabilizing force, seeking to maintain consistency in U.S. policy from administration to administration.

Initially, the Bush administration seemed to avoid the issue of Israeli-Palestinian violence, which was perceived as a political "hot potato." The post of U.S. Special Envoy to the Middle East, which had been filled by Dennis Ross, was eliminated, with the administration preferring to leave the two sides to "stew in their own juices" for a time. The key question was whether such an approach could be sustained over the long term. Crises left untreated in the Middle East have a tendency to balloon to proportions where they no longer can be ignored. Moreover, continued U.S. involvement in the region was first and foremost in the interest of the United States itself. This held true even if the new administration believed that Israeli-Palestinian conflict was fundamentally irresolvable, and that efforts should be refocused on containing the violence rather than resolving it. An escalation of the violence, or its spread to other Middle Eastern states, would likely have had an adverse effect on key U.S. interests in other parts of the region, not least the Gulf.

Perhaps for this reason, the administration was slowly forced into dealing with the ongoing Israeli-Palestinian violence. An early sign of this was the creation of the aforementioned three-person team of Martin Indyk, at the time Ambassador to Tel Aviv; William Burns, Assistant Secretary of State for Middle Eastern Affairs; and Ronald Schlicher, Consul General to Jerusalem. The task of the Indyk-Burns-Schlicher team was to clear the way for the implementation of the Mitchell report. In addition, President Bush sent CIA Director George Tenet, and later former Marines General Anthony Zinni, to the region in attempts to set up a cease-fire plan. All of these steps, it should be noted, reflected attempts to manage the conflict, rather than to resolve it. It was still too early to determine if this reflected the beginning of a deeper involvement by the Bush administration, or if it was an attempt to maintain appearances, after which the United States would return to a more hands-off approach.

Some observers suggested that Arafat decided not to reach an agreement with Israel in the framework of the negotiations that began at Camp David out of a desire to delay the final stage of talks until after U.S. elections. The logic behind this speculation was that Arafat considered Clinton emotionally tied to and overly supportive of Israel, and believed that the PA's negotiating position might improve with a new administration. If this speculation was correct, it reflected a massive miscalculation on the part of the Palestinian leadership. The PA's relations with the United States worsened dramatically after the Bush administration took office. In deciding to force a crisis between itself and Israel, the PA's leadership squandered one of the most important assets gained in recent years – its close ties with the U.S. government.

The deterioration in U.S.-PA relations could be tied to a number of factors. First, Arafat's personal conduct at the Camp David talks and during the violent confrontations that broke out thereafter made him a much-disliked figure among U.S. leaders. Second, conservatives in the new administration were predisposed to regard him skeptically even before their election to office, in light of his history of terrorism and his alliance with Saddam Hussein. Third, the new administration considered the outgoing president's close relations with Arafat a grave mistake. Investing in a questionable figure of his ilk was, in the eyes of many senior members of the Bush team, a gross misuse of the U.S. taxpayer's money. If anything, it seemed to them symptomatic of the kind of rose-tinted ultra-liberal ideology that characterized both Bill and Hillary Clinton.

By contrast, U.S.-Israel relations were not adversely affected, despite Sharon's long history of confrontation with the United States over policies that he has supported in the past. His restraint in the face of the ongoing Israeli-Palestinian violence was in clear accordance with U.S. interests and laid a solid basis for a working relationship between the two newly elected leaders. The difference in Israeli and Palestinian relations with the United States appeared in stark relief with the willingness of the new president to meet directly with Prime Minister Sharon and contrasted with his refusal to meet PA Chairman Arafat. Even so, there was potential for crisis in the U.S.-Israel relationship. Latent disagreement in relation to settlements or Israeli-initiated military offensives could easily have flared up into full-fledged crises between the two governments, and there have been a number of "close calls" in U.S.-Israel relations over the course of 2001.

U.S. policy toward Iraq appeared to suffer from a different problem. Here, the Bush team claimed to have new policy ideas that would be much more effective than those put in place by the previous administration. There was also an emotional element at work in their desire to find a solution for the Iraqi problem. Much of the team that was appointed to serve under George W. Bush was also involved in the Gulf War, serving under George Herbert Walker Bush. For both the President and senior figures like Cheney and Powell, it was difficult to accept that Saddam Hussein remained in power, and that Iraq was slowly emerging from the effects of the war.

However, in pursuing its desire to see Saddam Hussein's removal, the Bush administration had to face a number of real-world constraints. While the U.S. remained the world's sole superpower, the Middle East had changed since the end of the Gulf War in 1991. U.S. power was limited, and leaders like Saddam Hussein and Yasser Arafat were able to flout U.S. desires and survive. The Iraqi military threat was less palpable than it had been prior to the war, and Iraq's neighbors preferred to focus on whatever economic benefits could be derived from trading with it as it tried to rehabilitate its economy. Moreover, there was little confidence in U.S. determination among its regional allies, who were no longer certain that the United States would stand behind them if they adopted policies that exposed them to Saddam's wrath.

On a broader level, anti-American sentiment was spreading throughout the Middle East. Animosity toward the United States was spurred by a number of factors, including the Israeli-Palestinian conflict and the perception that U.S. sanctions were responsible for a humanitarian catastrophe in Iraq. These animosities were also related to the socioeconomic situation in the Arab world, an extension of perceptions regarding Western economic hegemony and globalization.

In addition, the credibility of U.S. resolve in the Middle East was further weakened by the realization on the part of regional powers that Europe was no longer behind the United States. Only the United Kingdom supported U.S. policy in Iraq. Russia and France both took consistent stands in favor of removing sanctions. It was hard to imagine that the United States would be able to rebuild the Gulf War coalition, given the positions of both the European powers and the states bordering Iraq. It was still too early, however, to determine if these constraints would force the Bush administration into a policy that was essentially similar to that of its predecessor, with perhaps some small changes (such as the aforementioned "smart sanctions"). Another possibility was that the Bush administration might try to promulgate a more aggressively anti-Iraqi agenda, for example by increasing funding to opposition Iraqi circles in the hopes that they would bring down the regime. The September 11 attacks and the U.S. victory in Afghanistan tilted the debate clearly in favor of the latter possibility.

In the case of formulating a new policy on Iran, the administration enjoyed greater latitude. It could easily disavow the Clinton-era policy of "dual containment," freeing it to seek improved relations with the Iranian regime. This was especially the case when the country's formal leader was an avowed reformist, such as Khatami. Some internal opposition to a conciliatory Iranian policy would likely have been encountered among the administration's neo-cons, given their tendency to divide the world into "good guys" and "bad guys" (with Iran, in their eyes, being an unquestioned "bad guy"). However, it was still possible that the more pragmatic approach espoused by Powell could take hold with regard to Iran, given that this was not a hot-button issue for the American right-wing. If so, the main issues that would have made relations between Iran and the United States difficult were the same ones that had been faced by the Clinton administration: Iran's unwillingness to "play the game" according to rules that the United States could accept. Indeed, these difficulties proved critical when the attempts to improve relations with Iran failed in early 2002.

The decision by the Bush foreign policy team to place NMD at the center of its foreign and security policy had a number of ramifications for the Middle East. On the one hand, it created a basis for deepening U.S.-Israeli security cooperation. Israel was already an important partner on this front, as it had been co-developing missile defense systems with the United States for many years. Israel also maintained operational co-operation with the United States on this issue, and provided important support for the administration by helping to enlist political backing for it within the United States. On the other hand, the policy adversely affected U.S. relations with China and Russia, and these two states might well respond by tampering with U.S. interests in the Middle East in the future. This could take a number of forms, such as interfering with U.S. policy initiatives, as they do already on matters relating to Iraq. Other possibilities include aiding the proliferation of non-conventional technologies in the region, as Russia has already done with Iran. The administration's recent difficulties with China could also provide that country's leadership with an increased motive for harming U.S. interests in the Middle East.

September 11 and its Middle East Aftermath

The attacks against the United States on September 11 had a clear effect on the region. First, they engendered a radical change in the U.S. national agenda. Second, and no less important, the attacks themselves were directly tied to the political situation in the Middle East. Finally, they played upon the complex, almost pathological, web of antipathies that existed between the Arab and Muslim world and the West.

Following the attacks of September 11, the Bush administration placed the war on terrorism at the center of its foreign and security policy agendas, providing a clear benchmark for its foreign relations. This meant that U.S. attitudes toward each state in the Middle East and elsewhere would be based on their degree of support for U.S. positions regarding the anti-terror campaign. In this, the Bush administration has enjoyed the undivided support of the American people. Willingness to join or support the coalition against terror thus became the standard for states that sought to develop or maintain good relations with the United States.

In the context of U.S. efforts to build a policy agenda after September 11, a number of developments were expected:

- As noted, the likelihood of a U.S.-led attack on Iraq increased.
- The United States became more actively involved in the Israeli-Palestinian context.
- Renewed efforts were made to stem anti-U.S. sentiment in the Middle East.
- Terrorism or other forms of behavior that were not in keeping with accepted international norms would not be tolerated. This created new tensions with certain Arab states, such as Egypt and Saudi Arabia.
- More coordination and cooperation with the EU and Russia was expected on policy initiatives affecting the region.

This placed the Arab and Muslim states of the Middle East in a quandary. The leaderships of most of these states understood that siding with the United States was in their national interest: the United States remained the world's sole superpower, and radical Islamic terrorism threatened many of them as well. At the same time, they had to face a domestic atmosphere which was generally sympathetic to Osama Bin Laden, and hostile or resentful toward the West and toward the status quo.

Since the attacks, there has been a tendency among some observers to find explanations for the depth of anti-western animosity in the Arab and Muslim world. Many have suggested that Arab and Muslim hostility, particularly toward the United States, was rooted in specific U.S. policies, such as supporting Israel or pressing for globalization. By acknowledging such misdeeds, these observers believed, it would be possible to understand this resentment and design policies to mollify it.

While there was certainly merit in this approach, it nevertheless seemed that the more fundamental reason for this animosity lay within the Middle East itself. Many Arab and Muslim states have simply proved unable to cope with modernization and were inclined to blame the West for their own domestic social, political, or economic maladies. While the United States, the EU, or Israel could perhaps have ameliorated the situation somewhat by altering certain policies, such alterations would not necessarily have led to profound or long-term improvements in relations between the Middle East and the West. For this, a deeper and more structural change would have had to take place, through which Middle Eastern regimes would have developed more effective ways to provide services, prosperity, and opportunity to their citizens. It is worth noting in this regard that the inordinate efforts made by the United States and the EU to protect Muslim ethnic groups in the Balkans did not substantially reduce Muslim resentment of the West. For these reasons, the Bush administration quickly concluded that the war on terrorism was unlikely to be brief.

At the same time, the United States felt that Arab and Muslim participation in its anti-terror coalition was imperative. Their reasons for this were both political and operational. From the political point of view, the United States wished to avoid having the "war on terrorism" be equated with a "war on Islam," as such a perception would only serve the interests of Bin Laden and others of his ilk. From the operational point of view, the cooperation of the Arab and Muslim states in fighting terrorism was clearer still: most of the terrorist organizations in question hailed from the Middle East, and many were still based there. Moreover, those states that provided support for terrorism were also largely situated in the greater Middle East. Any actions taken against these states would therefore have necessitated the support of their neighbors. Taken together, these factors led the United States to seek an improvement of its image in Arab popular perceptions and to seek out policies that would not inflame anti-Western sentiment further.

On the other hand, the United States became less tolerant of any kind of support for terrorism, no matter what the cause. This created problems for a great many Arab governments, because nearly all of them supported at least one terrorist organization. Saudi Arabia was an interesting case in point: on one hand, it was considered generally moderate, closely connected with the West, and supportive of the peace process. On the other hand, the regime's ruling style was based on a hard-line Islamic ideology, and both the Saudi regime and the Saudi people have financially supported a number of different organizations that used terror, such as the Palestinian Hamas. In the wake of

September 11, the United States seemed unwilling to stomach further Saudi ambivalence, and the Saudi leadership found itself in something of a bind. On a broader level, the United States was also disappointed by what it perceived as a general Arab reluctance to manifest real participation in the coalition against terror.

As noted, the reactions of the various states in the Middle East to the September 11 attacks were motivated in part by the need to show support for the United States, as the world's sole superpower. However, these states were also concerned with domestic reactions to such support. Moreover, they wished to use the changes that had taken place in both the U.S. and the international agendas to serve their own particular interests. In this, the Israeli-Palestinian example was particularly illustrative: both sides highly valued U.S. backing and therefore needed to demonstrate their support for its policies. Nevertheless, Israel regarded the attacks on the United States as an opportunity to improve its international standing *vis-à-vis* its fight against Palestinian terrorism and to corral greater international pressure on PA Chairman Arafat. For their part, the Palestinians could not afford to be seen as having cast their lot with the terrorists. Nevertheless, they continued to make use of controlled levels of violence as a political tool. Because the United States saw a clear need to appease Arab publics and mobilize Arab and Muslim support, the Palestinians believed that the aftermath of the attacks presented them with an opportunity to force U.S. pressure upon Israel to make concessions. In other words, each side supported the United States, while looking for ways to make the war on terrorism serve its own interests.

On another level, the attacks on the United States provided a clear demonstration of the massive potential posed by terrorist organizations that were able to combine suicide tactics, the wish to cause massive numbers of casualties, and the use of weapons of mass destruction. It was considered possible that Bin Laden's success could inspire other groups in the Middle East to emulate his methods, though the conditions in most Middle East states were less favorable to this kind of terrorism because of greater limitations on personal liberties. Paradoxically, it was easier for some Middle Eastern terrorist groups (among them, al-Qa'ida) to operate freely in the relatively permissive atmospheres of Europe and the United States than in the Middle East itself, where they were openly considered a threat to national security. Indeed, anti-terror crackdowns carried out by states like Egypt and Jordan had pushed many of the smaller groups that made up Bin Laden's network into Europe and the United States in the first place. An example of this was the prominent presence of Egyptian radicals among Bin Laden's top advisers. These Egyptians were members of radical Islamic groups that had tried to use terror to bring down the Egyptian regime. When the Egyptian security forces ultimately succeeded in suppressing these organizations, many of their surviving activists fled from Egypt to Europe, the United States, and elsewhere.

The dramatic events in the United States took place against a backdrop of much turmoil in the Middle East because of developments in the Israeli-Palestinian arena. Initially, there was considerable concern that the added tension of the war on terrorism would further burden Arab regimes that were in any case alienated from their domestic populations. There was a risk that Bin Laden's daring operations could fire the imagination of anti-regime elements throughout the region, and that such elements might be encouraged to intensify their efforts to overthrow their local leaders. By early 2002, it appeared however that these apprehensions were largely unwarranted.

Russia: Towards a Post–September 11 *Rapprochement* with the United States

Observers have pointed to a number of different factors that informed Russian President Putin's Middle East policy over 2000–2001. Putin clearly wished to rehabilitate Russia's great power status, in the context of which its historic role in the Middle East played a part. There were also a number of economic opportunities in the region. Finally, there were broader foreign policy problems that affected its position on regional issues, and internal problems within Russia that affected the Middle East.

Putin's major achievement since coming into office has been to strengthen the central government, thereby preventing further decomposition of Russia. In this context, he appeared to be seeking to return Russia to superpower status, based on nationalism rather than Soviet-style communism. Despite Russia's weakness both economically and militarily, this desire for a return to past glories spurred its drive to restore its influence in the Middle East, a region with a long history of Russian interest and presence.

In this context, Russia desired a role in the Middle East peace process. It may therefore have seen the Israeli-Palestinian violence as an opportunity both to improve its standing, and to demonstrate that it could influence the two sides. This was evident in Yasser Arafat's visit to Moscow in May 2001. However, Russia's desire to use the Middle East to rejuvenate its superpower status was tempered by a lack of resources. In the grand scheme of things, the Middle East was simply not that high on the Russian list of priorities, and demands on scarce resources placed sharp limits on Russian state *largesse*.

Given the weak state of Russia's economy, its interests in the Middle East were primarily commercial in 2001. This was the basis of its policies regarding Iraq and Iran, two oil-rich states with great economic potential. Russian interests in maintaining good relations with Iran were also essential for the maximization of profits from Caspian oil reserves, through both direct involvement in oil production and transshipment via pipelines through Russian territory. Economic interests were also what motivated Russia's liberal policy on arms sales, including strategically sensitive items such as surface-to-surface missiles and nuclear technologies.

Russia's faltering relations with the United States prior to the September 11 attacks also had an effect on the Middle East. Russia was concerned with U.S. policy regarding the developing of an NMD system. In its view, the implementation of U.S. decisions in this area constituted a fundamental violation of the Anti-Ballistic Missile (ABM) agreement, which was the basis for the strategic stability that existed between the United States and Russia. The deployment of such a system, Russian leaders claimed, would harm the effectiveness of the Russian nuclear deterrent, and would obligate large investments that the state could ill afford to make to ensure its future effectiveness. To this must be added a sense of encirclement that stemmed from the ongoing expansion of NATO, in addition to the anti-Russian rhetoric voiced by senior members of the Bush team. A continued decline in U.S.-Russian relations could well have motivated Russia to adopt a more provocative Middle East policy.

It would have been logical, moreover, for such provocations to take shape primarily through Russian relations with states that also had an interest in challenging U.S. regional hegemony, such as Iraq and Iran. However, the terrorist attacks in the United States appeared in late 2001 to have had a profound effect in the U.S.-Russian relationship, because it led to a convergence of interests between the two powers. The United States saw Russia as an important member of the anti-terror coalition. For its part, Russia saw the war on terrorism as an opportunity to get Western support – or at least Western acquiescence – to its war in Chechnya. As a first reconciliatory step toward Russia, President Bush decided to postpone NMD tests, which Russia had viewed as a violation of the ABM treaty.

Russia also had an interest in good relations with Israel. Such relations were part of preserving Moscow's self-image as a contender to superpower status with influence throughout the Middle East. These relations also had important economic benefits. By late 2001, however, it was still difficult to guess how Russia would balance its past desire to provoke the United States with the effects of the war on terrorism and its desire to maintain good relations with Israel. It was also difficult to foresee whether or not this would lead to a change in Russia's behavior regarding the proliferation of weapons of mass destruction. This was especially the case with regard to Iraq: given that Russia's anti-sanctions policy had adherents in Europe as well, it was not clear if it would be willing to fall in line behind the United States. The U.S. failure to obtain approval for smart sanctions, due in large part to Russian opposition, lent additional depth to this question.

The EU: Fifteen Actors in Search of a Role

During 2001 the European Union continued to forge its identity as a unified political entity with a common foreign and security policy and the tools to implement it. As such, it sought to enhance its role in the Middle East peace process, with particular emphasis on the Israeli-Palestinian track. The EU had maintained for some time that since it was bearing the majority of the economic burden in supporting the PA, it was due a greater political role in the negotiations between the two sides. This created certain tensions with the United States; to dispel these tensions, the Europeans made it repeatedly clear that they were not trying to undermine U.S. seniority in the process. Rather, they would have liked a larger role alongside the United States in finding a solution to the conflict. In this framework, Javier Solana, the EU High Representative for the Common Foreign and Security Policy, began to play a greater regional role by late 2000. This was apparent in the November 2000 Sharm el-Sheikh conference, in his participation as a member of the Mitchell commission, and in a series of visits that he conducted in the region.

Israel and the Palestinian Authority were divided over European involvement in the peace process. The Palestinians saw Europe as having greater sympathy for their interests, which could counterbalance U.S. support for Israel. Consequently, the PA wanted to see the EU become an important component in the international involvement that they were seeking to foster. Israel, for its part, looked in askance on greater European involvement for much the same reason. Despite its considerable support for many of the parties in the Middle East, the EU was unable to create a consensual basis for a more important regional role.

In June 2001, there was a sharp rise in the level of EU involvement in the peace process. This took place because of the role played by German Federal Minister for Foreign Affairs Joschka Fischer, who was in the region at the time of the Dolphinarium attack. Fischer took part in pressing Arafat to agree to a cease-fire, and promised European assistance in upholding it. The EU focused its attention on the PA, sending a delegation of security officials into Palestinian territory in order to advise the PA on steps that it needed to take in order to stop the violence, and to monitor their implementation. The activities of the EU delegation proved effective in this regard.

Chapter Five

Middle East Strategic Balances

As the analysis provided in the previous chapters makes clear, the Middle East experienced considerable change in 2001. The peace process fell into profound disarray, and the tone in the region became more hostile toward Israel and the United States. In practical terms, however, there were no major changes in the overall strategic balance of the Middle East as a whole, nor among any of the sub-regional conflicts within it.

The Arab-Israeli Balance

The developments that took place after the outbreak of violence between Israel and the Palestinians could have been seen as challenging the perception that the regional strategic balance favored Israel. Nevertheless, the manner in which various Arab actors reacted to that violence crisis reinforced the belief that the overall strategic balance had not altered significantly. The leaders of most Arab states continued to believe that Israel enjoyed decisive superiority. This belief was demonstrated by the widespread rejection of pressures to join the fight against Israel. In doing so, these leaders made it clear that they considered military options to be unrealistic, given the current distribution of forces in the region. These events also demonstrated the clear weaknesses of the Arab states in all of the traditional indicators of power. Those states or entities that sought to change the status quo were forced into adopting alternative tactics – such as guerilla warfare and terrorism – where Israel showed some vulnerability. For them, the prolonged fighting in Lebanon demonstrated that such tactics could hold Israel's battlefield superiority in check, meaning that its strategic strengths and deterrence capability would be correspondingly limited.

In contrast to the stagnation that took hold of most of the other armies in the region, the IDF had continuously and systematically upgraded its forces. It was the only armed force in the Middle East to have successfully tackled the revolution in military affairs (RMA). Moreover, Israeli technological capabilities placed it on the cutting edge of many of the developments relevant to exploiting the RMA's potential. Israel enjoyed the support of the world's sole superpower, the United States, while its rivals remained without a superpower patron. In addition, the Arab world was politically divided and could not easily have cobbled together an anti-Israel war coalition. To this was added Israel's great economic leap forward over the last decade of the twentieth century, and its integration into the global economy. When compared to the ongoing economic deadlock in the Arab world, it was easy to see why the Arab states believed that the strategic gap that had separated them from Israel continued to widen.

During 2001, there was no change in the level of arms transfers into the region. Among the states that immediately bordered Israel, only Egypt enjoyed an unimpeded supply of U.S. weapons. However, even in the Egyptian military, while there has been a continuous process of modernization, arms purchases continued to focus on traditional weapons systems. There was no sign that Egypt was trying to develop the capabilities needed to deal with the RMA.

The Syrian and Iraqi armies remained at a standstill, albeit for different reasons. In Syria, the military's stagnation was due to a lack of financial resources, while in Iraq, military modernization was blocked by UN sanctions. Attempts in Syria were underway to develop new operational concepts that would enable it to survive a military confrontation with Israel in spite of its lack of cutting-edge weapons. Nevertheless, this effort only highlighted a general recognition by the Syrian national command authorities of its military inferiority *vis-à-vis* Israel. Israel, for its part, continued to strengthen steadily, with an emphasis on those areas affected by the RMA. Two important stepping stones that took place in 2000–2001 were the introduction of the Arrow Missile Defense System into operational service in October 2000, and the successful replacement of a spy satellite that had come to the end of its operational life in December 2000. These developments strengthened Arab awareness regarding Israel's command of technology, and their own inability to compete in these areas.

Over the course of 2001 and early 2002, no increase was observed in the pace of military restructuring in the Arab world. Syria and Russia have apparently opened discussions which could lead to actual arms deals between them for the first time in a long while. Also, the erosion of UN sanctions could eventually lead to a renewal of weapons shipments to Iraq, despite U.S. efforts to forestall such an eventuality.

The constancy of the picture in the military realm was matched by strategic factors which were not of a purely military nature. Despite expectations on the part of some Arab actors, the Bush administration was as sympathetic to Israel as its predecessor, even if that sympathy was based on different, less emotional, bases. Hence, there was no reason to believe that it would seek to undo the strategic ties between Israel and the United States. Contrary to Palestinian expectations, the behavior of the PA since the outbreak of the violence engendered great anger in the United States, and actually strengthened the administration's support of Israel.

In the fields of economics and technology, Israel had to absorb a two-fold economic blow: the military confrontation with the Palestinians, which harmed a number of Israeli industries, and the international crisis in high-tech. The ability of the Israeli economy not to falter in the face of these developments, however, showed that its foundations were firm, and that it had a measure of resilience. While economic growth forecasts were downgraded sharply, the Israeli economy remained stable, and the international economic community did not lose its confidence in the Israeli market. Moreover, the conflict evinced a degree of resilience among the Israeli public that surprised many observers. At the same time, the ongoing violence did grave harm to the Palestinian and Jordanian economies, demonstrating their vulnerability.

Israel's growing pre-eminence in high-tech has deepened the Arab world's awareness of its inability to close the strategic gap. This has strengthened two tendencies among radical states and entities in the region: a move by some to consider low-intensity confrontations, and an emphasis by others on acquiring non-conventional weapons. This latter trend has been based on the assumption that, while here too Israel had an advantage, the gap was smaller, and it would be easier to reach mutual deterrence. Weapons of mass destruction (WMD) were thus seen as a kind of strategic equalizer. It would be possible to envision a situation in which Israel – generally considered a nuclear power – might find itself mired in a balance of terror with those Arab states that possessed chemical or biological capabilities. While Israeli capabilities in this area would be greater than those of the Arab states, so too would its tremendous vulnerabilities to such weapons because of its small size.

The Balance in the Gulf

Buoyed up by high oil prices, the military strength of the Gulf Cooperation Council (GCC) countries continued to grow. This growth shifted the military balance with Iraq, which remained under UN sanctions. It also shifted the military balance between the GCC and Iran, which had to divert growing sums to domestic-civilian needs, and which was also subject to a limited sanctions regime. Rising oil revenues affected all sides equally, however, and there were initial signs that Iran planned to increase the rate of its military build-up. As noted, Iran signed a multi-year, large-scale framework agreement with Russia, and some new deals have been closed in this context. While these deals would certainly affect Iranian military capabilities in the future, they had no bearing on the balance of forces in the Gulf in 2001.

If the ongoing presence of U.S. forces in the Gulf and in Turkey were added to this picture, as well as U.S. commitments to its allies, one would likely conclude that Iran and Iraq had no real capability to threaten their neighbors. *A priori*, Iraq's provocative attitude toward the United States, and its behavior since the outbreak of the Israeli-Palestinian violence, pointed to a growing sense of security, both military and political. Upon a deeper examination, however, it seems that Saddam's sense of security was based more on his improved political stature, and his assessment that the odds of a new coalition crystallizing against him were low. Therefore, Iraqi provocations in 2001 should not be regarded too seriously; they were primarily an act of showmanship with political goals, rather than a real demonstration of intent.

Weapons of Mass Destruction and Surface-to-Surface Missiles

No breakthroughs in regional programs to develop WMDs or surface-to-surface missiles took place during 2001. There were no significant increases in the capabilities of any of the countries armed with WMDs, nor any move toward disarmament or limitation. The dominant perception was that Israel enjoyed superiority in these areas, even if in principal its vulnerabilities to them were also greater, due to its small size and high population density.

Except for Israel, Iran continued to carry out the broadest-based efforts in this field. Its nuclear program appeared to proceed in 2001 at the same slow, cautious pace that had characterized it for some years. There was no evidence to suggest that Iran had set up either facilities for the enrichment of uranium or the special reactors and separation facilities required for the manufacture of weapons based on plutonium. Nevertheless, the process of building an overall nuclear infrastructure continues. Construction of the reactor at Bushehr was near completion by the end of 2001. Under this cover, Iran continued to obtain technologies and materials that would enable it to develop military nuclear applications in the future, should it choose to do so. An NPT signatory, Iran did not sign the treaty's improved verification protocol, 93+2. The signing of this protocol would have made it very difficult for Iran to move from a civilian nuclear program to a military one, given that military applications for nuclear technology require a considerable industrial capability for producing weapons-grade fissile materials and warheads.

No additional tests of the Iranian Shahab-3 missile (with a range of some 1,300 km – enough to strike Israel from Iranian territory) were noted in 2001. It would seem that the development of the missile was still mired in difficulties and it was not operational. There have been indications of advances in developing solid-fuelled missiles with a range of some 200 km. Nevertheless, this development affects the balance between Iran and its immediate neighbors only. Iran's main supplier for the needed technologies in these fields remained Russia. In that vein, U.S. intelligence services had accused Russia in mid–2001 of supplying Iran with a special type of reinforced aluminum that could be used for building centrifuges for uranium enrichment.

As a party to the CWC, Iran made the necessary reports on the chemical weapons in its possession to the Organization for the Prohibition of Chemical Weapons (OPCW). It was not known if this report had been full and complete, and as noted above, there were some signs that Iran had already violated the agreement by continuing to produce chemical agents. Iran also maintained a biological weapons project, though it was not known how much progress had been made in this regard.

Western countries estimated that Iraq succeeded in concealing from UN inspectors some of the means at its disposal for developing WMDs. Specifically, these estimates related to a small number of missiles and missile launchers, some biological agents such as anthrax, botulism, and possibly others, and perhaps some chemical agents as well. It thus seemed reasonable to assume that the absence of UNSCOM inspectors in Iraq since the end of 1998 had enabled Iraq to renew its WMD projects, based on the human infrastructure that remained at its disposal. If such projects did exist, however, they would naturally have been extremely well hidden, and it should not be surprising that no details on them would have come to light. In addition, the gradual erosion of the sanctions gave Iraq the financial resources necessary for renewing such projects, as well as purchases and smuggling of necessary materials or technologies.

Syria continued to focus on the development of chemical weapons (and to a limited degree, biological ones) and long range missiles. There have been no changes in the numbers of missile launchers at its disposal, but it has continued to manufacture SCUD Cs and Ds.

During 2001 there were no additional revelations regarding Israeli capabilities in the fields of WMD and surface-to-surface missiles. The overall perception in the region was that Israel possessed both a large nuclear arsenal and long-range missiles, implying that it enjoyed superiority *vis-à-vis* its potential rivals in these areas as well. Israel was also the only nation to make progress on the production of WMD defenses. Its first Arrow missile battery went operational in October 2000, and there were reports that Israel had developed effective inoculations against anthrax, a major component of biological weapons.

PART II

MILITARY FORCES

Yiftah Shapir

Introductory Note

This part of the *Middle East Military Balance* contains data on the arsenals and the orders-of-battle of 20 states and the Palestinian Authority. It also contains information on other security activities of these states — arms procurement, military production and security cooperation.

Appendices providing a glossary, technical data on weapon systems, a list of abbreviations, a comparative table and charts, appear at the end of this part of the book.

Definitions and Criteria

Data on military acquisitions and sales, as well as on security assistance, are limited to information pertaining to the past five years. The year in parentheses in these sections always refers to the most recent information on an entry.

Armor

Tanks are divided into two main categories: light tanks (under 25 tons) and main battle tanks (MBTs). High quality MBTs and other MBTs are also differentiated.
The criteria for "high quality" are any three of the following attributes:

- A 120mm (or higher) caliber gun
- A power plant of more than 900 hp and/or power-to-weight ratio of 19 hp/t or better
- Reactive or modular armor
- A capability to fire barrel launched anti-tank missiles
- An advanced fire control system, with tracking capability

Under this categorization, some versions of the T-72 MBT are categorized as "high quality," although they are not necessarily on par with tanks like the M1A1 or the Merkava Mk III.

Armored Fighting Vehicles (AFVs)

AFVs are divided into three categories:

- Armored personnel carriers — armored vehicles designed to carry several infantrymen, armed with light weapons only
- Infantry fighting vehicles — armored vehicles built to carry several infantrymen, armed with heavier weapons, such as guns or missiles
- Reconnaissance vehicles — armored vehicles of various sizes and armament, designed to carry a small crew of weapons operators, but not intended for dismounted infantry fighting

It should be noted that the dividing line between the categories is not well-defined, and sometimes it is difficult to decide how a certain vehicle should be categorized. For example, heavier reconnaissance vehicles can be categorized as light tanks, especially when they use tracks rather than wheels.

Air Defense

Some militaries in the region have a separate Air Defense arm. In other countries, air defense equipment is divided between the Air Force and the Ground Forces. In this volume, all air defense weapon systems are aggregated into one sub-section in each chapter, regardless of the organizational distribution of the weapons systems.

Air defense equipment is categorized as follows:

- Shoulder-launched missiles
- Light SAMs — with a range up to 12 km, self-propelled or towed.
- Mobile medium SAMs — self-propelled, with a range of 12 – 30 km.
- Medium to heavy SAMs — stationary or towed systems with a range of 12 – 30 km, or any system with a range of more than 30 km.
- Other systems — AA guns and combined systems.

Numbers are given according to the number of independent fire units. Thus, for example, the number of SA-2 (Guideline) will represent the number of batteries, but for SA-8 (Gecko) the number of launchers is given. However, an exception is made in the "Order-of-Battle" table at the beginning of the "Armed Forces" section for each country where only the number of batteries is calculated for the sake of brevity.

Combat Aircraft

Combat aircraft are divided into the following categories:

- Interceptors
- Multi-role (high quality and others)
- Ground attack
- Obsolete

Navy

Size and armament for each vessel appear in the tables for each country.

Non-Governmental Forces

Listed are only major non-governmental forces that might have military significance. There are two types of non-governmental forces. First, there are those opposing the government of the country in which they act. Second, there are those which are based in — and sometimes financed by — another country. These organizations are listed according to the host country.

Note on Symbols

In this volume several symbols are used to denote instances where accurate data is not available:

NA	Data not available. This symbol is used in the economic data tables only.
~	The tilde is used in front of a number to denote approximate number.
+	The weapon system is known to be in use, but the quantity is not known.
*	There is doubt whether the weapon system exists in the order-of-battle.
0	The weapon system exists but known to be not in use.

Economic Data

The tables on economic data include data on GDP (in current US dollars). Per capita GDP is derived from a simple division of the GDP by the size of the population.

Data on military expenditures in the Middle East are notoriously elusive. Hence such data should be regarded, at best, as indicators of trends.

Acknowledgments

The hard work of compiling, updating and setting the data was done by Yoel Kozak and Tamir Magal, to whom I owe a great debt of gratitude. Jacqueline Hahn-Efrati worked on the editing and proofreading. I alone, however, bear responsibility for any inaccuracies.

Yiftah S. Shapir
May 2002

1. ALGERIA

General Data

Official Name of the State: Democratic and Popular Republic of Algeria
Head of State: President of the High State Council Abd al-Aziz Buteflika
Prime Minister: Ali Benfils
Minister of Defense: Nureddin Zarhouni
Chief of General Staff: Major General Muhammad Lamari
Commander of the Ground Forces: Major General Salih Ahmad Jaid
Commander of the Air Force: Brigadier General Muhammad Ibn Suleiman
Commander of Air Defense Force: Brigadier General Achour Laoudi
Commander of the Navy: Admiral Brahim Dadci

Area: 2,460,500 sq. km.
Population: 31,300,000

Demography

Ethnic groups		
Arabs	24,570,500	78.5%
Berbers	6,072,200	19.4%
Europeans	313,000	1.0%
Others	344,300	1.1%
Religious groups		
Sunni Muslims	30,987,000	99.0%
Christians and Jews	313,000	1.0%

Economic Data

		1996	1997	1998	1999	2000
GDP (current prices)	$ bn	46.85	47.87	47.34	47.87	44.77
GDP per capita	$	1,638	1,645	1,589	1,554	1,430
Real GDP growth	%	3.8	1.1	5.1	3.3	3.8
Consumer price index	%	18.7	5.7	4.9	2.4	3.0
External debt	$ bn	33.4	30.9	30.7	28.1	25.0
Balance of payments						
• Exports fob	$ bn	13.22	13.82	10.14	12.32	19.53
• Imports fob	$ bn	9.1	8.13	8.63	8.96	9.5
• Current account balance (including services and income)	$ bn	1.25	3.45	-0.91	0.02	9.2

Economic Data *(continued)*

		1996	1997	1998	1999	2000
Government expenditure						
• Total expenditure	$ bn	13.23	14.65	14.9	14.44	15.72
• Defense expenditure	$ bn	1.37	1.68	1.83	1.88	NA
• Real change in defense expenditure	%	11.4	22.6	8.9	2.7	NA
• Defense expenditure /GDP	%	2.9	3.5	3.9	3.9	NA
Population	m	28.6	29.1	29.8	30.8	31.3
Official exchange rate	AD:$1	54.75	57.70	58.74	66.57	74.8

Sources: EIU Quarterly Report, EIU Country Profile, IMF International Financial Statistical Yearbook, SIPRI Yearbook

Arms Procurement and Security Assistance Received

Country	Type	Details
Belarus	• Arms transfers	MiG-29 aircraft
France	• Military training	Training of Gendarmerie
Qatar	• Arms transfers	Rapid deployment vehicles, night vision equipment
Russia	• Arms transfers	Kh-35 SSMs, Su-24 aircraft, upgrading of combat vessels
South Africa	• Arms transfers	UAV systems, upgrading of Mi-24 helicopters
UK	• Arms transfers	Naval vessels
US	• Arms transfers	C^3I system
	• Assistance	$125,000 for training program

Foreign Military Cooperation

Type	Details
• Forces deployed abroad	Ethiopia and Eritrea (UNMEE)
• Joint maneuvers	US maritime SAR and ASW exercises
• Security agreement	France, Russia, South Africa

Defense Production

	M	P	A
Army equipment			
• Trucks (in collaboration with France)		√	
• Small arms		√	
Naval craft			
• Tugs	√		
• Kebir class PBs		√	√

Note: M - manufacture (indigenously developed)
P - production under license
A - assembly

Weapons of Mass Destruction

NBC Capabilities

Nuclear capability
One 15 Mw nuclear reactor, probably upgraded to 40 Mw (from PRC), allegedly serves a clandestine nuclear weapons program; one 1 Mw nuclear research reactor (from Argentina); basic R&D; signatory to the NPT. Safeguards agreement with the IAEA in force. Signed and ratified the African Nuclear Weapons Free Zone Treaty (Treaty of Pelindaba).

Chemical weapons (CW) and protective equipment
No data on CW activities available. Signed and ratified the CWC.

Biological weapons (BW)
No data on BW activities available. Not a party to the BWC.

Armed Forces

Major Changes: No major change was recorded in the Algerian order-of-battle in 2000. The Algerian Air Force received its first upgraded Su-24 attack aircraft from Russia in November.

Order-of-Battle

Year	1996	1997	1999	2000	2001
General data					
•Personnel (regular)	152,500	124,000*	127,000	127,000	127,000
• SSM launchers	35	*			
Ground Forces					
• Divisions	5	5	5	5	5
• Total number of brigades	37	26*	26	26	26

Order-of-Battle *(continued)*

Year	1996	1997	1999	2000	2001
• Tanks	1,100	930*	860	860	860
		(1,060)	(1,060)	(1,060)	(1,060)
• APCs/AFVs	1,780	1,930	1,930	1,930	2,080*
• Artillery (including MRLs)	980	985	900 (985)	900 (985)	900 (985)
Air Force					
• Combat aircraft	205	205	187(205)*	187 (205)	184 (214)
• Transport aircraft	76	48*	39 (45)	39 (45)	41 (46)
• Helicopters	108	116	114	114	133(142)*
Air Defense Forces					
• Heavy SAM batteries	30	11*	11	11	11
• Medium SAM batteries	23	18*	18	18	18
• Light SAM launchers	+	40*	78*	78	78
Navy					
• Combat vessels	32	29	29	26	26
• Patrol crafts	28	21*	21	21	16
• Submarines	2	2	2	2	2

Note: Beginning with 1997, data refers to quantities in active service. The number in parentheses refers to the total inventory.
* Due to change in estimate.

Personnel

	Regular	Reserves	Total
Ground Forces	107,000	150,000	257,000
Air Force	14,000		14,000
Navy	6,000		6,000
Total	**127,000**	**150,000**	**277,000**
Paramilitary			
• National Security Force	16,000		16,000
• Republican Guards Brigade	1,200		1,200
• Gendarmerie	24,000		24,000

Ground Forces

Formations

	Divisions	Independent brigades/ groups	Independent battalions	Brigades in divisions
Armored	2	1		3 armd., 1 mech. each
Mechanized/Infantry	2			1 armd., 3 mech.each
Motorized/Infantry		5		
Special forces/ Airborne	1			
Artillery			7	
Air defense			5	
Engineers			4	
Total	**5**	**6**	**16**	

Tanks

Model	Quantity	In service	Since	Notes
MBTs				
High quality				
• T-72	300	285	1980	
Medium and low quality				
• T-62	330	300	1978	
• T-55/T-54	310	275	1964	
Subtotal	640	575		
Light tanks				
• PT-76	70	0	1985	Possibly phased out
• AMX-13	50	0	1962	Possibly phased out
Subtotal	120	0		
Total	**1,060**	**860**		

APCs/AFVs

Model	Quantity	In service	Since	Notes
APCs				
• OT-64	150	150	1993	
• Fahd	200	200	1992	
• BTR-50/60	445	445	1975	
• BTR-152	100	100	1965	
• M-3 (Panhard)	50	50	1983	
Subtotal	945	945		

APCs/AFVs *(continued)*

Model	Quantity	In service	Since	Notes
IFVs				
• BMP-2	230	230	1989	
• BMP-1	685	685	1981	
Subtotal	915	915		
Reconnaissance				
• BRDM-2	115	115	1980	
• Engesa EE-9	50	50	1981	
• AML-60	55	55	1963	
Subtotal	220	220		
Total	**2,080**	**2,080**		

Artillery

Model	Quantity	In service	Since	Notes
Self-propelled guns and howitzers				
• 152mm 2S3	35	+	1966	
• 122mm 2S1	150	+	1977	
Subtotal	185	~100		
Towed guns and howitzers				
• 152mm ML-20	20	20	1966	
• 130mm M-46/Type-59	10	10	1991	
• 122mm D-30	190	190	1984	
• 122mm D-74	}		1966	
• 122mm M-1931/37	}	~190	1984	Refers to all types
• 122mm M-30 (M-1938)	}		1983	
• 85 mm M-1945/ D-44 field/AT	80	80	1976	
Subtotal	~490	~490		
Mortars, over 160mm				
• 160mm M-43	60	60	1978	
Mortars, under 160mm				
• 120mm M-43	120	120	1974	
MRLs				
• 240mm BM-24	30	30	1962	
• 140mm BM-14-16	50	50	1962	
• 122mm BM-21	50	50	1980	
Subtotal	130	130		
Total	**~985**	**~900**		

Anti-Tank Missiles

Model	Quantity	In service	Since	Notes
• AT-3 (Sagger)	+	+	1975	Some mounted on BRDM-2 APCs
• AT-4 (Spigot)	+	+		
• AT-5 (Spandrel)	+	+		Mounted on BMP-2 APCs
• Milan	~200	~200	1982	
Total	**~1,400**	**~1,400**		

Anti-Tank Guns

Model	Quantity	In service	Since	Notes
• 76mm AT gun	50	0		Possibly phased out
• 107mm B-11 recoilless rifle	40	40		Unconfirmed
Total	**90**	**40**		

Air Force

Order-of-Battle

Category	Quantity	In service	Notes
• Combat	214	184	
• Transport	46	41	
• Helicopters	142	133	

Combat Aircraft

Model	Quantity	In service	Since	Notes
Interceptors				
• MiG-25 A/B/U (Foxbat)	20	12	1979	4 listed also under Miscellaneous Aircraft
• MiG-23MF/MS/U (Flogger B/E)	30	18	1978	
Subtotal	50	30		
Ground attack				
• Su-24 (Fencer C)	19	19	1991	4 listed also under Miscellaneous Aircraft

Combat Aircraft (*continued*)

Model	Quantity	In service	Since	Notes
• MiG-23BN (Flogger D/F)	40	38	1978	
• Su-20/22 (Fitter C)	15	15	1978	
Subtotal	74	72		
Obsolete				
• MiG-21 MF/bis/U (Fishbed)	90	82	1970	
Total	**214**	**184**		
Future procurement				
• Su-24	22			Delivery in progress; set to conclude by the end of 2001
• MiG-29	36			

Transport Aircraft

Model	Quantity	In service	Since	Notes
• An-12 (Cub)	5	5		
• Beechcraft Queen Air 80/King Air 100/ Super King Air B-200T	12	12	1977	2 employed in maritime patrol role
• C-130H/L-100-30 Hercules	17	14	1981	
• Fokker F-27 Mk 400/ Mk 600	3	1	1973	Employed in maritime patrol role
• Gulfstream III	3	3	1983	
• IL-76 (Candid)	4	4	1994	
• Mystère-Falcon 900	2	2	1990	Unconfirmed
Total	**46**	**41**		

Training and Liaison Aircraft

Model	Quantity	In service	Since	Notes
Jet trainers				
• L-39 Albatross	30	24	1987	
• CM-170 Fouga Magister	20	20	1971	
Subtotal	50	44		
Piston/Turbo-prop				
• Zlin 142	30	30	1990	
• Beechcraft Sierra 200	18	18	1976	
• Beechcraft T-34C (Turbine Mentor)	6	0	1978	Possibly phased out
Subtotal	54	48		
Total	**104**	**92**		

Helicopters

Model	Quantity	In service	Since	Notes
Attack helicopters				
• Mi-24/25 (Hind)	36	36	1978	Number unconfirmed
Medium transport				
• Mi-8/17 (Hip)	56	47	1975	
• SA-330 Puma	5	5	1971	
Subtotal	61	52		
Light transport				
• AS-350 Ecureuil	8	8	1995	
• Alouette II/III	6	6	1983	
• Bell 206	3	3	1988	
• Mi-2 *	28	28		
Subtotal	45	45		
Total	**142**	**133**		
Future procurement				
• Rooivalk				Under negotiation
• Mi-8/17	47			

* change of estimate

Miscellaneous Aircraft

Model	Quantity	In service	Since	Notes
Reconnaissance				
• Su-24MR	4	4	1991	Also listed under Combat Aircraft
• MiG-25R	4	3	1979	Also listed under Combat Aircraft
Maritime surveillance				
• Fokker F-27 Mk 400/ Mk 600	3	1	1973	Also listed under Transport Aircraft
• Super King Air B-200T	2	2	1986	Also listed under Transport Aircraft
UAVs and Mini-UAVs				
• Seeker	4-8		1998	

Advanced Armament

Air-to-air missiles

AA-2 (Atoll), AA-6 (Acrid), AA-7 (Apex), AA-11 (Archer)

Air-to-ground missiles

AT-2 (Swatter), AT-6 (Spiral), AS-10 (Karen), AS-14 (Kedge)

Air Force Infrastructure

Military airfields: **13**

Ain Ousira, Algiers, Amanas, Balida, Bechar, Biskra, Boufarik, Bousfear, Laghuat, Oran, Ouargla, Tafa Aoui, Tindouf

Air Defense Forces

Surface-to-Air Missiles

Model	Batteries	Launchers	Since	Notes
Heavy missiles				
• SA-2 (Guideline)	6		1970	
• SA-3 (Goa)	5		1982	
Total	**11**			
Medium missiles				
• SA-6 (Gainful)	10		1979	
• SA-8 (Gecko)		24	1986	
Total	**10**	**24**		
Light missiles				
• SA-9 (Gaskin)		46	1980	
• SA-13 (Gopher)		32		Unconfirmed
Total		**78**		
Shoulder-launched missiles				
• SA-7 (Grail)		180	1978	
Total		**180**		

Other Air Defense Systems

Model	Quantity	In service	Since	Notes
Short-range guns				
• 57mm ZSU 57x2 SP	+	+	1980	
• 57mm S-60	70	70	1974	
• 37mm M-1939	145	145	1986	
• 35mm KS-12	24	24		
• 23mm ZSU 23x4 SP (Gun Dish)	30	30	1980	
• 23mm ZU 23x2	50	50	1986	
• 20mm	100	100	1987	
Total	**~420**	**~420**		
Radars				
• AN/TPS-70	4	4	1999	Part of C^3I system

Navy

Submarines

Type	Quantity	Length (m.)/ displacement (t.)	Notes/ armament
• K class (Kilo)	2	73.8/3,076	6x533mm torpedoes or 24 mines

Combat Vessels

Type	Quantity	Length (m.)/ displacement (t.)	Notes/ armament
Missile corvette			
• Nanuchka II	3	59.3/660	4xSS-N-2B (Styx) 2xSA-N-4 (Gecko) 2x57mm guns
MFPBs			
• Ossa II	6	38.6/171	4xSS-N-2B (Styx) 4x30mm guns 3 possibly non-operational
ASW frigate			
• Mourad Rais (Koni)	3	96.4/1,440	2xSA-N-4 (Gecko) RBU 6000 ASW mortars 4x30mm guns 22 mines
Gun corvette			
• Djebel chinoise (Type 802)	2	58.4/496	1x76mm gun 2x40mm guns 4x23mm guns
Gunboats			
• Kebir class (Brooke Marine)	12	37.5/166	1x76mm gun 4x25mm guns
Total	**26**		
Future procurement			
• Kebir class	2		Total order of 15
• Kh-35 missiles	48		

Patrol Craft

Type	Quantity	Length (m.)/ displacement (t.)	Notes/ armament
• Al Mouderrib (Chui-E)	7	58.8/388	2xtwin 14.5mm MG
• Baglietto 20 GC	5	20.4/44	1x20mm gun
• Al Munkid	4		SAR ships
Total	**16**		

Landing Craft

Type	Quantity	Length (m.)/ displacement (t.)	Notes/ armament
• Polnochny class (Type 771)	1	75/760	180 troops; 6 tanks 2x140mm MRLs 2x30mm guns
• Kalaat Beni Hammad (Brooke Marine)	2	93/2,450	2x40mm guns 2x25mm guns
Total	**3**		

Auxiliary Vessels

Type	Quantity	Length (m.)/ displacement (t.)	Notes/ armament
• Poluchat I	1	29.6/70	

Coastal Defense

Type	Quantity	Notes
• SS-N-2 Styx	4	

Naval Infrastructure

Naval bases: **5**

Algiers, Annaba, Mers al-Kebir, Oran, Skikda

Ship maintenance and repair facilities: **8**

Three slipways belonging to Chantier Naval de Mers al-Kebir at Oran; 4,000-ton dry docks at Algiers; 3 small graving docks at Annaba; a small dry dock at Beni Saf.

Major Non-Governmental Paramilitary Forces

Personnel

	Active	Reserves
• Islamic Salvation Army (AIS)	+	+
• Armed Islamic Group (GIA)	+	+
Total	**1,000-1,500**	**1,000-1,500**

2. BAHRAIN

General Data

Official Name of the State: State of Bahrain
Head of State: Amir Shaykh Hamad bin Isa al-Khalifa
Prime Minister: Khalifa ibn Salman al-Khalifa
Minister of Defense: Lieutenant General Khalifa ibn Ahmad al-Khalifa
Commander in Chief of the Armed Forces: Salman bin Hamad al-Khalifa
Chief of Staff of the Bahraini Defense Forces: Major General Abdallah ibn Salman al-Khalifa
Commander of the Air Force: Hamad ibn Abdallah al-Khalifa
Commander of the Navy: Lieutenant Commander Yusuf al-Maluallah

Area: 620 sq. km.
Population: 700,000

Demography

Ethnic groups		
Arabs	511,000	73.0%
Southeast Asians	91,000	13.0%
Persians	56,000	8.0%
Others	42,000	6.0%
Religious groups		
Shi'ite Muslims	525,000	75.0%
Sunni Muslims	175,000	25.0%
National groups		
Bahrainis	441,000	63.0%
Southeast Asians	91,000	13.0%
Alien other Arabs	70,000	10.0%
Iranians	56,000	8.0%
Others	42,000	6.0%

Economic Data

		1996	1997	1998	1999	2000
GDP (current price)	$ bn	6.1	6.4	6.2	6.6	7.3
GDP per capita	$	10,166	10,666	10,333	9,428	10,428
Real GDP growth	%	3.9	3.1	4.8	4.0	5.2
Consumer price index	%	-0.5	2.5	-0.4	-1.3	2.0
External debt	$ bn	2.4	2.4	2.6	2.7	2.7

Economic Data *(continued)*

		1996	1997	1998	1999	2000
Balance of payments						
• Exports fob	$ bn	4.70	4.38	3.27	4.14	5.80
• Imports fob	$ bn	4.04	3.78	3.3	3.47	4.20
• Current account balance (including services and income)	$ bn	0.26	-0.03	-0.78	-0.34	0.67
Government expenditure						
• Total expenditures	$ bn	1.83	1.94	1.88	1.93	1.95
• Defense expenditure	$ bn	0.29	0.29	0.29	NA	NA
• Real change in defense expenditure	%	5.86	-0.69	2.43	NA	NA
• Defense expenditure /GDP	%	4.75	4.53	4.67	NA	NA
Population	m	0.6	0.6	0.6	0.7	0.7
Official exchange rate	BD:$1	0.38	0.38	0.38	0.38	0.38

Sources: EIU Quarterly Report, EIU Country Profile, IMF International Financial Statistical Yearbook, SIPRI Yearbook

Arms Procurement and Security Assistance Received

Country	Type	Details
Netherlands	• Arms transfers	AIFVs, armored CP, ARVs
Sweden	• Arms transfers	Early warning network
UK	• Arms transfers	Sealion ESM
	• Military training	A number of retired British officers hold senior positions in Bahraini force, training the new National Guard
US	• Arms transfers	F-16 aircraft, Black Hawk helicopters, AIM-120 AAMs, AGM-65G/F, MLRS, ATACMS, TOW ATGMs, early warning network, a missile frigate
	• Military training	Foreign advisers/instructors; trainees abroad
	• Maintenance	Foreign technicians

Arms Sales and Security Assistance Extended

Country	Type	Details
UK	• Facilities	Air force facilities
US	• Facilities	Naval facilities, storage facilities, prepositioning of army equipment and intelligence installations, HQ facilities for the US forces in the Gulf at Mina Salman

Foreign Military Cooperation

Type	Details
• Foreign forces	About 1,100 US soldiers
• Forces deployed abroad	Saudi Arabia (part of GCC "Desert Shield" Rapid Deployment Force)
• Joint maneuvers	Joint US Air Force, Navy and Special Forces exercises
• Security agreements	US, Britain, GCC countries

Weapons of Mass Destruction

NBC Capabilities

Nuclear capability

No known nuclear activity. Signatory to the NPT.

Chemical weapons (CW) and protective equipment

No known CW activities. Party to the CWC.

Biological weapons (BW)

No known BW activities. Party to the BWC.

Ballistic Missiles

Model	Launchers	Missiles	Since	Notes
Future procurement				
• ATACMS		30		

Armed Forces

Major Changes: Inauguration of the GCC joint communication network, which is part of the GCC joint early warning system. The USA has agreed to sell Bahrain ATACMS tactical ballistic missiles. The Bahraini Air Force received 10 new F-16 Block 40 aircraft, capable of carrying AMRAAM air to air missiles.

Order-of-Battle

Year	1996	1997	1999	2000	2001
General data					
• Personnel (regular)	7,400	7,400	7,400	7,400	7,400
• SSM launchers				9	9
Ground Forces					
• Total number of brigades	3	3	3	3	3
• Number of battalions	6	7	7	7	7
• Tanks	81	110	180	180	180
• APCs/AFVs	192	217(237)	277(297)	277(297)	277(297)
• Artillery (including MRLs)	44	44(50)	48(50)	48(50)	48(50)

Order-of-Battle *(continued)*

Year	1996	1997	1999	2000	2001
Air Force					
• Combat aircraft	24	24	24	34	34
• Transport aircraft	3–4	2	2	2	2
• Helicopters	23	41*	41	39(41)	39(41)
Air Defense Forces					
• Heavy SAM batteries	1	1	1	1	1
• Medium SAM batteries	7	2*	2	2	2
• Light SAM launchers	160	40*	40	40	40
Navy					
• Combat vessels	11	11	11	11	11
• Patrol boats	19	19	21	21	21

Note: Beginning with 1997, data refers to quantities in active service. The number in parentheses refers to the total inventory.
* Due to change in estimate.

Personnel

	Regular	Reserves	Total
Ground Forces	6,000		6,000
Air Force	700		700
Navy	700		700
Total	**7,400**		**7,400**
Paramilitary			
• Coast Guard and National Guard	2,000		2,000

Ground Forces

Formations

	Brigades	Independent battalions	Battalions in brigade
Armored	1		2 armd., 1 reconn.
Infantry	1		2 mech., 1 inf.
Artillery	1		6 batt.
Air Defense		1	
Special Forces		1	
Total	**3**	**2**	

Tanks

Model	Quantity	In service	Since	Notes
MBTs				
Medium and low quality				
• M60 A3	180	180	1987	
Total	**180**	**180**		

APCs/AFVs

Model	Quantity	In service	Since	Notes
APCs				
• M113	110	110	1990	
• M-3 (Panhard)	110	110	1979	
• AT-105 Saxon	10	10	1981	
Subtotal	230	230		
IFVs				
• YPR-765	25	25	1996	
Reconnaissance				
• AML-90	22	22	1979	
• Ferret	10	0	1972	Possibly phased out
• Saladin	10	0	1973	Possibly phased out
Subtotal	42	22		
Total	**297**	**277**		

Artillery

Model	Quantity	In service	Since	Notes
Self-propelled guns and howitzers				
• 203mm M110	13	13	1994	
Towed guns and howitzers				
• 155mm M198 A1	20	18	1984	
• 105mm L-118	8	8		
Subtotal	28	26		
MRLs				
• 227mm MLRS	9	9	1992	
Total	**50**	**48**		

Anti-Tank Missiles

Model	Launchers	Missiles	Since	Notes
• BGM-71C Improved TOW	15	+		
• BGM-71E (TOW 2A)	+	+		
Future procurement				
• BGM-71E/F (TOW 2A/B)				

Air Force

Order-of-Battle

Category	Quantity	In service	Notes
• Combat	34	34	
• Transport	2	2	
• Helicopters	41	39	

Combat Aircraft

Model	Quantity	In service	Since	Notes
Advanced multi-role				
• F-16C/D	22	22	1990	
Multi-role				
• F-5E/F	12	12	1985	
Total	**34**	**34**		

Transport Aircraft

Model	Quantity	In service	Since	Notes
• Gulfstream II	2	2	1977	

Helicopters

Model	Quantity	In service	Since	Notes
Ground attack				
• AH-1E	14	14	1996	
• 500MD	2	2	1981	
• MBB BO-105	5	3	1976	
Subtotal	21	19		
Medium transport				
• S-70A Black Hawk	3	3	1996	
• AB-212	12	12	1980	
• Bell 412	3	3	1982	With police
Subtotal	18	18		
Naval combat				
• SA-365 Dauphin	2	2	1988	
Total	**41**	**39**		

Advanced Armament

Air-to-air missiles

AIM-9P/L Sidewinder (150), AIM-7M Sparrow (48), AGM-65D Maverick (24)

Air-to-ground missiles

AS-15TT anti-ship missile

Advanced Armament *(continued)*

Future procurement
LANTIRN (3), AIM-120 AMRAAM (26)

Note: Numbers in parentheses refer to number of units purchased, not to current inventory levels.

Air Force Infrastructure

Military airfields: 1
Shaykh Isa

Air Defense Forces

Surface-to-Air Missiles

Model	Batteries	Launchers	Since	Notes
Heavy missiles				
• MIM-23B Improved HAWK	1		1994	
Medium missiles				
• Crotale	2		1995	Number unconfirmed
Light missiles				
• RBS-70		40	1980	
Shoulder launched missiles				
• FIM-92A Stinger		18	1987	400 missiles (number unconfirmed)

Other Air Defense Systems

Model	Quantity	In service	Since	Notes
Short range guns				
• 35mm Oerlikon	12	12		Possibly with Skyguard FCS

Navy

Combat Vessels

Type	Quantity	Length (m.)/ displacement (t.)	Notes/ armament
Missile frigates			
• Sabha (Oliver Hazard Perry class)	1	135.6/3,638	1xSH-2G helicopter 4xHarpoon SSM 36xStandard SM-1 6x324mm torpedoes 1x76mm gun 1x20mm Vulcan Phalanx gun
Missile corvettes			
• Al-Manama (Lürssen MGB-62)	2	63.0/632	4xExocet MM-40 1x76mm gun 1xtwin 40mm gun
MFPBs			
• Ahmad al-Fateh (Lürssen TNC-45)	4	44.9/259	4xExocet MM-40 1x76mm gun 1xtwin 40mm gun
• Al-Riffa (Lürssen FPB-38)	2	38.5/205	2xtwin 40mm guns 1x57mm rocket launcher
• Al-Jarim (Swift FPB-20)	2	19.2/33	1x20mm gun
Subtotal	8		
Total	**11**		

Patrol Craft

Type	Quantity	Length (m.)/ displacement (t.)	Notes/ armament
• Al- Muharraq (Wasp 30)	1	30/90	1x30mm gun
• Dera'a (Tracker)	1	19.5/31	
• Dera'a (Halmatic)	4	20.1/31.5	
• Dera'a (Wasp)	2	20/36.3	
• Saham 1 (Wasp)	3	11/7	
• Saif (Halmatic)	6	14.4/17	
• Saif (Fairey Marine Sword)	4	13.7/15	
Total	**21**		

Landing Craft

Type	Quantity	Length (m.)/ displacement (t.)	Notes/ armament
• LCU 1466	3	36.3/360	176 ton cargo
• Safra LCM (Fairey Marine)	1	22.5/150	
Total	**4**		

Auxiliary Vessels

Type	Quantity	Length (m.)/ displacement (t.)	Notes/ armament
• Ajeera class	1	39.6/420	200 ton fuel/water
• Safra	1	25.9/165	

Naval Infrastructure

Naval bases: **1**

Mina Salman

Ship maintenance and repair facilities

Arab Shipbuilding and Repair Yard (ASRY), a 500,000 dwt dry-dock engaged in repairs and construction (mainly supertankers; jointly owned by Bahrain, Kuwait, Qatar, Saudi Arabia, UAE-each 18.84%;Iraq-4.7%; and Libya-1.1%)

3. EGYPT

General Data

Official Name of the State: The Arab Republic of Egypt
Head of State: President Muhammad Husni Mubarak
Prime Minister: Atef Muhammad Ebeid
Minister of Defense and Military Production: Field Marshal Muhammad Hussayn Tantawi
Chief of General Staff: General Magdi Hatata
Commander of the Air Force: Lieutenant General Ahmad Muhammad Shafik
Commander of the Navy: Vice Admiral Ahmad Saber Salim

Area: 1,000,258 sq. km. (dispute with Sudan over "Halaib triangle" area)
Population: 68,500,000

Demography

Ethnic groups		
Arabs	67,404,000	98.4%
Greeks, Italians, Armenians	685,000	1.0%
Nubians	68,500	0.1%
Others	342,500	0.5%
Religious groups		
Sunni Muslims	64,390,000	94.0%
Copts, other Christians	4,110,000	6.0%

Economic Data

		1996	1997	1998	1999	2000
GDP (current price)	$ bn	67.3	75.6	82.7	89.0	93.1
GDP per capita	$	1,134	1,168	1,253	1,324	1,359
Real GDP growth	%	5.0	5.5	5.6	6.0	3.9
Consumer price index	%	7.2	4.6	4.2	3.1	2.9
External debt	$ bn	31.3	29.8	32.0	31.1	30.1
Balance of payments						
• Exports fob	$ bn	4.78	5.53	4.40	5.24	7.19
• Imports fob	$ bn	13.17	14.16	14.62	15.16	17.00
• Current account balance (including services and income)	$ bn	-0.19	-0.71	-2.57	-1.69	-1.05

Economic Data *(continued)*

		1996	1997	1998	1999	2000
Government expenditure						
• Total expenditure	$ bn	19.71	20.88	21.81	22.83	24.81
• Defense expenditure	$ bn	1.97	1.98	2.02	2.15	NA
• Real change in defense expenditure	%	0.0	0.86	1.96	6.11	NA
• Defense expenditure /GDP	%	2.92	2.62	2.45	2.41	NA
Population	m	59.3	64.7	66.0	67.2	68.5
Official exchange rate	E£: $1	3.39	3.39	3.39	3.40	3.47

Sources: EIU Quarterly Report, EIU Country Profile, IMF International Financial Statistical Yearbook, SIPRI Yearbook.

*Published defense expenditure data apparently does not include $1.3 bn annual foreign military assistance from the USA.

Arms Procurement and Security Assistance Received

Country	Type	Details
Finland	• Cooperation in arms production, assembly, R&D	Transfer of technology and production license of GH 52 APU 155mm gun
Germany	• Arms transfers	G 115EG basic trainer aircraft
	• Maintenance of equipment	anti-mine equipmen
India	• Arms transfers	Spare parts for Soviet-made aircraft
Italy	• Arms transfers	Upgrading of Ramadan-class fast attack craft
Netherlands	• Arms transfers	AIFVs
North Korea	• Arms transfers	Assistance to Egyptian production of SSMs (alleged)
PRC	• Arms transfers	K-8 training aircraft
Russia	• Arms transfers	Upgrading of SA-3 SAMs
UK	• Arms transfers	Naval radars, mortar-locating radar upgrade, Upgrading of Ramadan-class fast attack craft

Arms Procurement and Security Assistance Received *(continued)*

Country	Type	Details
US	• Arms transfers	F-16 C/D aircraft, upgrading AH-64A helicopters to AH-64D configuration, upgrading of AEW aircraft, SH-2G helicopters, CH-47D helicopters, AAMs, LANTIRN navigation and targeting system, airborne EW systems, UAVs, Avenger ADS, UMRAAM SAMs, F-16 simulators, M109 A3 guns, TOW ATGMs, missile frigates, Ambassador fast attack crafts, Harpoon anti-ship missiles, torpedoes, Moray-class submarines, AN/SPS-48E radars, upgrading of AN/TPS-59 radars
	• Assistance	$1.3 billion grant, some items from US drawdown, worth several hundred million dollars
	• Cooperation in arms production, assembly, R&D	Assembly of M1A1 tanks and M88A2 recovery vehicle, upgrading M113 APCs, AIFVs
	• Military training	Foreign advisers/instructors, trainees abroad

Arms Sales and Security Assistance Extended

Country	Type	Details
Bosnia	• Arms transfers	10 T-55 tanks and spare parts, artillery
Congo	• Military training	Advisers in country
Greece	• Military training	Foreign trainees
North Korea	• Cooperation in arms production assembly, R&D	Transfer of missile technology (alleged)
Oman	• Military training	Advisers in country
US	• Facilities	Use of airfields at Cairo West, Qena, Inshas, Hurghada

Foreign Military Cooperation

Type	Details
• Foreign forces	US forces as of September 2000 includes some 500 soldiers
• Forces deployed abroad	Bosnia (UNMIBH); Georgia (UNOMIG)
• Joint maneuvers	France, Germany, Greece, Italy, Jordan, Kuwait, Netherlands, Saudi Arabia, UAE, UK, US

Defense Production

	M	P	A
Weapons of mass destruction			
• Upgraded Scud B SSMs (with North Korean cooperation)	√		
• Chemical agents (unconfirmed)	√		
Ground forces equipment			
• M1A1 tanks, with cooperation from US (some parts will be produced in Egypt)			√
• M88 Armored Recovery Vehicles			√
• Fahd APCs (with FRG components and assistance)		√	
• 155mm GH 52 APU towed field gun (with Finnish assistance)		√	
• Conversion of 122mm D-30 howitzers to 122mm AR SP howitzers	√		
• 130mm artillery pieces		√	
• 122mm Saqr 18/30/36 MRLs	√		
• Mortars		√	
• Short-range SAMs (Saqr eye)			√
• Conversion of 23mm AAGs to Sinai 23 SP AA systems (with French assistance)	√		
• Soviet-design AAGs and small arms		√	
• Upgrading of Russian tanks (with British assistance)		√	
• Add-on armor to M113 APCs	√		
• Tank tracks		√	
• Minefield crossing systems (similar to Viper)		√	
• Trucks and jeeps (with US)		√	
• British tank guns		√	
• Mines, including scatterable	√	√	
• Ammunition for artillery, tanks, and small arms	√		
Air Force equipment			
• K-8 Karakorum basic trainer and light attack aircraft		√	
• Parts for F-16		√	
• Parts for Mirage 2000		√	
• Parts for Mystère-Falcon 50 executive aircraft		√	
• Aircraft fuel pods		√	
• CBUs (US design)		√	
• Aerial bombs		√	

Defense Production *(continued)*

	M	P	A
Navy equipment			
• Timsah patrol boats	√		
• Type 83 patrol boats	√		
Electronics			
• SAM electronics (in collaboration with UK)		√	
• Fire control system		√	
• Bassal artillery fire control system	√		
• Simulators for rifle firing	√		
Optronics			
• Night vision devices		√	

Note: M - manufacture (indigenously developed)
P - production under license
A - assembly

Weapons of Mass Destruction

NBC Capabilities

Nuclear capability

22 Mw research reactor from Argentina, completed 1997; 2 Mw research reactor from the USSR, in operation since 1961. Party to the NPT. Safeguards agreement with the IAEA in force. Signed, but not ratified, the African Nuclear Weapon Free Zone Treaty (Treaty of Pelindaba).

Chemical weapons (CW) and protective equipment

Alleged continued research and possible production of chemical warfare agents; Alleged stockpile of chemical agents (mustard and nerve agents); personal protective equipment; Soviet type decontamination units; Fuchs (Fox) ABC detection vehicle (12); SPW-40 P2Ch ABC detection vehicle (small numbers). Refused to sign the CWC.

Biological weapons (BW)

Suspected biological warfare program; no details available. Not a party to the BWC.

Ballistic Missiles

Model	Launchers	Missiles	Since	Notes
• SS-1 (Scud B/Scud C)	24	100	1973	Possibly some upgraded
Future procurement				
• Scud C/Project-T		90		Locally produced
• Vector				Unconfirmed
• No-Dong				Alleged

Note: See also under Rockets

Armed Forces

Major Changes: The Egyptian army received additional 24 SP122 self-propelled guns. The Egyptian Air Force received the last F-16 C/D aircraft of the Peace Vector V deal. Deliveries of the first 24 F-16 aircraft in the framework of the Peace Vector VI deal are due beginning 2001. The Air Force also decided to upgrade its 35 Apache AH-64A to the AH-64D standard, although Egypt will not receive the longbow radar. The Air Force will upgrade its 5 Hawkeye AEW aircraft and will get another aircraft from the US. The first of 74 G 115EG training aircraft from Germany has entered service. The Navy ordered two new Moray class submarines and 4 Ambassador Mk III missile patrol boats.

Order-of-Battle

Year	1996	1997	1999	2000	2001
General data					
• Personnel (regular)	424,000	421,000	450,000	450,000	450,000
• SSM launchers	9	9	24	24	24
Ground Forces					
• Divisions	12	12	12	12	12
• Total number of brigades	50	53	49	49	49
• Tanks	2,900	2,662 (3,162)	~2,750 (3,505)	~3,000 (3,505)	~3,000 (3,505)
• APCs/AFVs	5,180	3,025 (4,995)	~3,400 (~5,300)	~3,400 (~5,300)	~3,400 (~5,300)
• Artillery (including MRLs)	3,060	3,158	~3,550	~3,530 (~3,570)	~3,530 (~3,570)
Air Force					
• Combat aircraft	497	505	481(494)	481(494)	481(494)
• Transport aircraft	43	35*	44	44	44
• Helicopters	211	223	~225	~225	~225
Air Defense Forces					
• Heavy SAM batteries	122	105*	109	109	109
• Medium SAM batteries	48	48	44	44	44
• Light SAM launchers	50	50	50	105	105
Navy					
• Submarines	8	6	4	4	4
• Combat vessels	59	64	65	64	64
• Patrol crafts	70	83	104	104	104

Note: Beginning with 1997, data refers to quantities in active service. The number in parentheses refers to the total inventory.

* Due to change in estimate.

Personnel

	Regular	Reserves	Total
Ground Forces	320,000	150,000	470,000
Air Force	30,000	20,000	50,000
Air Defense	80,000	70,000	150,000
Navy	20,000	14,000	34,000
Total	**450,000**	**254,000**	**704,000**
Paramilitary			
• Coast Guard			2,000
• Frontier Corps			6,000
• Central Security Forces			325,000
• National Guard			60,000
• Border Guard			12,000

Ground Forces

Formations

	Corps/ armies	Divisions	Independent brigades/groups	Brigades in divisions
All Arms	2			
Armored		4	4	2 armd., 1 mech., 1 aty. each
Mechanized		7	4	2 mech., 1 armd., 1 aty. each
Infantry		1	2	
Airborne			1	
Paratroopers			1	
Special Forces			+	
Artillery			15	
SSM			2	
Total	**2**	**12**	**~30**	

Tanks

Model	Quantity	In service	Since	Notes
MBTs				
High quality				
• M1A1	555	500	1992	
Medium and low quality				
• M60 A3	850	835	1981	
• M60 A1	700	600	1990	

Tanks *(continued)*

Model	Quantity	In service	Since	Notes
• T-62	600	~550	1972	
• T-55	800	~500		Most in storage
Subtotal	2,950	~2,500		
Total	**3,505**	**~3,000**		
Future procurement				
• M1A1	100			

APCs/AFVs

Model	Quantity	In service	Since	Notes
APCs				
• M113 A2	1,768	1,000	1980	52 M901 ITV
• BMR-600	250	250	1983	
• Fahd	165	160	1986	
• OT-62/BTR-50	1,100	+		Possibly phased out
Subtotal	3,283	~1,410		
IFVs				
• YPR-765	600	600	1996	200 with TOW under armor
• BMP-1	220	220		
• V-150/V-300 commando	~180	~180		
Subtotal	~1,000	~1,000		
Reconnaissance				
• BRDM-2	300	300	1968	
• BTR-40/152	~675	~675		
Subtotal	~975	~975		
Total	**~5,300**	**~3,400**		

Artillery

Model	Quantity	In service	Since	Notes
Self-propelled guns and howitzers				
• 155mm M109 A2	200	164	1984	
• 122mm SP122	124	124	1987	
Subtotal	324	288		
Towed guns and howitzers				
• 130mm M-46/Type-59	+	+		
• 122mm D-30	+	+		
Subtotal	~970	~970		

Artillery *(continued)*

Model	Quantity	In service	Since	Notes
Mortars, over 160mm				
• 240mm	+	+		
• 160mm	60	60		
Subtotal	~60	~60		
Mortars, under 160mm				
• 120mm M-43	1,800	1,800		
• 107mm M30 SP	100	100		On M106 chassis
Subtotal	1,900	1,900		
MRLs				
• 122mm BM-11/BM-21	100	100		
• 122mm Saqr 18/30/36	200	200		
Subtotal	~300	~300		
Rockets				
• FROG-7	12	12		
• 210mm Saqr 80	*	*		
Subtotal	~12	~12		
Total	**~3,570**	**~3,530**		
Future procurement				
• 155mm GH 52 APU	+			To be produced in Egypt
• 155mm M109A2/A3	179			

Ground Radars

Model	Quantity	In service	Since	Notes
Artillery/mortar locating radars				
• AN/TPQ-36	6	6	1999	
• AN/TPQ-37	2	2	1989	
Future procurement				
• AN/TPQ-37				

Logistics and Engineering Equipment

Bar mine-laying system, EWK pontoon bridges, GSP self-propelled ferries, M-123 Viper minefield crossing system or al-Fatah Egyptian Viper-like system, MT-55 bridging tanks, MTU-55 bridging tanks, Egyptian bridging tanks (on T-34 chassis), mine-clearing rollers, PMP folding pontoon bridges, PRP motorized bridges, M88 ARV.

Anti-Tank Missiles

Model	Launchers	Missiles	Since	Notes
• BGM-71C Improved TOW/ BGM-71D TOW II	~600	+		
• M901 ITV	52	+		Also listed under APCs
• YPR-765 (TOW under armor)	200	+	1996	Also listed under APCs
• MILAN	250	+	1978	
• AT-3 (Sagger)		1,400	1972	
• Swingfire	200	+	1976	
Total	**~1,300**	**+**		
Future procurement				
• TOW IIA/B	540			

Air Force

Order-of-Battle

Category	Quantity	In service	Notes
• Combat	494	481	
• Transport	44	44	
• Helicopters	~225	~225	

Combat Aircraft

Model	Quantity	In service	Since	Notes
Advanced multi-role				
• F-16C/D	153	153	1986	
• F-16A/B	40	34	1982	Will be upgraded to F-16C/D standard
• Mirage 2000	18	18	1986	
Subtotal	211	205		
Multi-role				
• F-4E Phantom	32	25	1980	
Ground attack				
• Alpha Jet and Alpha Jet MS-2	42	42	1983	Defined in Egypt as CAS aircraft

Combat Aircraft *(continued)*

Model	Quantity	In service	Since	Notes
Obsolete				
• F-7 Shenyang/ MiG-21 MF	150	150	1972	14 listed also under reconnaissance
• Mirage 5	59	59	1974	6 listed also under reconnaissance
Subtotal	209	209		
Total	**494**	**481**		
Future procurement				
• F-16C/D	24			Deliveries to commence in 2001

Transport Aircraft

Model	Quantity	In service	Since	Notes
• Beechcraft 1900C	6	6	1988	4 in various surveillance roles
• Boeing 707	1	1	1974	
• C-130H/ C-130H-30 Hercules	21	21	1978/1990	2 in various surveillance roles
• DHC-5D Buffalo	9	9	1982	
• Gulfstream III/V	4	4	1985/1996	
• Mystère-Falcon 20	3	3		
Total	**44**	**44**		

Training and Liaison Aircraft

Model	Quantity	In service	Since	Notes
Jet trainers				
• Alpha Jet and Alpha Jet MS-2			1983	Also listed under Combat Aircraft
• L-59	48	48	1993	
• L-29 (Delfin)	60	60	1972	
• L-39 (Albatross)	10	10	1990	
Subtotal	118	118		
Piston/Turbo-prop				
• G 115EG	~40	~40	2000	
• Embraer EMB-312 (Tucano)	54	54	1984	
• al-Gumhuriya	36	36	1973	
Subtotal	130	130		
Total	**248**	**248**		
Future procurement				
• G 115EG	74			being delivered
• K-8 Karakorum	80			

Helicopters

Model	Quantity	In service	Since	Notes
Attack				
• AH-64A Apache	35	35	1995	
• SA-342 L/M Gazelle	65	65	1983	
Subtotal	100	100		
Heavy transport				
• CH-47C/D Chinook	19	19	1981	
Medium transport				
• Mi-8 (Hip)	~40	~40	1972	Some may be armed
• S-70A Black Hawk	2	2	1990	VIP service
• Westland Commando Mk 2	25	25	1974	
Subtotal	~65	~65		
Light transport				
• UH-12E Hiller	17	17	1982	
Naval combat				
• SH-2G Seasprite	10	10	1997	
• SA-342L Gazelle	9	9	1983	
• Westland Sea King Mk 47	5	5	1976	
Subtotal	24	24		
Total	**~225**	**~225**		
Future procurement				
• AH-64D Apache	35			Upgrading of existing AH-64A beginning 2003
• CH-47D Chinook	6			Upgrading of existing CH-47C
• S-70A Black Hawk	2			VIP

Miscellaneous Aircraft

Model	Quantity	In service	Since	Notes
Reconnaissance				
• MiG-21R	14	14		Also listed under Combat Aircraft
• Mirage 5DR	6	6	1974	Also listed under Combat Aircraft
AEW/AWACS				
• E-2C Hawkeye	6	6	1986	

Miscellaneous Aircraft *(continued)*

Model	Quantity	In service	Since	Notes
ELINT/maritime surveillance/ASW				
• Beechcraft 1900C	4	4	1992	Also listed under Transport Aircraft
• C-130H	2	2	1978	Also listed under Transport Aircraft
UAVs and mini-UAVs				
• Kader	+	+		
• R4E-50 Skyeye	48	48		
• 324 Scarab	50	50		
Target drones				
• CT-20	+	+		
• Beech AQM-37A	+	+		
• Beech MQM-107B	+	+		
• TTL BTT-3 Banshee	Several dozen	Several dozen		
Future procurement				
• Camcopter UAV				

Advanced Armament

Air-to-air missiles

AIM-7F/M Sparrow (550), AIM-9L/P Sidewinder (1,100), R-550 Magic, R-530D Super

Air-to-ground missiles

AGM-65 Maverick (1,100), AS-30L, AGM-114 Hellfire (1,000), HOT

Avionics

LANTIRN (30)

Future procurement

LANTIRN (15)

Note: Numbers in parentheses refer to number of units purchased, not to current inventory levels.

Air Force Infrastructure

Aircraft shelters

In all operational airfields, for combat aircraft

Military airfields: **28**

Abu Hammad, Abu Suweir, Alexandria, Aswan, Beni Suef, Bilbeis, Cairo International, Cairo West, Fayid, Hurghada, Inshas, Janaklis, Jebel al-Basour, Kabrit, Kom Awshim, Luxor, al-Maza, al-Minya, Mansura, Marsah Matruh, Qena, al-Qutamiya, Saqqara, Sidi Barani, Ras Banas, Salahiya, Tanta, al-Zaqaziq

Air Defense Forces

Surface-to-Air Missiles

Model	Batteries	Launchers	Since	Notes
Heavy missiles				
• MIM-23B Improved HAWK	16		1981	
• SA-2 (Guideline)	40		1965	
• SA-3 (Goa)	53		1965	Being upgraded
Total	**109**			
Medium missiles				
• Crotale	12		1977	
• SA-6 (Gainful)	14		1972	
• Sparrow	18			Included in Skyguard AA system
Total	**44**			
Light missiles				
• MIM-72A Chaparral		80		
• Avenger		25	2000	
Total		**105**		
Shoulder-launched missiles				
• Ain al-Saqr (Saqr Eye)		+		
• SA-7 (Grail)		~2,000	1972	
Future procurement				
• HUMRAAM				Under negotiations
• SA-3 (Goa)		50		Upgrade of launchers and missiles; to be delivered in 2003

Other Air Defense Systems

Model	Quantity	In service	Since	Notes
Air defense systems (missiles, radars and guns)				
• Skyguard AD system	18	18		Egyptian designation: Amoun
• Sinai 23mm AD system	~45	~45		
Total	**~65**	**~65**		
Short-range guns				
• 57mm ZSU 57x2 SP	40	40		

Other Air Defense Systems *(continued)*

Model	Quantity	In service	Since	Notes
• 35mm Oerlikon-Buhrle 35x2 GDF-002	36	36		Integral part of Skyguard AD systems
• 23mm ZSU 23x4 SP (Gun Dish)	360	360		
• 23mm ZU 23x2	117	117		
Total	**553**	**553**		
Radars				
• AN/TPS-59(V)2	5	5		Being upgraded to V(3) version
• AN/TPS-59/M34	8	8	1991	Being upgraded
• AN/TPS-63	42	42		
• P-15 Flat Face	+	+	1973	
• P-12 Spoon Rest	+	+	1973	
• TRS-2100 (Tiger S)	15	15		

Navy

Submarines

Type	Quantity	Length (m.)/ displacement (t.)	Notes/ armament
• R class (Romeo ex-Chinese)	4	76.6/1,830	Sub-Harpoon SSM 8x533mm torpedoes or 28 mines
Future procurement			
• Moray class	2		

Combat Vessels

Type	Quantity	Length (m.)/ displacement (t.)	Notes/ armament
Missile frigates			
• Descubierta class	2	88.8/1,233	8xHarpoon SSMs 24xAspide SAMs 6x324mm torpedoes 1x375mm ASW launcher 1x76mm gun 2x40mm guns

Combat Vessels *(continued)*

Type	Quantity	Length (m.)/ displacement (t.)	Notes/ armament
• Jianghu class	2	103.2/1,425	4xHai Ying-II SSMs 4x57mm guns 12x37mm guns 2 RBU 1200 ASW mortars
• Knox class	2	134/3,011	1x Seasprite helicopter 8xHarpoon SSMs 1x127mm gun 1x20mm phalanx 4x324mm torpedoes
• Oliver Hazard Perry	4	135.6/2,750	2xSeasprite helicopters 4xHarpoon SSMs 36xStandard SAM 1x76mm gun 1x20mm Phalanx 6x324mm torpedoes
Subtotal	10		
MFPBs			
• Hegu class	5	27.0/88	2xSY-1 SSMs or 2xSS-N-2 Styx 2x23mm guns 1 non-operational
• October (Komar)	6	25.5/82.0	2xOtomat SSMs 4x30mm guns
• Ossa I	4	38.6/171	4x SS-N-2A Styx SA-N-5 Grail 4x30mm guns 1 non-operational
• Ramadan (Vosper Thornycroft)	6	52.0/307	4xOtomat SSMs 1x76mm gun 2x40mm guns SA-N-5 portable SAMs Command and control systems to be upgraded
Subtotal	21		
Mine warfare vessels			
• T-43 class minesweeper	6	58.0/580	4x37mm guns 20 mines 2 non-operational

Combat Vessels *(continued)*

Type	Quantity	Length (m.)/ displacement (t.)	Notes/ armament
• Swiftships coastal minesweep	3	33.8/203	
• Yurka class minesweeper	4	52.4/540	4x30mm guns 10 mines
• Swiftships route survey	2	27.4/165	
Subtotal	15		
Gunboats			
• Hainan class	8	58.8/375	4x57mm guns 4x23mm guns 3 non- operational
• Shanghai II	4	38.8/113	4x37mm guns 4x23mm guns
• Shershen class	6	34.7/145	SA-N-5 portable SAM 4x30mm guns 2x122mm MRL
Subtotal	18		
Total	**64**		
Future procurement			
• Ambassador MFPBs	4		Delivery 2004

Patrol Craft

Type	Quantity	Length (m.)/ displacement (t.)	Notes/ armament
• Spectre	12	13.8/37	
• Peterson	9	13.9/18	
• Peterson	3	15.5/20	
• Crestitalia	6	21.0/36	2x30mm guns 1x20mm gun
• DC 35 type	29	10.7/4	
• Nisr class (de Castro)	5	31.0/110	2-4x25mm guns 1x122mm RL
• Swiftships	9	28.4/102	2x23mm guns 1x20mm gun
• Timsah class	22	30.5/106	2x30mm guns or 2x20mm guns
• Type 83	9	25.5/85	2x23mm guns 1x20mm gun
Total	**104**		

Landing Craft

Type	Quantity	Length (m.)/ displacement (t.)	Notes/ armament
• LCM	5		
• Polnochny class LSM	3	73.0/800	2x30mm guns 2x140mm MRL 6 tanks or 350 tons
• Vydra class LCU	9	54.8/425	4x37mm guns 200 troops or 250 tons
• Seafox	8	11/11.3	Swimmers' delivery craft
Total	**25**		
Future procurement			
• US-made landing ship			

Auxiliary Vessels

Type	Quantity	Length (m.)/ displacement (t.)	Notes/ armament
• Black Swan class frigate (training)	1	91.2/1,925	6x102mm guns 4x37mm guns no longer serviceable
• El Fateh (Zenith, Wessex)	1	110.6/1,730	2xSA-N-5 SAMs 4x115mm guns 6x37mm guns 2x40mm guns 8x533mm torpedoes used for training
• Niryat diving support	1		
• Okhtensky (tug)	6	47.6/930	
• Poluchat II torpedo recovery	2	29.6/100	
• Toplivo 2 class tanker	8	53.7/1,029	500 tons diesel
• Training ships	5		1 Sekstan, 14,650-ton, 13,008-ton, 2 others

Coastal Defense

Type	Quantity	Notes
• OTOMAT	3 batteries	
• HY-2	+	
Total	~30 launchers	Unconfirmed

Naval Infrastructure

Naval bases: **8**

Abu Qir (naval academy), Alexandria, Hurghada, Marsa Matruh, Port Said, Safaga, Suez, Berenice (Ras Banas)

Ship maintenance and repair facilities

Alexandria (including construction up to 20,000 dwt), Port Said, Ismailiya

4. IRAN

General Data

Official Name of the State: Islamic Republic of Iran
Supreme Religious and Political National Leader (Rahbar): Hojatolislam Ali Hoseini Khamenei
Head of State (formally subordinate to the National Leader): President Hojatolislam Seyyed Mohammed Khatami
Minister of Defense: Rear Admiral Ali Shamkhani
Commander in Chief of the Armed Forces: Major General Mohammad Salimi
Chief of the Joint Staff of the Armed Forces: Brigadier General Abdol Ali Pourshasb
Commander of the Ground Forces: Brigadier General Nasser Mohammadi-Far
Commander of the Air Force: Brigadier General Assad Abadi Habiballah Baqa'i
Commander of the Navy: Rear Admiral Abbas Mohtaj
Commander-in-Chief of the Islamic Revolutionary Guards Corps (IRGC): Major General Yahya Rahim Safavi
Chief of the Joint Staff of the IRGC: Rear Admiral Ali Akbar Ahmadian
Commander of the IRGC Ground Forces: Brigadier General Aziz Ja'afri
Commander of the IRGC Air Wing: Brigadier General Ahmad Kazemi
Commander of the IRGC Naval Wing: Rear Admiral Ali Morteza Saffari

Area: 1,647,240 sq. km. (not including Abu Musa Island and two Tunb islands; control disputed)
Population: 63,800,000 est.

Demography

Ethnic groups		
Persians	32,540,000	51.0%
Azeris	15,310,000	24.0%
Gilaki and Mazandarani	5,100,000	8.0%
Kurds	4,472,000	7.0%
Arabs	1,915,000	3.0%
Balouchis	1,275,000	2.0%
Turkmens	1,275,000	2.0%
Lurs	1,275,000	2.0%
Others	638,000	1.0%
Religious groups		
Shi'ite Muslims	56,782,000	89.0%
Sunni Muslims	6,380,000	10.0%
Christians, Zoroastrians, Jews, Baha'is and others	638,000	1.0%

Economic Data

		1996	1997	1998	1999	2000
GDP (current prices)	$ bn	78.4	92.6	59.7	52.9	66.4
GDP per capita	$	1,305	1,520	966	842	1,041
Real GDP growth	%	5.5	3.0	2.2	2.5	4.0
Consumer price index	%	28.9	17.4	17.8	20.1	16.0
External debt	$ bn	16.7	11.8	14.0	10.4	9.0
Balance of payments						
• Exports fob	$ bn	22.4	18.4	13.0	19.7	30.0
• Imports fob	$ bn	15.0	14.1	13.6	13.5	16.2
• Current account balance (including services and income)	$ bn	5.2	2.2	-1.9	4.7	12.2
Government expenditure						
• Total expenditure	$ bn	18.9	21.8	12.9	12.0	15.5
• Defense expenditure	$ bn	2.9	3.2	3.2	NA	NA
• Real change in defense expenditure	%	16.0	10.3	0.0	NA	NA
• Defense expenditure /GDP	%	3.7	3.5	5.4	NA	NA
Population	m	60.1	60.9	61.8	62.8	63.8
Official exchange rate	IR:$1	3,000	3,000	5,500	7,900	8,150

Sources: EIU Quarterly Report, EIU Country Profile, IMF International Financial Statistical Yearbook, SIPRI Yearbook

Arms Procurement and Security Assistance Received

Country	Type	Details
France	• Arms transfers	Socata training aircraft
Germany	• Arms transfers	Aircraft, missile parts, chemical and nuclear technology (unauthorized by government)
India	• Military training	Trainees in India
Israel	• Arms transfers	M113 APC parts (unauthorized by government)
North Korea	• Arms transfers	SSM technology
PRC	• Arms transfers	Missile technology, transport aircraft, Chemical weapons (CW) precursors alleged, FL-10 ASCMs
	• Foreign advisers	Nuclear technicians
	• Cooperation in R&D and arms production	solid fuel SSM technology

Arms Procurement and Security Assistance Received *(continued)*

Country	Type	Details
Russia	• Arms transfers	SSM technology, T-72S tank production under license, Kilo-class submarines, Igla SAMs, satellite technology, Tu-334 transport aircraft Mi-171 helicopter
	• Assistance	Training of nuclear technicians
	• Military training	Training of officers in Russia
Singapore	• Arms transfers	Spare parts for American-made weapons
Taiwan	• Arms transfers	Spare parts for American-made aircraft
Ukraine	• Arms transfers	Tanks, IL-140 transport aircraft
USA	• Arms transfers	Spare parts for American-made aircraft (unauthorized by government)

Arms Sales and Security Assistance Extended

Country	Type	Details
Bosnia	• Arms transfers	Chinese ATGMs, artillery shells
	• Military training	Several hundred IRGC fighters
KUP, KDP	• Arms transfers	Shoulder-launched SAMs
Lebanon	• Arms transfers	Hizbullah militia: artillery, MRLs, small arms, ATGMs, engineering equipment, Strela SAMs, night vision equipment
	• Assistance	Hizbullah militia: grant estimated at tens of millions of dollars annually
	• Military training	Some IRGC instructors with Hizbullah militia in Syrian-held Beka'
Libya	• Arms transfers	SSM technology
Palestinians	• Assistance	$20 million annually for Hamas
	• Military training	Palestinian Hamas and Islamic Jihad; PFLP-GC
Sudan	• Military training	A few IRGC personnel in the Sudanese Army and with People's Defense Forces
	• Arms transfers	Tanks, combat aircraft, MRL launchers
	• Assistance	Financial aid
Syria	• Cooperation in arms production, R&D	Joint development of Scud C SSMs

Foreign Military Cooperation

Type	Details
• Forces deployed abroad	300 IRGC troops in Lebanon
• Joint maneuvers	India, Pakistan (naval maneuvers), Kuwait (proposed naval maneuvers), Oman (observers)

Defense Production

	M	P	A
Weapons of mass destruction			
• Assembly and production of Scud C, Shehab 3, Shehab 4, and Kosar SSMs (with China, North Korea, Russia, and possibly also Pakistan)	√		√
• Chemical agents (mustard, attempts to produce nerve agents)	√		
Army equipment			
• Production of Russian T-72S tanks		√	
• Zulfikar and Towsan tanks	√	√	
• Upgrading of T-55 tanks to Iranian model Type 72Z	√		
• Upgrading of T-54 tanks to Iranian model Safir-74	√		
• Boragh, Cobra, Sayyad and BMT-2 APCs	√		
• Zelzal, Nazeat, Shahin and Fadjr rockets	√		
• 122, 160, and 240mm MRLs	√		
• 122 and 155mm SP guns	√	√	
• 81, 120, 130 and 320mm mortars and artillery ammunition	√		
• Raad (AT-3) Towsan (AT-5) and Toophan (TOW) ATGMs	√		
• Laser-guided AT missiles	√		
• RPG-7, Nafez and Saegheh ATRLs	√	√	
• ERA protection for various tanks	√		
• Gas masks	√		
• Spare parts, trucks	√		
Air Force equipment			
• Azarakhsh and Owaz fighter aircraft	√		
• Tondar and Dorneh training aircraft	√		
• An-140 and An-74 transport aircraft		√	√
• Zafar 300 attack helicopter, Sanjack light helicopter	√		
• Shahbaviz 2-75, Shahbaviz 2061 and Shahed 5 helicopters	√	√	
• Fajr-3 and Parasto light aircraft (probably still under development)	√		
• Ababil, Tallash, Saeqeh and Muhajer UAVs	√		
• Upgrading of F-4 , F-5 and F-14 aircraft	√		
• Upgrading of AB-206 helicopters with TOW/ Toophan ATGMs	√		
• Conversion of HAWK and Standard missiles to be carried on aircraft	√		
• ZU-23mm anti-aircraft guns		√	
• SAMs (assembly of Chinese HN-5A and HQ-2, unconfirmed)			√
• Misagh-1, Saeqeh and Sayyad-1 SAMs	√		
• Reverse engineering of Crotale and Rapier SAMs	√		
• Darya (C-802) ASCMs	√		
• Laser-guided missiles	√		

Defense Production *(continued)*

	M	P	A
• ARM missiles	√		
• TV-guided missiles	√		
• Spare parts for aircraft	√		
Electronics			
• Radio transceivers (copy of US model)	√		
• Laser detector	√		
• Night vision systems	√		
Naval equipment			
• Tareq patrol craft	√		
• MIG-S-1800, MIG-S-1900 and MIG-S-2600 patrol crafts	√		
• MIG-S-3700 LCU (Foque class)	√		
• Sabiha-15 midget submarines	√		
• Tondar (C-802) SSMs	√		
• Upgrading of Standard missiles to naval SAMs	√		
• Hendijan auxiliary vessels	√		
Space			
• Telecommunication satellite under development, to be launched with French cooperation	√		

Note: M - manufacture (indigenously developed)
P - production under license
A - assembly

Some of the weapons systems may be copies of foreign types and not indigenously developed. In addition, some may be only prototypes, which were displayed for propaganda purposes and are not in production.

Weapons of Mass Destruction

NBC Capabilities

Nuclear capability

One 5 Mw research reactor acquired from the US in the 1960s (in Tehran) and one small 27 kw miniature neutron source reactor (in Isfahan). One 1,000 Mw VVER power reactor under construction, under a contract with Russia, in Bushehr; suspected nuclear weapons program.

Party to the NPT. Safeguards agreement with the IAEA in force.

NBC Capabilities *(continued)*

Chemical weapons (CW) and protective equipment

Iran admitted in 1999 that it possessed Chemical weapons (CW) in the past. Party to the CWC, but nevertheless suspected of still producing and stockpiling Mustard, VX and other chemical agents. PRC and Russian firms and individuals allegedly provide assistance in CW technology and precursors. Personal protective equipment and munitions decontamination units for part of the armed forces.

Biological weapons (BW)

Suspected biological warfare program, no details available. Party to the BWC.

Ballistic Missiles

Model	Launchers	Missiles	Since	Notes
• SS-1 (Scud B/Scud C)	~20	300 Scud B, 100 Scud C		
• Shehab-3	~5			
• CSS-8	16			
Total	**~40**			
Future procurement				
• Shehab-4/Kosar				Under development

Note: See also under Rockets

Armed Forces

Major Changes: Iran test-fired the Shehab-3 MRBM and the Fateh-2 solid fuel missile. The Army continues to absorb the indigenously made Zulfikar tanks and Boragh APCs. The Air Force is adapting Bell 206 helicopters to a combat role, equipping them with ATGW missiles. The Air Defense received most of its new Igla (SA-18) shoulder-launched SAMs.

Order-of-Battle

Year	1996	1997	1999	2000	2001
General data					
• Personnel (regular)	410,000	~520,000*	~520,000	~520,000	~520,000
• SSM launchers	15	~30*	~30	~30	~40
Ground Forces					
• Divisions	32	32	32	32	32
• Total number of brigades	87	87	87	87	87
• Tanks	1,500	1,500	1,520	~1,500	~1,700
• APCs/AFVs	1,300	1,200	1,235	1,240	~1,570*
• Artillery (including MRLs)	1,500-2,000	2,640* (2,930)	2,640 (2,930)	~2,700 (~3,000)	~2,700 (~3,000)

Order-of-Battle *(continued)*

Year	1996	1997	1999	2000	2001
Air Force					
• Combat aircraft	214	226(318)	205(297)	205(333)	209(337)
• Transport aircraft	119	93(114)*	91(112)	92(111)	105(123)
• Helicopters	275	310(553)*	293(555)	300(560)	325(560)
Air Defense Forces					
• Heavy SAM batteries	30–35	30–35	30–35	30–35	29*
• Medium SAM batteries	+	+	+	+	+
• Light SAM launchers	110	95	95	95	95
Navy					
• Combat vessels	33	33	31	29	29
• Patrol craft	176	136	139	~120	~110
• Submarines	2	3	3	3	3

Note: Beginning with 1997, data refers to quantities in active service. The number in parentheses refers to the total inventory.
* Due to change in estimate.

Personnel

	Regular	Reserves	Total
Ground Forces	~350,000	350,000	~700,000
Air Force	18,000		18,000
Air Defense	12,000		12,000
Navy	~18,000		~18,000
IRGC-Ground Forces	100,000		100,000
IRGC-Navy	20,000		20,000
Total	**~520,000**	**350,000**	**~870,000**
Paramilitary			
• Baseej		2,000,000	

Ground Forces

Formations

	Corps/ armies	Divisions	Independent brigades/ groups	Brigades in divisions
All arms	4			
Armored		4	1	3 armd., 1 mech., 1 aty. each

Formations *(continued)*

	Corps/ armies	Divisions	Independent brigades/ groups	Brigades in divisions
Mechanized/ Infantry		6	1	4 inf., 1 aty. each
Airborne			1	
Special forces		2	5	3 commando each
Artillery			6	
Total	**4**	**12**	**14**	

IRGC Formations

	Divisions	Independent brigades/ groups	Brigades in divisions
Armored	4		
Mechanized/Infantry	16		
Special forces		3	
Artillery		6	
SSM		1–2	
Total	**20**	**10–11**	

Note: The IRGC has possibly reorganized as 26 divisions without independent brigades. IRGC divisions are smaller in size than army divisions, sometimes equivalent to the strength of one brigade.

Tanks

Model	Quantity	In service	Since	Notes
MBTs				
High quality				
• T-72 S/M1	422	422	1990	Indigenously Assembled tanks
• Zulfikar	~60	~60	1996	Based on estimated production rate of 20 per year
Subtotal	~480	~480		
Medium and low quality				
• Chieftain MK 3/MK 5	~100	~100	1973	
• T-62	150	150	1982	
• T-55 and derivatives	~550	~550	1985/1996	Type 69/Type 59/ Type 72Z/Safir 74
• M60 A1	150	150	1972	
• M48/M47	150	150	1958	
Subtotal	~1,100	~1,100		

Tanks *(continued)*

Model	Quantity	In service	Since	Notes
Light tanks				
• Scorpion	~80	~80	1977	
• Towsan	+	+	1998	
Subtotal	~80	~80		
Total	**~1,700**	**~1,700**		
Future procurement				
• Zulfikar				Being produced locally
• T-72S	578			578 out of 1000 kits not yet supplied

APCs/AFVs

Model	Quantity	In service	Since	Notes
APCs				
• M113	200	200	1968	
• Boragh	120	120	1996	Based on estimated production rate of 20 per year
• BTR-50/60	500	500	1967	
• MT-LB	+	+		
Subtotal	~820	~820		
IFVs				
• BMP-1	300	300	1977	
• BMP-2	413	413	1991	Indigenously assembled
Subtotal	713	713		
Reconnaissance				
• Engesa EE-9 Cascavel	35	35	1982	
Total	**~1,570**	**~1,570**		
Future procurement				
• BMP-2	1,087			1,087 out of 1,500 kits not yet supplied

Artillery

Model	Quantity	In service	Since	Notes
Self-propelled guns and howitzers				
• 203mm M110	~30	~30	1976	
• 175mm/170mm Koksan M-1978	~20	~20	1994	
• 175mm M107	25	25	1975	

Artillery *(continued)*

Model	Quantity	In service	Since	Notes
• 155mm M109	440	~150	1978	
• 155mm Thunder 2	+	+	1998	Indigenously developed; low production rate
• 122mm Thunder 1	+	+	1998	Indigenously developed; low production rate
• 122mm 2S1	60	~50	1993	
Subtotal	~600	~300		
Towed guns and howitzers				
• 203mm M115	30	~30	1974	
• 155mm G-5	30	30	1989	
• 155mm GHN-45	100	100	1988	
• 155mm M114	~100	~100	1970	
• 152mm (PRC)	30	30		
• 130mm M-46/Type 59	~800	~800	1973	
• 122mm D-30	~500	~500	1982	
• 122mm Type 54/60	~100	~100	1990	
• 105mm M101	~200	~200	1966	
Subtotal	~2,000	~2,000		
Mortars, over 160mm				
• 320mm	+	+		
Mortars, under 160mm				
• 120mm M-65	+	+	1980	
• 107mm M30	+	+	1981	
MRLs				
• 240mm Fadjr-3	+	+	1994	
• 230mm Oghab	+	+	1987	
• 122mm BM-21	~100	~100	1978	
• 122mm Hadid/ Azrash/Nur	50	50	1994	
• 107mm Type 63	100	100	1986	
Subtotal	~250	~250		
Rockets				
• 610mm Zelzal-2	+	+	1998	
• 355mm Nazeat	+	+	1988	
• 333mm Fadjr 5	+	+	1998	
• 333mm Shahin 2	+	+	1989	
Total	**~3,000**	**~2,700**		

Logistics and Engineering Equipment

Pontoon bridges, light infantry assault boats, self-propelled pontoons, AFV transporters (several hundred)

Anti-Tank Weapons

Missiles

AT-11 (Spandrel), AT-4 (Spigot), AT-3 (Sagger), BGM-71A TOW, SS-11/SS-12, Towsan, Toophan, Raad

Guns

106mm M40 A1C recoilless rifle (200)

Air Force

Order-of-Battle

Category	Quantity	In service	Notes
• Combat	337	209	
• Transport	123	105	
• Helicopters	560	325	

Note: all figures include aircraft with army and navy aviation.

Combat Aircraft

Model	Quantity	In service	Since	Notes
Interceptors				
• F-14A Tomcat	60	25	1972	
• MiG-29	35	35	1990	
Subtotal	95	60		
Multi-role				
• F-4 D/E/RF Phantom	70	40	1968	
• Mirage F1-E	24	12	1991	
Subtotal	94	52		
Ground attack				
• Azarakhsh	4	4	2000	Indigenously developed; low production rate
• Su-24	24	24	1991	
Subtotal	28	28		
Obsolete				
• F-7	60	24	1987	
• F-5 A/B/E	60	45	1974	
Subtotal	120	69		
Total	**337**	**209**		

Combat Aircraft *(continued)*

Model	Quantity	In service	Since	Notes
Future procurement				
• Azarakhsh				Indigenously developed; low production rate
• Su-25				Negotiations with Georgia
• Su-27				Negotiations with Russia

Transport Aircraft

Model	Quantity	In service	Since	Notes
• Iran-140	+	+	2000	Low production rate
• An-74	12	12	1999	
• C-130 E/H Hercules	48	~30	1970	Including 2-3 in electronic surveillance role
• Boeing 747	9	9	1976	
• Boeing 707 and KC-707 tanker	15	14	1973	Including Boeing 707s in electronic surveillance/ECM/ECCM role
• Aero Commander 690	3	3	1978	
• Dornier Do-228	4	4		Employed in maritime surveillance role
• Fokker F-27 400M/600	18	18	1972	
• Mystère-Falcon 20	13	13	1991	
• Jetstar	1	1		
Total	**123**	**~105**		
Future procurement				
• Iran-140	45			

Training and Liaison Aircraft

Model	Quantity	In service	Since	Notes
Jet trainers				
• T-33	9	9	1968	
Piston/Turbo-prop				
• Beechcraft Bonanza F-33	~25	~25	1974	
• Cessna 185/180/150	45	45	1978	
• Embraer EMB-312 (Tucano)	25	25	1989	

Training and Liaison Aircraft *(continued)*

Model	Quantity	In service	Since	Notes
• Mushshak (PAC Mushshak)	25	25	1991	
• Socata TB 21/TB 200 (Trinidad/Tobago)	12	12	1996	
• Pilatus PC-7 Turbo-trainer	45	45	1983	
• Pilatus PC-6	15	15	1982	
Subtotal	192	192		
Total	**201**	**201**		

Helicopters

Model	Quantity	In service	Since	Notes
Attack helicopters				
• AH-1J Cobra	100	70	1974	
• AB-206 Jetranger	90	40	1969	Possibly armed
Subtotal	190	110		
Naval combat				
• SH-3D	3	+	1977	
Heavy transport				
• CH-47C Chinook	45	35	1973	
• RH-53D/SH-53D	~25	10	1976	
Subtotal	~70	~45		
Medium transport				
• AB-214A	~200	~70	1974	
• AB-205/Shahbaviz 2061	50	50	1969	
• AB-212/Shahbaviz 2-75	28	28	1971	
• Mi-171	5	5	2000	
• SA-330/IAR-330 Puma	+	+		
• AS-61	2	2	1978	
Subtotal	~285	~155		
Light transport				
• IAR-316	12	12	1994	
• IAR-317	+	+		
Subtotal	~12	~12		
Total	**~560**	**~325**		
Future procurement				
• Mi-171	20			Under negotiation
• Shahbaviz 2-75/Shahed 5				Production of 2-4 helicopters annually
• Shahbaviz 2061				Production of 2-4 helicopters annually

Miscellaneous Aircraft

Model	Quantity	In service	Since	Notes
Electronic surveillance				
• RC-130	3	3		Also listed under Transport Aircraft
Maritime surveillance				
• Dornier DO-228	4	4		Also listed under Transport Aircraft
• P-3 Orion	5	2	1974	
Target drones				
• Tallah I/II	+	+	1996	
• Saeqeh I/II	+	+	1996	
UAVs				
• Ababil-S	*	*	1999	
• Ababil-T	*	*	1999	
• Mohajer III (Dorne)	+	+	1997	
• Mohajer IV (Hodhod)	+	+	1997	

Advanced Armament

Air-to-air missiles

AA-10 (Alamo), AA-11 (Archer), AIM-54A Phoenix (280), AIM-9L Sidewinder (1,270), AIM-7 Sparrow (430), PL-2 (540), PL-7 (360)

Air-to-ground missiles

AGM-65 Maverick, AS-10 (Karen), AS-12, C-801 Fajr e-Darya(C-802)

Future procurement

AA-11 (Archer), AA-12

Note: Number in parentheses refers to quantity of missiles purchased, not current inventory levels

Air Force Infrastructure

Aircraft shelters:

In all operational airfields

Military airfields: **13**

Bandar Abbas, Birjand, Bushehr, Ghaleh-Marghi, Isfahan, Kerman, Kharg Island, Mehrabad, Mashhad, Qeshm, Shiraz, Tabriz, Tehran.

Air Defense Forces

Surface-to-Air Missiles

Model	Batteries	Launchers	Since	Notes
Heavy missiles				
• HAWK/MIM-23B Improved HAWK	~15		1964	
• SA-2 (Guideline)/ HQ-2J	~10		1986	May be under control of IRGC
• SA-5 (Gammon)	4		1995	
Total	**~30**			
Medium missiles				
• SA-6 (Gainful)	+		1974	
Light missiles				
• Rapier		30	1971	To be upgraded
• RBS-70		50	1984	
• Tigercat		15	1968	
Total		**95**		
Shoulder-launched missiles				
• Igla (SA-18)		325	2000	Total 700 being delivered
• FIM-92A Stinger		+	1987	With IRGC
• SA-7 (Grail)/ HN-5A/SA-14		+	1974	
Future procurement				
• Igla (SA-18)		700		Being delivered
• S-300 PMU				Under negotiation

Other Air Defense Systems

Model	Quantity	In service	Since	Notes
Air defense systems (missiles, radars and guns)				
• 35mm Contraves Skyguard ADS	100	24		
Short-range guns				
• 57mm ZSU 57x2 SP	100	100	1974	
• 57mm S-60	50	50	1966	
• 40mm L-70	95	95		
• 40mm M1	20	20	1968	
• 23mm ZSU 23x4 SP (Gun Dish)	75	75	1974	
• 23mm ZU 23x2	500	500	1977	
Total	**840**	**840**		
Radars				
• AR-3D	+	+		

Navy

Submarines

Type	Quantity	Length (m.)/ displacement (t.)	Notes/ armament
• Kilo class (Type 877)	3	73.8/3,076	6x533 torpedoes 24 mines
• Iranian midget submarines	3	9.2/90	Serviceability unknown
Total	**6**		

Combat Vessels

Type	Quantity	Length (m.)/ displacement (t.)	Notes/ armament
Missile frigate			
• Alvand class (Vosper Mk 5)	3	94.5/1,100	4xC-802 SSMs/ 1xSeakiller II SSM 1xMk-10 ASW mortar 1x114mm gun 2x35mm guns 3x20mm guns
MFPBs			
• Kaman class (Combattante II)	10	47.0 /249	4xC-802/Harpoon SSMs standard SAMs 1x76mm gun 1x40mm gun 4 non-operational
• Thondor class (Houdong)	10	36.6/171	4xC-802 SSMs 2x30mm guns
• China cat class	2		C-802 SSMs 2x25mm guns
Subtotal	22		
Gun corvettes			
• Bayandor class (PF-103)	2	84/900	2x76mm guns 2x40mm guns 2x20mm guns
Mine warfare vessels			
• MSC 292 and MSC 268 class	2	44.5/384	Acoustic and magnetic sweep 2x20mm guns
Total	**29**		

Patrol Craft

Type	Quantity	Length (m.)/ displacement (t.)	Notes/ armament
• Parvin class (PGM-71)	3	30.8/98	4 depth charges 1x40mm gun 2x20mm guns 2x12.7mm MGs
• MIG-S-2600	6	26.2/85	1x107mm MRL 2x23mm guns
• PBI (Peterson)	30	15.2/20.1	1xTigercat SSM 2x12.7mm MGs
• US Mk II	6	15.2/22.9	2x12.7mm MGs
• US Mk III	9	19.8/41.6	1x20mm gun 1x12.7mm MG
• MIG-S-1800	6	18.7/60	1x20mm gun 1x12.7mm MG
• MIG-G-1900	10	19.5/30	2x23mm guns
• Boghammar	20	13/6.4	1x107mm MRL 1x106mm RCL 3x12.7mm MGs RPG 7
• Boston Whaler craft type 1	20	6.7/1.3	1x107mm MRL 1x12.7mm MG
• Various other small craft	+	5-7 m	Some with 12.7mm MGs
Total	**~110**		

Landing Craft

Type	Quantity	Length (m.)/ displacement (t.)	Notes/ armament
• Wellington class hovercraft (BH-7 class)	0	23.9/53.6	6 non-operational
• Hengam class	4	93/2,540	Up to 9 tanks or 227 troops 4x40mm guns 8x23mm guns 2x12.7mm MGs
• Iran Hormuz 24 class	3	73.1/2,014	9 tanks or 140 troops
• Iran Hormuz 21 class	3	65/1,280	600 ton
• Fouque class (MIG-S-3700)	3	37/276	140 ton
Total	**13**		

Auxiliary Vessels

Type	Quantity	Length (m.)/ displacement (t.)	Notes/ armament
• Delvar class support ship	7	64/890	765 dwt 2x23mm guns
• Luhring Yard-supply ship	2	108/4,673	3,250 dwt 1xAB 212 helicopter 3x20mm guns
• Kangan class water tanker (Mazagon)	4	148/12,000	9,430 dwt 2x23mm guns
• Swan Hunter replenishment ship	1	207.2/33,014	9,367 dwt 3 Sea king helicopter 1x76mm gun
• Hendijan (MIG-S-4700)	12	50.8/460	40 ton on deck and 95m³ liquid
• Damen 1550	10	16/25	

Coastal Defense

Type	Batteries	Missiles	Notes
• HY-2 (Silkworm)	~12	300	
• C-801/802	15–25	~100	
• SS-N-22 (Sunburn)			Alleged; Probably non-existent
Total	**25-30**	**400**	

Naval Infrastructure

Naval bases: **9**

Bandar Abbas, Bandar Anzelli, Bandar Khomeini, Bandar Lengeh, Bushehr, Chah Bahar, Farsi Island, Jask, Kharg Island.

IRGC naval bases: **10**

Abadan oil terminal, Abu Musa Island, al-Fayisiyah Island, Cyrus oilfield, Halul Island platform (unconfirmed), Larak Island, Qeshm Island, Rostam Island oilfield, Sir Abu Nuair, Sirri Island.

Ship maintenance and repair facilities: **1**

MAN Nordhaman 28,000-ton floating dock

Major Non-Governmental Paramilitary Forces

Pro-government organizations

Personnel

	Active
• Ismael Khan (Afghans)	1,000–2,000
• Supreme Council for Islamic Revolution in Iraq (SCIRI)	15,000

Anti-government organizations

Personnel

	Active
• Democratic Party of Iranian Kurdistan (DPIK)	10,000

5. IRAQ

General Data

Official Name of the State: The Republic of Iraq
Head of State: President Saddam Hussein
Prime Minister: Saddam Hussein
Minister of Defense: Lieutenant General Sultan Hashim Ahmad al-Jabburi Tai
Supreme Commander of the Armed Forces: President Saddam Hussein
Chief of Staff of Ground Forces: General Ibrahim Abd al-Sattar Mohammad al-Takriti
Commander of the Air Force: Lieutenant General Khaldoun Khatab Bakr
Commander of the Navy: Rear Admiral Khalid Baqer Khadar

Area: 432,162 sq. km.
Population: 23,500,000 est.

Demography

Ethnic groups		
Arabs	17,272,500	73.5%
Kurds	5,076,000	21.6%
Turkmens	564,000	2.4%
Assyrians and others	587,500	2.5%
Religious groups		
Shi'ite Muslims	12,925,000	55.0%
Sunni Muslims	9,870,000	42.0%
Christians, Yazidis, and others	705,000	3.0%

Economic Data

		1996	1997	1998	1999	2000
Balance of payments						
• Exports fob	$ bn	0.95	5.68	6.5	11.6	NA
• Imports fob	$ bn	1.73	4.18	4.4	7.9	NA
• Current account balance (including services and income)	$ bn	-0.25	0.2	-0.5	-0.4	NA
Population	m	21.3	22.0	22.5	23.0	23.5
Official exchange rate	ID: $1	0.311	0.311	0.311	0.311	0.311

Sources: EIU Quarterly Report, EIU Country Profile, IMF International Financial Statistical Yearbook, SIPRI Yearbook

Note: economic data on Iraq are scarce and unreliable.

Arms Procurement and Security Assistance Received

Country	Type	Details
Belarus	• Cooperation in arms production	Alleged Upgrading of Iraqi AD systems and fighter aircraft
Czech Republic	• Arms transfers	Alleged SP guns
France	• Cooperation in arms production	Alleged AD systems (unauthorized by government)
Germany	• Arms transfers	Alleged assistance in SSM and CW technologies
India	• Arms transfers	Alleged assistance in CW technologies
PRC	• Arms transfers	Optical-wire communication system
Romania	• Arms transfers	Alleged Guidance systems for SSMs
Russia	• Arms transfers	Alleged Igla SAMs
	• Advisers	Alleged 15 Russian experts
	• Cooperation in arms production	Alleged Upgrading of Iraqi AD systems and fighter aircraft
Yugoslavia	• Arms transfers	Alleged Chemical protection equipment
	• Cooperation in arms production	Alleged Upgrading of Iraqi AD systems and fighter aircraft

Note: Since the Gulf War data is scarce.

Arms Sales and Security Assistance Extended

Note: Since the Gulf War data is scarce.

Defense Production

	M	P	A
Weapons of mass destruction			
• SSMs under development	√		
• Chemical agents	√		
• Biological agents	√		
Army equipment			
• Tanks		√	
• Artillery		√	
• MRLs		√	
• Land mines, including scatterable	√		
• ATRLs		√	
• Small arms and artillery ammunition	√		
• Electronics	√		

Defense Production *(continued)*

	M	P	A
Air Force equipment			
• Conversion of aircraft to UAVs	√	√	
• Mini-UAVs	√		
• AD systems	√		
• Aerial bombs	√	√	
Naval equipment			
• Small PBs	√		
• Rubber boats	√		
• Naval mines based on Soviet designs		√	

Note: M - manufacture (indigenously developed)
P - production under license
A - assembly

Weapons of Mass Destruction

NBC Capabilities

Nuclear capability

Since the Gulf War, all known Iraqi facilities have been destroyed by the UN's and IAEA's facility-destruction and monitoring teams. Inspections were suspended in 1998.

Since then, nuclear weapons development has likely resumed. Party to the NPT.

Chemical weapons (CW) and protective equipment

Production of chemical agents has probably been renewed since the suspension of UNSCOM inspections in Iraq.

Chemical agents produced in the past included Mustard (sulfur mustard and purified mustard), Sarin, Tabun, Soman, VX, Hydrogen Cyanide (unconfirmed); large quantities of chemical agents were destroyed by UN missions, but some may have remained.

Delivery systems: SSM warheads, artillery shells, mortar bombs, MRL rockets, aerial bombs and land mines.

Personal protective equipment, Soviet-type unit decontamination equipment.

Not a party to the CWC.

Biological weapons (BW)

Production and development of biological agents probably have been renewed since the suspension of UNSCOM inspections in Iraq.

Biological agents produced in the past included Anthrax, Aflatoxin, Botulinum and Typhoid. Iraq claims that they were destroyed, but stocks were largely unaffected by UN inspectors' activity. Experiments were also carried out with other agents.

Delivery systems: SSM warheads, aerial bombs, and airborne spraying-tanks for combat aircraft, helicopters and UAVs.

Party to the BWC.

Ballistic Missiles

Model	Launchers	Missiles	Notes
• al-Hussein	5	20 – 30	Production probably resumed
• al-Samoud	+	+	
Total	~5		

Armed Forces

Major Changes: No major change was recorded in the Iraqi order-of-battle due to the sanctions on Iraq. International monitoring of Iraq's proscribed activities in developing and producing WMD was not resumed. Production of ballistic missiles, chemical and Biological weapons (BW) is assumed to have resumed.

Order-of-Battle

Year	1996	1997	1999	2000	2001
General data					
• Personnel (regular)	400,000	391,800	432,500	432,500	432,500
• SSM launchers	5	5	5	5**	5**
Ground Forces					
• Divisions	23	23	23	23	23
• Tanks	2,100	2,000	2,000 (2,300)	2,000 (2,400)	2,000 (2,400)
• APCs/AFVs	3,300	2,000* (3,300)	2,000 (2,900)	2,000 (2,900)	2,000 (2,900)
• Artillery (including MRLs)	1,800	2,050*	2,050	2,100	2,100
Air Force					
• Combat aircraft	380	215* (333)	215 (333)	215 (333)	200 (333)
• Transport aircraft	+	+	+	+	+
• Helicopters	400	370(460)*	370 (460)	360 (460)	360 (460)
Air Defense Forces					
• Heavy SAM batteries	NA	60*	60	60	60
• Medium SAM batteries	NA	NA	NA	NA	10
• Light SAM launchers	NA	NA	130	130	130
Navy					
• Combat vessels	7	5	2	0	0
• Patrol craft	9	9	0	0	0

Note: Beginning with 1997, data refers to quantities in active service. The number in parentheses refers to the total inventory.

* Due to change in estimate.

** Number does not include unguided rocket launchers.

Personnel

	Regular	Reserves	Total
Ground Forces	400,000	650,000	1,050,000
Air Force	15,000		15,000
Air Defense	15,000		15,000
Navy	2,500		2,500
Total	**432,500**	**650,000**	**1,082,500**
Paramilitary			
• Border guards	20,000		20,000
• Security forces	25,000–45,000		25,000–45,000
• Special Republican Guard	26,000		26,000

Ground Forces

Formations

	Corps/ armies	Divisions	Independent brigades/ groups	Brigades in divisions
All arms	5+2*			
Armored		6		
Mechanized		4		
Infantry		13		
Special forces			2	
Total	**5**	**23**	**2**	

* 5 corps and 2 corps HQs.

Tanks

Model	Quantity	In service	Since	Notes
MBTs				
High quality				
• T-72/T-72M	700	700	1982	
• Assad Babil (T-72 M1)	+	+	1989	
Subtotal	~800	~800		
Medium and low quality				
• T-62	+	+	1973	
• T-55/Type 59/ Type 69/M-77	+	+	1962/1982	Some upgraded
Subtotal	~1,600	~1,200		
Total	**~2,400**	**~2,000**		

APCs/AFVs

Model	Quantity	In service	Since	Notes
APCs				
• YW-531	+	+	1990	
• M60P	+	+	1986	
• Engesa EE-11	+	+	1981	
• BTR-40/50/60	+	+	1974	
• FUG-70/PSZH-IV	+	+	1981	
• M-3 (Panhard)	+	+	1981	
• OT-62/OT-64	+	+	1977	
• MT-LB	+	+		
IFVs				
• BMP-1	}	900	1977	
• BMP-2			1990	
• BMD	+	+	1978	
Reconnaissance				
• BRDM-2	+	+	1982	
• Engesa EE-9	+	+	1981	
• AML-90/60	+	+	1969	
Total	**2,900**	**2,000**		

Artillery

Model	Quantity	In service	Since	Notes
Self-propelled guns and howitzers				
• 155mm GCT	+	+	1985	
• 155mm M109	+	+	1984	
• 155mm Majnoon	+	+	1982	
• 152mm M-1973	+	+	1975	
• 122mm M-1974	+	+	1977	
Subtotal	150	150		
Towed guns and howitzers				
• 180mm S-23	+	+	1974	
• 155mm G-5	+	+	1986	
• 155mm GHN-45	+	+	1984	
• 155mm M114 A1	+	+	1983	
• 152mm M-1976 (2A36)	+	+	1986	
• 152mm D-20	+	+	1977	
• 152mm M-1943 (D-1)	+	+	1974	
• 130mm M-46/Type 59	+	+	1962	
• 122mm D-30/Saddam	+	+	1984	
• 122mm M-1938	+	+	1977	

Artillery *(continued)*

Model	Quantity	In service	Since	Notes
• 105mm M56	+	+	1982	
• 105mm M102	+	+	1984	
• 85mm field/AT	+	+	1974	
Subtotal	1,800	1,800		
Mortars, over 160mm				
• 160mm mortar	+	+	1975	
Mortars, under 160mm				
• 120mm SP	+	+		
• 120mm M43	+	+	1975	
Rockets				
• FROG - 7	29	29		
• Laith 90	+	+	1988	
Subtotal	~30	~30		
MRLs				
• Ababil	+	+	1988	262mm Ababil-50, 400mm Ababil-100
• Astros II	+	+	1986	127mm SS-30, 180mm SS-40, 300mm SS-60
• 132mm BM-13	+	+	1986	
• 130mm	+	+		
• 128mm M-63	+	+		
• 122mm BM-21/BM-11	+	+	1977	
• 122mm Firos-25	+	+		
• 107mm	+	+	1986	
Subtotal	130	130		
Total	**~2,100**	**~2,100**		

Ground Radars

Model	Quantity	In service	Since	Notes
Artillery/mortar locating radars				
• Cymbeline	+	+		
• Rasit	+	+		

Logistics and Engineering Equipment

BLG-60, MTU-55 bridging tanks, GSP self-propelled ferries, mine-clearing rollers, minefield crossing system, PMP pontoon bridges, TPP pontoon bridges, Soviet-model tank-towed bridges, AFV transporters (1,500-2,000)

Anti-Tank Weapons

Missiles

AT-3 (Sagger), AT-4 (Spigot), BGM-71A TOW, MILAN, AT-5 (Spandrel) mounted on BMP-2, BRDM-2 (carrying AT-3) SP, M-3 (carrying HOT) SP, VCR/TH (carrying HOT) SP, M901 ITV

Total	**1,500**
Guns	
• 107mm B-11	+

Air Force

Order-of-Battle

Category	Quantity	In service	Notes
• Combat	~333	~200	119 additional planes flown to Iran during the Gulf War (1991)
• Transport	+	+	
• Helicopters	460	360	

Combat Aircraft

Model	Quantity	In service	Since	Notes
Interceptors				
• MiG-29 (Fulcrum)	15	+	1988	Additional 4 in Iran
• MiG-25 (Foxbat)	15	~10	1982	Additional 4 in Iran
• MiG-23 MF/ML	30	~20	1976	
Subtotal	60	~30		
Multi-role				
• Mirage F-1B/EQ5/EQ2/EQ4	30	30	1980	Additional 24 in Iran
Ground attack				
• Su-24 (Fencer C)	6	1	1989	Additional 24 in Iran
• MiG-23 B (Flogger)/MiG-27	30	25	1976	Additional 12 in Iran
• Su-20/22 (Fitter C/H)	45	30	1974	Additional 24 in Iran
• Su-25 (Frogfoot)	25	~15	1985	Additional 7 in Iran
Subtotal	106	~70		

Combat Aircraft *(continued)*

Model	Quantity	In service	Since	Notes
Obsolete				
• MiG-21 MF/ BIS/U (Fishbed)/F-7	130	~70	1974	
• Su-7B (Fitter A)	*	*	1969	Possibly phased out
Subtotal	130	~70		
Bombers				
• Tu-22 (Blinder)	6	0	1973	Additional 20 in Iran
• Tu-16 (Badger)/ An-6 (B-6D)	1	0	1987	
Subtotal	**7**	**0**		
Total	**~333**	**~200**		

Transport Aircraft

Model	Quantity	In service	Since	Notes
• An-12 (Cub)	5	5	1966	
• An-24 (Coke)	+	+	1967	
• An-26 (Curl)	+	+	1977	
• Il-76 (Candid)	+	1	1989	Including some tankers
• Mystère-Falcon 20/ Falcon 50	+	+		
• Tu-124A/Tu-134 (Crusty)	+	+	1962	
Total	**small number**	**small number**		

Note: Additional 15 aircraft in Iran, 6 in Kuwait and 8 in Jordan.

Training and Liaison Aircraft

Model	Quantity	In service	Since	Notes
Jet trainers				
• L-29 (Delfin)	~20	~20	1974	
• L-39 (Albatross)	~30	~30	1975	
• Embraer EMB-312 (Tucano)	~60	~60	1985	
Subtotal	~110	~110		
Piston/Turbo-prop				
• MBB-223 Flamingo/ AS 202 Braud/Zlin 326	~35	~35	1979	
• Pilatus PC-7	25	25	1980	
• Pilatus PC-9	30	30	1987	
Subtotal	~90	~90		
Total	**~200**	**~200**		

Helicopters

Model	Quantity	In service	Since	Notes
Attack				
• Mi-24/Mi-25 (Hind)	30	30	1982	
• SA-342 Gazelle	50	50	1977	
• MBB BO-105	40	40	1979	Number unconfirmed
• Alouette III (armed)	30	30	1971	
Subtotal	150	150		
Heavy transport				
• Mi-6 (Hook)	15	~10	1974	
Medium transport				
• Bell 214	40	~20	1985	
• AS-61	5	3	1982	
• Mi-8/Mi-17 (Hip)	100	100	1974	
• AS-332 Super Puma	+	+		
• SA-330 Puma	20	10	1977	
• Mi-2 (Hoplite)	+	+		
• SA-321 Super Frelon	10	10	1976	Also employed in naval combat role
Subtotal	~180	~150		
Light transport				
• BK-117	~25	~20	1988	
• Hughes 500D	30	10	1983	
• Hughes 300C	30	10	1983	
• Hughes 530F	25	16	1985	
Subtotal	~110	~50		
Total	**~460**	**~360**		

Miscellaneous Aircraft

Model	Quantity	In service	Notes
AEW/AWACS			
Adnan-1/Adnan-2 AEW	2	1-2	2 Adnan-2 flown to Iran
UAVs and mini-UAVs			
Mirach 100	+	+	

Advanced Armament

Air-to-air missiles

AA-2 (840), AA-6, AA-7 (96), AA-8 (304), R-530 (267), R-550 Magic (680), Super 530D/F.

Advanced Armament *(continued)*

Air-to-ground missiles

AM-39 Exocet (750), Armat (750), AS-2 (Kipper), AS-4 (Kitchen), AS-5 (Kelt), AS-6 (Kingfish), AS-7 (Kerry), AS-9 (Kyle), AS-10, AS-12, AS-14 (40), AS-15TT (50), AS-20, AS-30L (180), AT-2 (Swatter), C-601, HOT, LX, X-23.

Bombs

Belouga CBU, Cardoen CBU, fuel-air explosive (FAE)

Note: Number in parentheses refers to quantity of missiles purchased, not to current inventory levels.

Air Force Infrastructure

Aircraft shelters

For all combat aircraft (some damaged)

Military airfields: **28**

Abu-Ajal, al-Assad, al-Bakr, Balad, Basra, H-2, H-3, Habbaniyah, Irbil, Jalibah, Khalid, Kirkuk, Kut al-Amarah, Kut al-Amarah new field, Mosul, Mudaysis, Muthanah, al-Nasiriyah, al-Qadisiyah, al-Rashid, al-Rumaylah, Saddam, Salman, al-Shuaiba, al-Tallil, al-Taqaddum, al-Tuz, Wadi al-Khir.

Air Defense Forces

Surface-to-Air Missiles

Model	Batteries	Launchers	Since	Notes
Heavy missiles				
• SA-2 (Guideline)/ SA-3 (Goa)	60		1972	
Total	**60**			
Medium missiles				
• SA-6 (Gainful)	10		1974	
• SA-8 (Gecko)		20	1987	
Total	**10**	**20**		
Light missiles				
• Roland I/II		100	1981	
• SA-9 (Gaskin)		+	1981	
• SA-13 (Gopher)		30	1989	
Total		**130**		

Surface-to-Air Missiles *(continued)*

Model	Batteries	Launchers	Since	Notes
Shoulder-launched missiles				
• SA-7 (Grail)		400	1975	
• SA-14 (Gremlin)		+	1989	
• SA-16 (Gimlet)		+	1992	
Total		**~400**		

Note: Serviceability of missile batteries is uncertain due to American bombing (40% were damaged).

Other Air Defense Systems

Model	Quantity	In service	Since	Notes
Short-range guns				
• 57mm ZSU 57x2 SP	+	+	1977	
• 57mm S-60	+	+	1972	
• 37mm M-1939	+	+	1972	
• 23mm ZSU 23x4 SP (Gun Dish)	+	+	1977	
• 23mm ZU 23x2	+	+	1972	
Total		**~2,500**		
Radars				
• P-35/37 Barlock	+	+		
• P-15/P-18 Flat Face	+	+		
• P-15M Squat Eye	+	+		
• P-14 Tall King	+	+		
• P-12 Spoon Rest	+	+		
• TRS-2215	+	+		
• TRS-2230	+	+		

Navy

Combat Vessels

Type	Quantity	Length (m.)/ displacement (t.)	Notes/ armament
The following vessels are currently non-operational:			
2 Assad corvettes, 20 Sawari PBs, 2 Vosper PBRs, 2 PB-90, 1 Bogomol, 2 Zhuk, 1 Osa-I, 3 SRN-6			

Naval Infrastructure

Naval bases:	**4**
Basra, Umm Qasr, Faw, al-Zubayir	
Ship maintenance and repair facilities:	**1**
6,000-ton capacity floating dock, held in Egypt	

Major Non-Governmental Paramilitary Forces

Anti-Governmental Organizations

Personnel

	Active	Reserves	Total
• Kurdish Democratic Party (KDP)	25,000	30,000	55,000
• Kurdish Workers Party (PKK)	20,000		20,000
• Patriotic Union of Kurdistan (PUK)	18,000		18,000
• Supreme Assembly of the Islamic Revolution In Iraq (SAIRI)	2,000		2,000

Pro-Governmental Organizations

Personnel

	Active	Reserves	Total
• National Liberation Army (NLA - Mujahedin Khalq)	15,000		15,000

Equipment

Organization	Category	System	Quantity	Notes
NLA	Tanks	• Chieftain	36	
		• T-54/55	160	
	APCs	• BMP-1		
		• M113		
		• Scorpion		
	Artillery	• 155mm SPH		
		• 130mm		
		• 122mm		
		• 106mm M40		
	MRLs	• 122mm BM-21		
	Helicopters	• Mi-17		
		• MD-530		
PUK	Tanks	• T-54/55		

6. ISRAEL

General Data

Official Name of the State: State of Israel
Head of State: President Moshe Katsav
Prime Minister: Ariel Sharon
Minister of Defense: Binyamin Ben-Eliezer
Chief of General Staff: Lieutenant General Shaul Mofaz
Commander of the Air Force: Major General Dan Halutz
Commander of Army HQ: Major General Yiftah Rontal
Commander of the Navy: Rear Admiral Yedidia Ya'ari

Area: 22,145 sq. km, including East Jerusalem and vicinity, and the Golan Heights.
Population: 6,200,000

Demography

Ethnic groups		
Jews	5,047,000	81.4%
Arabs, Druze, and others	1,153,000	18.6%
Religious groups		
Jews	5,047,000	81.4%
Muslims	874,000	14.1%
Christians	173,500	2.8%
Druze and others	105,500	1.7%

Economic Data

		1996	1997	1998	1999	2000
GDP (current price)	$ bn	95.1	100.0	100.7	100.8	110.2
GDP per capita	$	16,684	17,241	16,783	16,524	17,774
Real GDP growth (at 1995 prices)	%	4.6	4.4	3.9	2.2	5.9
Consumer price index	%	11.3	9.0	5.5	5.2	1.2
External debt	$ bn	32.7	34.8	36.1	37.1	37.8
Balance of payments						
• Exports fob	$ bn	21.33	22.7	22.97	25.57	31.49
• Imports fob	$ bn	28.43	27.82	26.2	29.97	35.05
• Current account balance (including services and income)	$ bn	-5.44	-3.66	-0.96	-1.88	-1.48

Economic Data *(continued)*

		1996	1997	1998	1999	2000
Government expenditure						
• Total expenditure	$ bn	44.80	44.41	38.44	39.83	43.00
• Defense expenditure	$ bn	8.15	8.26	7.84	8.78	8.91
• Real change in defense expenditure	%	7.14	1.32	4.55	-0.13	6.57
• Defense expenditure /GDP	%	8.31	8.01	8.31	8.29	8.08
Population	m	5.70	5.83	5.97	6.12	6.20
Official exchange rate	NIS:$1	3.19	3.45	3.80	4.14	4.07

Sources: EIU Quarterly Report, EIU Country Profile, IMF International Financial Statistical Yearbook, SIPRI Yearbook

Arms Procurement and Security Assistance Received

Country	Type	Details
France	• Arms transfers	Spare parts, Socata training aircraft, CW detectors
Germany	• Arms transfers	NBC detection vehicles, CW personal protection gear, 3 Dolphin submarines, Seahake heavy torpedoes
	• Assistance	Partial financial support for 3 submarines constructed in Germany
India	• Arms transfers	Possible purchase of UAVs
Netherlands	• Arms transfers	CW personal protection gear
	• Cooperation in arms production	Cooperation in building patrol boats
South Africa	• Arms transfers	Patrol boats
Turkey	• Arms transfers	Akrep reconnaissance vehicle
US	• Arms transfers	F-15I combat aircraft, F-16I combat aircraft , S-70A helicopters, AH-64D helicopters, King Air B200-T aircraft, SAMs, JDAMs guided bombs, missile corvettes, SP artillery, naval SSMs, MLRS, upgrading of MLRS, tank transporters, heavy trucks, HMMWVs light combat vehicles, ATGMs, MIM-120 AAMs
	• Assistance	$1.98 bn grant, will be gradually increased up to $2.4 bn in 2008 (additional $1.2 bn between 1999-2001 within the framework of Wye River Memorandum)
	• Cooperation in arms production, assembly, R&D	Finance and assistance for Arrow ATBM, THEL defense system (Nautilus) and other projects
	• Military training	Trainees abroad

Arms Sales and Security Assistance Extended

Country	Type	Details
Argentina*	• Arms transfers	Radars and electronic reconnaissance systems for maritime patrol aircraft, upgrading of Pampa training aircraft
Australia	• Arms transfers	ESM for Australian C-130 aircraft, Popeye AGMs, ESM for helicopters, night vision equipment for helicopters, ESM for frigates, ECM pods for F-111 aircraft
Austria	• Arms transfers	Command and control systems
Belgium	• Arms transfers	Hunter UAVs, EHUD air combat debriefing system
Brazil*	• Arms transfers	HUD and avionics for trainer aircraft, avionics suit for ALX attack aircraft, upgrading of F-5 combat training aircraft
Canada	• Arms transfers	Overhead weapons stations for M113 APCs
Chile*	• Arms transfers	Sa'ar 4 missile patrol boats, Patrol boats, AAMs, AAGs, artillery, components for upgrading of F-5 combat aircraft, tanker aircraft
Colombia*	• Cooperation in arms production	Co-production of Galil assault rifle
Croatia	• Arms transfers	Upgrading of MiG-21 aircraft (possibly suspended)
Cyprus	• Arms transfers	Torpedo boats, electronic communication systems, flak jackets
Czech Republic	• Cooperation in arms production, assembly, R&D	Upgrading T-72 tanks
Denmark	• Arms transfers	Helmet-mounted cueing system, Thermal imaging systems
Ecuador*	• Arms transfers	Kfir combat aircraft
Eritrea*	• Arms transfers	Fast patrol boats
Ethiopia	• Arms transfers	Upgrading MiG-21 combat aircraft (temporarily suspended)
Finland	• Arms transfers	AD command and control system, Ranger UAVs, Spike ATGMs, communication equipment
France	• Arms transfers	Hunter UAVs, hand-held SAR systems, EHUD air combat debriefing system
	• Cooperation in arms production, assembly, R&D	Military communications, Litening designator pods for combat aircraft

* According to Foreign publications, as cited by Israeli publications.

Arms Sales and Security Assistance Extended *(continued)*

Country	Type	Details
Germany	• Arms transfers	Litening designator pods for combat aircraft, EHUD air combat debriefing system, upgrading of CH-53 helicopters
	• Cooperation in arms production, assembly, R&D	EW systems for Tornado aircraft, Litening pods for NATO, development of a satellite, NT series ATGMs, upgrading of F-4 Phantom aircraft for Greece, upgrading of MiG-29 aircraft
Greece	• Arms transfers	Upgrading F-4 aircraft, installation of EW systems in F-16 aircraft
Georgia	• Cooperation in arms production, assembly, R&D	Upgrading Su-25 combat aircraft
India*	• Arms transfers	Searcher-2 and Heron UAVs, Harpy anti-radar drone, executive jets, EL/M-2032 radar for Jaguar aircraft, Litening pods, communication equipment, Green Pine detection radar, Super-Dvora patrol boats, Barak SSMs, M-46 guns, upgrading of artillery, avionics for upgrade of combat aircraft
	• Cooperation in arms production, assembly, R&D	Battlefield surveillance radar, UAVs
Indonesia	• Arms transfers	Mini-UAVs
Italy	• Arms transfers	Opher guiding kit for bombs, airborne SAR system, Litening designator pods, EHUD air combat debriefing system
	• Cooperation in arms production, assembly, R&D	Joint upgrading of A-129 Mangusta attack helicopter
Myanmar (Burma)	• Arms transfers	Alleged upgrading of F-7 fighter aircraft, including AA missiles, Litening designator pods, laser guided bombs, alleged supplying of 155mm guns, alleged upgrading of corvettes
Nepal	• Arms transfers	Galil assault rifles
Netherlands	• Arms transfers	Gill ATGMs, Artillery C^2 systems, EHUD air combat debriefing system
	• Cooperation in arms production, assembly, R&D	Training simulators

* According to Foreign publications, as cited by Israeli publications.

Arms Sales and Security Assistance Extended *(continued)*

Country	Type	Details
Nicaragua	• Arms transfers	Dabur patrol boats
Poland	• Cooperation in arms production, assembly, R&D	Possible upgrading of Su-22 combat aircraft
Portugal	• Arms transfers	EHUD air combat debriefing systems, ESM systems
PRC*	• Arms transfers	Phalcon AEW system (suspended)
Romania	• Arms transfers	OWS-25 weapon system for APCs, ground radar system, upgrading of tanks
	• Cooperation in arms production, assembly, R&D	Upgrading of MiG-29 aircraft, night vision equipment for Romanian IAR-330 Puma helicopters, upgrading Dracula attack helicopters, upgrading of MiG-21s in Romania, upgrading IAR-99/109 trainer aircraft, upgrading of MRLs
Russia	• Cooperation in arms production, assembly, R&D	KA 50/52 attack helicopter, Su-30 MKI
Singapore*	• Arms transfers	Upgrading of F-5 combat aircraft, EHUD air combat debriefing system, Searcher UAVs, NT-S ATGMs, Overhead weapon stations, reconnaissance satellite
	• Cooperation in arms production, assembly, R&D	Upgrading Turkish F-5 combat aircraft
Slovenia	• Arms transfers	155mm guns, 120 mm mortars, upgrading of PC-9 training aircraft
South Africa	• Arms transfers	Upgrading Boeing 707 to SIGINT configuration
South Korea*	• Arms transfers	Popeye-2 AGM, Harpy anti-radar drones, night vision systems, EHUD air combat debriefing systems, EL/M-2022 maritime surveillance radar, satellite reconnaissance equipment
Spain*	• Arms transfers	Upgrading of F-5 and T-38 aircraft, Litening designator pods, military communications, ground surveillance radar
Sri Lanka	• Arms transfers	Kfir aircraft, Sa'ar 4.5 MFPBs, Superhawk UAVs, mine detection radar, ESM systems
Sweden	• Arms transfers	120mm ammunition for tanks, ground penetrating radar

* According to Foreign publications, as cited by Israeli publications.

Arms Sales and Security Assistance Extended *(continued)*

Country	Type	Details
	• Cooperation in arms production, assembly, R&D	NBC protection for civilians, explosives detection system
Switzerland*	• Arms transfers	Communication intelligence systems
	• Cooperation in arms production, assembly, R&D	Ranger UAVs, C^3I simulators, Protected Weapons Stations systems
Thailand	• Arms transfers	Searcher mini-UAVs, Popeye AGM (temporarily suspended), upgrading F-5 aircraft, upgrading L-39 training aircraft, conversion of transport aircraft to tanker (temporarily suspended), ARS-700 SAR systems
Turkey	• Arms transfers	Upgrading F-4 and F-5 aircraft, upgrading of M60 tanks, Popeye AGMs, EHUD air combat debriefing system, aerial reconnaissance systems, ARS-700 SAR systems, ground penetrating radar
	• Cooperation in arms production, assembly, R&D	Popeye AGMs, Delila anti-radar missile
Uganda	• Arms transfers	Upgrading of MiG-21 aircraft (temporarily suspended)
UK	• Arms transfers	Artillery and infantry ammunition, NT-G ATGMs (for evaluation), CATS and ACE simulators, ESM for Nimrod 2000, EHUD air combat debriefing systems
US	• Arms transfers and cooperation in arms production	**Air Force equipment:** Python 4 AAMs , Popeye AGMs, F-15I fuselage parts, engine parts for F-15/F-16 aircraft, digital mapping systems for V-22 aircraft, Helmet Mounted Cueing-system, Litening designation pods, laser designators for the Comanche helicopter, upgrading UH-1 helicopters, airborne SAR, tactical air-launched decoys, image processing technology, joint research on Arrow ATBM, upgrading of T-38 aircraft, Astra SPX aircraft, production and marketing of satellite launchers, EROS reconnaissance satellite. **Ground Forces equipment:** central computer for Bradley AFVs, 120mm mortars,

* According to Foreign publications, as cited by Israeli publications.

Arms Sales and Security Assistance Extended *(continued)*

Country	Type	Details
		Enhanced Applique Armor kits for APCs, upgrading MLRS, mine clearing systems, joint research on THEL laser weapon
Venezuela	• Arms transfers	Radars and combat management systems for frigates, Litening designation pods, Barak SAMs (ground based version)
Zambia	• Arms transfers	Upgrading MiG-21 aircraft (temporarily suspended)

* According to foreign publications, as cited by Israeli publications.

Foreign Military Cooperation

Type	Details
• Pre-positioning of equipment	$200 million worth of stockpiled US military equipment
• Cooperation in military training	US and Turkish use of Israeli airfields and airspace for training; Israeli use of Turkish airspace and airfields for training
• Joint maneuvers	Jordan – SAR, Turkey – SAR and joint air force maneuvers, US

Defense Production

	M	P	A
Ground Forces equipment			
• THEL system	√		
• Merkava MBTs	√		
• Self propelled and towed artillery pieces	√		
• Several types of ACVs (some based on old tank hulls)	√		
• SP AAGs (Soviet gun, US carrier)			√
• Tank guns	√		
• NT-G, NT-S, NT-D and Lahat ATGMs	√		
• ATRLs	√		
• Overhead weapon systems for IFVs	√		
• Tread-width mine plows for tanks (TWMP)	√		
• Tank-towed bridges (TAB)	√		
• Upgrading of M60 tanks	√		
• Mines	√		
• Small arms	√		
• Artillery, mortar and small arms ammunition	√		
Air force equipment (some joint ventures with US companies)			
• Arrow ATBM	√		

Defense Production *(continued)*

	M	P	A
• Upgrading of combat aircraft	√		
• Upgrading of helicopters	√		
• AEW aircraft conversion	√		
• AAMs	√		
• AGMs	√		
• CBUs	√		
• TV and laser guided bombs	√		
• Airborne and target designation pods	√		
• UAVs and mini-UAVs	√		
• Air-launched decoys	√		
• Operational flight trainer systems	√		
• Radars	√		
• Refueling system for aircraft	√		
• Helicopter parts		√	
• Combat aircraft parts		√	
Navy equipment			
• LCTs	√		
• MFPBs	√	√	
• PBs	√		
• SSMs	√		
• Torpedo components		√	
Electronics			
• Radars – early warning, missile detection, naval, ground surveillance	√		
• Search and rescue system	√		
• ELINT equipment	√		
• EW jammers	√		
• Audio/video microwave transceivers	√		
• Radio voice scramblers and encryption units	√		
• Airborne ESM systems	√		
Optronics			
• Night vision devices	√		
• Laser rangefinders and target designators	√		
Space			
• Shavit satellite launcher	√		
• Ofeq series imaging satellite	√		
• Amos communications satellite	√		
• EROS imaging satellite	√		

Note: M - manufacture (indigenously developed)
P - production under license
A - assembly

Weapons of Mass Destruction

NBC Capabilities

Nuclear capabilities

Two nuclear research reactors; alleged stockpile of nuclear weapons*

Not a party to the NPT.

Chemical weapons (CW) and protective equipment

Personal protective equipment; Unit decontamination equipment.

Fuchs (Fox) NBC detection vehicles (8 vehicles); SPW-40 P2Ch NBC detection vehicles (50 vehicles); AP-2C CW detectors.

Signed but not yet ratified the CWC.

BW capabilities

Not a party to BWC.

* According to foreign publications, as cited by Israeli publications.

Ballistic Missiles

Model	Launchers	Missiles	Since	Notes
• MGM-52C (Lance)	12		1976	
• Jericho Mk 1/2/3*	+			
Total	+			

* According to foreign publications, as cited by Israeli publications.

Armed Forces

Major Changes: The Israeli Army has disbanded the HQ responsible for coordination of the activities of the SLA, after Israel's withdrawal from Southern Lebanon in May 2000. The Army is in the process of integrating some of its independent infantry brigades into the armored divisions. The armor corps continues the slow process of absorbing new Merkava Mk 3 MBTs, and withdrawing older models of MBTs from service. The Air Force received its first Beech King Air B200T out of an order of 14. It withdrew from service its WWII vintage C-47 transport aircraft. The Air Force also ordered 50 more F-16I combat aircraft and 8 AH-64D attack helicopters. The navy received its 3rd Dolphin submarine. Its older Gal class submarines, are to be sold.

Order-of-Battle

Year	1996	1997	1999	2000	2001
General data					
• Personnel (regular)	187,000	187,000	186,500	186,500	186,500
• SSM launchers	+	+	+	+	+
Ground Forces					
• Divisions	16	16	16	16	16
• Total number of brigades	77	77	77	76	76
• Tanks	3,870	3,900	3,895	3,930	3,930
• APCs/AFVs	8,010	8,010	8,040	8,040	8,040
• Artillery (including MRLs)	1,292	1,312 (1,912)	1,348 (1,948)	1,348 (1,948)	1,348 (1,948)
Air Force					
• Combat aircraft	640	613(780)	624(801)	628(800)	533(798)
• Transport aircraft	83	83(93)	77(87)	77(87)	64(87)
• Helicopters	285	278(288)	289(299)	287(297)	232(297)
Air Defense Forces					
• Heavy SAM batteries	4+	21*	22	22	22
• Light SAM launchers	50	50	~70	~70	~70
Navy					
• Submarines	3	4	4	6	6
• Combat vessels	22	21	21	20	20
• Patrol craft	36	35	35	32	32

Note: Beginning with 1997, data refers to quantities in active service. The number in parentheses refers to the total inventory.
* Due to change in estimate.

Personnel

	Regular	Reserves	Total
Ground Forces	141,000	380,000	521,000
Air Force	36,000	55,000	91,000
Navy	9,500	10,000	19,500
Total	**186,500**	**445,000**	**631,500**
Paramilitary			
• Border Police	7,650		7,650

Ground Forces

Formations

	Corps/HQ	Divisions	Independent brigades/groups	Brigades in divisions
All arms	3*			
Armored		12		2-3 armd., 1 mech., 1 aty. Each
Mechanized/ Infantry/Territorial		4	8	
Airborne			4	
Total		**16**	**12**	

Anti-guerrilla HQ: 3 divisional HQ for control of units engaged in anti-guerrilla activities in Samaria and Gaza (after May 1994, Gaza HQ stationed in Jewish settlements) and on the Lebanese border. In emergency, the HQ are to be reinforced by armor, infantry, helicopters, engineering and anti-tank forces.
* According to foreign publications, as cited by Israeli publications.

Tanks

Model	Quantity	In service	Since	Notes
MBTs				
High quality				
• Merkava Mk I/Mk II/ Mk III	1,280	1,280	1979/1983/ 1989	
Medium and low quality				
• Centurion/ upgraded Centurion	1,000	1,000	1965	
• M60 A3/upgraded M60/Magach 7	1,040	1,040	1980	
• M60/M60 A1	360	360	1970	
• M48 A5	200	200		
• T-62	50	50	1974	
Subtotal	2,650	2,650		
Total	**3,930**	**3,930**		
Future procurement				
• Merkava Mk III/Mk IV				

APCs/AFVs

Model	Quantity	In service	Since	Notes
• Achzarit	+	+	1994	
• M113 (various marks)	+	+		
• Nagmashot*	100	100	1989	
• Nagmachon	+	+		
• Nakpadon	15	15		
• M2 and M3 halftrack	2,685	2,685		Some phased out
• Akrep	30	30	1998	
• RBY	+	+		
Total	**8,040**	**8,040**		

* According to foreign publications, as cited by Israeli publications.

Artillery

Model	Quantity	In service	Since	Notes
Self-propelled guns and howitzers				
• 203mm M110	+	+	1975	
• 175mm M107	+	+	1974	
• 155mm M109 A1/A2	}			
• 155mm M109 Doher	}	600		
• 155mm M-50	+	+		
• 155mm L-33	+	+		
Subtotal	900	900		
Towed guns and howitzers				
• 155mm M-71	+	+		
• 130mm M-46	+	+		
• 122mm D-30	+	+		
Mortars, over 160mm				
• 160mm SP	+	+		
Mortars, under 160mm				
• 120mm	250	250		
MRLs				
• 240mm	+	+	1974	
• 140mm	+	+		
• 122mm BM-21	+	+		
• 227mm MLRS	48	48		
Rockets				
• 290mm MAR 290	+	+		
• Keres anti-radar missile	+	+		
• Kachlilit anti-radar missile	+	+		
Total	**1,948**	**1,348**		

Ground Radars

Model	Quantity	In service	Since	Notes
Artillery/mortar-locating radars				
• AN/TPQ-37	+	+		
• AN/PPS-15	+	+		
• Shilem	+	+		

Logistics and Engineering Equipment

Gilois motorized bridges, M-123 Viper minefield crossing system, M60 AVLB, mine-clearing rollers, mine layers, Pomins II portable mine neutralization system*, Puma ECVs, TAB (towed assault bridge, towed by tanks), TLB (trailer-launched bridge), TWMP (tread-width mine plows), M-1000 heavy equipment transporters

* According to foreign publications, as cited by Israeli publications.

Anti-Tank Missiles

Spike, Gil and Dandy* AT missiles (NT-S, NT-G, NT-D), BGM-71A TOW and BGM-71C Improved TOW, Mapats SP, Nimrod, Israeli BGM-71C Improved TOW SP, M-47 Dragon, AT-3 (Sagger)

Future procurement

BGM-71E (TOW 2A)

* According to foreign publications, as cited by Israeli publications.

Air Force

Order-of-Battle

Category	Quantity	In service	Notes
• Combat	798	533	Including aircraft in operational storage
• Transport	87	64	
• Helicopters	297	232	

Combat Aircraft

Model	Quantity	In service	Since	Notes
Advanced multi-role				
• F-15I	25	25	1998	
• F-15 A/B	72	72	1976	
• F-16 A/B	108	108	1980/1986	
• F-16 C/D	138	138		
Subtotal	343	343		

Combat Aircraft *(continued)*

Model	Quantity	In service	Since	Notes
Multi-role				
• F-4E/RF-4E Phantom and Phantom 2000	140	140	1969	
• A-4 Skyhawk	175	50	1967	The rest are in operational storage
• Kfir C-2/TC-2/ C-7/TC-7	140	0	1976	In operational storage
Subtotal	455	190		
Total	**798**	**533**		
Future procurement				
• F-16I	100			Delivery 2003-2009

Transport Aircraft

Model	Quantity	In service	Since	Notes
• Arava	10	10	1984	
• Beech Queen Air 80	6	6	1978	
• Boeing 707	10	10	1973	Some in EW role
• Boeing 707 tanker	3	3		
• C-130E/H Hercules	22	17	1970	5 in storage
• DC-3 Dakota (C-47)	18	0	1948	In storage, to be sold
• Dornier Do-28	15	15	1971	
• KC-130 tanker	3	3	1976	
Total	**87**	**64**		
Future procurement				
• C-130J	12			Under negotiations
• C-27J	10			Under negotiations

Training and Liaison Aircraft

Model	Quantity	In service	Since	Notes
Jet trainers				
• CM-170 Fouga Magister/Tzukit	80	40	1960	The rest are in operational storage
Piston/Turbo-prop				
• Socata Trinidad TB-21	22	22	1995	
• Cessna U-206 (Stationair-6)	21	0		In storage, for sale
• Piper Cub	35	35		
Subtotal	78	57		
Total	**158**	**97**		

Helicopters

Model	Quantity	In service	Since	Notes
Attack				
• AH-64A Apache	41	40	1990	One to be upgraded
• AH-1G/1S Cobra	64	40	1981	
• 500MD Defender	30	0	1979	
Subtotal	135	80		
Heavy transport				
• CH-53	39	39	1970	Including CH-53-2000
Medium transport				
• Bell 212	55	45		10 in storage for sale
• S-70A	25	25	1994	
Subtotal	80	70		
Light transport				
• Bell 206 JetRanger	38	38		
Naval combat				
• AS 536 Panther	5	5	1995	
Total	**297**	**232**		
Future procurement				
• AH-64D Apache	8			Delivery 2003
• S-70A	24			Delivery beginning 2002

Miscellaneous Aircraft

Model	Quantity	In service	Since	Notes
Reconnaissance				
• RF-4E	+	+		Also listed under Combat Aircraft
AEW/AWACS				
• E-2C Hawkeye	4	4	1978	
• Boeing 707 AEW*	+	+		Also listed under Transport Aircraft
ELINT and EW				
• Boeing 707 ELINT*	+	+		
• Boeing 707 EW*	+	+		
• Beech King Air A200CT (RC-12D)	6	6	1990	
• Beech King Air B-200T	+	+	2001	Being delivered
Maritime surveillance aircraft				
• Seascan (Westwind 1124N)	3	3		
• Beech King Air B-200T	4	4		

Miscellaneous Aircraft *(continued)*

Model	Quantity	In service	Since	Notes
UAVs and mini-UAVs				
Hermes 450S, Hermes 450 High Altitude*, Mastiff, Pioneer, Scout, Searcher				
Target drones				
Beech AQM-37A; Beech BQM-107B, MQM-74C Chuckar II, Teledyne Ryan 1241				
Future procurement				
• Beech King Air B-200T	14			Total order. 10 for EW 4 for maritime patrol; delivery in process
• Hunter UAV, Heron UAV				

* According to foreign publications, as cited by Israeli publications.

Advanced Armament

Air-to-air missiles

AIM-9L/M Sidewinder, AIM-7 Sparrow, Python 3, Python 4, Shafrir, AIM-120 AMRAAM

Air-to-ground missiles

AGM-78D Standard ARM, AGM-65 Maverick, AGM-62A Walleye, AGM-45A/B Shrike, AGM-114 Hellfire, Delilah ALCM, AGM-142 Popeye*, NT-D ATGM*

Bombs

CBU (including Tal-1, ATA-1000, ATA-500), runway-penetration bombs, Pyramid, Griffin, Harpy anti-radar drone*, Guillotine, Opher

EW and ECM

Chaff and flare dispensers for combat aircraft, Samson AN/ADM-141 TALD, EL/L-8202 ECM pod, EL/L-8230 ECM system, EL/L-8231 ECM system, EL/L-8240 ECM system, EL/M-2160 warning system, LWS-20 system, SRS-25 airborne receiver, SPS-20 self protection system, SPS-65 self protection system, SPS-200 airborne self protection system, SPS-1000 EW system, SPS-2000 self protection system, Sky-Jam 200 jammer, AN/ALQ 131 electronic countermeasure systems (20)

Future procurement

AIM-9M AAM, Star-1 AGM/cruise missile (under development), AIM-120B AMRAAM (57), JDAMs guided bombs (700), AGM-114L3 Hellfire II (480)

* According to foreign publications, as cited by Israeli publications.

Air Force Infrastructure

Aircraft shelters
In all operational airfields, for combat aircraft
Military airfields: 11
Haifa, Hatzerim, Hatzor, Lod, Nevatim, Palmachim, Ramat David, Ramon, Tel Aviv, Tel Nof, Uvda
Aircraft maintenance and repair capability
Maintenance on all models in service, partly in airfields, partly at Israel Aircraft Industries facilities

Air Defense Forces

Surface-to-Air Missiles

Model	Batteries	Launchers	Since	Notes
Heavy missiles				
• MIM-23B Improved HAWK	17		1965	
• MIM-104 Patriot	4		1991	
• Arrow ATBM	1	8	1998	Including Green Pine radar and Citrus Tree command post
Total	**22**			
Light missiles				
• MIM-72A Chaparral		~50		
• Mahbet SP		~ 20	1997	M163 Vulcan with Stinger SAMs
Total		**~70**		
Shoulder-launched missiles				
• FIM-92C Stinger		500 missiles		
• MIM-43A Redeye		+	1975	
Future procurement				
• MIM-104 Patriot	3			Under negotiation
• Arrow ATBMs	2			Total order of 3

Other Air Defense Systems

Model	Quantity	In service	Since	Notes
Short-range guns				
• 40mm Bofors L70	+	+		
• 23mm ZU 23x2	+	+		
• 20mm M163 A1 Vulcan SP	20	20		Being converted to Mahbet
• 20mm TCM-20 Hispano Suiza SP	+	+		
• 20mm Hispano Suiza	+	+		
Total	**~900**	**~900**		
Radars				
• Ramit, FPS-100, AN/TPS-43, Green Pine, Alufa-3				
Aerostats with airborne radars				
• Status				

Navy

Submarines

Type	Quantity	Length (m.)/ displacement (t.)	Notes/ armament
•Dolphin (Thyssen)	3	57.3/1,900	Sub-Harpoon SSMs 6x533mm torpedoes total of 16 torpedoes/missiles
• GAL (Type 540)	3	45/600	Sub-Harpoon SSMs 8x533mm torpedoes total of 10 missiles/ torpedoes (to be sold)
Total	**6**		

Combat vessels

Type	Quantity	Length (m.)/ displacement (t.)	Notes/ armament
Missile corvettes			
• Eilat class (Sa'ar 5)	3	86.4/1,075	1xSA-536 helicopter 8xHarpoon SSMs 8xGabriel II SSMs 64xBarak-1 SAMs 1x76mm gun 2x25mm Sea Vulcans 6x324mm torpedoes

Combat vessels *(continued)*

Type	Quantity	Length (m.)/ displacement (t.)	Notes/ armament
MFPBs			
• Aliya class (Sa'ar 4.5)	5	61.7/498	1xSA-536 helicopter 8xHarpoon SSMs 4xGabriel II SSMs 2x20mm guns 1x20mm Vulcan Phalanx 2x12.7mm MGs
• Hetz class (Sa'ar 4.5)	6	61.7/488	8xHarpoon SSMs 6xGabriel II SSMs 32xBarak I SAMs 1x76mm gun 1x20mm Vulcan Phalanx 2x12.7mm MGs
Subtotal	11		
ASW vessels			
• Reshef class (Sa'ar 4)	5	58/415	4xHarpoon SSMs 4-6xGabriel II SSMs 1-2x76mm guns 2x20mm guns 1x20mm Vulcan Phalanx 2x12.7mm MGs In ASW role: 2-3x324mm torpedoes sonar
• Mivtach class	1	45/250	5xGabriel II SSMs 2-3x324 torpedoes sonar
Subtotal	6		
Total	**20**		
Future procurement			
• Hetz class			Upgrading of Sa'ar 4 class to improved Sa'ar 4.5/Nirit level

Patrol Craft

Type	Quantity	Length (m.)/ displacement (t.)	Notes/ armament
• Super Dvora	14	21.6/54	2x20mm or 2x25mm guns 2x12.7mm MGs 1x84mm MRL depth charges
• Dabur	15	19.8/39	2x20mm guns 2x12.7mm MGs 2x324mm torpedoes 1x84mm MRL depth charges
• Nahshol (Bobcat)	3	22/36.5	1x20mm gun
Total	**32**		
Future procurement			
• Super Dvora	2		

Landing Craft

Type	Quantity	Length (m.)/ displacement (t.)	Notes/ armament
• Ashdod class LCT	3	62.7/400	In reserve
• LCM	2		
Total	**5**		
Future procurement			
• Newport LST	1		

Auxiliary Vessels

Type	Quantity	Length (m.)/ displacement (t.)	Notes/ armament
• Ro-Ro	1		
• Bat Sheva support ship	1	95.1/1,150	4x20mm guns 4x12.7mm MGs

Special Maritime Forces

Midget submarines; Zaharon fast boats

Naval Infrastructure

Naval bases: 3

Ashdod, Eilat, Haifa

Ship maintenance and repair facilities

Repair and maintenance of all naval vessels at Haifa, partly in conjunction with Israel Dockyards

7. JORDAN

General Data

Official Name of the State: The Hashemite Kingdom of Jordan
Head of State: King Abdullah bin Hussein al-Hashimi
Prime Minister: Ali Abu al-Ragheb
Minister of Defense: Ali Abu al-Ragheb
Inspector General of the Armed Forces: Major General Abd Khalaf al-Najada
Chief of the Joint Staff of the Armed Forces: Major General Mohammad Malkawi
Commander of the Air Force: Major General Saud Nuseirat
Commander of the Navy: Commodore Ali Mahmoud al-Khasawna

Area: 90,700 sq. km.
Population: 6,700,000

Demography

Ethnic groups		
Arabs	6,566,000	98.0%
Circassians and Armenians	134,000	2.0%
Religious groups		
Sunni Muslims	6,432,000	96.0%
Greek Orthodox and other Christians	268,000	4.0%

Economic Data

		1996	1997	1998	1999	2000
GDP (current prices)	$ bn	7.0	7.3	8.0	8.1	8.3
GDP per capita	$	1,186	1,197	1,270	1,246	1,239
Real GDP growth	%	1.4	1.3	1.2	1.6	2.5
Consumer price index	%	6.5	3.0	4.5	0.6	0.7
External debt	$ bn	8.1	8.2	8.5	8.2	8.0
Balance of payments						
• Exports fob	$ bn	1.82	1.83	1.8	1.83	1.97
• Imports fob	$ bn	3.82	3.65	3.4	3.3	3.96
• Current account balance (including services and income)	$ bn	-0.22	0.03	0.015	0.4	-0.09

Economic Data *(continued)*

		1996	1997	1998	1999	2000
Government expenditure						
• Total expenditure	$ bn	2.53	2.5	2.9	3.0	2.84
• Defense expenditure	$ bn	0.57	0.59	0.63	0.65	NA
• Real change in defense expenditure	%	3.6	3.5	6.8	3.2	NA
• Defense expenditure /GDP	%	8.1	8.1	7.9	8.0	NA
Population	m	5.9	6.1	6.3	6.5	6.7
Official exchange rate	JD:$1	0.709	0.709	0.709	0.709	0.709

Sources: EIU Quarterly Report, EIU Country Profile, IMF International Financial Statistical Yearbook, SIPRI Yearbook

Arms Procurement and Security Assistance Received

Country	Type	Details
Belgium	• Arms transfers	Spartan APCs
Canada	• Arms transfers	Avionics upgrade for C-130
Georgia	• Arms transfers	Possible co-production of Su-25
Taiwan	• Military training	Trainees abroad
Turkey	• Arms transfers	CN-235 aircraft
	• Military training	Flight simulation, training of helicopter pilots
UK	• Arms transfers	Challenger MBTs, Mine-clearing flail
	• Military training	Trainees abroad
Ukraine	• Arms transfers	BTR-94 APCs
US	• Arms transfers	F-16 combat aircraft, M-60 MBTs, helicopters, M110 SP guns, aircraft simulators, Mk 3 patrol boats, TOW ATGMs, border control system, TPS-117 radar
	• Assistance	$176.7 million military aid
	• Military training	Advisers

Arms Sales and Security Assistance Extended

Country	Type	Details
Bahrain	• Military training	Training of fighter pilots
Philippines	• Arms transfers	F-5 aircraft
Oman	• Military training	Training of infantry soldiers
Qatar	• Military training	Training of Special Forces
UAE	• Cooperation in arms production	AB17 Tiger APCs
	• Military training	Training of F-16 pilots
US	• Facilities	Use of airfields by combat aircraft

Foreign Military Cooperation

Type	Details
• Cooperation in military training	Turkey (use of facilities and airspace for training of pilots)
• Forces deployed abroad	Small contingency force in Bosnia (UNMIBH); Ethiopia and Eritrea (UNMEE); observers in Georgia (UNOMIG) and Tajikistan
• Joint maneuvers	Egypt, Israel (SAR), France, Oman, Qatar, Turkey, UAE, UK, US
• Security agreements	Saudi Arabia, Turkey, US

Defense Production

	M	P	A
Army equipment			
• Upgrading of Khalid and al-Hussein MBTs	√	√	
• Upgrading of M60 and Tariq MBTs	√	√	
• Upgrading of Scorpion light tanks	√		
• Conversion of M47 tanks to ARVs	√		
• Conversion of Tariq MBTs to IFVs	√		
• Badia and Tiger APCs and Sangyong vehicles	√		
• Black Iris light reconnaissance vehicle	√		
• Production of modified Land Rover APCs		√	
• High explosives (with assistance from India)	√		
Electronics			
• Upgrading of avionics (joint venture)	√		
Optronics			
• Night vision equipment		√	

Note: M - manufacture (indigenously developed)
P - production under license
A - assembly

Weapons of Mass Destruction

NBC Capabilities

Nuclear capability

No known capability; Party to the NPT.

Chemical weapons (CW) and protective equipment

No known CW activities

Personal protective and decontamination equipment; Party to the CWC.

Biological weapons (BW)

No known BW capability; party to BWC.

Armed Forces

Major Changes: The Jordanian Army received 96 Challenger MBTs from Great Britain out of 288 ordered. It also received 50 Spartan APCs from Belgium, 50 BTR-94 IFVs from the Ukraine, 50 M106 mortars and 23 M901 ITVs from the USA. Jordan revealed this year several indigenous programs for the upgrading of older models of MBTs and converting old MBTs to IFVs or to ARVs.

Order-of-Battle

Year	1996	1997	1999	2000	2001
General data					
• Personnel (regular)	94,000	94,200	94,200	94,200	94,200
Ground Forces					
• Divisions	4	4	4	4	4
• Total number of brigades	15	14	14	14	14
• Tanks	815	834	~900	~900	~920
		(1,226)	(~1,200)	(~1,200)	(~1,270)
• APCs/AFVs	1,480	1,475	1,475	1,500	1,500
		(1,575)	(1,575)	(1,600)	(1,750)
• Artillery (including MRLs)	450	770(795)*	788(813)	788(813)	838(863)
Air Force					
• Combat aircraft	85	91	101	100	91(100)
• Transport aircraft	12	11(13)	12(14)	14(16)	12
• Helicopters	60	68	68	68	74
Air Defense Forces					
• Heavy SAM batteries	14	14	14	14	14
• Medium SAM batteries	50	50	50	50	50
• Light SAM launchers	+	50*	50	50	50
Navy					
• Patrol crafts	12	10	10	13	13

Note: Beginning with 1997, data refers to quantities in active service. The number in parentheses refers to the total inventory.
* Due to change in estimate.

Personnel

	Regular	Reserves	Total
Ground Forces	85,000	60,000	145,000
Air Force	8,500		8,500
Navy	700		700
Total	**94,200**	**60,000**	**154,200**

Personnel *(continued)*

	Regular	Reserves	Total
Paramilitary			
• General Security Forces (including Desert Patrol)	25,000		
• Popular Army		200,000-250,000	

Note: The Popular Army is not regarded as a fighting force.

Ground Forces

Formations

	Divisions	Independent brigades/ groups	Brigades in divisions
Armored	2		3 armd., 1 aty., 1 AD each
Mechanized	2		1 Inf., 2 mech., 1 aty., 1 AD each
Infantry/Royal Guard		1	
Special forces		1	
Artillery		5	
Total	**4**	**7**	

Tanks

Model	Quantity	In service	Since	Notes
MBTs				
High quality				
• Al-Hussein	96	44	1999	Challenger I Out of 288 ordered
• Khalid	275	275	1984	Improved Chieftain
Subtotal	~370	~320		
Medium and low quality				
• Tariq	290	290	1980	Improved Centurion
• M60 A1/A3	288	288	1980	
• Chieftain	90	0		In storage
• M48 A1	212	0	1966	
Subtotal	880	578		

Tanks *(continued)*

Model	Quantity	In service	Since	Notes
Light Tanks				
• Scorpion	19	19		With Desert Patrol
Total	**~1,270**	**~920**		
Future procurement				
• Challenger I	288			Some already delivered

APCs/AFVs

Model	Quantity	In service	Since	Notes
APCs				
• M113 A1/A2	1,315	1,315	1968	Including M106 M30, M901 ITV
• Engesa EE-11	100	100	1987	With General Security Forces
• Spartan	50	+	2000	Being upgraded
• Saracen	+	0	1963	Included under Saladin
Subtotal	1,465	1,415		
IFVs				
• BTR-94	50	50	1999	
• BMP-2	35	35	1989	
Subtotal	85	85		
Reconnaissance				
• Saladin	60	0	1963	Quantity includes both Saracen and Saladin
• Ferret	140	0	1955	In storage
Subtotal	200	0		
Total	**1,750**	**1,500**		
Future procurement				
• AB3 Black Iris	100			
• AB2 Aigis	4			
• AB5	14			
• AB6 Spartan	130			50 already delivered

Artillery

Model	Quantity	In service	Since	Notes
Self-propelled guns and howitzers				
• 203mm M110 A2	128	128	1980	
• 155mm M109 A2	220	220	1980	
Subtotal	348	348		
Towed guns and howitzers				
• 203mm M115	25	0	1965	
• 155mm M114	30	30	1970	
• 155mm M-59 (Long Tom)	10	10	1965	
• 105mm M102 A1	50	50	1970	
Subtotal	115	90		
Mortars, under 160mm				
• 120mm	300	300	1975	
• 107mm M30	100	100	1975	50 M106 SP
Subtotal	400	400		
Total	**863**	**838**		

Ground Radars

Model	Quantity	In service	Since	Notes
Artillery/mortar locating radars				
• AN/TPQ-36/37	7	7	1990	
Future procurement				
• Border control system	+	+	2000	Including ground radars, IR cameras and aerostats

Logistics and Engineering Equipment

Aardvark Mk 2 flail (6), Aardvark Mk 3 flail (4), bridges, mine-clearing plows and bulldozers, UDK-1, AFV transporters (200), M578 recovery vehicles (30)

Future procurement

M47 ARVs (20) , Aardvark Mk 3 flail (3)

Anti-Tank Missiles

Model	Quantity	In service	Since	Notes
• BGM-71A/C TOW/ improved TOW	260	260	1974	
• M901 ITV	93	93	1988	
• M47 Dragon	310	310	1976	
Total	**663**	**663**		
Future procurement				
• Tow II	+			

Anti-Tank Guns

Model	Quantity	In service	Since	Notes
• 106mm M40	330	330	1987	
PGMs				
• 155mm Copperhead projectiles (CLGP)	100	100		

Air Force

Order-of-Battle

Category	Quantity	In service	Notes
• Combat	100	91	
• Transport	12	12	
• Helicopters	74	74	

Combat Aircraft

Model	Quantity	In service	Since	Notes
Advanced multi-role				
• F-16 A/B	16	16	1997	
Multi-role				
• Mirage F1-C/E	29	25	1981	
• F-5 E/F	55	50	1975	To be upgraded for training purposes
Subtotal	84	75		
Total	**100**	**91**		
Future procurement				
• F-16 A/B	8			Under negotiation
• A-10				Under negotiation

Transport Aircraft

Model	Quantity	In service	Since	Notes
• C-130 Hercules	5	5	1972	Upgraded
• CASA C-212	2	2	1975	
• CN-235	2	2	1998	
• Gulfstream III/IV	2	2	1986	
• L-1011-500	1	1	1984	
Total	**12**	**12**		
Future procurement				
• Challenger 604	2			Delivery in 2001

Training and Liaison Aircraft

Model	Quantity	In service	Since	Notes
Jet trainers				
• CASA C-101	13	13	1987	
Piston/Turbo-prop				
• TB-20 Socata	2	2	2000	
• BAe-SA-3-125 Bulldog	15	15	1978	
Subtotal	17	17		
Total	**30**	**30**		

Helicopters

Model	Quantity	In service	Since	Notes
Attack				
• AH-1G/F/S Cobra	26	26	1985	
Medium transport				
• Bell 205/UH-1H	18	18	1995	
• S-70A Black Hawk	3	3	1987	
• AS-332 Super Puma	12	12	1986	
Subtotal	33	33		
Light transport				
• Alouette III	1	1	1977	
• MD 500D	8	8	1980	
• MBB BO-105	3	3		With general security forces
• BK-117	3	3		
Subtotal	15	15		
Total	**74**	**74**		
Future procurement				
• S-70A Black Hawk	4			Under negotiation

Miscellaneous Aircraft

Future procurement

TTL BTT-3 Banshee target drones (82), 2 launchers

Advanced Armament

Air-to-air missiles

AIM-9J/M/P Sidewinder (750), AIM-7M Sparrow (96), R-550 Magic

Air-to-ground missiles

AS-30L (10), AGM-65C Maverick (60)

Advanced Armament *(continued)*

Bombs

Belouga CBU, Durandal anti-runway bombs

Future procurement

Night vision systems

Note: Number in parentheses refers to the quantity of missiles purchased, not to current inventory levels.

Air Force Infrastructure

Aircraft shelters

For all combat aircraft

Military airfields: 6

Amman (Marka), Azrak, H-4, H-5, Jaafar, Mafraq

Air Defense Forces

Surface-to-Air Missiles

Model	Batteries	Launchers	Since	Notes
Heavy missiles				
• MIM-23B Improved HAWK	14		1978	
Total	**14**			
Medium missiles				
• SA-8 (Gecko)		50	1982	
Total		**50**		
Light missiles				
• SA-13 (Gopher)		50	1986	
Total		**50**		
Shoulder-launched missiles				
• Javelin		+		
• MIM-43A Redeye		270	1977	
• SA-14 (Gremlin)		300	1987	
• SA-18 (Igla)		240	1991	
Total		**~800**		

Other Air Defense Systems

Model	Quantity	In service	Since	Notes
Short-range guns				
• 40mm M-42 SP	200	0	1966	To be phased out
• 23mm ZSU 23x4 SP (Gun Dish)	45	16	1983	
• 20mm M163 Vulcan SP	100	100	1976	
Total	**345**	**116**		
Radars				
• AN/TPS-43	2	2		
• AN/TPS-63	5	5		
• S-711	5	5		
Future Procurement				
• TPS-117	2			

Navy

Patrol Craft

Type	Quantity	Length (m.)/ displacement (t.)	Notes/ armament
• Feysal class (Bertram)	4	11.6/8	1x12.7mm MGs
• Al-Hussein class (VT Hawk)	3	30.5/124	2x30mm guns 1x20mm gun 2x12.7mm MGs
• Al-Hashim class (type 412)	3	12.7/9	In Dead Sea 1x12.7mm MG
• MK-3	3	19.8/41.6	1x20mm gun 1x12.7mm MG
Total	**13**		

Naval Infrastructure

Naval bases:	2
Aqaba, Hingat al-Ramat	

8. KUWAIT

General Data

Official Name of the State: State of Kuwait
Head of State: Jabir al-Ahmad al-Jabir al-Sabah
Prime Minister: Saad Abdallah al-Salim al-Sabah
Minister of Defense: Jabir Mubarak al-Hamad al-Sabah
Chief of General Staff: Major General Ali al-Mumin
Commander of the Air Force and Air Defense Forces: Brigadier General Sabir al-Suwaidan
Commander of the Navy: Commodore Ahmad Yousuf al-Mualla

Area: 17,820 sq. km. (including 2,590 sq. km. of the Neutral Zone)
Population: 2,200,000

Demography

Ethnic groups		
Kuwaitis	990,000	45.0%
Other Arabs	770,000	35.0%
Southeast Asians	198,000	9.0%
Persians/Iranians	88,000	4.0%
Others	154,000	7.0%
Religious groups		
Sunni Muslims	990,000	45.0%
Shi'ite Muslims	880,000	40.0%
Christians, Parsis, Hindus, and others	330,000	15.0%

Economic Data

		1996	1997	1998	1999	2000
GDP (current price)	$ bn	31.1	30.0	25.3	29.7	40.3
GDP per capita	$	16,368	15,000	12,650	14,142	18,318
Real GDP growth (1984 prices)	%	-3.3	2.3	2.0	-2.4	4.1
Consumer price index	%	3.6	0.6	0.2	3.0	3.0
External debt	$ bn	7.5	9.4	9.4	8.9	6.9
Balance of payments						
• Exports fob	$ bn	14.95	14.28	9.62	12.28	23.22
• Imports cif	$ bn	7.95	7.75	7.71	6.71	7.63

Economic Data *(continued)*

		1996	1997	1998	1999	2000
• Current account balance (including services and income)	$ bn	7.11	7.94	2.22	5.06	15.05
Government expenditure						
• Total expenditure	$ bn	13.01	13.13	13.25	14.13	15.60
• Defense expenditure	$ bn	3.14	2.4	2.3	2.26	NA
• Real change in defense expenditure	%	-14.78	-23.72	-4.05	-1.69	NA
• Defense expenditure /GDP	%	10.09	7.98	9.08	7.60	NA
Population	m	1.9	2.0	2.0	2.1	2.2
Official exchange rate	KD:$1	0.30	0.30	0.31	0.30	0.31

Sources: EIU Quarterly Report, EIU Country Profile, IMF International Financial Statistical Yearbook, SIPRI Yearbook

Arms Procurement and Security Assistance Received

Country	Type	Details
Belgium	• Arms transfers	90mm ammunition, 90mm turrets for AFVs
Finland	• Arms transfers	CW protective equipment
France	• Arms transfers	Radars, SAMs, MFPBs, MM-40 anti-ship missiles
	• Military training	Trainees abroad
Germany	• Arms transfers	Fuchs nuclear, biological and chemical reconnaissance vehicle
PRC	• Arms transfers	155mm PLZ-45 SP artillery
South Africa	• Arms transfers	Mortars, laser range-finders, light armament
Sweden	• Arms transfers	Early warning network
UK	• Arms transfers	APCs, Starburst shoulder-launched SAMs, Sea-Skua anti-ship missiles
	• Military training	Foreign advisers/instructors, trainees abroad
	• Maintenance aid	Desert warrior IFVs
US	• Arms transfers	TOW-2B ATGMs, early warning network
	• Maintenance aid	M88 ARVs, M1A2 tanks, M113 APCs, tanks and artillery ammunition
	• Infrastructure	Upgrading of 2 air bases and construction of one brigade HQ

Arms Sales and Security Assistance Extended

Country	Type	Details
Brazil	• Arms transfers	A-4 combat aircraft
UN	• Assistance	$35 million for UNIKOM force
US	• Assistance	Annual grant for US force in Kuwait
	• Facilities	Facilities for US forces

Foreign Military Cooperation

Type	Details
• Foreign forces	Some 4,600 US soldiers, 2 batteries of MIM-104 Patriot SAMs, pre-positioning of US tanks (110), APCs (110) and artillery pieces (equipment for one brigade); 24 US A-10 attack aircraft stationed in Kuwait; 12 UK Tornado GR1/1A aircraft; 900 UNIKOM troops and 200 observers
• Joint maneuvers	US (amphibious, command post and naval exercises), UK (marines), GCC countries, France, Egypt, Syria, Iran
• Security agreements	France, GCC countries, Italy, PRC, Russia, UK, US

Weapons of Mass Destruction

NBC Capabilities

Nuclear capability

No known nuclear activity. Party to the NPT.

Chemical weapons (CW) and protective equipment

No known CW activities. Party to the CWC.

Personal protective equipment; unit decontamination equipment

Biological weapons (BW)

No known BW activities. Party to the BWC.

Armed Forces

Major Changes: Inauguration of the GCC joint communication network, part of the GCC joint early warning system. The Kuwaiti Army received 10 new 90mm LCTS turrets for its Pandur AFVs. It also received 27 155mm PLZ-45 self-propelled guns. No major change was recorded in the Air Force or Navy.

Order-of-Battle

Year	1996	1997	1999	2000	2001
General data					
• Personnel (regular)	32,500	15,500*	19,500	19,500	19,500
Ground Forces					
• Number of brigades	6	6	6	6	6
• Number of battalions	1	1	1	1	1
• Tanks	700	318(455)*	318(483)	318(483)	318(483)
• APCs/AFVs	50	455(515)*	436(715)	~490(755)	~530(797)*
• Artillery (including MRLs)	24	75(128)	75(128)	~70(~125)	~100(~150)
Air Force					
• Combat aircraft	59	40(59)	40(59)	40(59)	40(59)
• Transport aircraft	6	5	5	5	5
• Helicopters	18-21	24-27	24-27	~25	23(28)
Air Defense Forces					
• Heavy SAM batteries	12	12	12	12	12
Navy					
• Combat vessels	2	4	6	10	10
• Patrol craft	33	54*	51	69	69

Note: Beginning with 1997, data refers to quantities in active service. The number in parentheses refers to the total inventory.
* Due to change in estimate.

Personnel

	Regular	Reserves	Total
Ground Forces	15,000	24,000	39,000
Air Force	2,500		2,500
Navy	2,000		2,000
Total	**19,500**	**24,000**	**43,500**
Paramilitary			
• National Guard	5,000		5,000
• Civil Defense	2,000		2,000

Ground Forces

Formations

	Independent brigades/ groups	Independent battalions
Armored	2	
Mechanized	2	
Artillery	1	
Border Defense	1	
Royal Guard	1	
Commando		1
Total	7	1

Tanks

Model	Quantity	In service	Since	Notes
MBTs				
High quality				
• M1A2 Abrams	218	218	1994	
• M-84	200	100	1990	
Subtotal	418	318		
Medium and low quality				
• Chieftain	45	0	1977	
• Vickers Mk 1	20	0	1970	
Subtotal	65	0		
Total	483	318		

APCs/AFVs

Model	Quantity	In service	Since	Notes
APCs				
• M113	230	60	1981	8 M901 ITV
• Fahd	60	+	1994	
• Shorland S600	22	22	1998	With National Guard
• M577	40	40	1995	Artillery command post vehicle
Subtotal	352	~125		
IFVs				
• Pandur	60	60	1998	Various models
• BMP-3	55	20	1995	
• BMP-2	46	40	1988	
• Desert Warrior	254	254	1994	
Subtotal	415	374		

APCs/AFVs *(continued)*

Model	Quantity	In service	Since	Notes
Reconnaissance				
• Pandur LCT 90mm	10	10	2000	
• Panhard VBL	20	20	1997	
Subtotal	30	30		
Total	**797**	**~530**		
Future procurement				
• Pandur				Option for up to 200 vehicles

Artillery

Model	Quantity	In service	Since	Notes
Self-propelled guns and howitzers				
• 155mm PLZ-45	27	27	2000	Being deliverd
• 155mm M109 A3	24	24		
• 155mm M109 A2	23	0	1986	Damaged during the Gulf War, being overhauled
• 155mm AMX-13 F-3	18	0		In storage, for sale
• 155mm GCT AuF-1	12	0	1992	In storage, for sale
Subtotal	104	51		
Mortars, under 160mm				
• 120mm RTF-1	~15	~15		
• 107mm	6	6		
Subtotal	~20	~20		
Rockets				
• 300mm Smerch (BM9A52-2)	27	27	1995	
Total	**~150**	**~100**		
Future procurements				
• 155mm PLZ-45	75			27 ordered in 1997, total requirement for 75
• 120mm SP mortars	30-100			
• M109 A6 Paladin	48			Under negotiation

Logistics and Engineering Equipment

Aardvark Mk.3 flail, M88 ARVs (14)

Anti-Tank Missiles

Model	Launchers	Missiles	Since	Notes
• AT-4 Spigot	+	80	1994	
• AT-5 Spandrel	+	240	1994	
• AT-10 Bastion	+	600	1995	
• BGM-71A/B TOW	82	+	1977	
• BGM-71C	*	*		Status unknown
• M901 ITV	8	+		
• M-47 Dragon	+	+		
Future procurement				
• BGM-71F (TOW 2B)		728		

Air Force

Order-of-Battle

Category	Quantity	In service	Notes
• Combat	59	40	
• Transport	5	5	
• Helicopters	28	23	

Combat Aircraft

Model	Quantity	In service	Since	Notes
Advanced multi-role				
• F/A-18C/D	40	40	1992	Fewer pilots than aircraft
Multi-role				
• Mirage F1-B/C	19	0	1976	Not in service
Total	**59**	**40**		

Transport Aircraft

Model	Quantity	In service	Since	Notes
• Boeing 737-200	1	1		
• C-130-30 Hercules/ L-100-30	3	3	1971	
• DC-9	1	1	1976	
Total	**5**	**5**		
Future procurement				
• C-130J	2			

Training and Liaison Aircraft

Model	Quantity	In service	Since	Notes
Jet trainers				
• BAC-167	8	0	1969	
• Hawk	12	0	1985	
Subtotal	20	0		
Piston/Turbo-prop				
• S-312 (Shorts Tucano)	18	8	1995	
Total	**38**	**8**		

Helicopters

Model	Quantity	In service	Since	Notes
Attack				
• SA-342K Gazelle	16	13	1974	
Medium transport				
• AS-330 Puma	7	5	1975	
Naval combat				
• AS-332 Super Puma	5	5	1985	
Total	**28**	**23**		

Miscellaneous Aircraft

Model	Quantity	In service	Since	Notes
Future procurement				
• Skyeye UAVs				3 systems, 12 UAVs under negotiation

Advanced Armament

Air-to-air missiles

AIM-9M Sidewinder, AIM-7F Sparrow (200)

Air-to-ground missiles

AGM-65G Maverick (300), AGM-84 Harpoon (40), AS-11, AS-12, HOT

Bombs

Paveway II laser-guided

Note: Numbers in parentheses refer to the number of missiles purchased, not to current inventory levels.

Air Force Infrastructure

Aircraft shelters

In airfields; for combat aircraft; under reconstruction

Military airfields: **3**

Al-Ahmadi, al-Jahra (Ali al-Salam), Kuwait International Airport

Air Defense Forces

Surface-to-Air Missiles

Model	Batteries	Launchers	Since	Notes
Heavy missiles				
• MIM-23B Improved HAWK	6		1977	
• Aspide	6			Part of Skyguard AD
Total	**12**			
Shoulder-launched missiles				
• FIM-92A Stinger		+		
• Starburst		48	1997	Approx. 250 missiles
Total		**~50**		

Note: The Kuwaiti Air Defense also relies on two US Army Patriot batteries.

Other Air Defense Systems

Model	Quantity	In service	Since	Notes
Air defense systems (missiles, radars and guns)				
• Skyguard AD system (Egyptian Amoun)	6	1		Each battery with 2xAspide launchers 2xOerlikon 35mm
Short-range guns				
• 40mm Bofors L-70/L-60	+	+		Unconfirmed
• Oerlikon-Buhrle 2x35 GDF-002	+	+		Part of Skyguard AD
• 23mm ZSU 23x4 SP (Gun Dish)	+	+		
• 20mm Oerlikon GAI	+	+		
Radars				
• AN/FPS-117 (Seek Igloo)	1	1		
• AN/TPS-32	1	1		
• Tiger (TRS-2100)	1	1		
• TRS 22XX	+	+		
• AD command and control unit (ADGE)	1	1		
Aerostat with airborne radars				
• LASS	1	1		

Navy

Combat Vessels

Type	Quantity	Length (m.)/ displacement (t.)	Notes/ armament
MFPBs			
• Istiklal (FPB-57)	1	58.1/410	4xExocet MM40 SSMs 1x76mm gun 2x40mm guns mines
• Sanbouk (TNC-45)	1	44.9/255	4xExocet MM40 SSMs 1x76mm gun 2x40mm guns
• Um-almaradim (P-37 BRL)	8	42/245	4xSea Skua SSMs 1x40mm gun 1x20mm gun
Total	**10**		

Patrol Craft

Type	Quantity	Length (m.)/ displacement (t.)	Notes/ armament
• Inttisar (OPV-310)	4	31.5/150	1x20mm gun 1x12.7mm MG
• Manta	12	14/10	3x12.7mm MGs
• Shaheed (100K FPB)	2	33.3/104	1x20mm gun 2x12.7mm MGs
• Various small patrol boats	51	10-12m	Cougar and al-Shaali class PBs carrying 12.7mm MGs
Total	**69**		
Future procurements			
• Magnum Sedan PBs	20		
• 2,000 ton OMV corvettes	4		

Landing Craft

Type	Quantity	Length (m.)/ displacement (t.)	Notes/ armament
• al-Tahaddy LCT	2	45/215	80 tons
Total	**2**		

Auxiliary Vessels

Type	Quantity	Length (m.)/ displacement (t.)	Notes/ armament
• Logistic support ship	2	32.3/320	170 tons
• Logistic support ship	1	27/170	40 tons equipment
• Support ship	1	55.4/545	2x12.7mm MGs

Naval Infrastructure

Naval bases (including Coast Guard): **6**

Kuwait City (Shuwaikh), al-Qulaya (Ras al-Qalaya), Umm al-Hainam, al-Bida, Verba, al-Harian

Ship maintenance and repair facilities:

190-meter floating dock at Kuwait City, repair capacity 35,000 dwt

9. LEBANON

General Data

Official Name of the State: Republic of Lebanon
Head of State: President Emile Lahoud
Prime Minister: Rafiq al-Hariri
Minister of Defense: Ghazi Zaitar
Commander-in-Chief of the Armed Forces: Lieutenant General Michel Sulayman
Chief of General Staff: Brigadier General Fady Abu-Shakra
Commander of the Air Force: Brigadier General George Shaàban
Commander of the Navy: Rear Admiral George Maàlouf

Area: 10,452 sq. km.
Population: 3,400,000

Demography

Ethnic groups		
Arabs	3,230,000	95.0%
Armenians	136,000	4.0%
Others	34,000	1.0%
Religious groups		
Shi'ite Muslims	1,088,000	32.0%
Sunni Muslims	714,000	21.0%
Druze	204,000	6.0%
Alawis	34,000	1.0%
Christians:		
Maronites	714,000	21.0%
Greek Orthodox	272,000	8.0%
Greek Catholic	170,000	5.0%
Armenians (Orthodox and Catholic)	136,000	4.0%
Others	68,000	2.0%

Economic Data

		1996	1997	1998	1999	2000
GDP (current prices)	$ bn	13.0	15.0	16.7	16.6	16.4
GDP per capita	$	4,193	4,839	5,219	5,030	4,823
Real GDP growth	%	4.0	4.0	2.0	-1.0	-0.5
Consumer price index	%	8.9	5.2	3.8	0.5	-1.0
External debt	$ bn	4.0	5.0	6.7	8.4	9.2

Economic Data *(continued)*

		1996	1997	1998	1999	2000
Balance of payments						
• Exports fob	$ bn	0.74	0.63	0.72	0.68	0.7
• Imports fob	$ bn	7.0	7.5	7.1	6.2	6.2
• Current account balance (including services and income)	$ bn	-3.7	-3.8	-3.3	-2.3	-2.1
Government expenditure						
• Total expenditure	$ bn	4.61	5.95	5.15	5.6	6.9
• Defense expenditure	$ bn	0.43	0.38	0.41	NA	NA
• Real change in defense expenditure	%	-12.3	-11.7	7.9	NA	NA
• Defense expenditure /GDP	%	3.3	2.5	2.4	NA	NA
Population	m	3.08	3.14	3.2	3.3	3.4
Official exchange rate	L£:$1	1,571	1,539	1,516	1,507	1,507

Sources: EIU Quarterly Report, EIU Country Profile, IMF International Financial Statistical Yearbook, SIPRI Yearbook

Arms Procurement and Security Assistance Received

Country	Type	Details
Arab League	• Assistance	$50 million for mine-clearing project
France	• Arms transfers	AMX-30 tanks
Iran	• Assistance	$100 million annually to Hizbullah and Islamic Jihad
Syria	• Military training	Advisers; approx. 50 trainees in Syria annually
UAE	• Assistance	Finance of mine-clearing project
US	• Arms transfers	Jeeps, trucks, M113 APCs, helicopters
	• Assistance	Approx. $575,000 for training in 2001
	• Military training	Advisers; few dozen trainees in US

Arms Sales and Security Assistance Extended

Country	Type	Details
Pakistan	• Arms transfers	Mirage III aircraft

Foreign Military Cooperation

Type	Details
• Foreign forces in country	Syria (25,000 in Beka', Tripoli area, and Beirut); Palestinian organizations; 300 Iranian Islamic Revolution Guards Corps (IRGC), several instructors with Hizbullah non-government militia in the Syrian-held Beka', UNIFIL force in south Lebanon (4,500 from Fiji, Finland, France, Ghana, Italy, India, Nepal, and Ukraine)

Weapons of Mass Destruction

NBC Capabilities

Nuclear capability

No nuclear capability. Party to the NPT.

Chemical weapons (CW) and protective equipment

No known CW activity. Not a party to the CWC.

Biological weapons (BW)

No known BW activities. Party to the BWC.

Armed Forces

Major Changes: No major change was recorded in the Lebanese order-of-battle. The Israeli supported South Lebanese Army ceased to exist after Israel's withdrawal from Lebanon. The Lebanese Army is receiving AMX-30 MBTs from Saudi Arabia.

Order-of-Battle

Year	1996	1997	1999	2000	2001
General data					
• Personnel (regular)	52,000	51,400	51,400	51,400	51,400
Ground Forces					
• Number of brigades	17	17	13*	13	13
• Tanks	350	320 (350)	280(350)*	280 (350)	280 (350)
• APCs/AFVs	670	730 (875)*	730 (875) (1,380)	1,235* (1,380)	1235
• Artillery (including MRLs)	190	328(331)*	~330	~330	~330
Air Force					
• Combat aircraft	16	(16)	(16)	(16)	(6)
• Transport aircraft	1	(2)	(2)	(1)	(1)
• Helicopters	40	16(34)*	16(34)	16(38)	16(38)

Order-of-Battle *(continued)*

Year	1996	1997	1999	2000	2001
Navy					
• Patrol crafts	36	39(43)	39(41)	32(35)	32(35)

Note: Beginning with 1997, data refers to quantities in active service. The number in parentheses refers to the total inventory.
* Due to change in estimate.

Personnel

	Regular	Total
Ground Forces	50,000	50,000
Air Force	1,000	1,000
Navy	400	400
Total	**51,400**	**51,400**
Paramilitary		
• Gendarmerie/ internal security	13,000	

Ground Forces

Formations

	Independent brigades/groups	Independent battalions
Mechanized/Infantry	11	
Presidential guard	1	
Special forces/ Airborne/Intervention	1	6
Artillery	2	
Support/Logistics/Medical	3	
Total	**18**	6

Tanks

Model	Quantity	In service	Since	Notes
MBTs				
Medium and low quality				
• T-55/upgraded T-54	180	180	1985	
• M48 A1/A5	130	60	1983	
Subtotal	310	240		

Tanks *(continued)*

Model	Quantity	In service	Since	Notes
Light tanks				
• AMX-13/105mm gun	20	20	1982	
• AMX-13/75mm gun	20	20	1981	
Subtotal	40	40		
Total	**350**	**280**		
Future procurement				
• AMX-30	62			

APCs/AFVs

Model	Quantity	In service	Since	Notes
APCs				
• M113 A1/A2	1,100	1,100	1970	
• M-3 (Panhard VIT)	15	15	1976	
Subtotal	1,115	1,115		
IFVs				
• VAB - VCI/VTT	75	75	1984	
• V-150 Commando	50	0	1981	
Subtotal	125	75		
Reconnaissance				
• AML-90	80	45	1993	
• Saracen/Saladin	60	0	1979	Possibly phased out
Subtotal	140	45		
Total	**1,380**	**1,235**		
Future procurement				
• M113 A1/A3	500			

Artillery

Model	Quantity	In service	Since	Notes
Towed guns and howitzers				
• 155mm M198	36	36	1984	
• 155mm M114	20	20	1980	
• 155mm M50	12	12	1970	
• 130mm M-46	20	20	1986	
• 122mm D-30	24	24	1985	
• 122mm M-1938	36	36	1973	
• 105mm M 101A1	15	15	1982	
• 105mm M 102	10	10	1983	
Subtotal	173	173		
Mortars, under 160mm				
• 120mm Brandt M-50 and M-60	130	130	1973	

Artillery *(continued)*

Model	Quantity	In service	Since	Notes
MRLs				
• 122mm BM-21/BM-11	30	~30	1993	
Total	**~330**	**~330**		

Logistics and Engineering Equipment

- M578 recovery vehicles (25)

Anti-Tank Missiles

Model	Quantity	In service	Since	Notes
• BGM-71A TOW	24	24	1975	
• MILAN	+	+	1979	
Total	**~80**	**~80**		

Anti-Tank Guns

Model	Quantity	In service	Since	Notes
• 106mm M-40 A2 recoilless rifle	+	+	1977	
• 85mm M-1945/D-44	+	+	1984	

Air Force

Order-of-Battle

Category	Quantity	In service	Notes
• Combat	6	0	
• Transport	1	0	
• Helicopters	38	16	

Combat Aircraft

Model	Quantity	In service	Since	Notes
Obsolete				
• Hawker Hunter F-70/T-66	6	0	1965	

Transport Aircraft

Model	Quantity	In service	Since	Notes
• Dove	1	0		

Training and Liaison Aircraft

Model	Quantity	In service	Since	Notes
Jet trainers				
• CM-170 Fouga Magister	5	0	1966	
Piston/Turbo-prop				
• BAe SA-3-120/126 Bulldog	5	0	1975	
Total	**10**	**0**		

Helicopters

Model	Quantity	In service	Since	Notes
Attack				
• SA-342 Gazelle	5	0	1980	
Medium transport				
• UH-1H (Bell 205)	16	16	1995	
• AB-212	5	0	1973	
• SA-330 Puma (possibly IAR-330)	5	0	1980	
Subtotal	26	16		
Light transport				
• Alouette II/III	7	0	1960	
Total	**38**	**16**		

Advanced Armament

Air-to-ground-missiles

• SS-11/12 (96)

Note: Number in parentheses refers to the quantity of missiles purchased, not to current inventory levels.

Air Force Infrastructure

Military airfields: **3**

Rayaq, Kleiat, Beirut

Air Defense Forces

Surface-to-Air Missiles

Model	Launchers	Since	Notes
Shoulder-launched missiles			
• SA-7 (Grail)	+		

Other Air Defense Systems

Model	Quantity	In service	Since	Notes
Short-range guns				
• 40mm M42 SP	10 – 12	10 – 12	1966	Probably in storage
• 23mm ZU 23x2	+	+	1981	
• 23mm ZU 23x2 SP	+	+	1985	On M113
• 20mm	+	+	1984	Probably in storage
Total	**~75**	**~75**		

Navy

Patrol Craft

Type	Quantity	Length (m.)/ displacement (t.)	Notes/ armament
• Tracker II class	0	19.3/31	2x12.7mm MGs 2 unserviceable
• Attacker	5	20/38	2x12.7mm MGs
• Fairey Marine small patrol craft	27	8.2/6	
Total	**32**		

Landing Craft

Type	Quantity	Length (m.)/ displacement (t.)	Notes/ armament
• EDIC class LCT	2	59/ 670	16 Troops 8 APCs 1x81mm MRL 2x20mm guns

Naval Infrastructure

Naval bases: 5

Beirut, Junieh, Sidon, Tripoli, Tyre

Ship maintenance and repair facilities

55 meter slipway for light craft repairs in Junieh

Major Non-Governmental Paramilitary Forces

Personnel

	Active	Reserves	Total
• Hizbullah	600–800	3,000–5,000	5,800
• Popular Liberation Army (Druze)		10,000	10,000
• Amal		10,000	10,000

Equipment

Organization	Category	System	Quantity	Notes
Hizbullah	APCs	• M113	several	
	Aircraft	• Ultra-light aircraft		
	Air Defense	• SA-7		
		• SA-18		
		• Stinger		
		• ZU-23x2		
		• 57mm		
	ATGMs	• AT-3 Sagger		
		• AT-4 Fagot		
		• TOW		
	Artillery guns	• 106mm		
	Mortars	• 81mm		
		• 120mm		
	MRLs	• 122mm BM-21		
	Artillery rockets	• 240mm Fajr-3		Alleged
		• 333mm Fajr-5		Alleged

10. LIBYA

General Data

Official Name of the State: The Great Socialist People's Libyan Arab Jamahiriya
Head of State: Colonel Muammar al-Qaddafi
Prime Minister: Mohammad Ahmad al-Manqush (official title: Secretary-General of the General People's Committee)
Minister of Defense: Colonel Abu-Bakr Yunis Jaber
Inspector General of the Armed Forces: Colonel Mustapha al-Kharrubi
Commander-in-Chief of the Armed Forces: Colonel Abu-Bakr Yunis Jaber
Commander of the Air Force and Air Defense Forces: Brigadier General Ali Riffi al-Sharif

Area: 1,759,540 sq. km
Population: 5,650,000

Demography

Ethnic groups		
Arabs and Berbers	5,480,000	97.0%
Others:	170,000	3.0%
Greeks, Maltese, Italians, Egyptians, Pakistanis, Indians, Tunisians, Turks		
Religious groups		
Sunni Muslims	5,480,000	97.0%
Christians and others	170,000	3.0%

Economic Data

		1996	1997	1998	1999	2000
GDP (current price)	$ bn	33.2	34.2	31.8	32.3	35.4
GDP per capita	$	5,928	5,896	6,000	5,872	6,321
Real GDP growth	%	1.1	0.5	-2.0	5.4	6.5
Consumer price index	%	38.9	25.0	24.2	18.0	12.0
External debt	$ bn	3.3	3.7	3.7	3.6	3.8
Balance of payments						
• Exports fob	$ bn	9.58	9.88	6.33	7.28	13.41
• Imports fob	$ bn	7.06	7.16	5.86	4.30	7.74
• Current account balance (including services and income)	$ bn	1.48	1.88	-0.39	2.14	3.89

Economic Data *(continued)*

		1996	1997	1998	1999	2000
Government expenditure						
• Total expenditure	$ bn	12.48	14.09	13.48	10.56	NA
• Defense expenditure	$ bn	NA	NA	NA	NA	NA
• Real change in defense expenditure	%	NA	NA	NA	NA	NA
• Defense expenditure/ GDP	%	NA	NA	NA	NA	NA
Population	m	5.59	5.78	5.34	5.47	5.65
Official exchange rate	LD:$1	0.36	0.38	0.39	0.46	0.50

Sources: EIU Quarterly Report, EIU Country Profile, IMF International Financial Statistical Yearbook, SIPRI Yearbook

Arms Procurement and Security Assistance Received

Country	Type	Details
Egypt	• Cooperation in arms production	Alleged involvement in SSMs development
Iran	• Cooperation in arms production	Alleged involvement in SSMs development
Iraq	• Assistance	Alleged involvement in SSMs development
North Korea	• Arms transfers	Alleged sale of SSMs
	• Military training	Foreign advisers/instructors
PRC	• Arms transfers	Alleged sale of SSM parts and technology
Russia	• Arms transfers	Alleged sale of SSM parts and technology
Ukraine	• Arms transfers	Alleged sale of SSMs
Yugoslavia	• Cooperation in arms production	Alleged involvement in SSMs development

Arms Sales and Security Assistance Extended

Country	Type	Details
Niger	• Arms transfers	Antonov cargo aircraft

Defense Production

	M	P	A
Weapons of mass destruction			
• Toxic chemical agents	√		
• Plans to upgrade SSMs, with assistance by foreign experts, and efforts to produce an indigenous SSM (al-Fatah), not yet operational	√		
Army equipment			
• Tank upgrading facility, with assistance of Czech Republic		√	

Note: M - manufacture (indigenously developed)
P - production under license
A - assembly

Weapons of Mass Destruction

NBC Capabilities

Nuclear capabilities

5Mw Soviet-made research reactor at Tadjoura; basic R&D. Party to the NPT. Safeguards agreement with the IAEA in force. Signed but not ratified the African Nuclear Weapon Free Zone treaty (Treaty of Pelindaba).

Chemical weapons (CW) and protective equipment

CW production facilities, stockpile of chemical agents, nerve gas and Mustard gas. Personal protective equipment; Soviet type decontamination units.
Not a party to the CWC.

Biological weapons (BW)

Alleged production of toxins and other Biological weapons (BW) (unconfirmed). Party to the BWC.

Ballistic Missiles

Model	Launchers	Missiles	Since	Notes
• Scud B/C	80	500	1976/1999	In storage
• No-Dong	+	+	2000	Allegedly being delivered
Total	**~80**			
Future procurement				
• No-Dong	7	50		Allegedly being delivered

Note: See also under Rockets

Armed Forces

Major Changes: Libya received its first No-Dong IRBMs from North Korea. No other major change was recorded in the Libyan armed forces.

Order-of-Battle

Year	1996	1997	1999	2000	2001
General data					
• Personnel	76,000	76,000	76,000	76,000	76,000
• SSM launchers	110	110	128	80*	~80
Ground Forces					
• Number of brigades	+	5	1*	1	1
• Number of battalions	+	46	46	46	46
• Tanks	2,700	950	600-700*	~650	~650
		(2,700)	(2,210)	(2,210)	(2,210)
• APCs/AFVs	3,000	2,750	~2,750	~2,750	~2,750
		(2,970)	(2,970)	(2,970)	(2,970)
• Artillery (including MRLs)	2,600-	2,245	2,220	~2,270	~2,320
	3,000	(2,325)	(2,300)	(~2,350)	(~2,400)
Air Force					
• Combat aircraft	483	~360(483)	~360(443)	~360(443)	~360(443)
• Transport aircraft	106	85(90)	85(90)	85(90)	85(90)
• Helicopters	210	164(212)	127(204)	127(204)	127(204)
Air Defense Forces					
• Heavy SAM batteries	90	~30*	~30	~30	~30
• Medium SAM batteries	35	~10*	~10	~10	~10
• Light SAM launchers	55	55	55	55	55
Navy					
• Submarines	6	4	0(4)	0(4)	0(4)
• Combat vessels	43	34	34	24	24
• Patrol craft	9	2	2	0	0

Note: Beginning with 1997, data refers to quantities in active service. The number in parentheses refers to the total inventory.

* Due to change in estimate.

Personnel

	Regular	Reserves	Total
Ground Forces	50,000		50,000
Air Force and Air Defense	18,000		18,000
Navy	8,000		8,000
Total	**76,000**		**76,000**
Paramilitary			
• People's Militia		40,000	40,000
• Revolutionary Guards (part of the People's Militia)	3,000		3,000
• Islamic Pan African Legion (part of the People's Militia)	2,500		2,500

Ground Forces

Formations

	Independent brigades/ groups	Independent battalions
Presidential Security Force	1	
Armored		10
Mechanized/Infantry		21
Artillery		22
Paratroops		15
Air Defense		8
SSM	5	
Total	**6**	**76**

Tanks

Model	Quantity	In service	Since	Notes
MBTs				
High quality				
• T-72/T-72M	360	150	1979	
Medium and low quality				
• T-62	600	+	1975	
• T-55	1,250	+	1974	
Subtotal	1,850	~500		
Total	**2,210**	**~650**		

APCs/AFVs

Model	Quantity	In service	Since	Notes
APC				
• Oto-Breda 6614/6616	400	400	1980	
• Engesa EE-9/11	300	200	1975/1977	
• BTR-50/60	750	750	1970	
• M113 A1	50	~30	1972	
• OT-62/OT-64	200	100	1975	
Subtotal	1,700	~1,480		
IFV				
• BMP-1/BMP-2	1,050	1,050	1972	
Reconnaissance				
• BRDM-2	220	220		
• Oto-Breda 6616			1980	Also listed under APCs
• Engesa EE-9			1975	Also listed under APCs
Total	**2,970**	**~2,750**		

Artillery

Model	Quantity	In service	Since	Notes
Self-propelled guns and howitzers				
• 155mm Palmaria	210	210	1983	
• 155mm M109	20	0	1973	
• 152mm ZTS Dana	80	80	1986	
• 152mm M-1973	60	60	1982	
• 122mm M-1974	130	130	1980	
Subtotal	500	480		
Towed guns and howitzers				
• 130mm M-46	330	330	1978	
• 122mm D-30	245	245		
• 122mm D-74	60	60		
• 105mm M101	60	0	1970	
Subtotal	695	635		
Mortars, over 160mm				
• 240mm	120	120		
• 160mm	24	24		
Subtotal	144	144		
Mortars, under 160mm				
• 120mm	48	48		
• 107mm	64	64		
Subtotal	112	112		

Artillery *(continued)*

Model	Quantity	In service	Since	Notes
MRLs				
• 140mm	+	+		
• 130mm M-51	+	+	1980	
• 122mm BM-21/ RM-70/BM-11	600	600	1980	
• 107mm Type 63	300	300	1979	
Subtotal	~900	~900		
Rockets				
• FROG-7	48	48		
Total	**~2,400**	**~2,320**		

Anti-Tank Missiles

Model	Launchers	Missiles	Since	Notes
• AT-3 (Sagger)	+	620	1977	
• AT-4 (Spigot)	+	+	1990	
• AT-5 (Spandrel)	+	+		
• BRDM-2	40			Carrying AT-3
• MILAN	+	400	1981	
Total	**+**	**3,000**		

Anti-Tank Guns

Model	Quantity	In service	Since	Notes
• 106mm recoilless rifle	220	220		
• 84mm Carl Gustav	400	400		

Air Force

Order-of-Battle

Category	Quantity	In service	Notes
• Combat	443	~360	
• Transport	90	85	
• Helicopters	204	127	

Combat Aircraft

Model	Quantity	In service	Since	Notes
Interceptors				
• MiG-25/25R (Foxbat)	80	~70	1980	
• MiG-23	170	~125	1976	Also listed under Ground Attack
Subtotal	250	~195		
Multi-role				
• Mirage F-1	30	30	1979	
Ground attack				
• Su-24 (Fencer C)	6	6	1989	
• Su-20/22 (Fitter C)	40	40		
• MiG-23/27 (Flogger)				Also listed under Interceptors
Subtotal	46	46		
Bombers				
• Tu-22 (Blinder)	7	5	1974	
Obsolete				
• MiG-21 bis (Fishbed)	70	45		
• Mirage V	40	40	1971	
Subtotal	110	85		
Total	**443**	**~360**		

Transport Aircraft

Model	Quantity	In service	Since	Notes
• An-26 (Curl)	15	10	1983	
• C-130H Hercules/ L-100-20/L100-30	10	10	1970	
• C-140 Jetstar	1	1		
• Fokker F-27-400/600	9	9	1981	
• G-222L	19	19	1980	
• IL-76 (Candid)	19	19	1979	Including about 4 tankers
• L-410 UVP	15	15		
• Mystère-Falcon 20/50	2	2	1981	
Total	**90**	**85**		

Training and Liaison Aircraft

Model	Quantity	In service	Since	Notes
Jet trainers				
• G-2AE Galeb/ J-1E Jastreb	120	80	1975	
• L-39 Albatross	177	110	1978	
• CM-170 Fouga Magister	12	0	1971	
Subtotal	309	190		
Piston/Turbo-prop				
• SF-260 M/L/W	70	20	1977	
Total	**379**	**210**		

Helicopters

Model	Quantity	In service	Since	Notes
Attack				
• Mi-24/25	56	30	1978	Number unconfirmed
• Mi-35	13	13	1990	
Subtotal	69	43		
Heavy transport				
• CH-47C Chinook	15	15	1976	
Medium transport				
• Mi-8/17 (Hip)	25	25	1975	
• AB-212/205	2	2	1974	
• SA-321 Super Frelon	10	10	1971	Also employed in naval combat role
Subtotal	37	37		
Light transport				
• Alouette III	14	14	1971	Possibly with police
• Mi-2 (Hoplite)	35	0		
• AB-206	4	4	1970	
• A-109	2	2		
Subtotal	55	20		
Naval combat				
• Mi-14 (Haze)	28	12	1983	
Total	**204**	**127**		

Advanced Armament

Air-to-air missiles

AA-2 (Atoll), AA-6 (Acrid), AA-7 (Apex), AA-8 (Aphid), AA-11 (Archer), R-530 (75), R-550 Magic (130), Super 530D/F

Air-to-ground missiles

AS-9 (Kyle), AS-10 (Karen), AS-14 (Kedge), AT-2 (Swatter), AT-6 (Spiral) (unconfirmed)

Note: The number in parenthesis refers to the quantity of missiles purchased, not to current inventory levels.

Air Force Infrastructure

Military airfields: **13**

Al-Adem (Tobruk), Benghazi (Baninah), Beni Walid, al-Bumbah, Ghurdabiyah (Surt), Jufra, Kufra, Maatan al-Sarra, Misratha, Ouqba ben Nafi (Al-Watiya), Sabhah, Tripoli International (Idriss), Umm al-Tika.

Air Defense Forces

Surface-to-Air Missiles

Model	Batteries	Launchers	Since	Notes
Heavy missiles				
• SA-2 (Guideline)	~15		1975	
• SA-3 (Goa)	~10		1975	
• SA-5 (Gammon)	4		1985	
Total	**~30**			
Medium missiles				
• Crotale	+		1974	
• SA-6 (Gainful)	6		1975	
• SA-8 (Gecko)		20		
Total	**~10**	**20**		
Light missiles				
• SA-9 (Gaskin)/ SA-13 (Gopher)		55	1981	
Shoulder-launched missiles				
• SA-7 (Grail)		400	1979	
• SA-14 (Gremlin)		+		
Total		**~400**		

Note: Serviceability of air defense systems is unclear.

Other Air Defense Systems

Model	Quantity	In service	Since	Notes
Short-range guns				
• 57mm S-60	90	90		
• 40mm Bofors L-70	50	0		
• 30mm 30x2 M-53/59 SP	240	0		
• 23mm ZSU 23x4 SP (Gun Dish)	250	250		
• 23mm ZU 23x2	100	100		
Total	**730**	**440**		

Navy

Submarines

Type	Quantity	Length (m.)/ displacement (t.)	Notes/ armament
• F class (Foxtrot, Type 641)	0	91/2,475	4 non-operational 10x533mm torpedoes 44 mines
Total	**0**		

Combat Vessels

Type	Quantity	Length (m.)/ displacement (t.)	Notes/ armament
Missile frigates			
• Koni class (Type 1159)	2	96.4/1,440	4xSS-N-2C Styx SSMs 2xSA-N-4 SAMs 4x76mm guns 4x30mm guns 4x406mm torpedoes 1xRBU 6000 ASW mortar 20 mines
Missile corvettes			
• Nanuchka class	3	59.3/660	4xSS-N-2C Styx SSMs 2xSA-N-4 SAMs 2x57mm guns

Combat Vessels *(continued)*

Type	Quantity	Length (m.)/ displacement (t.)	Notes/ armament
MFPBs			
• Combattante II	5	49.0/311	4xOtomat SSMs 1x76mm gun 2x40mm guns 4 aditional non-operational
• Ossa II	6	38.6/245	4xSS-N-2C Styx SSMs 4x30mm guns 6 additional non-operational
Subtotal	11		
Mine warfare vessels			
• Natya class minesweepers (Type 266ME)	8	61.0/804	4x30mm guns 4x25mm guns 2xRBU 1200 ASW mortars 10 mines Acoustic & Magnetic sweep
Total	**24**		

Landing Craft

Type	Quantity	Length (m.)/ displacement (t.)	Notes/ armament
• Turkish type	3	56.0/280	100 troops; 350 tons 1x80mm mortar
• PS-700 class LST	2	99.5/2,800	240 troops; 11 tanks 6x40mm guns 1x SA-316 Helicopter
• Polnochny class LCT (Type 773U)	2	83.9/1,305	4x30mm guns 2x140mm MRLs 100 mines 1 non-operational
Total	7		

Auxiliary Vessels

Type	Quantity	Length (m.)/ displacement (t.)	Notes/ armament
• Vosper (Tobruk)	1	54.0/500	1x102mm gun 2x40mm guns used for training
• Zeltin (LSD type)	1	98.8/2,200	2x40mm guns Maintenance and repair craft
• Yelva	1	40.9/300	Diving-support ship
• Spasilac class	1	55.5/1,590	Yugoslav salvage ship 4x12.7mm MGs
• Transporters (Ro-Ro)	10	166.5/2,412	

Coastal Defense

Type	Quantity	Notes
• SS-2C Styx	+	In 3 sites

Naval Infrastructure

Naval bases : **6**

Al-Khums, Benghazi, Misratah, Tobruk, Tripoli, Derna

Ship maintenance and repair facilities

Facilities at Tripoli with foreign technicians for repair of vessels of up to 6,000 dwt; a 3,200-ton lift floating dock; floating docks at Benghazi and Tobruk

11. MOROCCO

General Data

Official Name of the State: Kingdom of Morocco
Head of State: King Mohammed VI
Prime Minister: Abd al-Rahmane Youssoufi
Minister of Defense: King Mohammed VI
Secretary General of National Defense Administration: Abdel Rahaman Sbai
Commander-in-Chief of the Armed Forces: King Mohammed VI
Inspector General of the Armed Forces: General Abd al-Kader Loubarisi
Commander of the Air Force: Ali Abd al-Aziz al-Omrani
Commander of the Navy: Captain Muhammad al-Tariqi

Area: 622,012 sq. km., including the former Spanish Sahara
Population: 28,700,000

Demography

Ethnic groups		
Arabs	17,105,000	59.6%
Berbers	11,336,000	39.5%
Europeans and others	259,000	0.9%
Religious groups		
Sunni Muslims	28,326,900	98.7%
Christians	315,700	1.1%
Jews	57,400	0.2%

Economic Data

		1996	1997	1998	1999	2000
GDP (current prices)	$ bn	36.6	33.4	35.7	35.0	34.3
GDP per capita	$	1,361	1,223	1,284	1,241	1,195
Real GDP growth	%	12.2	-2.3	6.5	-0.4	0.8
Consumer price index	%	3.0	0.9	2.9	0.7	2.0
External debt	$ bn	21.9	20.2	20.7	19.4	18.1
Balance of payments						
• Exports fob	$ bn	6.89	7.04	7.14	7.5	7.27
• Imports cif	$ bn	9.1	8.9	9.46	9.95	11.4
• Current account balance(including services and income)	$ bn	0.06	-0.17	-0.14	-0.17	-1.44

Economic Data *(continued)*

		1996	1997	1998	1999	2000
Government expenditure						
• Total expenditure	$ bn	9.9	9.23	10.21	10.45	NA
• Defense expenditure	$ bn	1.43	NA	NA	NA	NA
• Real change in defense expenditure	%	-7.8	NA	NA	NA	NA
• Defense expenditure / GDP	%	3.9	NA	NA	NA	NA
Population	m	26.9	27.3	27.8	28.2	28.7
Official exchange rate	Dh:$1	8.72	9.53	9.6	9.8	10.6

Sources: EIU Quarterly Report, EIU Country Profile, IMF International Financial Statistical Yearbook, SIPRI Yearbook

Arms Procurement and Security Assistance Received

Country	Type	Details
Belarus	• Arms transfers	T-72 tanks
France	• Arms transfers	OPV 64 patrol ships
UK	• Arms transfers	Upgrading of 105mm guns
US	• Arms transfers	T-37 aircraft
	• Assistance	$3.45 million grant in 2001

Arms Sales and Security Assistance Extended

Country	Type	Details
US	• Facilities	Use of Sidi Slimane, Marrakech and Casablanca airfields in emergency; permission for space shuttle to land at Marrakech AFB; use of communications center at Kenitra; storage and use of naval facilities at Mohammedia

Foreign Military Cooperation

Type	Details
• Forces deployed abroad	Small contingency force in Bosnia and Croatia
• Joint maneuvers	France, US
• Security agreements	Tunisia

Defense Production

	M	P	A
Army equipment			
• Small arms ammunition	√		
• Assembly of trucks			√

Note: M - manufacture (indigenously developed)
P - production under license
A - assembly

Weapons of Mass Destruction

NBC Capabilities

Nuclear capability
No nuclear capability. Party to the NPT.

Chemical weapons (CW) and protective equipment
No known CW activity. Party to the CWC.

Biological weapons (BW)
No known BW activities. Signed but not ratified the BWC.

Armed Forces

Major Changes: The Moroccan Army received 48 refurbished T-72 MBTs from Belarus, and 32 M106 (107mm SP mortars) from US Army draw-down during 2000.

Order-of-Battle

Year	1996	1997	1999	2000	2001
General data					
• Personnel (regular)	141,000	196,500	145,500	145,500	145,500
Ground Forces					
• Number of brigades	12	7*	6	6	6
• Tanks	415	364*	379	540*	588
• APCs/AFVs	1,500	1,200*	1,074	1,120*	1,120
		(1,537)	(1,374)	(1,420)	(1,420)
• Artillery (including MRLs)	386	970*	967	1,027*	1,060
		(1,020)	(1,017)		

Order-of-Battle *(continued)*

Year	1996	1997	1999	2000	2001
Air Force					
• Combat aircraft	74	72	72	72	59(72)
• Transport aircraft	48	45	43	43	41(43)
• Helicopters	127	129	130	130	121(131)
Air Defense Forces					
• Light SAM launchers	+	37*	37	37	37
Navy					
• Combat vessels	13	13	13	13	13
• Patrol craft	52	49	48	52	52

Note: Beginning with 1997, data refers to quantities in active service. The number in parentheses refers to the total inventory.
* Due to change in estimate.

Personnel

	Regular	Reserves	Total
Ground Forces	125,000	150,000	275,000
Air Force	13,500		13,500
Navy and Marines	7,000		7,000
Total	**145,500**	**150,000**	**295,500**
Paramilitary			
• Gendarmerie Royale	10,000		10,000
• Force Auxiliere	25,000		25,000
• Mobile Intervention Corps	5,000		5,000

Ground Forces

Formations

	Independent brigades/ groups	Independent battalions
Armored		10
Mechanized	3	19
Infantry		35
Light Security	1	
Camel Corps		5
Paratroops	2	
Airborne/Commando		2+4
Artillery		12
Air Defense		1
Total	**6**	**88**

Tanks

Model	Quantity	In service	Since	Notes
MBTs				
High quality				
• T-72	48	48	2000	
Medium and low quality				
• M60 A1/A3	250	250	1981/93	
• M48 A5	185	185	1974	
Subtotal	435	435		
Light tanks				
• SK-105 (Kürassier)	105	105	1985	
Total	**588**	**588**		

APCs/AFVs

Model	Quantity	In service	Since	Notes
APCs				
• M113 A1/A2	383	383	1979	Including 23 M901 Also listed under Anti-Tank Weapons
• M-3 (Panhard)	30	30	1981	Unconfirmed
• UR-416	55	55	1977	Also listed under Anti-Tank Weapons
• OT-62	150	0	1968	
• M-3 half-track	50	0	1966	
Subtotal	668	468		
IFVs				
• Ratel 20/90	60	60	1981	
• VAB-VCI/VTT	290	290	1979	
• Engesa EE-11	+	0	1981	Included with Engesa EE-9
Subtotal	350	350		
Reconnaissance				
• AMX-10 R/CM	110	110	1981	
• Engesa EE-9	50	0	1981	Quantity includes Engesa EE-11
• BRDM-2	50	0	1992	Including 36 listed under Anti-Tank Weapons
• EBR-75	16	16	1970	
• AML-90/AML-60	175	175	1966	
Subtotal	401	301		
Total	**1,420**	**1,120**		

Artillery

Model	Quantity	In service	Since	Notes
Self-propelled guns and howitzers				
• 203mm M110 A2	60	60	1996	
• 155mm Mk F-3 (AMX)	100	100	1980	
• 155mm M109 A1	40	40	1978	
• 105mm Mk 61	5	5	1963	
Subtotal	205	205		
Towed guns and howitzers				
• 155mm FH-70	30	30	1993	
• 155mm M114	20	20	1976	
• 155mm M198	35	35		
• 130mm M-46	18	18	1981	
• 105mm L-118 light gun	30	30	1980	To be upgraded
• 105mm M-1950	35	35	1972	
• 105mm M101/M101 A1	18	18	1970	
Subtotal	186	186		
Mortars, under 160mm				
• 120mm	600	600	1972	20 SP mounted on VAB
• 107mm M30 SP	32	32	2000	Mounted on M106
Subtotal	632	632		
MRLs				
• 122mm BM-21	36	36	1980	
Total	**1,060**	**1,060**		
Future procurement				
• 105mm L-118	6		2001	

Logistics and Engineering Equipment

M578 recovery vehicles (60), SK-105 ARVs (10)

Anti-Tank Missiles

Model	Quantity	In service	Since	Notes
• BGM-71A TOW	150	150	1978	
• M901 ITV	23	23	1999	Also listed under APCs
• AT-3 (Sagger) SP	36	0	1992	Mounted on BRDM-2
• Cobra SP	42	42	1979	Mounted on UR-416
• M47 Dragon	480	480	1978	
• MILAN	80	80	1982	
Total	**811**	**775**		

Anti-Tank Guns

Model	Quantity	In service	Since	Notes
• 106mm M40 A2	350	350	1977	
• 90mm M-56	28	28	1975	
Total	**378**	**378**		

Air Force

Order-of-Battle

Category	Quantity	In service	Notes
• Combat	72	59	
• Transport	43	41	
• Helicopters	131	121	

Combat Aircraft

Model	Quantity	In service	Since	Notes
Multi-role				
• F-5E/F	22	15	1981	
• Mirage F1	34	28	1979	
Subtotal	56	43		
Ground attack				
• OV-10 Bronco	3	3	1981	
Obsolete				
• F-5A/B	13	13	1967	
Total	**72**	**59**		

Transport Aircraft

Model	Quantity	In service	Since	Notes
• Beechcraft King Air 100	5	5	1975	
• Beechcraft Super King Air 200	5	5	1983	
• Beechcraft Super King Air 300	1	1	1991	
• Boeing 707	2	2	1982	
• C-130H Hercules	15	15	1974	Including 2 employed in electronic surveillance and 2 tankers
• CN-235	7	7	1990	
• Dornier DO-28 D-2	3	2	1981	
• Gulfstream II/III	2	1	1976	

Transport Aircraft *(continued)*

Model	Quantity	In service	Since	Notes
• Mystère-Falcon 50	1	1	1980	
• Mystère-Falcon 20	2	2	1968	Electronic countermeasures
Total	**43**	**41**		

Training and Liaison Aircraft

Model	Quantity	In service	Since	Notes
Jet trainers				
• Cessna 318 (T-37)	14	14	1996	
• Alpha jet	22	22	1979	
• Beechcraft T-34C	12	10	1977	
• CM-170 Fouga Magister	22	22	1964	
Subtotal	70	68		
Piston/Turbo-prop				
• AS-202/18A Bravo	10	10	1978	
• CAP 10/232	9	9	1983	Aerobatic team
Subtotal	19	19		
Total	**89**	**87**		

Helicopters

Model	Quantity	In service	Since	Notes
Attack helicopters				
• SA-342 Gazelle	22	22	1976	Of which 6 with gendarmerie
Heavy transport				
• CH-47C Chinook	8	8	1979	
Medium transport				
• SA-330 Puma	28	28	1976	Of which 6 with gendarmerie
• AB-205	32	32	1969	
• AB-212	5	5	1973	
• AS-365 Dauphin II	2	2	1983	With gendarmerie
Subtotal	67	67		
Light transport				
• Alouette II/III	5	5	1981	With gendarmerie
• Bell 206 JetRanger	26	16	1975	
• SA-315B Lama	3	3		With gendarmerie
Subtotal	34	24		
Total	**131**	**121**		

Miscellaneous Aircraft

Model	Quantity	In service	Since	Notes
Reconnaissance				
• RF-5	2	1	1981	Also listed under Combat Aircraft
• C-130H	2	2	1974	Also listed under Transport Aircraft
Tanker				
• KC-130	2	2	1974	Also listed under Transport Aircraft
Electronic warfare				
• Mystère 20F	2	2	1968	Also listed under Transport Aircraft
Maritime surveillance				
• BN-2T Defender	7	7	1993	Possibly in fishery protection role
UAVs and mini-UAVs				
• Skyeye R4E-50	+	+	1990	

Advanced Armament

Air-to-air missiles

AIM-9J Sidewinder (320), R-530, R-550 Magic (300), Super 530D

Air-to-ground missiles

AGM-65 Maverick (380), HOT

Note: Number in parentheses refers to the quantity of missiles purchased, not to current inventory levels.

Air Force Infrastructure

Military airfields: 10

Agadir, Casablanca (Nouasseur), Fez, Kenitra, Larache, L'Ayoun, Marrakech, Meknes, Rabat, Sidi Slimane

Air Defense Forces

Surface-to-Air Missiles

Model	Batteries	Launchers	Since	Notes
Light missiles				
• MIM-72A Chaparral		37	1977	
Shoulder-launched missiles				
• SA-7 (Grail)		70	1978	

Other Air Defense Systems

Model	Quantity	In service	Since	Notes
Short-range guns				
• 37mm M-1939	100	14	1972	
• 23mm ZU 23x2	90	30	1986	
• 20mm M163 Vulcan SP	115	115	1983	
• 20mm M167 SP	40	40	1993	
Total	**345**	**199**		
Radars				
• AN/TPS-43	8	8		
• AN/TPS-63	8	8		Upgraded

Navy

Combat Vessels

Type	Quantity	Length (m.)/ displacement (t.)	Notes/ armament
Missile frigates			
• Descubierta	1	88.8/1,233	4xMM38 Exocet SSMs 1x8 Aspide SAMs 6x324mm torpedoes 1xSR 375 ASW mortar 1x76mm gun 1x40mm gun
MFPBs			
• Lazaga	4	58.1/524	4xMM38 Exocet SSMs 1x76mm gun 1x40mm gun 2x20mm guns

Combat Vessels *(continued)*

Type	Quantity	Length (m.)/ displacement (t.)	Notes/ armament
Gunboats			
• Okba class (PR-72)	2	57.5/375	1x76mm gun 1x40mm gun
• Cormoran class (P-200D Vigilance)	6	58.1/425	1x40mm gun
Subtotal	8		
Total	**13**		
Future procurement			
• Floreal frigates	2	93.5/2,950	To be delivered in 2001

Patrol Craft

Type	Quantity	Length (m.)/ displacement (t.)	Notes/ armament
• Al Wacil/Erraid (P-32)	10	32/74	6 Al Wacil class, 4 Erraid class 4 with customs/ Coast Guard 1x20mm gun
• Rais Bargech (OPV 64)	5	64/580	1x40mm gun 1x20mm gun 4x14.5mm MGs
• Osprey mk II	4	54.8/475	2x20mm guns
• Arcor 46	18	14.5/15	With customs/Coast Guard 2x12.7mm MGs
• Arcor 53	15	16/17	With customs/Coast Guard 1x12.7mm MG
Total	**52**		

Landing Craft

Type	Quantity	Length (m.)/ displacement (t.)	Notes/ armament
• Batral LSL	3	80/750	140 troops, 12 vehicles Helicopter pod 2x81mm mortars 4x40mm guns

Landing Craft *(continued)*

Type	Quantity	Length (m.)/ displacement (t.)	Notes/ armament
• EDIC LCT	1	59/250	11 vehicles 1x120mm mortar 2x20mm guns
• Newport class LST	1	159.2/8,450	400 troops, 500-ton vehicles 4xLCVP/LCPL boats 1x20mm Phalanx gun
Total	**5**		

Auxiliary Vessels

Type	Quantity	Length (m.)/ displacement (t.)	Notes/ armament
• Cargo ship	1	77/1,500	2x14.5mm MGs
• Agor survey ship (Robert D. Conrad)	1	67.3/1,370	
• Dakhla support ship	1	69/800	
• SAR craft	3	19.4/40	With Coast Guard
Total	**6**		

Naval Infrastructure

Naval bases: 7

Agadir, al-Hoceima, Casablanca, Kenitra, Dakhla, Safi, Tangier

Ship maintenance and repair facilities

156-meter dry-dock at Casablanca, repair ships of up to 10,000 dwt; facility for minor repairs at Agadir

12. OMAN

General Data

Official Name of the State: Sultanate of Oman
Head of State: Sultan Qabus ibn Said al-Said
Prime Minister: Sultan Qabus ibn Said al-Said
Minister of Defense: Sultan Qabus ibn Said al-Said
Minister of Defense Affairs: Badr bin Saud bin Harib al-Busaidi
Chief of General Staff: Lieutenant General Khamis bin Humaid bin Salim al-Kalabani
Commander of the Ground Forces: Major General Ahmad bin Harith bin Naser al-Nabhani
Commander of the Air Force: Major General Mohammad Ibn Mahfoodh al-Ardhi
Commander of the Navy: Rear Admiral Said Shiab bin Tareq al-Said

Area: 212,000 sq. km.
Population: 2,400,000

Demography

Ethnic groups		
Arabs	2,174,000	90.6%
Others (Africans, Persians, Southeast Asians)	226,000	9.4%
Religious groups		
Ibadi Muslims	1,800,000	75.0%
Sunni Muslims	451,000	18.8%
Shi'ite Muslims, Hindus	149,000	6.2%

Economic Data

		1996	1997	1998	1999	2000
GDP (current price)	$ bn.	15.28	15.84	14.09	15.61	19.58
GDP per capita	$	6,944	6,886	6,124	6,784	8,156
Real GDP growth	%	2.9	6.1	2.7	-1.0	4.6
Consumer price index	%	0.1	0.1	-0.8	0.4	-0.8
External debt	$ bn	3.15	3.9	4.58	4.61	4.49

Economic Data *(continued)*

		1996	1997	1998	1999	2000
Balance of payments						
• Exports fob	$ bn	7.34	7.63	5.51	7.22	11.06
• Imports fob	$ bn	4.38	4.65	5.22	4.30	4.5
• Current account balance (including services and income)	$ bn	0.18	-0.04	-2.97	-0.19	3.20
Government expenditure						
• Total expenditure	$ bn	5.85	5.99	5.77	5.88	6.34
• Defense expenditure	$ bn	1.91	1.81	1.82	1.61	NA
• Real change in defense expenditure	%	-4.97	-5.23	0.55	-11.53	NA
• Defense expenditure / GDP	%	12.50	11.42	12.92	10.31	NA
Population	m	2.2	2.3	2.3	2.3	2.4
Official exchange rate	OR:$1	0.39	0.39	0.39	0.39	0.39

Sources: EIU Quarterly Report, EIU Country Profile, IMF International Financial Statistical Yearbook, SIPRI Yearbook

Arms Procurement and Security Assistance Received

Country	Type	Details
France	• Arms transfers	Mistral-2 air defense systems
Italy	• Arms transfers	A-109 Helicopters for security services (with Britain)
Jordan	• Military training	Trainees abroad
Netherlands	• Arms transfers	Surveillance radar, fire control radar
Sweden	• Arms transfers	Early warning network
Switzerland	• Arms transfers	Pilatus PC-9 trainer aircraft
UK	• Arms transfers	Challenger tanks, Piranha APCs, Lynx 300 helicopters (with Italy), Martello 743D air defense radar (with Italy), missile corvettes, upgrading Jaguar aircraft, early warning network, early warning simulators
US	• Arms transfers	Tank ammunition, early warning network
	• Military training	Foreign advisers/instructors/serving personnel

Arms Sales and Security Assistance Extended

Country	Type	Details
UK	• Facilities	Use of airfields
US	• Facilities	Airfields at Masira, Seeb, al-Khasb, Thamarit; storage facilities and prepositioning of US Army and Air Force support equipment; naval facilities at Masira and Ghanam Peninsula; communications center

Foreign Military Cooperation

Type	Details
• Foreign forces	Some 250 US soldiers
• Joint maneuvers	Egypt, GCC countries, UK, US
• Security agreement	GCC countries, Iran, US

Weapons of Mass Destruction

NBC Capabilities

Nuclear capability

No known nuclear activity. Signatory to the NPT.

Chemical weapons (CW) and protective equipment

No known CW activities. Party to the CWC.

Biological weapons (BW)

No known BW activities. Party to the BWC.

Armed Forces

Major Changes: Inauguration of the GCC joint communication network, part of the GCC joint early warning system. The Omani Army received 20 new Challenger II MBTs.

Order-of-Battle

Year	1996	1997	1999	2000	2001
General data					
• Personnel (regular)	29,600	34,000*	34,000	34,000	34,000
Ground Forces					
• Number of brigades	4	4	4	4	4
• Total number of battalions	22	18*	18	18	18

Order-of-Battle *(continued)*

Year	1996	1997	1999	2000	2001
• Tanks	156	178	131(181)	131(181)	151(201)
• APCs/AFVs	142	135 (166)	135 (166)	~135 (~165)	~225* (~255)
• Artillery	177	148(154)*	148(154)	148(154)	148 (154)
Air Force					
• Combat aircraft	37	31(47)	31(47)	31	29(30)
• Transport aircraft	44	38(42)	38(42)	38(42)	41(45)
• Helicopters	37	37	37	35	41
Air Defense Forces					
• Light SAM launchers	54	58	58	58	58
Navy					
• Combat vessels	14	9	9	9	9
• Patrol craft	18	23	23	22	22

Note: Beginning with 1997, data refers to quantities in active service. The number in parentheses refers to the total inventory.
*Due to change in estimate.

Personnel

	Regular	Reserves	Total
Ground Forces	25,000		25,000
Air Force	5,000		5,000
Navy	4,000		4,000
Total	**34,000**		**34,000**
Paramilitary			
• Tribal force (Firqat)	3,500		3,500
• Police/border police (operating aircraft, helicopters and PBs)			7,000
• Royal Household (including Royal Guard, Royal Yachts and Royal Flight)			6,500

Ground Forces

Formations

	Independent brigades/groups	Independent battalions/ Regiments
Royal Guard	1 HQ	
Armored	1 HQ	2+1 royal guard
Infantry (Partly Mechanized)	2 HQ	8+2 royal guard
Reconnaissance		2 (1 inf.+1 armd.)
Paratroops/ Special Forces		1+2 royal guard
Artillery		4
Air Defense		1
Total	**4**	**23**

Tanks

Model	Quantity	In service	Since	Notes
MBTs				
High quality				
• Challenger-2	38	38	1995	
Medium and low quality				
• M60 A3	93	43	1990	
• M60 A1	6	6	1980	
• Chieftain	27	27	1982	
Subtotal	126	76		
Light tanks				
• Scorpion	37	37	1980	Being upgraded
Total	**201**	**151**		

APCs/AFVs

Model	Quantity	In service	Since	Notes
APCs				
• GKN-Defense Piranha	80	80	1995	
• BTR-80	+	+	1994	Small number
• AT-105 Saxon	15	15	1986	
• Fahd	31	+		Unconfirmed
• Spartan	23	23	1980	Including 3 Samson ARVs, 4 Sultan CPs
• VAB	23	23	1986	9 are also listed under Air Defense
Subtotal	~175	~145		

APCs/AFVs *(continued)*

Model	Quantity	In service	Since	Notes
IFVs				
• V-150 Commando	20	20	1982	
Reconnaissance				
• VBL	51	51	1996	
• VBC-90	9	9	1986	
Subtotal	60	60		
Total	**~255**	**~225**		
Future procurement				
• Piranha	80			Delivery to begin in 2001

Artillery

Model	Quantity	In service	Since	Notes
Self-propelled guns and howitzers				
• 155mm G-6	24	24	1995	
• 155mm M109 A2	15	15	1986	
Subtotal	39	39		
Towed guns and howitzers				
• 155mm FH-70	12	12	1986	
• 130mm Type 59	12	12	1981	
• 122mm D-30	25	25		
• 105mm L-118	42	36	1976	
Subtotal	91	85		
Mortars, under 160mm				
• 120mm	12	12	1976	
• 107mm M30 SP	12	12	1986	Mounted on M106
Subtotal	24	24		
Total	**154**	**148**		

Logistics and Engineering Equipment

Challenger ARVs (4); Samson ARVs (3); tank transporters (9)

Anti-Tank Missiles

Model	Launchers	Missiles	Since	Notes
• BGM-71A TOW	18	+		
• MILAN	32	+	1984	
Total	**50**			
Future procurement				
• TOW-2A				Delivery until 2003

Air Force

Order-of-Battle

Category	Quantity	In service	Notes
• Combat	30	29	
• Transport	45	41	
• Helicopters	41	41	

Combat Aircraft

Model	Quantity	In service	Since	Notes
Multi-role				
• SEPECAT Jaguar S(O) Mk 1/Mk 2/T2	19	18	1977	To be upgraded to Jaguar 97 standard
• HAWK Mk-203	11	11	1994	
Total	**30**	**29**		
Future procurement				
• F-16				Under negotiations

Transport Aircraft

Model	Quantity	In service	Since	Notes
• BAe-111	3	3	1974	
• BN-2 Defender/Islander	4	0	1974	
• C-130H Hercules	3	3	1981	
• CN-235	3	3	1993	With police
• DC-8	1	1	1982	
• DC-10	1	1		
• DHC-5D Buffalo	4	4	1982	
• Dornier Do-228-100	2	2	1984	Used by police air wing for maritime surveillance and border patrol
• Gulfstream	1	1	1992	
• Learjet	1	1	1981	With police service
• Mystère-Falcon 20	1	1	1983	
• Mystère-Falcon 10	1	1	1980	
• Mystère-Falcon 900	2	2		
• Skyvan Srs 3M	18	18	1970	7 employed in maritime patrol role
Total	**45**	**41**		

Training and Liaison Aircraft

Model	Quantity	In service	Since	Notes
Jet trainers				
• BAC-167 Strikemaster Mk 82	12	12	1967	
• Hawk Mk-103	4	4	1993	
Subtotal	16	16		
Piston/Turbo-prop				
• AS-202 Bravo	4	4	1976	
• Mushshak	3	3	1994	
• MFI-17 Safari	7	7		
Subtotal	14	14		
Total	**30**	**30**		
Future procurement				
• PC-9	12			

Helicopters

Model	Quantity	In service	Since	Notes
Medium transport				
• AB-205	20	20	1970	
• Bell 212	3	3	1976	
• AB-214	10	10	1974	
• AS-332 Super Puma/ SA-330 Puma	5	5	1982	
Subtotal	38	38		
Light transport				
• Bell 206 JetRanger	3	3	1970	
Total	**41**	**41**		
Future procurement				
• A-109				
• Super Lynx 300				

Miscellaneous Aircraft

Model	Quantity	In service	Since	Notes
Maritime surveillance				
• Skyvan Srs 3M	7	7	1970	Also listed under Transport Aircraft
• Dornier DO-228-100	2	2	1984	Also listed under Transport Aircraft
Target drones				
• TTL BTT-3 Banshee	53	+		

Advanced Armament

Air-to-air missiles

R-550 Magic (70), AIM-9P/J Sidewinder (330)

Bombs

BL-755 CBU

Note: Numbers in parentheses refer to number of units purchased, not to current inventory levels.

Air Force Infrastructure

Aircraft shelters

For all combat aircraft, at Masira and Thamarit

Military airfields: **6**

Bureimi, Dukha, Masira, Muscat (Seeb), Salala, Thamarit

Air Defense Forces

Surface-to-Air Missiles

Model	Batteries	Launchers	Since	Notes
Light missiles				
• Rapier Mk2		28		Upgraded
• Javelin		30	1989	
• Tigercat		*		
Total		**58**		
Shoulder- launched missiles				
• Blowpipe		+	1982	
• SA-7 (Grail)		34	1988	
Total		**~35**		
Future procurement				
• Mistral-2				On Panhard VBL

Other Air Defense Systems

Model	Quantity	In service	Since	Notes
Air defense systems (missiles, radars and guns)				
• Skyguard AD system	+	+	1995	With 35mm guns
Short-range guns				
• 40mm Bofors L-60	12	12	1987	
• 35mm Oerlikon Contraves	+	+	1995	With Skyguard
• 23mm ZU 23x2	4	4	1980	
• 20mm 20x2 VDAA SP	9	9	1986	On VAB
Total	**25**	**25**		

Other Air Defense Systems *(continued)*

Model	Quantity	In service	Since	Notes
Radars				
• AR-15	+	+		
• S-713 Martello 3D	2	2		
• S-600	+	+		
• Watchman	+	+		

Navy

Combat Vessels

Type	Quantity	Length (m.)/ displacement (t.)	Notes/ armament
Missile corvettes			
• Qahir class (Vosper Thornycroft)	2	83.7/1,450	1xHelicopter 8xExocet MM40 SSMs 1x8 Crotale-NG 1x76mm gun 2x20mm guns 6x324mm torpedoes
MFPBs			
• Dhofar class (Province class)	4	56.7/394	6-8 Exocet MM40 SSMs 1x76mm gun 2x40mm guns 2x12.7mm MGs
Gunboats			
• al-Bushra (P-400)	3	54.5/475	1x76mm gun 1x40mm gun 2x20mm guns 2x12.7mm MGs
Total	**9**		

Patrol Craft

Type	Quantity	Length (m.)/ displacement (t.)	Notes/ armament
• CG-29	3	28.9/84	2x20mm guns with police
• CG-27	1	24/53	1x20mm gun with police
• Seeb (Vosper Thornycroft)	4	25/60.7	1x20mm gun 2x7.62mm MGs
• Zahra (Emsworth type)	2	16.0/18	2x7.62mm MGs with police
• Zahra (Watercraft type)	3	13.9/16	2x7.62mm MG with police
• P-2000	1	20.8/80	1x12.7mm MG with police
• P-1903	1	19.2/26	2x12.7mm MGs with police
• Vosper Thornycroft	5	22.9/50	1x20mm gun with police
• Dheeb al Bahar (D-59116)	2	23/65	1x12.7mm MG with police
Total	**22**		

Landing Craft

Type	Quantity	Length (m.)/ displacement (t.)	Notes/ armament
• Nasr al Bahar (Brooke Marine LST)	1	93/2,500	Helicopter deck 4x40mm guns 2x20mm guns 2x12.7mm MGs 400 tons or 7 tanks; 240 troops; 2 LCVP
• Al-Neemran (LCU)	1	25.5/30	
• Vosper 230ton LCM	3	33.0/230	100 tons
Total	**5**		

Auxiliary Vessels

Type	Quantity	Length (m.)/ displacement (t.)	Notes/ armament
• Mabrukah (Brooke Marine training ship)	1	62/900	1x40mm gun 2x20mm guns helicopter deck ex-royal yacht
• Al-Sultan (Conoship Groningen)	1	65.7/1,380 dwt	
• Coastal freighter	1		
• Survey craft	1	15.5/23.6	
• Diving craft	1	18/13	
• Harbor craft	3	18/13	

Naval Infrastructure

Naval bases: 4

Mina Raysut (Salala), al-Khasb, Muscat, Wuddam

Ship maintenance and repair facilities

Muscat

13. PALESTINIAN AUTHORITY

General Data

This section includes information on the Palestinian Authority and Palestinian security organizations inside the Palestinian Authority. It does not cover Palestinians living elsewhere.

Official Name: Palestinian National Authority (PA)
Chairman: Yasser Arafat
Chief of Security Forces: formally General Abd al-Rizak al-Majaida

Area: 400 sq. km. (Gaza), 5,800 sq. km. (West Bank). By the terms of the Interim Agreement, the West Bank is divided into three areas, designated A, B, and C. The PA has civilian responsibility for Palestinians in all three areas, exclusive internal security responsibility for Area A (18.2%), and shared security responsibility for Area B (24.8%). Israel maintains full security responsibility for the remaining 57% (area C).
Population: Gaza - 1,120,000 (estimate); West Bank-2,000,000 (estimate)

Demography

Religious groups		
Sunni Muslims	2,808,000	90%
Christians	312,000	10%

Economic Data

		1996	1997	1998	1999	2000
GDP (current price)	$ bn	3.90	3.95	4.03	4.75	4.60
GDP per capita	$	1,470	1,406	1,394	1,578	1,474
Real GDP growth (at 1986 prices)	%	-1.7	-0.8	3.8	6.0	-7.5
Consumer price index	%	7.7	6.1	5.6	5.5	2.8
External debt	$ bn	NA	NA	NA	NA	NA
Balance of payments						
• Exports fob	$ bn	0.51	0.48	0.4	NA	NA
• Imports cif	$ bn	2.53	2.25	2.38	NA	NA
• Current account balance	$ bn	-0.9	-0.76	-0.75	NA	NA

Economic Data *(continued)*

		1996	1997	1998	1999	2000
Government expenditure						
• Total expenditure	$ bn	0.78	0.87	0.87	0.96	0.96
• Security expenditure	$ bn	0.25	0.25	0.30	0.50	NA
• Real change in security expenditure	%	45.9	0.8	20.0	66.6	NA
• Security expenditure/ GDP	%	6.36	6.32	7.44	10.52	NA
Population	m	2.65	2.81	2.89	3.01	3.12
Official exchange rate (Israeli currency)	NIS:$1	3.19	3.45	3.80	4.15	4.07

Sources: EIU Quarterly Report, EIU Country Profile, IMF International Financial Statistical Yearbook, SIPRI Yearbook

Arms Procurement and Security Assistance Received

Country	Type	Details
Afganistan	• Military training	Trainees abroad
Algeria	• Military training	Trainees abroad
Egypt	• Military training	Trainees abroad (police, and civil defense)
Iran	• Military training	Trainees abroad
Libya	• Military training	Trainees abroad
Morocco	• Military training	Trainees abroad
Netherlands	• Arms transfers	Light arms
Pakistan	• Military training	Trainees abroad
Tunisia	• Military training	Trainees abroad
Yemen	• Military training	Trainees abroad

Defense Production

	M	P	A
Army equipment			
• 120mm, 82mm, 60mm mortars and mortars ammunition	√		
• Various explosive charges	√		

Note: M - manufacture (indigenously developed)
P - production under license
A - assembly

Security Forces

Major Changes: Since the outbreak of the events in September 2000, Palestinian forces operated several types of weapons, including mortars and LAW anti-tank missiles. They also acquired 107mm MRLs and Strela (SA-7) shoulder launched SAMs. Their existing inventory of BRDM armored vehicles suffered damage and their number decreased. The Palestinian forces are reportedly organized in 6 regiments of unknown size. An important role is played by the Fatah's Tanzim, a popular militia force which is not an official part of the PA but loyal to Yasser Arafat.

Order-of-Battle

Year	1996	1997	1999	2000	2001
General data					
• Personnel (regular)	~30,000	~34,000	~34,000	~36,000	~45,000
Ground Forces					
• Regiments					6
• APCs/AFVs	45	45	45	45	~40
Aerial Police					
• Helicopters	2	2 (4)	2 (4)	2 (4)	2 (4)
Coastal Police					
• Patrol craft	-	7	13	10	13

Note: Beginning with 1997, data refers to quantities in active service. The number in parentheses refers to the total inventory.

Personnel

	Gaza	West Bank	Total	Notes
General Security Service branches				
Public Security	+	+	14,000	Also referred to as the "National Security Force"
Coastal Police	+	+	1,000	
Aerial Police	+	+	+	Rudimentary unit operating VIP helicopters
Civil Police	+	+	10,000	The "Blue Police" — a law enforcement agency;

Personnel *(continued)*

	Gaza	West Bank	Total	Notes
				operates the 700-strong "rapid deployment special police"
Preventive Security Force	+	+	5,000	Plainclothes internal security force
General Intelligence	+	+	3,000	Intelligence gathering organization
Military Intelligence	+	+	+	Unrecognized preventive security force; includes the Military Police.
Civil Defense	+	+	+	Emergency and rescue service
Additional security forces				
Presidential Security	+	+	3,000	Elite unit responsible for Arafat's personal security
Special Security Force	+	+	+	Unrecognized intelligence organization
Total	**~25,000**	**~20,000**	**~45,000**	

Note: The Palestinian security services include several organizations under the "Palestinian Directorate of Police Force", recognized in the Cairo and Washington agreements. In addition, there are some organizations that report directly to Arafat. Some of the security organizations (particularly the "Blue Police") have little or no military significance. They are mentioned here because of PA's unique organizational structure, and because it is difficult to estimate the size of the total forces that do have military significance. See also under "non-governmental organizations".

Ground Forces

Formations

	Divisional HQ	Regiments	Notes
Infantry	1	6	
Total	**1**	**6**	

APCs/AFVs

Model	Quantity	In service	Since	Notes
Reconnaissance				
• BRDM-2	45	~40	1995	Some damaged

Artillery

Model	Quantity	In service	Since	Notes
Mortars, under 160mm				
• 120mm	+	+	2000	
• 81mm	+	+	2000	
• 52mm/60mm	+	+	2000	
MRLs				
•107mm	+	+	2000	
Total	+	+		

Anti-Tank Missiles

Model	Launchers	Missiles	Since	Notes
• RPG-7	+		2000	
• LAW	+		2000	

Aerial Police

Helicopters

Model	Quantity	In service	Since	Notes
Medium transport				
•Mi-8/17	4	2	1996	

Air Defense Forces

Surface-to-Air Missiles

Model	Batteries	Launchers	Since	Notes
Shoulder-launched missiles				
• SA-7		+	2000	
• FIM-92 Stinger		*	2000	Alleged

Other Air Defense Systems

Model	Quantity	In service	Since	Notes
Short-range guns				
• 23mm AD guns	+	+		Alleged

Coastal Police

Patrol Craft

Type	Quantity	Length (m.)/ displacement (t.)	Notes/ armament
• Gindallah	1		
• P-76	1		
• Volvo	2	8.0/5	7.62mm MG 2 non-operational
• Zodiak Mk 3	0		3 non-operational
• Zodiak Mk 5	4	5.8m	7.62mm MG 6 non-operational
• Zodiak Mk 7	2		
• Sillinger	3		
Total	**13**		

Note: some of the boats were damaged during the events since September 2000

Major Non-Governmental Paramilitary Forces

Pro-governmental Organizations

Name	Active	Notes
• Tanzim (al-Fatah)	Several thousand	Loyal to Yasser Arafat, but not an official organ of the PA

Anti-governmental Organizations

Name	Active	Notes
• Hamas	several hundred	
• Islamic Jihad	several hundred	

14. QATAR

General Data

Official Name of the State: State of Qatar
Head of State: Shaykh Hamad ibn Khalifa al-Thani
Prime Minister: Abdallah ibn Khalifa al-Thani
Minister of Defense: Shaykh Hamad ibn Khalifa al-Thani
Commander in Chief of the Armed Forces: Shaykh Hamad ibn Khalifa al-Thani
Chief of General Staff: Brigadier General Hamad bin Ali al-Attiyah
Commander of the Ground Forces: Colonel Saif Ali al-Hajiri
Commander of the Air Force: General Ali Saeed al-Hawal al-Marri
Commander of the Navy: Captain Said al-Suwaydi

Area: 11,437 sq. km.
Population: 600,000

Demography

Ethnic groups		
Arabs	240,000	40.0%
Pakistanis	108,000	18.0%
Indians	108,000	18.0%
Persians	60,000	10.0%
Others (mostly Southeast Asians)	84,000	14.0%
Religious groups		
Sunni Muslims	421,800	70.3%
Shi'ite Muslims	145,800	24.3%
Others	32,400	5.4%

Economic Data

		1996	1997	1998	1999	2000
GDP (current prices)	$ bn	9.1	11.3	10.5	14.1	16.4
GDP per capita	$	15,167	18,833	17,500	23,500	27,333
Real GDP growth	%	4.8	24.0	2.0	0.2	4.3
Consumer price index	%	7.4	2.8	2.6	2.1	1.0
External debt	$ bn	7.2	9.0	9.8	11.0	13.0

Economic Data *(continued)*

		1996	1997	1998	1999	2000
Balance of payments						
• Exports fob	$ bn	3.83	3.85	5.03	7.21	10.29
• Imports fob	$ bn	2.58	3.0	3.1	2.25	3.1
• Current account balance (including services and income)	$ bn	-1.33	-1.68	-0.46	2.17	3.82
Government expenditure						
• Total expenditure	$ bn	4.5	4.84	4.12	4.23	4.23
• Defense expenditure	$ bn	NA	NA	NA	NA	NA
• Real change in defense expenditure	%	NA	NA	NA	NA	NA
• Defense expenditure /GDP	%	NA	NA	NA	NA	NA
Population	m	0.6	0.6	0.6	0.6	0.6
Official exchange rate	QR: $1	3.64	3.64	3.64	3.64	3.64

Sources: EIU Quarterly Report, EIU Country Profile, IMF International Financial Statistical Yearbook, SIPRI Yearbook.

Arms Procurement and Security Assistance Received

Country	Type	Details
France	• Military training	Advisers
	• Arms transfers	APCs, combat aircraft, AMX-30 MBTs, Crotale SAMs, Mica and Magic II AAMs
Jordan	• Arms transfers	AB-2 Aigis armored vehicles
Sweden	• Arms transfers	GCC early warning system
UK	• Arms transfers	Rapier SAMs, combat vessels, aircraft, APCs
	• Military training	Advisers/instructors
US	• Arms transfers	GCC early warning system
	• Military training	Advisers, trainees abroad
	• Facilities	Construction and upgrading of air base

Arms Sales and Security Assistance Extended

Country	Type	Details
Algeria	• Arms transfers	Vehicles, night vision equipment
France	• Facilities	Training facilities, deployment of equipment
Spain	• Arms transfers	F-5 aircraft
US	• Facilities	Transportation equipment, deployment of maritime patrol aircraft, pre-positioning for an armored brigade

Foreign Military Cooperation

Type	Details
• Forces deployed abroad	Troops part of GCC "Peninsula Shield" rapid deployment force in Saudi Arabia
• Foreign forces in country	50 US troops
• Joint maneuvers	France, GCC countries, Italy, UK, US, Yemen
• Security agreement	Bahrain, France, Italy, Iran, Kuwait, Oman, Saudi Arabia

Weapons of Mass Destruction

NBC Capabilities

Nuclear capability

No known nuclear activity. Party to the NPT.

Chemical weapons and protective equipment

No known CW activities. Party to the CWC.

Biological weapons

No known BW activities. Party to the BWC.

Armed Forces

Major Changes: Inauguration of the GCC joint communication network, which is part of the GCC joint early warning system. No other major change was recorded in the Qatari order-of-battle.

Order-of-Battle

Year	1996	1997	1999	2000	2001
General data					
• Personnel (regular)	10,300	11,800	11,800	11,800	11,800
Ground Forces					
• Number of brigades		1*	1	2	2
• Number of regiments	1	1	1		
• Total number of battalions	7	10*	10	11	11
• Tanks	24	24	44	44	44
• APCs/AFVs	310	230(310)*	222(302)	~260(338)	~260(338)
• Artillery (including MRLs)	37	56*	56	56	56

Order-of-Battle *(continued)*

Year	1996	1997	1999	2000	2001
Air Force					
• Combat aircraft	14	9	14	18	18
• Transport aircraft	7	8	8	8	7 (8)
• Helicopters	41	32*	31	31	30(31)
Air Defense Forces					
• Light SAM launchers	29	48*	48	48	51
Navy					
• Combat vessels	5	7	7	7	7
• Patrol crafts	48	44	36	26	26

Note: Beginning with 1997, data refers to quantities in active service. The number in parentheses refers to the total inventory.
* Due to change in estimate.

Personnel

	Regular	Total
Ground Forces	8,500	8,500
Air Force	1,500	1,500
Navy (including Marine Police)	1,800	1,800
Total	**11,800**	**11,800**
Paramilitary		
• Armed Police	8,000	

Ground Forces

Formations

	Independent brigades/groups	Independent battalions	Battalions in brigades
Armored	1		1 armd., 1 mech., 1 aty.
Mechanized		4	
Royal Guard	1		3 inf.
Special forces		1	
Artillery		2	
Total	**2**	7	

Tanks

Model	Quantity	In service	Since	Notes
MBTs				
Medium and low quality				
• AMX-30	44	44	1978/1996	
Total	**44**	**44**		
Future procurement				
• Challenger	50			Under negotiation
• Leclerc	50-100			Under negotiation

APCs/AFVs

Model	Quantity	In service	Since	Notes
APCs				
• VAB	134	134	1978	4 mortar carriers, 24 mounted with HOT ATGM
• Fahd	10	~6		
• Saracen	25	6	1970	
Subtotal	169	~150		
IFVs				
• Piranha II	40	40	1998	36 with LAV 90mm guns, 2 CMP and 2 ARV
• AMX-10P/VCI	45	45	1978	
• V-150 Commando	8	8	1986	
Subtotal	93	93		
Reconnaissance				
• VBL	16	16	1994	
• AMX 10RC			1981	Included with other models of AMX-10
• Engesa EE-9	20	0	1978	
• Saladin	30	0	1970	
• Ferret	10	0	1968	
Subtotal	76	16		
Total	**338**	**~260**		
Future procurement				
• AB-2 Aigis	+			Under negotiations

Artillery

Model	Quantity	In service	Since	Notes
Self-propelled guns and howitzers				
• 155mm Mk F-3 (AMX)	22	22	1984	
Towed guns and howitzers				
• 155mm G-5	12	12	1991	
Mortars, under 160mm				
• 120mm Brandt	15	15	1993	
• 81mm VPM SP	4	4	1977	Mounted on VAB APCs
Subtotal	19	19		
MRLs				
• 122mm BM-21	+	+		
• Astros II	3	3	1992	127mm SS-30 or 180mm SS-40
Total	**56**	**56**		

Anti-Tank Missiles

Model	Launchers	Missiles	Since	Notes
• HOT	48	+	1978	24 are mounted on VAB
• MILAN	60-100	+	1987	
Total	**~108**			

Anti-Tank Guns

Model	Quantity	In Service	Since	Notes
• 84mm Carl Gustav light recoilless rifle	+	+	1978	

Air Force

Order-of-Battle

Category	Quantity	In service	Notes
• Combat	18	18	
• Transport	8	7	
• Helicopters	31	30	

Combat Aircraft

Model	Quantity	In service	Since	Notes
Advanced multi-role				
• Mirage 2000	12	12	1997	
Multi-role				
• Mirage F1-E/B	6	6	1984	To be sold; 7 planes already sold to Spain
Total	**18**	**18**		

Transport Aircraft

Model	Quantity	In service	Since	Notes
• Airbus 340	1	1	1993	
• Boeing 727	1	1	1979	
• Boeing 707	2	2	1977	
• BN-2 Islander	1	1	1986	
• Mystère-Falcon 900	3	2	1991	
Total	**8**	**7**		

Training and Liaison Aircraft

Model	Quantity	In service	Since	Notes
Jet trainers				
• Alpha jet	6	6	1980	
Total	**6**	**6**		
Future procurement				
• Hawk 100	15-18		1996	Not finalized

Helicopters

Model	Quantity	In service	Since	Notes
Attack				
• SA-342 Gazelle	13	12	1983	2 employed as light helicopters with police
Medium transport				
• AS-332 Super Puma/ AS-532 Cougar	6	6	1987	
• Westland Commando Mk 2/Mk 3	4	4	1982	4 out of 12 used for VIP transport
Subtotal	10	10		
Naval combat				
• Westland Commando Mk 2/ Mk 3	8	8	1982	
Total	**31**	**30**		
Future procurement				
• Naval combat helicopter				

Miscellaneous Aircraft

Model	Quantity	In service	Since	Notes
Target drones				
• TTL BTT-3 Banshee	+	+		Unconfirmed

Advanced Armament

Air-to-air missiles
Mica (144), R-550 Magic II (272), R-530 (128)
Air-to-ground missiles
AM-39 Exocet, AS-30L (128)

Note: Number in parentheses refers to the quantity of missiles purchased, not to current inventory levels.

Air Force Infrastructure

Military airfields: **2**
Doha; Al Ghariyeh

Air Defense Forces

Surface-to-Air Missiles

Model	Launchers	Since	Notes
Light missiles			
• Mistral	24	1995	
• Rapier	18	1984	
• Roland 2	9	1988	Number unconfirmed
Total	**51**		
Shoulder-launched missiles			
• FIM-92A Stinger	12	1989	
• Blowpipe	6	1986	
Total	**18**		
Command and Control			
• GCC Aerial Early Warning System	+	+	
Future procurement			
• Patriot PAC-3			Under negotiation
• Shorts Starburst			Suspended

Navy

Combat Vessels

Type	Quantity	Length (m.)/ displacement (t.)	Notes/ armament
MFPBs			
• Barzan class (Vita Vosper Thornycroft)	4	56.3/376	8xMM 40 Exocet SSMs 8xMistral SAMs 1x76mm gun 1x30mm gun
• Damsah class (Combattante III)	3	56/345	8xMM 40 Exocet SSMs 1x76mm gun 2x40mm guns 4x30mm guns
Total	7		

Patrol Craft

Type	Quantity	Length (m.)/ displacement (t.)	Notes/ armament
• Helmatic (M-160)	3	16/20	
• Damen (Polycat 1450)	3	14.5/18	1x20mm gun
• Crestitalia (MV-45)	4	14.5/17	1x20mm gun with police
• Spear class	12	9.1/4.3	
• P-1200	3	11.9/12.7	with police
Total	**26**		

Coastal Defense

Type	Batteries	Notes
• MM-40 Exocet	3-4	

Naval Infrastructure

Naval bases:	**2**
Doha, Halul Island	

15. SAUDI ARABIA

General Data

Official Name of the State: The Kingdom of Saudi Arabia
Head of State: King Fahd ibn Abd al-Aziz al-Saud
Prime Minister: King Fahd ibn Abd al-Aziz al-Saud
First Deputy Prime Minister and Heir Apparent: Crown Prince Abdallah ibn Abd al-Aziz al-Saud
Defense and Aviation Minister: Prince Sultan ibn Abd al-Aziz al-Saud
Chief of General Staff: General Salih ibn Ali al-Muhaya
Commander of the Ground Forces: Lieutenant General Sultan ibn Ali al-Mutayri
Commander of the National Guard: Crown Prince Abdallah ibn Abd al-Aziz al-Saud
Commander of the Air Force: Lieutenant General Muhammad ibn Abd al-Aziz al-Hunaydi
Commander of the Air Defense Forces: Lieutenant General Majid ibn Talhab al-Qutaibi
Commander of the Navy: Vice Admiral Talal ibn Salem al-Mufadhi

Area: 2,331,000 sq. km.
Population: 20,500,000

Demography

Ethnic groups		
Arabs	18,737,000	91.4%
Afro-Arabs	1,025,000	5.0%
Others	738,000	3.6%
Religious groups		
Sunni Muslims	18,880,000	92.1%
Shi'ite Muslims	1,025,000	5.0%
Others (mainly Christians)	595,000	2.9%
Nationality		
Saudis	14,904,000	72.7%
Others	5,596,000	27.3%

Economic Data

		1996	1997	1998	1999	2000
GDP (current price)	$ bn	141.3	146.5	128.4	142.9	165.1
GDP per capita	$	7,515	7,512	6,356	7,180	8,053
Real GDP growth	%	1.4	2.7	1.6	0.4	4.1
Consumer price index	%	1.2	0.1	-0.4	-1.6	-0.7
External debt	$ bn	17.7	24.4	28.5	28.5	28.5
Balance of payments						
Exports fob	$ bn	60.7	60.7	38.8	50.7	77.1
Imports fob	$ bn	25.4	26.4	27.5	25.7	31.7
Current account balance (including services and income)	$ bn	0.7	0.3	-13.1	0.4	14.8
Government expenditure						
Total expenditure	$ bn	40.05	48.33	52.34	48.27	54.13
Defense expenditure	$ bn	13.20	17.93	16.41	14.52	NA
Real change in defense expenditure	%	-0.10	35.76	-8.46	-11.49	NA
Defense expenditure/ GDP	%	9.34	12.23	12.77	10.16	NA
Population	m	18.8	19.5	20.2	19.9	20.5
Official exchange rate	SR:1$	3.75	3.75	3.75	3.75	3.75

Sources: EIU Quarterly Report, EIU Country Profile, IMF International Financial Statistical Yearbook, SIPRI Yearbook

Arms Procurement and Security Assistance Received

Country	Type	Details
Belgium	• Arms transfers	Turrets for LAV IFVs
Canada	• Arms transfers	LAV APCs/IFVs, naval simulators
France	• Arms transfers	Upgrading SAMs, upgrading F-2000 missile frigates, Lafayette missile frigates
	• Military training	Foreign advisers/instructors/serving personnel; trainees abroad for Cougar helicopters
	• Maintenance aid	Naval vessels
Germany	• Arms transfers	Cougar helicopters
Italy	• Arms transfers	AB 412 helicopters
PRC	• Military training	Foreign advisers/instructors/serving personnel for CSS-2 missiles (unconfirmed)
Sweden	• Arms transfers	Early warning network

Arms Procurement and Security Assistance Received *(continued)*

Country	Type	Details
UK	• Arms transfers	Mortars, ARM missiles
	• Military training	Foreign advisers/instructors/serving personnel; trainees abroad
US	• Arms transfers	F-15 combat aircraft, AIM-120 AAMs, ATGMs, SAMs, M1A2 tanks, surveillance radars, early warning network, upgrading of AIM-9L and AIM-7M AAMs, upgrading of GBU-10 bombs, medium-caliber ammunition, radio systems
	• Maintenance aid	Technical assistance and maintenance
	• Military training	Foreign advisers/instructors/serving personnel; trainees abroad

Arms Sales and Security Assistance Extended

Country	Type	Details
Lebanon	• Arms transfers	AMX-30 tanks
Tunisia	• Arms transfers	AMX-30 tanks
US	• Facilities	HQ at Riyadh, facilities for combat aircraft at Taif and Dhahran air bases

Foreign Military Cooperation

Type	Details
• Joint maneuvers	Egypt, France, GCC countries, Pakistan, UK, US
• Foreign forces	GCC "Peninsula Shield" rapid deployment force: 7,000-10,000 at Hafr al-Batin; mostly Saudis and soldiers from other GCC countries. As of September 2000, there are some 7,000 US soldiers stationed in Saudi Arabia.

Defense Production

	M	P	A
Army equipment			
• al-Fahd 8x8 APC	√		
• Small arms ammunition	√		
Air Force equipment			
• Some accessories and components for foreign-made aircraft, flares and chaff		√	

Defense Production (continued)

	M	P	A
Electronics			
• Radio transceivers			√
• parts for EW equipment			√
• Components of aircraft radars			√
• Hand-held thermal imager/binocular		√	

Note: M - manufacture (indigenously developed)
P - production under license
A - assembly

Weapons of Mass Destruction

NBC Capabilities

Nuclear capability

No known nuclear activity. Party to the NPT.

Chemical weapons and protective equipment

No known CW activities. Party to the CWC.

Personal protective equipment; decontamination units; US-made CAM chemical detection systems; Fuchs (Fox) NBC detection vehicles

Biological weapons

No known BW activities. Party to the BWC.

Ballistic Missiles

Model	Launchers	Missiles	Since	Notes
• CSS-2	8-12	30-50	1988	Number of launchers unconfirmed

Armed Forces

Major Changes: Inauguration of the GCC joint communication network, which is part of the GCC joint early warning system. The Saudi Arabian National Guard received its 90mm-armed LAVs – the last of an order of 1,117. The Saudi Arabian Army will receive almost two thousand TOW-2B ATGMs. Saudi Arabia agreed to sell some of its old AMX-30 MBTs to Lebanon and Tunisia. The Air Force received its first AB-412 helicopters out of an order of 44. The Navy saw the launching of its first of three Al-Riad type missile frigates. The ship will be delivered in 2002.

Order-of-Battle

Year	1996	1997	1999	2000	2001
General data					
• Personnel (regular)	161,000	165,000	165,000	171,500	171,500
• SSM launchers	8-12	8-12	8-12	8-12	8-12
Ground Forces					
• Number of brigades	18	18	20	20	20
• Tanks	1,015	865	865	750	750
		(1,015)	(1,015)	(1,015)	(1,015)
• APCs/AFVs	~4,100	5,220*	~5,310	~5,300	~4,500
			(~5,440)	(~5,440)	(~5,300)
• Artillery (incl. MRLs)	770	~410	~410	~410	~410
		(~580)*	(~780)	(~780)	(~780)
Air Force					
• Combat aircraft	249	321*	~345	~355	~360
					(~365)
• Transport aircraft	76	61	61	61	42(55)
• Helicopters	180	175	160	160	214(216)
Air Defense Forces					
• Heavy SAM batteries	23	22	22	22	25
• Medium SAM batteries	16	16	16	16	21
Navy					
• Combat vessels	27	24	24	24	24
• Patrol craft	102	92*	80	74	74

Note: Beginning with 1997, data refers to quantities in active service. The number in parentheses refers to the total inventory.

* Due to change in estimate.

Personnel

	Regular	Reserves	Total
Ground Forces	75,000		75,000
Air Force	20,000		20,000
Air Defense	4,000		4,000
Navy (including a marine unit)	13,500		13,500
National Guard	57,000	20,000	77,000
Royal Guard	2,000		2,000
Total	**171,500**	**20,000**	**191,500**
Paramilitary			
• Mujahidun (affiliated with National Guard)			30,000
• Coast Guard	4,500		4,500
• Frontier Corps	10,500		10,500

Ground Forces

Formations

	Independent Brigades/Groups	Independent Battalions
Armored (Ground Forces)	4	
Mechanized (5 Ground Forces, 3 National Guard)	8	
Infantry (Royal Guard)	1	
Infantry (National Guard)	6	19
Marines		2
Airborne/ Special Forces (Ground Forces)	1	
Total	**20**	**21**

Note: Saudi ground forces comprise 10 brigades (5 mechanized, 4 armored, 1 airborne/infantry), plus one Royal Guard brigade; the National Guard has 9 brigades (3 mechanized, 6 infantry)

Tanks

Model	Quantity	In service	Since	Notes
MBTs				
High quality				
• M1A2	315	200	1993	115 in storage
Medium and low quality				
• M60 A3	400	400	1985	
• AMX-30	300	150	1975	
Subtotal	700	550		
Total	**1,015**	**750**		
Future procurement				
• Leclerc MBTs	355			Under negotiation

APCs/AFVs

Model	Quantity	In service	Since	Notes
APCs				
• Piranha APC	420	420	2000	Of which 34 are ENGs and 67 ARVs
• M113 A1/A2	1,600	1,600	1976/1981	
• AMX-10/AMX-10P	500	500	1975	Of which 90 are carrying ATGMs
• BMR-600	140	140	1985	With marines

APCs/AFVs *(continued)*

Model	Quantity	In service	Since	Notes
• Engesa EE-11 Urutu	+	+		
• M-3 (Panhard)	150	150		
Subtotal	~2,800	~2,800		
IFVs				
• Piranha IFV	570	570	1992	Of which 73 are 120mm TDA and 111 are ITVs
• M-2/M-3 Bradley	400	400		
• V-150 Commando	980	290	1977	690 in storage
• AML-60/90	350	~225	1969	
• Fox/Ferret	200	200		Possibly phased out
Subtotal	2,500	~1,700		
Total	**~5,300**	**~4,500**		
Future procurement				
• Al-Fahd AD-40-8-1	100			
• Piranha LAV-AG	130			

Artillery

Model	Quantity	In service	Since	Notes
Self-propelled guns and howitzers				
• 155mm M109 A2	280	110		
• 155mm GCT	51	51	1980	
Subtotal	331	161		
Towed guns and howitzers				
• 155mm M198	90	60	1982	
• 155mm M114	50	50	1980	
• 155mm FH-70	72	0		
• 105mm M102/ M101	100	0	1975	
Subtotal	312	110		
Mortars, under 160mm				
• 120mm TDA SP	73	73	2000	On Piranha
• 107mm M30	+	+	1981	
MRLs				
• Astros II	60	60		180mm SS-40 or 127mm SS-30
Total	**~780**	**~410**		
Artillery/mortar-locating radars				
• AN/TPQ-37	+	+		

Logistics and Engineering Equipment

M-123 Viper minefield crossing system, Aardvark Mk 3 flail, M-69 A1 bridging tanks, bridging equipment, AFV transporters (600), Piranha ARVs (67), Piranha ENG (34)

Anti-Tank Missiles

Model	Launchers	Missiles	Since	Notes
• Piranha ITV	111	+	2001	Listed also under APCs
• AMX-10P SP	90	+	1982	Listed also under APCs; carrying HOT
• VCC-1 SP	200	+		Carrying TOW
• BGM-71C Improved TOW/BGM-71D TOW II	750	+	1988	
• M-47 Dragon	1,000	+	1977	
Total	**2,150**	+		
Future procurement				
• TOW-2A		1,827		

Anti-Tank Guns

Model	Quantity	In service	Since	Notes
• 106mm M-40	50	50		
recoilless rifle				
• 84mm Carl Gustav light recoilless rifle	300	300		

Air Force

Order-of-Battle

Category	Quantity	In service	Notes
• Combat	~365	~360	
• Transport	55	42	
• Helicopters	216	214	

Combat Aircraft

Model	Quantity	In service	Since	Notes
Interceptors				
• F-15 C/D Eagle	91	85	1982	
• Tornado ADV (F Mk 3)	21	21	1989	
Subtotal	112	106		

Combat Aircraft *(continued)*

Model	Quantity	In service	Since	Notes
Advanced multi-role				
• F-15S	72	72	1995	
Multi-role				
• Tornado IDS (GR Mk 1/GR-1A)	90	90	1986	12 of which are reconnaissance
• F-5E/F	~75	~ 75	1973	Some also listed under reconnaissance
Subtotal	~165	~165		
Obsolete				
• F-5A/B	15	15		Mostly employed as trainer aircraft
Total	**~365**	**~360**		

Transport Aircraft

Model	Quantity	In service	Since	Notes
• C-130E/H Hercules	46	33	1970/1980	
• CN-235	5	5	1987	
• Mystère-Falcon 20	2	2		
• VC-140 JetStar	2	2	1969	
Total	**55**	**42**		

Training and Liaison Aircraft

Model	Quantity	In service	Since	Notes
Jet trainers				
• Hawk Mk65	28	28	1987	
• BAC-167 Strikemaster	30	0	1968	Possibly phased out
Subtotal	58	28		
Piston/Turbo-prop				
• Pilatus PC-9	50	50	1987	
• BAe Jetstream 31	2	2	1987	
• Cessna 172 G/H/L	12	12	1967	
Subtotal	64	64		
Total	**122**	**92**		
Future procurement				
• Hawk 100/200	20			Under negotiation

Helicopters

Model	Quantity	In service	Since	Notes
Attack				
• Bell 406CS	15	15	1990	In army aviation
• AH-64A Apache	12	12	1993	In army aviation
Subtotal	27	27		
Naval combat				
• AS-365 Dauphin 2/ AS-565MA	27	25	1986	Including 6 in Medevac role
• AS-532 SC Cougar	6	6	1992	
Subtotal	33	31		
Medium transport				
• S-70A Black Hawk/ Desert Hawk	37	37	1990	16 of which are Medevac
• AS-532 UC Cougar	18	18		At least 6 belong to Navy
• KV-107/KV-107 IIA	18	18	1979	
• AB-412	2	2	2001	Out of 16 ordered
• AB-212	29	29	1977	Number unconfirmed
• Bell 205	24	24		
Subtotal	128	128		
Light transport				
• AB-206 JetRanger	28	28	1967	
Total	**216**	**214**		
Future procurement				
• AB-412	16			Total order, being delivered

Miscellaneous Aircraft

Model	Quantity	In service	Since	Notes
Reconnaissance				
• Tornado IDS	12	12	1986	Also listed under Combat Aircraft
• RF-5E	8	8	1973	Also listed under Combat Aircraft
AEW/AWACS				
• E-3A AWACS	5	5	1986	
Tankers				
• KC-130H	7	7	1973	
• KE-3/Boeing 707	8	8	1986	
Target drones				
• TTL BTT-3 Banshee	+	+		
• MQM-74C Chukar II	+	+		

Advanced Armament

Air-to-air missiles
AIM-7F Sparrow (1,100); AIM-7M (1,000); AIM-9J/P Sidewinder (1,800); AIM-9L/M Sidewinder (1,500); AIM-9S (150); Red Top; Sky Flash (550)
Air-to-ground missiles
AGM-65A/D/G Maverick (1,700); ALARM (200); AM-39 Exocet; AS-15TT (220); Sea Eagle (350)
Bombs
CBU-86; CBU-87; BL-755 CBU; Paveway III (100); GBU-10/12/15
Future procurement
AIM-120 AMRAAM (500)

Note: Numbers in parentheses refer to quantity of units purchased, not to current inventory levels.

Air Force Infrastructure

Aircraft shelters
For combat aircraft
Military airfields : **15**
Abqaiq, al-Ahsa, Dhahran, Gizan, al-Hufuf, Jidda, Jubail, Khamis Mushayt, al-Kharj, Medina, Riyadh, Sharawra, al-Sulayyil, Tabuk, Taif.

Air Defense Forces

Surface-to-Air Missiles

Model	Batteries	Launchers	Since	Notes
Heavy missiles				
• MIM-104 Patriot	8		1991	
• MIM-23B Improved HAWK	17		1982	One used for training
Total	**25**			
Medium missiles				
• Crotale	16			Some are shelter-mounted for fixed sites
• Shahine I/II	5		1981	To be upgraded
Total	**21**			

Surface-to-Air Missiles *(continued)*

Model	Batteries	Launchers	Since	Notes
Shoulder-launched missiles				
• FIM-92A/C Stinger		400	1984	
• MIM-43A Redeye		500		
• Mistral		900		
Total		**1,800**		
Future procurement				
• FIM-92C Stinger		50		
• Crotale NG II				
• Mistral				

Other Air Defense Systems

Model	Quantity	In service	Since	Notes
Air defense systems (missiles, radars and guns)				
• 35mm Skyguard AD system	60	60		
Short-range guns				
• 35mm Oerlikon-Buhrle 35x2 GDF	156	156		Included in Skyguard
• 20mm M163 Vulcan SP	~100	~100		
• 30mm AMX-30 SA	52	18		
Total	**~310**	**~280**		
Radars				
• AN/FPS-117 (Seek Igloo)	17	17		
• AN/TPS-43G	28	28		
• AN/TPS-59	+	+		
• AN/TPS-63	35	35		
• AN/TPS-70	+	+		
Command and control system				
• GCC Aerial Early Warning system				Currently installed
Aerostat with airborne radars				
• LASS	+	+		

Navy

Combat Vessels

Type	Quantity	Length (m.)/ displacement (t.)	Notes/ armament
Missile frigates			
• Madina class (F-2000)	4	115.0/2,000	In process of upgrading (2 already upgraded) 1xSA-365 helicopter 8xOtomat SSMs 1x8 Crotale Naval SAMs 1x100mm gun 4x40mm guns 4x533mm torpedoes
Missile corvettes			
• Badr class (PCG-1 class)	4	74.7/870	8xHarpoon SSMs 1x76mm gun 2x20mm AD guns 1x20mm Phalanx 6x324mm torpedoes
MFPBs			
• Al-Siddiq (PGG-1 class)	9	58.1/425	4xHarpoon SSMs 1x76mm gun 2x20mm AD guns 1x20mm Phalanx
Mine warfare vessels			
• Addriyah (MSC-322 class minesweeper)	4	46.6/320	1x20mm AD gun magnetic sweepers
• al-Jawf (Sandown class)	3	52.7/450	2x30mm guns 2 PAP 104 Mk 5
Subtotal	7		
Total	**24**		
Future procurement			
• Lafayette class frigates (Type 3000)	3	128/4,100	Delivery in 2001 and 2003 1xAS-365 helicopter 8xMM40 SSM 8xCrotale Naval 1x100mm gun 2x20mm guns 4x533mm torpedoes

Patrol Craft

Type	Quantity	Length (m.)/ displacement (t.)	Notes/ armament
• Al-Jubatel (Abeking-Rasmussen)	2	26.2/96	1x20mm gun (with Coast Guard)
• Al-Jouf (Blohm & Voss)	4	38.6/210	2x20mm guns (with Coast Guard)
• Halter type	17	23.8/56	2x25mm guns
• Sea Guard	2	22.5/56	2x20mm guns (with Coast Guard)
• Simonneu Type 51	39	15.8/22	1x20mm gun
• Skorpion class	10	17.0/33	Light armament (with Coast Guard)
Total	**74**		

Note: Coast Guard has some 650 additional small patrol craft.

Landing Craft

Type	Quantity	Length (m.) / displacement (t.)	Notes / armament
• LCM-6 class	4	17.1/62	34 tons or 80 troops
• Slingsby SAH 2200 hovercraft	3	10.6	2.2 tons or 24 troops (with Coast Guard)
• US 1610 class LCU	4	41.1/375	170 tons or 120 troops
Total	**11**		
Future procurement			
• Slingsby SAH 2200 hovercraft	5		

Auxiliary Vessels

Type	Quantity	Length (m.)/ displacement (t.)	Notes/ armament
• Tabouk training ship	1	60/585	1x20mm gun
• Dammam (Jaguar class)	3	42.5/160	Ex-gunboat now used for training
• Royal yacht	1	1,450 dwt	
• Royal yacht	1	670 ton	
• Royal yacht al-Yamama	1		
• Royal yacht	1	112 ton	
• Royal yacht Pegasus	1		
• Durance class tanker	2	135.0/11,200	4x40mm guns 2 helicopter pads
• Ocean tugs	3	680 ton	

Auxiliary Vessels *(continued)*

Type	Quantity	Length (m.)/ displacement (t.)	Notes/ armament
• Coastal tugs	13		
• Small tankers	3	28.7/233	
• Training ship	1	21.4/75	With Coast Guard
• Brooke marine	1	24.5/82	Fire fighting craft With Coast Guard

Coastal Defense

Type	Quantity	Notes
• Otomat	4	

Naval Infrastructure

Naval bases (including coast guard): 13

Aziziya (Coast Guard), al-Dammam, al-Haql (Coast Guard), Jidda, Jizan, Jubayl, Makna (Coast Guard), al-Qatif, Ras al-Mishaab, Ras Tanura, al-Sharma, al-Wajh, Yanbu

Ship maintenance and repair facilities

Repair of vessels dependent on foreign experts; 22,000-ton and 62,000-ton floating docks at Dammam; 45,000-ton and 16,000-ton floating docks at Jidda

16. SUDAN

General Data

Official Name of the State: The Republic of Sudan
Head of State: President Omar Hassan Ahmad al-Bashir
Defense Minister: Major General Bakri Hassan Sallah
Chief of General Staff: General Abbas Arabi
Commander of the Air Force: Major General Ali Mahjoub Mardi
Commander of the Navy: Commodore Abbas al-Said Othman

Area: 2,504,530 sq. km.
Population: 29,500,000

Demography

Ethnic groups		
Arabs	11,505,000	39%
Nilotics	15,340,000	52%
Beja	1,770,000	6%
Foreigners	590,000	2%
Others	295,000	1%
Religious groups		
Sunni Muslims	20,650,000	70%
Indigenous beliefs	7,375,000	25%
Christians (Coptic, Greek Orthodox, Catholic, Protestant)	1,475,000	5%

Economic Data

		1996	1997	1998	1999	2000
GDP (current price)	$ bn	8.3	10.6	10.3	10.0	12.3
GDP per capita	$	305.1	382.7	363.9	346.0	416.9
Real GDP growth	%	4.0	6.7	5.0	6.0	7.2
Consumer price index	%	132.8	46.7	17.1	16.0	10.0
External debt	$ bn	17.0	16.3	16.8	16.4	16.4
Balance of payments						
• Exports fob	$ bn	0.62	0.59	0.6	0.78	1.73
• Imports fob	$ bn	1.34	1.42	1.73	1.26	1.19
• Current account balance (including services and income)	$ bn	-0.83	-0.83	-0.96	-0.47	-0.09

Economic Data *(continued)*

		1996	1997	1998	1999	2000
Government expenditure						
• Defense expenditure	$ bn	0.070	0.082	NA	NA	NA
• Real change in defense expenditure	%	-49.64	17.14	NA	NA	NA
• Defense expenditure/ GDP	%	0.84	0.77	NA	NA	NA
Population	m	27.2	27.7	28.3	28.9	29.5
Official exchange rate	SD:$1	125.1	157.6	200.8	252.6	257.1

Sources: EIU Quarterly Report, EIU Country Profile, IMF International Financial Statistical Yearbook, SIPRI Yearbook

Arms Procurement and Security Assistance Received

Country	Type	Details
Iran	• Arms transfers	Small arms, ammunition, EW equipment, vehicles, spare parts for Soviet and Chinese arms, 122mm rocket systems, tanks, aircraft, CW (alleged)
	• Military training	Technicians and IRGC; trainees abroad
Belarus	• Arms transfers	Mi-24 combat helicopters
Egypt	• Military training	Advisers and military training
Poland	• Arms transfers	T-55 tanks (via Yemen; unauthorized by Poland)
PRC	• Arms transfers	F-7 combat aircraft
	• Military training	Military advisers (alleged)

Arms Sales and Security Assistance Extended

Country	Type	Details
Iran	• Facilities	Iranian IRGC; facilities for Iranian ships at Port Sudan
Lebanon	• Facilities	Lebanese militia, camps with the popular defense forces

Foreign Military Cooperation

Type	Details
• Security agreements	Syria , Egypt
• Foreign Forces	PRC (alleged presence of forces for the defense of Chinese-operated oil fields)

Weapons of Mass Destruction

NBC Capabilities

Nuclear capability
No known nuclear activity. Party to the NPT.
Chemical weapons and protective equipment
Alleged CW from Iran (unsubstantiated); Alleged production of CW (unsubstantiated); Party to the CWC.
Personal protective equipment; unit decontamination equipment.
Biological weapons
No known BW activities. Party to the BWC.

Armed Forces

Major Changes: No major changes have been recorded in the Sudanese armed forces.

Order-of-Battle

Year	1996	1997	1999	2000	2001
General data					
• Personnel (regular)	86,500	84,500	103,000*	103,000	103,000
Ground Forces					
• Divisions	10	9*	9	9	9
• Total number of brigades	+	58*	61	61	61
• Tanks	450	~320*	~320	~350	~350
• APCs/AFVs	950	~560 (~700)*	~560 (~700)	~560 (~700)	~560 (~700)
• Artillery (including MRLs)	360	753 (765)*	~760 (~770)	~760 (~770)	~760 (~770)
Air Force					
• Combat aircraft	45	~35(~55)	~35(~55)	~35(~55)	~35(~55)
• Transport aircraft	25	26	26	25	24
• Helicopters	53	~55(67)	~60(69)	~60(69)	57 (73)
Air Defense Forces					
• Heavy SAM batteries	5	5	5	5	20
Navy					
• Patrol craft	23	22	22	18	18

Note: Beginning with 1997, data refers to quantities in active service. The number in parentheses refers to the total inventory.
* Due to change in estimate.

Personnel

	Regular	Reserves	Total
Ground Forces	100,000		100,000
Air Force	2,000		2,000
Navy	1,000		1,000
Total	**103,000**		**103,000**
Paramilitary			
• People's Defense Forces	15,000	85,000	100,000
• Border Guard	2,500		2,500

Ground Forces

Formations

	Divisions	Independent brigades/ groups
Armored	1	
Mechanized/Infantry	7	24
Airborne	1	
Artillery		3
Reconnaissance		1
Engineering	1	
Total	**10**	**28**

Tanks

Model	Quantity	In service	Since	Notes
MBTs				
Medium and low quality				
• M60 A3	20	20	1981	
• T-54/T-55/Type 59	~250	~250	1969	Number unconfirmed
• Type 62	70	70	1972	
Total	**~350**	**~350**		

APCs/AFVs

Model	Quantity	In service	Since	Notes
APCs				
• al-Walid	150	100	1986	
• M113	80	36	1982	
• BTR-152	80	80	1960	
• BTR-50	20	20	1970	
• Fahd	*	*	1989	

APCs/AFVs *(continued)*

Model	Quantity	In service	Since	Notes
• M-3 (Panhard)	*	*	1983	
• OT-62	20	20		
• OT-64	55	55	1973	
Subtotal	~420	~320		
IFVs				
• V-150 Commando	100	55	1984	
• BMP-2	6	6		
• AMX-VCI	+	+		
Subtotal	106	61		
Reconnaissance				
• BRDM 1/2	60	60		
• Ferret	60	60	1960	
• Saladin	50	50	1961	
• AML-90	5	5		
Subtotal	175	175		
Total	**~700**	**~560**		

Artillery

Model	Quantity	In service	Since	Notes
Self-propelled guns and howitzers				
• 155mm Mk F-3 (AMX)	10	6	1984	
Towed guns and howitzers				
• 155mm M114	20	12	1981	
• 130mm Type 59/M-46	75	75		
• 105mm M101	20	20		
Subtotal	115	107		
Mortars, under 160mm				
• 120mm	+	+	1970	
MRLs				
• 122mm BM-21	90	90	1989	
• 122mm Saqer	50	50	1986	
• 107mm Type 63	500	500		
Subtotal	640	640		
Total	**~770**	**~760**		

Anti-Tank Missiles

Model	Launchers	Missiles	Since	Notes
• BGM-71C improved TOW	+	+		Not all serviceable
• AT-3 (Sagger)	+	+		

Anti-Tank Guns

Model	Quantity	In service	Since	Notes
• 100mm M-1955 field/AT	+	+		
• 100mm M-1944	50	0	1975	
• 85mm M-1945/ D-44 field/AT	100	0	1973	
• 76mm M-1942	+	0		

Air Force

Order-of-Battle

Category	Quantity	In service	Notes
• Combat	55	~35	
• Transport	24	24	
• Helicopters	73	57	

Combat Aircraft

Model	Quantity	In service	Since	Notes
Interceptors				
• MiG-23	2	2	1987	
Multi-role				
• F-5E/F	8	0	1984/1982	
Obsolete				
• A-5 (Fantan)/Q-5	10	10		
• F-6 Shenyang/J-6	12	12	1981	
• MiG-21 (Fishbed)/F-7	23	~10	1970	
Subtotal	45	~32		
Total	**55**	**~35**		

Transport Aircraft

Model	Quantity	In service	Since	Notes
• An-24 (Coke)/An-26	4	4		
• C-130H Hercules	4	4	1978	
• DHC-5D Buffalo	3	3	1978	
• Fokker F-27	1	1	1974	
• Mystère-Falcon 50	1	1	1983	
• Mystère-Falcon 20	1	1	1978	
• C-212	4	4	1986	
• EMB-110P	6	6	1980	
Total	**24**	**24**		

Training and Liaison Aircraft

Model	Quantity	In service	Since	Notes
Jet trainers				
• BAC-145 Jet Provost	5	5	1969	
• BAC-167 Strikemaster	5	3	1984	
Total	**10**	**8**		

Helicopters

Model	Quantity	In service	Since	Notes
Attack				
• Mi-24	7	7	1991	
Medium transport				
• Mi-4 (Hound)	4	4	1974	Possibly phased out
• Mi-8 (Hip)	14	5		
• SA-330/IAR-330 Puma	12	12	1985	
• Bell 212/AB-212	5	0	1982	
• AB-412	10	8	1990	
Subtotal	45	29		
Light transport				
• MBB BO-105	18	18	1980	Some serving with police
• Bell 206	3	3	1992	
Subtotal	21	21		
Total	**73**	**57**		

Advanced Armament

Air-to-air missiles

AA-2 (Atoll)

Air Force Infrastructure

Military airfields : **13**

Atbara, al-Fasher, al-Geneina, Juba, Khartoum, Malakal, Merowe, al-Obeid, Port Sudan, Port Sudan (new), Wad Medani, Wadi Sayidina, Wau

Air Defense Forces

Surface-to-Air Missiles

Model	Batteries	Launchers	Since	Notes
Heavy missiles				
• SA-2 (Guideline)	20		1981	
Shoulder-launched missiles				
• SA-7 (Grail)		250	1980	
• MIM-43A Redeye		25	1984	
Total		**275**		

Other Air Defense Systems

Model	Quantity	In service	Since	Notes
Short-range guns				
• 57mm	+	+		
• 40mm	60	60		
• 37mm M-1939	110	80	1973	
• 23mm ZU 23x2	50	50	1984	
• 20mm M-3 VDA SP	12	12		
• 20mm M163A1 Vulcan SP	8	8	1986	
• 20mm M167 Vulcan	16	16	1986	
Total	**~260**	**~230**		

Navy

Patrol Craft

Type	Quantity	Length (m.)/ displacement (t.)	Notes/ armament
• Kadir class (Abeking and Rasmussen)	2	22.9/70	C-801 SSM 1x20mm gun
• Ashoora I class	8	8.1/3	
• Sewart class	4	12.9/9.1	1x12.7mm MG
• Kurmuk (Yugoslav type 15)	4	16.9/19.5	1x20mm gun
Total	**18**		

Auxiliary Vessels

Type	Quantity	Length (m.)/ displacement (t.)	Notes/ armament
• Yugoslav supply ships	2	47.3/410	1x20mm gun 2x12.7mm MG

Naval Infrastructure

Naval bases : **3**

Port Sudan, Flamingo Bay, Khartoum

Major Non-Governmental Paramilitary Forces

Personnel

	Regular	Reserves	Total	Notes
• National Democratic Alliance (NDA)				A coordinating organization of all active opposition organizations
• Sudan People's Liberation Army (SPLA)	30,000	100,000	130,000	The main non-governmental military organization, active in southern Sudan
• South Sudan Independence Movement (SSIM)	10,000		10,000	Also known as SPLA United; in 1996 signed a truce with the government
• Sudan Alliance Forces	1,000-2,000		1,000-2,000	Active in eastern Sudan
• Beja Congress Forces	500		500	Active in eastern Sudan
• New Sudan Brigade	2,000		2,000	Recent activity unknown

Equipment

Organization	Category	System	Notes
SPLA	Tanks	• T-54/55	
	MRLs	• BM-21	
	Artillery guns	• +	
	Mortars	• 120mm	
		• 60mm	
	Air Defense	• SA-7 SAM	
		• 14.5mm AAG	

17. SYRIA

General Data

Official Name of the State: The Arab Republic of Syria
Head of State: President Bashar al-Assad
Prime Minister: Mohammed Mustafa Miro
Minister of Defense: Lieutenant General Mustafa al-Tlass
Chief of General Staff: Major General Ali Aslan
Commander of the Air Force: Major General Kamal Makhafut
Commander of the Navy: Vice Admiral Wa'il Nasser

Area: 185,180 sq. km
Population: 16,600,000

Demography

Ethnic groups		
Arabs	14,990,000	90.3%
Kurds, Armenians and others	1,610,000	9.7%
Religious groups		
Sunni Muslims	12,284,000	74.0%
Alawis, Druze, and Shi'ite Muslims	2,656,000	16.0%
Christians (Greek Orthodox, Gregorian, Armenian, Catholics, Syrian Orthodox, Greek Catholics)	1,660,000	10.0%

Economic Data

		1996	1997	1998	1999	2000
GDP (current prices)	$ bn	16.1	16.8	17.2	16.5	16.8
GDP per capita	$	1,103	1,113	1,103	1,025	1,012
Real GDP growth	%	7.3	2.5	7.8	-1.5	1.5
Consumer price index	%	8.3	2.3	-0.5	-2.7	0.5
External debt	$ bn	21.4	20.9	22.4	22.6	22.0
Balance of payments						
• Exports fob	$ bn	4.18	4.06	3.14	3.8	4.66
• Imports fob	$ bn	4.52	3.6	3.32	3.6	3.57

Economic Data *(continued)*

		1996	1997	1998	1999	2000
• Current account balance (including services and income)	$ bn	0.04	0.46	0.06	0.2	1.38
Government expenditure						
• Total expenditure	$ bn	4.38	4.74	5.13	5.51	5.95
• Defense expenditure	$ bn	3.53	3.44	3.65	NA	NA
• Real change in defense expenditure	%	-7.0	3.0	5.9	NA	NA
• Defense expenditure/ GDP	%	20.5	20.2	20.9	NA	NA
Population	m	14.6	15.1	15.6	16.1	16.6
Official exchange rate	S£:$1	42.9	44.5	46.3	46.3	46.3

Sources: EIU Quarterly Report, EIU Country Profile, IMF International Financial Statistical Yearbook, SIPRI Yearbook

Arms Procurement and Security Assistance Received

Country	Type	Details
India	• Arms transfers	Aircraft spare parts; CW precursors
Iran	• Arms transfers	Assistance in MBT upgrade
	• Assistance	Promised guarantees for debts to Russia
	• Cooperation in arms production	Cooperation in production of SSMs
North Korea	• Arms transfers	Scud C SSMs, including assistance in production
PRC	• Cooperation in arms production, R&D	Scud D SSM production
Russia	• Arms transfers	Kornet ATGMs
	• Facilities	Repairs of naval base
	• Military training	Approx. 50 advisers; 70 trainees in Russia
Ukraine	• Arms transfers	Upgraded T-55 MBTs

Arms Sales and Security Assistance Extended

Country	Type	Details
Lebanon	• Military training	Approx. 200 trainees annually, advisers
Palestinian organizations	• Facilities	Camps for rejectionist front groups
	• Assistance	Grant for Fatah-Intifada, al-Saiqa, PPSF, PLF and PFLP-GC

Foreign Military Cooperation

Type	Details
• Forces deployed abroad	25,000 in Beka', northern Lebanon (Tripoli area) and Beirut

Defense Production

	M	P	A
Weapons of mass destruction			
• Production and upgrading of SSMs (in cooperation with North Korea and Iran)		√	√
• Production of chemical and biological agents, chemical warheads for SSMs	√		
Army equipment			
• Upgrading of tanks		√	
• Ammunition	√		

Note: M - manufacture (indigenously developed)
P - production under license
A - assembly

Weapons of Mass Destruction

NBC Capabilities

Nuclear capability

Basic research. Alleged deal with Russia for a 24 Mw reactor. Deals with China for a 27 kw reactor and with Argentina for a 3 Mw research reactor, both probably cancelled. Party to the NPT; Safeguards agreement with the IAEA in force.

Chemical weapons and protective equipment

Stockpiles of nerve gas, including Sarin, Mustard, and VX.
Delivery vehicles include chemical warheads for SSMs and aerial bombs.
Personal protective equipment; Soviet-type unit decontamination equipment;
Not a party to the CWC.

Biological weapons

Biological weapons and toxins (unconfirmed).
Signed but not ratified the BWC.

Ballistic Missiles

Model	Launchers	Missiles	Since	Notes
• SS-1 (Scud B)	18	200	1974	
• SS-1 (Scud C)	8	60	1992	variant from North Korea)
• SS-21 (Scarab)	18		1983	
Total	**44**			
Future procurement				
• Scud D	+			Under development

Note: See also under Rockets.

Armed Forces

Major Changes: Syria tested its first Scud D ballistic missile (with a range of 700km). No other major changes have been recorded in the Syrian armed forces.

Order-of-Battle

Year	1996	1997	1999	2000	2001
General data					
• Personnel (regular)	390,000	380,000	380,000	380,000	380,000
• SSM launchers	44	44	44	44	44
Ground Forces					
• Divisions	12	12	12	12	12
• Total number of brigades	59	67*	67	67	67
• Tanks	4,800	3,700* (4,800)	3,700 (4,800)	3,700 (4,800)	3,700 (4,800)
• APCs/AFVs	4,980	4,980	4,980	~5,000	~5,000
• Artillery (including MRLs)	2,500	2,575 (~2,975)*	2,575 (~2,975)	~2,600 (~3,000)	~2,600 (~3,000)
Air Force					
• Combat aircraft	515	520	520	520	490
• Transport aircraft	23	23(25)	23(25)	23(25)	23(25)
• Helicopters	285	295*	295	295	285
Air Defense Forces					
• Heavy SAM batteries	108	108	108	108	108
• Medium SAM batteries	70	65	65	64	64
• Light SAM launchers	+	55*	55	55	55

Order-of-Battle *(continued)*

Year	1996	1997	1999	2000	2001
Navy					
• Submarines	3	0(3)*	0(3)	0(3)	0(3)
• Combat vessels	32	25(30)*	24(27)	14*	14
• Patrol craft	16	8*	8	8	8

Note: Beginning with 1997, data refers to quantities in active service. The number in parentheses refers to the total inventory.
* Due to change in estimate.

Personnel

	Regular	Reserves	Total
Ground Forces	306,000	100,000	406,000
Air Force	30,000	10,000	40,000
Air Defense	40,000	20,000	60,000
Navy	4,000	2,500	6,500
Total	**380,000**	**132,500**	**512,500**
Paramilitary			
• Gendarmerie	8,000		8,000
• Workers' Militia		400,000	400,000

Ground Forces

Formations

	Corps/ armies	Divisions	Independent Brigades/ groups	brigades in divisions
All arms	3			
Armored		7	1	3 armd., 1 mech., 1 aty. each
Mechanized		3	1	2 mech., 2 armd.,1 aty. each
Republican Guard		1		3 armd., 1 mech., 1 aty.
Infantry/Special Forces		1	3	
Airborne/Special Forces			8-10	

Formations *(continued)*

	Corps/ armies	Divisions	Independent Brigades/ groups	brigades in divisions
Artillery			2	
SSM forces			3	
Anti-tank/ Infantry			2	
Total	**3**	**12**	**20-22**	

Note: One armored division is a reserve unit.

Tanks

Model	Quantity	In service	Since	Notes
MBTs				
High quality				
• T-72/T-72M	1,600	1,600	1979/1993	
Medium and low quality				
• T-62	1,000	1,000	1974	
• T-55/T-54	~2,200	1,100	1957	Some upgraded to MV standard
Subtotal	~3,200	2,100		
Total	**~4,800**	**3,700**		

APCs/AFVs

Model	Quantity	In service	Since	Notes
APCs				
• BTR-152	560	560	1967	
• BTR-40/50/60	1,000	1,000	1956	
Subtotal	1,560	1,560		
IFVs				
• BMP-1	2,450	2,450	1977	
• BMP-2	~ 70	~ 70	1988	
Subtotal	~2,520	~2,520		
Reconnaissance				
• BRDM-2	900	900	1978	Also listed under Anti-Tank Weapons
Total	**~5,000**	**~5,000**		

Artillery

Model	Quantity	In service	Since	Notes
Self-propelled guns and howitzers				
• 152mm 2S3	50	50	1984	
• 122mm 2S1	400	400	1982	
• 122mm D30	55	55	1986	Syrian-made
Subtotal	505	505		
Towed guns and howitzers				
• 180mm S-23	10	10	1975	
• 152mm M-1943	50	50	1987	
• 152mm D-20	20	20	1982	
• 130mm M-46	800	800	1970	
• 122mm D-30	500	500	1984	
• 122mm D-74	400	0		
• 122mm M-1938	150	150	1976	
Subtotal	1,930	1,530		
Mortars, over 160mm				
• 240mm	10	10	1986	
• 160mm	80	80	1976	
Subtotal	90	90		
Mortars, under 160mm				
• 120mm	+	+	1975	
Rockets				
• FROG-7	18	18	1971	
MRLs				
• 122mm BM-21	250	250	1979	
• 107mm Type 63	200	200	1994	
Subtotal	450	450		
Total	**~3,000**	**~2,600**		

Logistics and Engineering Equipment

MTU-67 bridging tanks, MT-55 bridging tanks (90), tank-towed bridges, mine clearing rollers, AFV transporters (800)

Anti-Tank Missiles

Model	Quantity	In service	Since	Notes
• AT-14 (Kornet)	1,000	1,000	1998	Being delivered
• AT-4 (Spigot)	150	150	1980	
• AT-5 (Spandrel)	40	40	1995	
• AT-3 (Sagger) SP	3,000	3,000	1974	Mounted on BRDM-2 and BMP-1
• MILAN	200	200	1980	
Total	**4,390**	**4,390**		

Air Force

Order-of-Battle

Category	Quantity	In service	Notes
• Combat	490	490	
• Transport	25	23	
• Helicopters	285	285	

Combat Aircraft

Model	Quantity	In service	Since	Notes
Interceptors				
• MiG-25 (Foxbat)	35	35	1980	
• MiG-29 (Fulcrum)	20	20	1987	
• MiG-23 ML/MF	51	51	1974	
Subtotal	106	106		
Ground attack				
• Su-24 (Fencer)	20	20	1988	
• MiG-23 U/BN (Flogger)	56	56	1978	
• Su-20/22 (Fitter C/D)	100	100	1978	
Subtotal	176	176		
Obsolete				
• MiG-21 MF/BIS/U (Fishbed)	~210	~210	1966	Some possibly phased out
Total	**~490**	**~490**		
Future procurement				
• Su-24 (Fencer)				Unconfirmed
• MiG-29 (Fulcrum)				Unconfirmed
• Su-27				Unconfirmed

Transport Aircraft

Model	Quantity	In service	Since	Notes
• An-24/26 (Coke/Curl)	6	6	1979	
• IL-76 (Candid)	4	4	1983	
• Tu-134	2	2	1985	
• Mystère-Falcon 20/900	5	3	1980	
• Piper Navajo	2	2		
• Yak-40 (Codling)	6	6	1989	
Total	**25**	**23**		

Training and Liaison Aircraft

Model	Quantity	In service	Since	Notes
Jet trainers				
• L-39 Albatross	90	90	1980	
Piston/Turbo-prop				
• MBB 223 Flamingo	40	40	1976	
• Mushshak	6	6	1994	
Subtotal	46	46		
Total	**136**	**136**		

Helicopters

Model	Quantity	In service	Since	Notes
Attack				
• Mi-25 (Hind)	52	52	1980	
• SA-342 Gazelle	38	38	1976	
Subtotal	90	90		
Medium transport				
• Mi-8/17 (Hip H)	160	160	1971	
• Mi-2	10	10	1975	
Subtotal	170	170		
Naval combat				
• Ka-28 (Helix)	5	5	1990	
• Mi-14 (Haze)	20	20	1984	
Subtotal	25	25		
Total	**285**	**285**		

Miscellaneous Aircraft

Model	Quantity	In service	Since	Notes
Reconnaissance				
• MiG-25 R	7	7	1985	
UAVs and mini-UAVs				
• Shmel/Malachit	+	+		

Advanced Armament

Air-to-air missiles

AA-2 (610), AA-6 (150), AA-7 (470), AA-8 (1,120), AA-10, AA-11

Air-to-ground missiles

AS-7, AS-9, AS-10, AS-11, AS-12, AS-14, AT-2, HOT

Note: Number in parentheses refers to the quantity of missiles purchased, not to current inventory levels.

Air Force Infrastructure

Aircraft shelters
In all airfields, for combat aircraft
Military airfields: **21**
Abu Duhur, Afis North, Aleppo, Damascus (International), Damascus (Meze), Dir ez-Zor, Dumayr, Hama, Jarah, Khalkhala, Latakia, Marj-royal (Bley), Nassiriyah, al-Qusayr, Rasm al-Aboud, Sayqal, Shayarat, al-Suweida, T-4, Tabaka, Tudmur

Air Defense Forces

Surface-to-Air Missiles

Model	Batteries	Launchers	Since	Notes
Heavy missiles				
• SA-2 (Guideline)/ SA-3 (Goa)	100		1971	
• SA-5 (Gammon)	8		1983	
Total	**108**			
Medium missiles				
• SA-8 (Gecko)		56	1982	
• SA-6 (Gainful)	50		1973	
Total	**50**	**56**		
Light missiles				
• SA-9 (Gaskin)		20	1975	
• SA-13 (Gopher)		35	1986	
Total		**55**		
Shoulder-launched missiles				
• SA-7 (Grail)		+	1973	
• SA-14 (Gremlin)		+		
• SA-16		+		
Future procurement				
• SA-10 (Grumble)				

Other Air Defense Systems

Model	Quantity	In service	Since	Notes
Short-range guns				
• 57mm S-60	700	~400	1973	Partly phased out
• 37mm M-1939	300	0	1973	
• 23mm ZSU 23x4 SP (Gun Dish)	400	400	1977	
• 23mm ZU 23x2	600	~300	1986	
Total	**2,000**	**~1,100**		

Other Air Defense Systems *(continued)*

Radars
Long Track, P-14 (Tall King), P-15 (Flat Face), P-12 (Spoon Rest), P-30, P-35, P-80, PRV-13, PRV-16.

Navy

Submarines

Type	Quantity	Length (m.)/ displacement (t.)	Notes/ armament
• R class (Type 633)	0	76.6/1,830	8x533mm torpedoes 28 mines 3 unserviceable

Combat Vessels

Type	Quantity	Length (m.)/ displacement (t.)	Notes/ armament
MFPBs			
• Ossa II	8	38.6/245	4xSS-N-2C Styx SSM 4x30mm guns
ASW vessels			
• Petya II	2	81.8/950	5-16x400mm torpedoes 4xRBU 2500 ASW mortars 3x76mm guns 22 mines
Mine warfare vessels			
• Sonya class (Type 1265)	1	48/450	2x30mm guns 2x25mm guns 8 mines
• Yevgenia class	3	24.6/77	2x25mm guns 2x14.5mm MGs
Subtotal	4		
Total	**14**		

Patrol Craft

Type	Quantity	Length (m.)/ displacement (t.)	Notes/ armament
• Zhuk class (Type 1400M)	8	24/39	4x14.5mm MGs

Landing Craft

Type	Quantity	Length (m.)/ displacement (t.)	Notes/ armament
• Polnochny B-class LCT (Type 771)	3	75/760	180 troops or 350 tons 2x140mm MRLs 4x30mm guns

Auxiliary Vessels

Type	Quantity	Length (m.)/ displacement (t.)	Notes/ armament
• al-Assad	1	105/3,500	Training ship
• Natya (Type 226)	1	61/804	2xSA-N-5 (Grail) SAMs 4x30mm guns formerly a minesweeper, now converted to oceanographic research
• T 43 class	1	60/580	16 mines 4x37mm guns 4x14.5mm MGs
• Sekstan class	1	40.8/400	115 tons
• Poluchat	1	29.6/100	2x14.5mm MGs formerly a torpedo recovery vessel
Total	5		

Coastal Defense

Type	Batteries	Since	Notes
Missiles			
• SSC-1B Sepal	12		
• SSC-3	12	1966	Armed with SS-N-2C missiles
Guns			
• 130mm	36		

Naval Infrastructure

Naval bases: **3**

Latakia, Minat al-Baida, Tartus

Ship maintenance and repair facilities

Repairs at Latakia

18. TUNISIA

General Data

Official Name of the State: The Republic of Tunisia
Head of State: President Zayn al-Abedine Bin Ali
Prime Minister: Mohamed Ghannouchi
Minister of Defense: Dali Jazi
Secretary of State for National Defense: Chokri Ayachi
Commander of the Ground Forces: Lieutenant General Muhammad Hadi Bin Hassin
Commander of the Air Force: Major General Rida Hamuda Atar
Commander of the Navy: Commodore al-Shadli Sharif

Area: 164,206 sq. km.
Population: 9,600,000

Demography

Ethnic groups		
Arabs/Berbers	9,408,000	98.0%
Europeans	96,000	1.0%
Others	96,000	1.0%
Religious groups		
Sunni Muslims	9,408,000	98.0%
Christians	96,000	1.0%
Others	96,000	1.0%

Economic Data

		1996	1997	1998	1999	2000
GDP (current prices)	$ bn	19.6	18.9	19.8	20.9	20.0
GDP per capita	$	2,153	2,054	2,129	2,200	2,083
Real GDP growth	%	7.1	5.4	4.8	6.2	5.0
Consumer price index	%	3.7	3.7	3.2	2.7	2.9
External debt	$ bn	11.4	11.2	10.9	11.9	10.4
Balance of payments						
• Exports fob	$ bn	5.52	5.56	5.72	5.87	5.96
• Imports fob	$ bn	7.28	7.51	7.87	8.02	8.33
• Current account balance (including services and income)	$ bn	-0.48	-0.6	-0.68	-0.44	-0.74

Economic Data *(continued)*

		1996	1997	1998	1999	2000
Government expenditure						
• Total expenditure	$ bn	6.95	6.15	6.34	6.6	6.4
• Defense expenditure	$ bn	0.35	0.36	0.38	NA	NA
• Real change in defense expenditure	%	0.0	2.8	5.5	NA	NA
• Defense expenditure/ GDP	%	1.8	1.9	1.9	NA	NA
Population	m	9.1	9.2	9.3	9.5	9.6
Official exchange rate	TD:$1	0.973	1.106	1.139	1.186	1.344

Sources: EIU Quarterly Report, EIU Country Profile, IMF International Financial Statistical Yearbook, SIPRI Yearbook.

Arms Procurement and Security Assistance Received

Country	Type	Details
Czech Republic	• Arms transfers	Trainer and transport aircraft
	• Military training	Training of technicians
Saudi Arabia	• Arms transfers	AMX-30 tanks
US	• Assistance	$3.45 million grant in 2001

Foreign Military Cooperation

Type	Details
• Joint maneuvers	France, Spain (unconfirmed), US
• Forces deployed abroad	Bosnia and Herzgovina (UNMIBH)
• Security cooperation	Greece, Morocco

Defense Production

	M	P	A
Naval Craft			
• 20 meter patrol craft, with assistance from South Korea		√	

Note: M - manufacture (indigenously developed)
P - production under license
A - assembly

Weapons of Mass Destruction

NBC Capabilities

Nuclear capability

No known nuclear activity. Signatory to the NPT.

Chemical weapons and protective equipment

No known CW activities. Party to the CWC.

Biological weapons

No known BW activities. Party to the BWC.

Armed Forces

Major Changes: No major change was recorded in the Tunisian order-of-battle.

Order-of-Battle

Year	1996	1997	1999	2000	2001
General data					
• Personnel (regular)	35,500	35,500	35,500	35,500	35,500
Ground Forces					
• Number of brigades	8	5	5	5	5
• Tanks	200	139(144)*	139(144)	139(144)	139(144)
• APCs/AFVs	316	316	316	316	316
• Artillery (including MRLs)	91	205(215)*	205(215)	205(215)	205(215)
Air Force					
• Combat aircraft	13	12	12	12	18
• Transport aircraft	11	10(11)	10(11)	10(11)	9(11)
• Helicopters	35	40	40	44	51
Air Defense Forces					
• Light SAM launchers	+	73*	73	83	83
Navy					
• Combat vessels	19	11*	11	9	9
• Patrol crafts	17	36*	36	37	37

Note: Beginning with 1997, data refers to quantities in active service. The number in parentheses refers to the total inventory.

* Due to change in estimate.

Personnel

	Regular	Total
Ground Forces	27,000	27,000
Air Force	4,000	4,000
Navy	4,500	4,500
Total	**35,500**	**35,500**
Paramilitary		
• Gendarmerie	2,000	2,000
• National Guard	7,000	7,000

Ground Forces

Formations

	Independent brigades groups	Regiments in Brigades
Mechanized/Infantry	3	1 armd., 2 mech., 1 aty. each
Commando/Paratroops	1	
Sahara brigade	1	
Total	**5**	

Tanks

Model	Quantity	In service	Since	Notes
MBTs				
Medium and low quality				
• M60 A1/A3	89	84	1984	
Light tanks				
• SK-105 (Kürassier)	55	55	1983	
Total	**144**	**139**		
Future procurement				
• AMX-30	30			From Saudi Arabia

APCs/AFVs

Model	Quantity	In service	Since	Notes
APCs				
• M113 A1/A2/ M125/M577	120	120	1980	35 M901 ITV listed under Anti-Tank Weapons

APCs/AFVs *(continued)*

Model	Quantity	In service	Since	Notes
• Fiat Type 6614	110	110	1980	
Subtotal	230	230		
IFVs				
• Engesa EE-11	+	+	1982	Included with Engesa EE-9
Reconnaissance				
• Engesa EE-9	36	36	1982	
• Saladin	20	20	1962	
• AML-60/90	30	30	1969	
Subtotal	86	86		
Total	**316**	**316**		

Artillery

Model	Quantity	In service	Since	Notes
Self-propelled guns and howitzers				
• 105mm M108	10	0	1950	Possibly phased out
Towed guns and howitzers				
• 155mm M198	48	48	1987	
• 155mm M114	18	18	1970	
• 105mm M101	45	45	1980	
Subtotal	111	111		
Mortars, under 160mm				
• 120mm Brandt	18	18	1987	
• 107mm	40	40	1980	
• 107mm SP	36	36	1987	Mounted on M106
Subtotal	94	94		
Total	**215**	**205**		

Logistics and Engineering Equipment

M728 ECV (4), SK-105 ARVs (5)

Anti-Tank Missiles

Model	Quantity	In service	Since	Notes
• BGM-71A TOW	100	100	1982	
• M901 ITV SP	35	35	1987	Also listed under APCs
• MILAN	500	500	1982	
Total	**635**	**635**		

Anti-Tank Guns

Model	Quantity	In service	Since	Notes
• 106mm M40 A1	70	70	1990	Recoilless rifle

Air Force

Order-of-Battle

Category	Quantity	In service	Notes
• Combat	18	18	
• Transport	11	9	
• Helicopters	51	51	

Combat Aircraft

Model	Quantity	In service	Since	Notes
Multi-role				
• F-5 E/F	18	18	1984	
Total	**18**	**18**		

Transport Aircraft

Model	Quantity	In service	Since	Notes
• C-130B Hercules	8	7	1985	
• L-410	3	2	1994	
Total	**11**	**9**		

Training and Liaison Aircraft

Model	Quantity	In service	Since	Notes
Jet trainers				
• L-59	12	12	1995	
• Aermacchi MB-326 B/KT/LT	11	11	1974	
Subtotal	23	23		
Piston/Turbo-prop				
• SF-260WT/C	20	20	1974	
• S 208A/M	2	2	1979	
• Piper Cub	10	10		
Subtotal	32	32		
Total	**55**	**55**		

Helicopters

Model	Quantity	In service	Since	Notes
Attack				
• SA-342 Gazelle	5	5	1991	
Medium transport				
• AB-205/UH-1H	24	24	1978	
• S-61R/HH-3E	4	4	1994	
• AS 365 Dauphin II	1	1	1986	
Subtotal	29	29		
Light transport				
• Alouette II/III	11	11	1964	
• AS-350 Ecureuil	6	6	1982	
Subtotal	17	17		
Total	**51**	**51**		

Advanced Armament

Air-to-air missiles

AIM-9J Sidewinder

Air Force Infrastructure

Military airfields: 4

Bizerta (Sidi Ahmad), Gabes, Gafsa, Sfax

Air Defense Forces

Surface-to-Air Missiles

Model	Launchers	Since	Notes
Light missiles			
• MIM-72A Chaparral	35	1977	
• RBS-70	48	1982	
Total	**83**		
Shoulder-launched missiles			
• SA-7 (Grail)	+		

Other Air Defense Systems

Model	Quantity	In service	Since	Notes
Short-range guns				
• 40mm	12	12	1964	
• 37mm M-1939	15	10	1980	

Other Air Defense Systems *(continued)*

Model	Quantity	In service	Since	Notes
• 20mm M-55	100	90	1990	
Total	**127**	**112**		
Radars				
• TRS-2230	+	+		
• TRS-2100 Tiger S	6	6	1988	

Navy

Combat Vessels

Type	Quantity	Length (m.)/ displacement (t.)	Notes/ armament
MFPBs			
• Combatante III	3	56/345	8xMM40 Exocet SSMs 1x76mm gun 2x40mm guns 4x30mm guns
• Bizerte class (P-48)	3	48/250	8xSS-12M SSMs 4x37mm guns
Subtotal	6		
Gunboats			
• Modified Haizhui class	3	35/120	4x25mm guns
Total	**9**		

Patrol Craft

Type	Quantity	Length (m.)/ displacement (t.)	Notes/ armament
• Kondor I class	5	51.9/377	2x25mm guns formerly a minesweeper, now with Coast Guard
• Coastal patrol craft	4	31.5/60	2x20mm guns
• Tazarka class	2	31.4/125	2x20mm guns 2x14.5mm MGs with Coast Guard
• Coastal patrol craft	6	25/38	1x20mm gun
• Bremse class	5	22.6/42	2x14.5mm MGs with Coast Guard
• Coastal patrol craft (Socomena)	11	20.5/32	1x12.7mm MG with Coast Guard
• Gabes class	4	12.9/18	2x12.7mm MGs with Coast Guard
Total	**37**		

Auxiliary Vessels

Type	Quantity	Length (m.)/ displacement (t.)	Notes/ armament
• Robert Conrad class	1	63.7/1,370	Survey ship
• Wilkes (T-AGS-33)	1	87/2,843	Survey ship
• White Sumac	2	40.5/485	
• Guesette class	4	11/8.5	Survey ship
Total	8		

Naval Infrastructure

Naval bases: **6**

Bizerta, Kelibia, La Goulette , Sfax, Sousse, Tunis

Ship maintenance and repair facilities

4 dry-docks and 1 slipway in Bizerta; 2 pontoons and 1 floating dock at Sfax. Capability for maintenance and repair of existing vessels.

19. TURKEY

General Data

Official Name of the State: Republic of Turkey
Head of State: President Ahmet Necdet Sezer
Prime Minister: Bülent Ecevit
Minister of National Defense: Sabahattin Cakmakoglu
Chief of General Staff: General Huseyin Kivrikoglu
Commander of the Ground Forces: General Hilmi Ozkok
Commander of the Air Force: General Ergin Celasin
Commander of the Navy: Admiral Ilhami Erdil

Area: 780,580 sq. km.
Population: 63,500,000

Demography

Ethnic group		
Turkish	50,800,000	80%
Kurdish	12,700,000	20%
Religious group		
Sunni Muslims	50,673,000	79.8%
Alevis (Shi'ite Muslims)	12,700,000	20.0%
Other (Christians and Jews)	127,000	0.2%

Economic Data

		1996	1997	1998	1999	2000
GDP (current prices)	$ bn	175.9	189.1	205.3	195.8	200.5
GDP per capita	$	2,860	3,026	3,233	3,040	3,070
Real GDP growth	%	7.3	7.6	3.2	-4.7	7.1
Consumer price index	%	80.4	85.7	84.6	65.1	54.9
External debt	$ bn	79.6	84.8	97.2	101.8	114.3
Balance of payments						
• Exports fob	$ bn	32.4	32.6	31.2	29.3	31.2
• Imports fob	$ bn	43.0	48.0	45.3	39.8	53.5
• Current account balance (including services and income)	$ bn	-2.4	-2.6	-2.1	-1.4	-9.8

Economic Data *(continued)*

		1996	1997	1998	1999	2000
Government expenditure						
• Total expenditure	$ bn	48.7	53.0	59.9	66.9	74.5
• Defense expenditure	$ bn	7.4	7.7	8.1	9.6	NA
• Real change in defense expenditure	%	12.1	4.0	5.2	18.5	NA
• Defense expenditure/ GDP	%	4.2	4.1	3.9	4.9	NA
Population	m	61.5	62.5	63.5	64.4	65.3
Official exchange rate	TL:$1	81,405	151,865	260,724	418,783	625,218

Sources: EIU Quarterly Report, EIU Country Profile, IMF International Financial Statistical Yearbook, SIPRI Yearbook.

Arms Procurement and Security Assistance Received

Country	Type	Details
Australia	• Arms transfers	Mine warfare system
France	• Arms transfers	Helicopters, Circe minesweepers, ECMs (possibly suspended), D'orves frigates
	• Cooperation in arms production	Eryx ATGMs
Germany	• Arms transfers	Meko frigates, Preveze submarine, Frankenthal minehunters
Israel	• Arms transfers	Upgrade of F-4s and F-5s, radars, missile warning systems, LOROPS reconnaissance pods, upgrade of M60 tanks, Harpy drones
	• Military training	SAR training
Italy	• Arms transfers	AB-412 helicopters (possibly suspended)
Norway	• Arms transfers	Penguin ASCMs
PRC	• Cooperation in assembly/R&D	WS-1 artillery rockets
Romania	• Arms transfers	Bombs
Russia	• Arms transfers	Mi-17 helicopters
Spain	• Cooperation in arms production	CN-235 aircraft
South Korea	• Cooperation in arms production	Production of artillery and SP guns
UK	• Arms transfers	Satellite communications system, Rapier SAM launchers
	• Cooperation in arms production	Upgrading Rapier SAMs

Arms Procurement and Security Assistance Received *(continued)*

Country	Type	Details
US	• Arms transfers	Knox frigates, ATACM SSMs, Blackhawk helicopters, APCs, Harpoon missiles, AMRAAM missiles, LANTIRN pods, Maverick missiles, TPQ-36 radars, Hellfire II ATGMs, CH-53E helicopters (possibly suspended), F-16 aircraft, AH-1Z King Cobra helicopters, I-Hawk SAMs, MPQ-64 radars, ALQ-144 MCMs, L-3 sonars, Stinger SAM launchers, MD-600 helicopters (possibly suspended)
	• Assistance	$1.6 million US foreign military aid

Note: due to the financial crisis many arms procurement programs were cancelled or suspended.

Arms Sales and Security Assistance Extended

Country	Type	Details
Albania	• Assistance	$80 million military aid
	• Military training	Advisers, trainees in Turkey, special forces training
Algeria	• Arms transfers	Armored Land Rovers
Azerbaijan	• Assistance	$3.45 million military aid
	• Arms transfers	SAR boat
	• Military training	Trainees in Turkey
Bosnia	• Assistance	$10 million
	• Military training	Trainees in Turkey
Croatia	• Arms transfers	CN-235 aircraft
Egypt	• Arms transfers	F-16 aircraft
EU	• Cooperation in arms production	Participation in the A400M transport aircraft program
Georgia	• Arms transfers	Gunboats
	• Assistance	$4 million aid for military modernization
	• Military training	Trainees in Turkey
Israel	• Cooperation in assembly/R&D	Joint development of ATBM project
	• Arms transfers	Armored Land Rovers
Jordan	• Arms transfers	CN-235 aircraft (on lease)
	• Military training	Flight simulation, training of helicopter pilots
KDP (Kurds)	• Arms transfers	Tanks, small arms
	• Assistance	Financial aid
Kyrgyzstan	• Assistance	$0.24 million in 2000 and $2.5 million in 2001
Kazakhstan	• Military training	Assistance in upgrading military capability

Arms Sales and Security Assistance Extended *(continued)*

Country	Type	Details
Malaysia	• Arms transfers	FNSS ACVs
Mali	• Military training	Training of armed policemen
Macedonia	• Arms transfers	F-5 aircraft
NATO	• Facilities	HQ LANDSOUTHEAST, HQ 6 ATAF
Pakistan	• Arms transfers	Armored Land Rovers, tactical radio communications
UAE	• Arms transfers	FNSS ACVs
US	• Cooperation in arms production	Participation in JSF program
Uzbekistan	• Military training	Counter terrorism training

Foreign Military Cooperation

Type	Details
• Cooperation in training	Albania, Azerbaijan, Israel (mutual use of airspace and training facilities), Jordan (mutual use of airspace and training facilities; joint training of infantry), Georgia, PRC
• Forces deployed abroad	Albania; Cyprus (30,000 troops); northern Iraq (1,000 troops); Bosnia (UNMIBH); Georgia (UNOMIG); Iraq/Kuwait (UNIKOM); Italy (F-16 aircraft, part of KFOR); Kosovo (150 troops in KFOR); Israel (TIPH)
• Foreign forces	Italy, UK, US (2,000 troops)
• Joint maneuvers	Albania (naval), Bulgaria (part of multinational peacekeeping brigade), Georgia (naval), Israel, Jordan, Macedonia (part of multinational peacekeeping brigade), NATO member states, Pakistan, Poland, Romania (part of multinational peacekeeping brigade), US
• Security agreements	Croatia, France, Georgia, Kazakhstan, Latvia

Defense Production

	M	P	A
Army equipment			
• Land Rover APCs, FNSS ACVs and AIFVs	√		
• Cobra reconnaissance AFVs	√		
• Chinese WS-1 rockets	√	√	
• Toros 230mm and 260mm MRLs	√		
• 155mm SP guns	√		
• Upgrade of 105mm and 155mm SP guns	√		
• 120mm SP mortars	√		

Defense Production *(continued)*

	M	P	A
• 107mm and 122mm MRLs	√		
• M48 tank guns	√		
• 25mm guns			√
• Eryx ATGMs		√	
• Hellfire ATGM mounted on ACVs	√	√	
• Trucks and wheeled tactical vehicles	√		
• Small arms	√		
• Explosives	√		
Air Force equipment			
• F-16 aircraft		√	
• Cougar helicopters		√	
• SF-260D basic trainers		√	
• CN-235 light transport aircraft		√	
• Participation in production of MD Explorer helicopter		√	
• UAVs	√		
• Modification of S-2E maritime patrol aircraft	√		
• Bora, Atiligan and Zipkin air defense systems	√	√	
• 35mm Oerlikon anti-aircraft guns		√	
• Jet engines		√	
• Popeye AGMs		√	
• Paveway II laser-guided bombs		√	
• Rapier surface-to-air missiles		√	√
Naval equipment			
• Atilay class submarines			√
• Berk class missile frigates			√
• Yildiz class and Dogan class MFPBs			√
• Minehunters		√	
• Yonca PBs	√		
• Osman Gazi landing craft			√
Electronics			
• Land-based and naval EW sets	√		
• Navigation systems	√		
• Ground surveillance radars	√		
• Tactical communication systems	√	√	
• Artillery fire-control systems	√		
• HF/SSB radios		√	
• ALQ-178 EW systems for F-4s and F-16s		√	
• Fast-16 EW systems for F-16s		√	
• TRS-22XX air surveillance radars		√	
• P-STAR air surveillance radars		√	
• C^3I systems		√	

Defense Production *(continued)*

	M	P	A
Optronics			
• Optical targeting devices/FLIR		√	
• Night-vision equipment	√	√	
• Laser range-finders	√		

Note: M - manufacture (indigenously developed)
P - production under license
A - assembly

Weapons of Mass Destruction

NBC Capabilities

Nuclear capability
One 5Mw TR-2 research reactor at Cekmerce and one 250kw ITV-TRR research reactor at Istanbul. Turkey intends to order a 1,000Mw reactor. As a member of NATO, nuclear weapons were deployed in Turkey in the past, and might be deployed again. Party to the NPT. Safeguards agreement with the IAEA in force.

Chemical weapons and protective equipment
Personal protective suits; portable chemical detectors; Fox detection vehicles. Party to the CWC.

Biological weapons
No known BW activity. Party to the BWC.

Ballistic Missiles

Model	Launchers	Missiles	Since	Notes
• ATACMS	28	72	1997	Using MLRS launchers

See also under Rockets.

Armed Forces

Major Changes: The economic crisis that began in March 2001 and the collapse of the Turkish currency forced the Armed Forces to declare that many of its procurement programs would be either cancelled, reduced or postponed. It is still unclear which of the programs will remain and which will be postponed or cancelled. The Air Force continues to absorb upgraded F-4E aircraft from Israel, as well as Blackhawk helicopters from the US and indigenously assembled Cougar helicopters. The Navy received its 7th Oliver Hazard Perry class frigate from the US.

Order-of-Battle

Year	1996	1997	1999	2000	2001
General data					
• Personnel (regular)	515,800	639,000*	633,000	633,000	610,000
• SSM launchers		28	28	28	28
Ground Forces					
• Divisions	2 - 3	5	5	5	5
• Total number of brigades	63	67	67	67	67
• Tanks	4,280	4,115* (4,190)	4,115 (4,190)	4,205 (4,280)	2,600 (4,255)
• APCs/AFVs	4,046	4,743*	4,520	5,460	5,460
• Artillery (including MRLs)	4,128	4,113 (4,412)	4,312 (4,611)	~4,350 (~4,650)	~4,350 (~4,650)
Air Force					
• Combat aircraft	434	461*	416	485	~445(465)
• Transport aircraft	62	87*	87	92	90 (94)
• Helicopters	304	381*	381	395	407
Air Defense Forces					
• Heavy SAM batteries	30	24*	24	24	24
• Light SAM launchers	24	86*	86	86	86
Navy					
• Combat vessels	63	75	51	65	78
• Patrol crafts	32	96*	88	108	103
• Submarines	16	17	16	15	14

Note: Beginning with 1997, data refers to quantities in active service. The number in parentheses refers to the total inventory.
* Due to change in estimate.

Personnel

	Regular	Reserves	Total
Ground Forces	500,000	259,000	759,000
Air Force	57,000	74,000	131,000
Navy	53,000	65,000	118,000
Total	**610,000**	**398,000**	**1,008,000**
Paramilitary			
• Coast Guard	2,200		2,200
• Gendarmerie/ National Guard	180,000	50,000	230,000

Ground Forces

Formations

	Corps/ armies	Divisions	Independent Brigades/ groups	Independent Battalions	Brigades in Divisions
All arms	4 armies 9 corps				
Armored			15		
Mechanized		2	18		1 armd., 2 mech., 1 aty. each
Infantry		3	9		4 inf., 1 aty. each
Commando			4		
Presidential Guard			1 (reg.)		
Border Defense			5 (reg.)	26	
Coastal Defense (reserve)			4		
Marines			1		
Total		**5**	**57**	**26**	

Tanks

Model	Quantity	In service	Since	Notes
MBTs				
Medium and low quality				
• Leopard A1/A3	397	397	1982	
• M60 A1/A3	906	906	1992	
• M48T	2,876	~1,300	1984	Some possibly in storage
• M47	75	0	1970	
Total	**4,255**	**~2,600**		
Future procurement				
• M1A1	100			Negotiation on lease
• Leopard 1	170			Upgrading program
• M60A1	170			Upgrading program under negotiation

APCs/AFVs

Model	Quantity	In service	Since	Notes
APCs				
• ACV AAPC	830	830	1997	
• M113 A1/A2	2,815	2,815	1975	
• BTR-80	240	240	1993	
• BTR-60	340	340	1991	
• S-55	40	40	1995	
Subtotal	4,265	4,265		
IFVs				
• Condor	25	25	1988	
• UR-416	35	35	1984	
• ACV AIFV	868	868	1997	Including 170 AMVs and 48 ATVs
Subtotal	928	928		
Reconnaissance				
• Cobra	~5	~5	1999	
• Akrep	260	260	1994	
Subtotal	~265	~265		
Total	**~5,460**	**~5,460**		
Future procurement				
• ACV	551			Delivery up to 2004

Artillery

Model	Quantity	In service	Since	Notes
Self-propelled guns and howitzers				
• 203mm M110	219	219	1981	
• 203mm M-55	9	9	1978	
• 175mm M107	36	36	1976	
• 155mm M44T	222	222	1992	
• 155mm M52T	365	365	1995	
• 105mm M108	26	26	1982	
Subtotal	877	877		
Towed guns and howitzers				
• 203mm M115	162	162	1983	
• 155mm M114	517	517	1979	
• 155mm M59	171	0	1975	
• 150mm Skoda	128	0	1976	
• 105mm M101/ M102	640	640	1974	
Subtotal	1,618	1,319		

Artillery *(continued)*

Model	Quantity	In service	Since	Notes
Mortars, under 160mm				
• 120mm	578	578	1981	
• 107mm M30	1,265	1,265	1974	
• 107mm M106 SP	+	+	1984	
• 81mm AMV SP	170	170	1997	Mounted on ACV
Subtotal	~2,050	~2,050		
Rockets				
• WS-1	~30	~30	1997	
MRLs				
• 227mm MLRS	28	28	1988	
• 122mm T-122	+	+		
• 107mm	48	48	1975	
Subtotal	~80	~80		
Total	**~4,650**	**~4,350**		
Future procurement				
• Toros 230/260mm				
• 155mm SP2000/ 155mm K9	400			Under development
• 155mm towed				Under development

Ground Radars

Model	Quantity	In service	Since	Notes
Artillery/mortar locating radars				
• AN/TPQ-37	4	4	1997	
• AN/TPQ-36	7	7	1988	
• Stentor	5	5	1988	
• Blindfire	13	13	1996	
• ARS-2000	+	+	1996	

Logistics and Engineering Equipment

Mine laying and clearing, bar mine-clearing system, crossing equipment, M48 ECVs (20)

Anti-Tank Missiles

Model	Launchers	Missiles	Since	Notes
• Milan	392	+	1984	
• TOW SP	365	+	1980	48 of which are on ACV ATV
• Cobra	186	+	1977	
Total	**943**			

Anti-Tank Missiles *(continued)*

Model	Launchers	Missiles	Since	Notes
Future procurement				
• Eryx		10,000		Delivery until 2009

Anti-Tank Guns

Model	Quantity	In service	Since	Notes
• 106mm M40 A1	2,330	2,330	1975	
• 75mm	620	620	1975	
• 57mm M-18	925	925	1976	
Total	**3,875**	**3,875**		

Air Force

Order-of-Battle

Category	Quantity	In service	Notes
• Combat	465	~445	
• Transport	94	90	
• Helicopters	407	407	

Combat Aircraft

Model	Quantity	In service	Since	Notes
Advanced multi-role				
• F-16C/D	225	225	1987	
Multi-role				
• Phantom 2000	15	15	1999	Out of total of 54; 1 plane per month
• F-4E	119	~100	1973	Some in the process of upgrading
Subtotal	134	~115		
Obsolete				
• F-5A/B	106	106	1965	
Total	**465**	**~445**		

Combat Aircraft *(continued)*

Model	Quantity	In service	Since	Notes
Future procurement				
• F-15E				Under negotiation
• F-16 C/D	32			Total order
• F-5	48			To be upgraded
• F-4E	54			Being upgraded to Phantom 2000 standard

Transport Aircraft

Model	Quantity	In service	Since	Notes
• C-160D	19	19	1971	
• KC-135R	9	7	1995	Tanker
• C-130E	7	7	1964	
• C-130B	7	5	1991	To be converted to EW role
• Citation (VIP)	5	5	1985	
• CN-235	47	47	1991	2 employed in EW role
Total	**94**	**90**		
Future procurement				
• A-400M	12			
• CN-235	12			Being delivered; 9 for maritime patrol

Training and Liaison Aircraft

Model	Quantity	In service	Since	Notes
Jet trainers				
• T-33	34	34	1975	
• T-38 (F-5)	70	70	1965	
• Cessna 318 (T-37)	60	60	1960	
Subtotal	164	164		
Piston/Turbo-prop				
• SF-260D	39	39	1990	
• Cessna 172 (T-41)	51	51	1972	26 with Army Aviation
Subtotal	90	90		
Total	**254**	**254**		

Helicopters

Model	Quantity	In service	Since	Notes
Attack				
• AH-1W/P	37	37	1990	With Army Aviation
Medium transport				
• AS-532 Cougar	26	26	1995	With Army Aviation
• Mi-17	19	19	1995	With gendarmerie
• S-70A Blackhawk	60	60	1992	35 with gendarmerie
• AB-212	15	15	1985	13 with Navy, in ASW role and 3 with Army Aviation
• UH-1H/AB-204/ AB-205	187	187	1966	160 with Army Aviation and 3 with Navy
Subtotal	307	307		
Light transport				
• Bell 206	32	32	1968	3 with Coast Guard
• H-300C	28	28	1982	With Army Aviation
• OH-58B	3	3	1994	With Army Aviation
Subtotal	63	63		
Total	**407**	**407**		
Future procurement				
• AB-412	9			Possibly suspended
• MD-600N	10			Possibly suspended
• CH-53/S-80E	4			Possibly suspended
• CH-60S Knighthawk	4			Possibly suspended
• AH-1Z King Cobra	50			Delivery in 2003
• S-70 Blackhawk	50			Total order; 24 already delivered
• S-70B Seahawk	8			Additional order of 8 possibly suspended

Helicopters *(continued)*

Model	Quantity	In service	Since	Notes
• Cougar AS-532	30			Delivery up to 2005; additional 20 under negotiation for police

Miscellaneous Aircraft

Model	Quantity	In service	Since	Notes
Reconnaissance				
• RF-4E	20	20	1977	Also listed under Combat Aircraft
• RF-5	20	20	1965	Also listed under Combat Aircraft
ELINT/EW				
• CN-235	2	2	1991	Also listed under Transport Aircraft
Maritime surveillance				
• Maule MX 7	1	1	1993	With Coast Guard
• S-2A/E Tracker	9	0	1970	
UAVs and mini-UAVs				
• CL-89	+	+		
• Gnat 750	6	6		
• Harphy attack drones	+	+	2000	
Future procurement				
• AEW aircraft	6			Probably to be postponed indefinitely
• UAVs	19			Tender has not been decided
• CN-235	9			Maritime surveillance

Advanced Armament

Air-to-air missiles

AIM-120 AMRAAM (138), AIM-9E/F Sidewinder (210), AIM-9J/M/S/P Sidewinder (1,460), AIM-7E Sparrow (690)

Air-to-ground missiles

AGM-88 HARM (100), AGM-65 A/G Maverick (300), AGM-142 Popeye (50), Sea Skua (36), BLU-107 Durandal (523)

Advanced Armament *(continued)*

Avionics
LANTIRN 24

Future procurement
LANTIRN (20), Hellfire II (84), AGM-65 G/F Maverick, Popeye II (Light), LOROPS, Penguin (16)

Note: Number in parentheses refers to the quantity of missiles purchased, not to current inventory levels.

Air Force Infrastructure

Military airfields: 23

Adnan-Menderes, Afyon, Akhisar, Akinci, Ankara-Güvercinlik, Balikesit, Bandirma, Dalaman, Diyarbakir, Elazig, Erhac, Erkilet, Erzincan, Eskisehir, Istanbul-Sarigazi, Izmir-Kaklic, Kayseri, Konya, Malatya, Merzifon, Murted, Yalova, Yesilkoy

Air Defense Forces

Surface-to-Air Missiles

Model	Batteries	Launchers	Since	Notes
Heavy missiles				
• Nike Hercules	24		1970	8 squadrons, 24 batteries
Light missiles				
• Rapier B1X		78	1999	Upgraded
• Rapier		8	1984	
Total		**86**		
Shoulder-launched missiles				
• Stinger		108	1991	
• Redeye		790	1986	
Total		**898**		
Future procurement				
• I-Hawk PIP-2	18			
• Rapier B1X		12		Under negotiations
• Armored Stinger SP		300		Under development

Other Air Defense Systems

Model	Quantity	In service	Since	Notes
Short-range guns				
• 40mm L60/70	800	800	1970	
• 40mm T1	40	40		
• 40mm M42 A1 SP	260	260	1976	
• 35mm GDF-003	120	120	1984	
• 20mm GAI-DO1	440	440	1975	
Total	**1,660**	**1,660**		
Radars				
• AN/FPS-117	1	1	1993	
• HR-3000 (Hadr)	3	3	1990	
• TRS-2100 (Tiger)	2	2	1988	
• MPQ-64 Sentinel	4	4	1998	
• TRS-22XX	14	14	1993	
• TRS-2000	4	4	1999	
• RAT-31	+	+	1996	
• AN/TPS-59	+	+		
Future procurement				
• MPQ-64 Sentinel	10	10		
• P-STAR	+	+		

Navy

Submarines

Type	Quantity	Length (m.)/ displacement (t.)	Notes/ armament
• Atilay (Type 1200)	6	61.2/1,185	8x533mm torpedoes
• Burakreist (Guppy II A)	2	93.2/2,440	10x533mm torpedoes 40 mines
• Hizzirreis (Tang)	2	87.4/2,700	8x533mm torpedoes mines
• Preveze (Type 1400)	4	62/1,586	2xSub Harpoon SSMs 8x533mm torpedoes mines
Total	**14**		
Future procurement			
• Gur class submarines	4		Delivery 2003-2006

Combat Vessels

Type	Quantity	Length (m.)/ displacement (t.)	Notes/ armament
Frigates			
• Barbaros (MEKO 200 track II-A/B)	4	116.7/3,350	1xAB-212 helicopter 8xHarpoon SSMs 2xSeasparrow 8 SAMs 6x324mm torpedoes 1x127mm gun 3x25mm Oerlicon AD gun
• Berk	1	95/1,450	Helicopter pad 2xHedgehog Mk11 24 ASW rocket launchers 6x324mm torpedoes 4x76mm guns
• Gaziantep (Oliver Perry class)	6	135.6/3,638	2xAB-212 helicopters 4xHarpoon SSMs 36xStandard SAMs 6x324mm torpedoes 1x76mm gun 1x20mm Phalanx AD gun
• Tepe (Knox class)	8	134/3,011	1xAB-212 helicopter 8xHarpoon SSMs 1xASROC Mk112 8 torpedo launcher 4x324mm torpedoes 1x20mm Vulcan Phalanx AD gun 1x127mm gun
• Yavuz (MEKO 200)	4	115.5/2,414	1xAB-212 helicopter 8xHarpoon SSMs 6x324mm torpedoes 8xSeasparrow SAMs 1x127mm gun 3xOerlicon 25mm AD guns
Subtotal	23		
MFPBs			
• Doğan class	8	58.1/436	8xHarpoon SSMs 1x76mm gun 2x35mm guns

Combat Vessels *(continued)*

Type	Quantity	Length (m.)/ displacement (t.)	Notes/ armament
• Kiliç class	3	57.8/433	8xHarpoon SSMs 1x76mm gun 1x40mm gun
• Yildiz class	2	57.8/433	8xHarpoon SSMs 1x76mm gun 2x35mm guns
• Kartal (Jaguar class)	8	42.5/160	2-4xPenguin SSMs 2x533mm torpedoes 2x40mm guns 4 mines
Subtotal	21		
Mine warfare vessels			
• Nusret	1	77/1,880	4x76mm guns 400 mines
• Mehmecik (YMP class)	1	39.6/540	
• Adjutant (MSC 268/294)	9	43/320	Sonar search 2x20mm guns
• Karamürsel (Vegasack class)	3	47.3/362	Active mine detectors 2x20mm guns
• Edincik (Circé class)	5	50.9/495	Robot seeker/destroyer 1x20mm gun
• Foça (Cove class)	4	34/180	1x12.7 MG
• Dalgiç (Mine hunting tenders)	8	21.8/70	1x12.7 MG
• Şamandira	3	19.6/72	
Subtotal	34		
Total	**78**		
Future procurement			
• D'orves class frigates	6		Upgraded for delivery 2002
• Type 332MJ minehunters	6	54.5/715	Delivery up to 2007

Patrol Craft

Type	Quantity	Length (m.)/ displacement (t.)	Notes/ armament
• Girne class	1	58.1/341	2xMousetrap Mk 20 4 ASW rocket launchers 2x40mm guns 2x20mm guns
• Bora class (Ashville)	1	50.1/225	1x76mm gun 1x40mm gun 4x12.7mm MGs
• Hisar class (PC–1638)	6	53/325	1xHedgehog Mk 15 24 ASW rocket launchers 1x40mm gun 4x20mm guns
• Trabzon class	3	50/370	1x40mm gun 2x12.7mm MGs
• Turk class	9	40.2/170	1xMousetrap Mk 20 4 ASW rocket launcher 2x40mm guns 1x20mm gun 2x12.7mm MGs
• PGM -71 class	4	30.8/130	2xMousetrap Mk 22 8 ASW rocket launchers 1x40mm gun 4x20mm guns
• Coast guard type	4	25.3/63	2xMousetrap Mk 20 8 ASW rocket launchers 2x20mm guns
• Taşkiçak (Large patrol craft)	12	40.7/195	1x40mm gun 2x12.7mm MGs
• Gölcük (Large patrol craft)	14	40.2/180	1x40mm gun 2x12.7mm MGs
• SAR 33 Type	10	34.6/180	1x40mm gun 2x12.7mm MGs
• SAR 35 Type	4	36.6/210	1x40mm gun 2x12.7mm MGs
• KW 15 class	8	28.9/70	1x40mm gun 2x20mm guns
• Kaan (Yonca)	12	15.1/19	2x12.7mm MGs
• Coastal patrol craft	12	14.6/29	1x25mm or 1x12.7mm MG

Patrol Craft

Type	Quantity	Length (m.)/ displacement (t.)	Notes/ armament
• Inshore patrol craft	1	11.6/10	1x12.7mm MG
• Harbor patrol craft	2	17/15	
Total	**103**		
Future procurement			
• Seaguard	10	29.6/90	Delivery to commence in 2000

Landing Craft

Type	Quantity	Length (m.)/ displacement (t.)	Notes/ armament
• Osman Gazi LST	1	105/3,773	900 troops, 15 tanks 4 LCVPs 3x40mm guns 2x35mm guns 2x20mm guns
• Sarucabey LST	2	92/2,600	600 troops, 11 tanks 2 LCVPs 3x40mm guns 4x20mm guns
• Ertuğrul (Terrebonne Parish LST)	2	117.1/5,800	395 troops, 2,200 ton 4 LCVPs 6x76mm guns
• LCM-8	20	22/113	140 troops or 60 ton 2x12.7mm MGs
• LCT	26	59.6/600	100 troops, 5 tanks 2x20mm guns 2x12.7mm MGs
• Edic Type LCT	4	57/580	100 troops, 5 tanks 2x20mm guns 2x12.7mm MGs
• Bayraktar LST	2	100/1,653	6x40mm guns 2x20mm guns
Total	**57**		

Auxiliary Vessels

Type	Quantity	Length (m.)/ displacement (t.)	Notes/ armament
• Tankers	4	1,440-19,000	2x20mm guns
• Water tankers	14	300-1,200 tons	
• Salvage/Rescue	3	1,200-1,600 tons	20mm guns 76mm guns 40mm guns
• Survey	3	680 tons	2x20mm guns
• Intelligence vessel	1	1,497 tons	
• Rhein training ships	2	98.2/2,370	2x100mm guns 4x40mm guns
• Training craft	6	28.8/94	
• Transport	40	Various sizes	
• Tugs	12	750; 1,235 tons	
• Floating docks	10		400-16,000 ton. Lift
• Boom defense	2	560-780 tons	3-4 20mm, 76mm or 40mm guns

Naval Infrastructure

Naval bases: **18**

Aksaz, Aksaz Bay, Ankara (HQ), Antalya, Bartin, Çanakkale, Erdek, Ereğli, Foça, Gölcük, Iskanderun, Istanbul, Izmir, Karamürsel (training), Marmaris, Mersin, Samsun, Trabzon

Naval aviation bases: **4**

Antalia, Cigli, Topel, Trabzon

Ship maintenance and repair facilities: **3**

Gölcük, Taşkiçak, Pendik

Major Non-Governmental Paramilitary Forces

Personnel

	Active
• PKK	8,000

Equipment

Organization	Category	System	Quantity	Notes
PKK	Air defense	• SA - 7 (Grail)	+	

20. UNITED ARAB EMIRATES (UAE)

General Data

Official Name of the State: United Arab Emirates
Head of State: Shaykh Zayid ibn Sultan al-Nuhayan, Emir of Abu Dhabi
Prime Minister: Shaykh Maktum ibn Rashid al-Maktum, Emir of Dubai
Minister of Defense: Shaykh Muhammad ibn Rashid al-Maktum
Chief of General Staff: HRH Lieutenant General Muhammad ibn Zayid al-Nuhayan
Commander of the Air Force and Air Defense Forces: Brigadier General Khalid bin Abdullah Al-Buainnain
Commander of the Navy: Captain Muhammad al-Muhairi

Area: 82,900 sq. km. (estimate)
Population: 3,000,000 (estimate)

Note: The UAE consists of seven principalities: Abu Dhabi, Dubai, Ras al-Khaima, Sharja, Umm al-Qaiwain, Fujaira, and Ajman

Demography

Ethnic and national groups		
South Asians	1,500,000	50%
Other Arabs and Iranians	690,000	23%
Emiri	570,000	19%
Westerners and East Asians	240,000	8%
Religious groups		
Sunni Muslims	2,400,000	80%
Shi'ite Muslims	480,000	16%
Others	120,000	4%

Economic Data

		1996	1997	1998	1999	2000
GDP (current price)	$ bn	48.0	50.4	47.4	52.1	60.5
GDP per capita	$	20,000	19,384	16,928	17,965	20,166
Real GDP growth (at constant 1990 prices)	%	10.1	2.1	1.2	2.5	6.0
Consumer price index	%	2.6	2.1	2.0	2.0	2.5
External debt	$ bn	10.9	12.3	18.2	15.8	12.5

Economic Data *(continued)*

		1996	1997	1998	1999	2000
Balance of payments						
• Exports fob	$ bn	35.2	38.1	33.8	39.9	43.3
• Imports cif	$ bn	25.0	28.5	30.5	32.8	31.9
• Current account balance (including services and income)	$ bn	5.3	4.4	-2.9	0.6	9.2
Government expenditure						
• Consolidated government expenditure	$ bn	20.89	17.55	19.47	19.62	20.60
• Defense expenditure	$ bn	1.59	1.52	1.48	1.42	NA
• Real change in defense expenditure	%	-3.22	-4.21	-3.02	-3.79	NA
• Defense expenditure /GDP	%	3.31	3.01	3.11	2.72	NA
Population	m	2.4	2.6	2.8	2.9	3.0
Official exchange rate	Dh:1$	3.67	3.67	3.67	3.67	3.67

Sources: EIU Quarterly Report, EIU Country Profile, IMF International Financial Statistical Yearbook, SIPRI Yearbook

Note: Some clarification regarding nomenclature of UAE goverment expenditures should be made. From 2000, the consolidated government expenditure figures are used in the above data. Prior to 2000, the Federal government expenditure figures are used.

Arms Procurement and Security Assistance Received

Country	Type	Details
Australia	• Arms transfers	Communication systems for navy
France	• Arms transfers	Mirage 2000-9 combat aircraft, Panther helicopters, AS-350B light helicopters, Leclerc tanks, radio sets, thermal imaging night vision systems, shoulder-launched SAMs, ARVs, torpedoes, anti ship missiles, C^3I systems, upgrading TNC-45 naval combat vessels
	• Cooperation in arms production, assembly, R&D	Combattante fast attack craft
	• Military training	Trainees abroad
Germany	• Arms transfers	tank transporters, Terrier APCs
	• Military training	Trainees abroad, Foreign advisers/instructors

Arms Procurement and Security Assistance Received *(continued)*

Country	Type	Details
Indonesia	• Maintenance of equipment	CN-235 maritime patrol aircraft
Jordan	• Cooperation in arms production, assembly, R&D	Joint development of a 4x4 tactical utility vehicle
Netherlands	• Arms transfers	Kortenaer frigates, artillery surveillance radar, upgrading of SP howitzers
	• Military training	Trainees abroad
Norway	• Arms transfers	Navy simulator
Russia	• Arms transfers	BMP-3 IFVs, upgrading of BMP-3 IFVs, Pantzyr-S1 self propelled air defense systems
South Africa	• Arms transfers	Upgrading of self propelled artillery
Spain	• Arms transfers	C-295 maritime patrol aircraft
Sweden	• Arms transfers	Early warning network
Switzerland	• Arms transfers	Training simulators for BMP-3 IFVs
Turkey	• Arms transfers	AAOV APCs
UK	• Arms transfers	Sonar, Black Shahin AGMs
US	• Arms transfers	F-16 Block 60 aircraft, AMRAAM AAMs, JDAMs guided bombs, Sea Sparrow naval SAMs, early warning network, tactical radio equipment
	• Military training	Foreign advisers/instructors/serving personnel (some civilians); trainees abroad

Arms Sales and Security Assistance Extended

Country	Type	Details
Bosnia	• Arms transfers	AMX-30 MBTs
Lebanon	• Assistance	Finance for demining project
UK	• Facilities	Logistical facilities
Unknown customer	• Arms transfers	Nibbio UAVs
US	• Facilities	Storage facilities for naval equipment at Jebel Ali and Fujaira, and pre-positioning of equipment for an armored brigade under negotiation

Foreign Military Cooperation

Type	Details
• Foreign forces	Some 400 US soldiers
• Forces deployed abroad	In Saudi Arabia (part of GCC "Peninsula Shield" rapid deployment force); 1,250 soldiers with NATOs KFOR peacekeeping force in Kosovo
• Joint maneuvers	France, GCC countries, India, US
• Security agreement	France, Germany, Slovak Republic

Defense Production

	M	P	A
Air force equipment			
• Falco target drone	√		
• Nibbio mini-UAV	√		
• al-Shabah UAV	√		
Naval equipment			
• Fast attack craft		√	
• Construction of patrol boats at Ajman (with British cooperation)		√	
• Upgrading of TNC-45 Patrol Boats	√		
• Swimmer delivery vehicles	√		

Note: M - manufacture (indigenously developed)
P - production under license
A - assembly

Weapons of Mass Destruction

NBC Capabilities

Nuclear capability

No known nuclear activity. Signatory to the NPT.

Chemical weapons and protective equipment

No known CW activities. Signed and ratified the CWC.

Personal protective equipment; unit decontamination equipment.

Biological weapons

No known BW activities. Signed but not ratified the BWC.

Ballistic Missiles

Model	Launchers	Missiles	Since	Notes
• Scud B	6		1991	Owned by Dubai; unconfirmed

Armed Forces

Major Changes: Inauguration of the GCC joint communication network, which is part of the GCC joint early warning system. Delivery of Leclerc MBTs will resume, after a dispute with the manufacturer is resolved. The Emiri Army is absorbing its newly upgraded 155mm M109 and G6 guns. It is also absorbing the last of its ACVs from Turkey and new Terrier light APCs from Germany. The Emiri Air Force concluded the deal to acquire 80 F-16 block 60 combat aircraft (which will be delivered between 2004-2008). The Emiri Navy began the process of upgrading its TNC-45 MFPBs.

Order-of-Battle

Year	1996	1997	1999	2000	2001
General data					
• Personnel (regular)	46,500	46,500	46,500	46,500	46,500
• SSM launchers	6	6	6	6	6
Ground forces					
• Number of brigades	6	9	8	8	8
• Tanks	216	~370 (~430)	~330 (~430)*	~430 (~470)	~400 (~470)
• APCs/AFVs	1,100	~960 (~1,120)	~960 (~1,120)	~1,250 (~1,400)	~1,250 (~1,410)
• Artillery (including MRLs)	264	411(434)*	411(434)	399(422)	399(422)
Air Force					
• Combat aircraft	66	54(66)	54(66)	54(66)	54(66)
• Transport aircraft	36	31(34)	31(34)	31(34)	33(36)
• Helicopters	85	93(95)*	93(95)	100(102)	91(103)
Air Defense Forces					
• Heavy SAM batteries	~7	~7	~7	5	5
• Medium SAM batteries	3	6*	6	6	6
• Light SAM launchers	+	113	113	~115	~115
Navy					
• Combat vessels	10	12	12	12	12
• Patrol craft	121	119	105	110	112

Note: Beginning with data for 1997, we refer to quantities in active service. The number in parentheses refers to the total inventory.

*Due to changes in estimate.

Personnel

	Regular	Reserves	Total
Ground Forces	40,000		40,000
Air Force	4,500		4,500
Navy	2,000		2,000
Total	**46,500**		**46,500**
Paramilitary			
• Coast Guard			+
• Frontier Corps			+

Ground Forces

Formations

	Independent Brigades/groups
Armored	3
Mechanized	4
Royal Guard	1
Artillery	1
Total	**9**

Note: includes two mechanized brigades under Dubai National Command.

Tanks

Model	Quantity	In service	Since	Notes
MBTs				
High quality				
• Leclerc	~250	~250	1995	Estimated number supplied, out of total number of 436
Medium and low quality				
• AMX-30	100	64	1981	
• OF-40 Lion Mk 2	36	0	1982	
Subtotal	136	64		
Light tanks				
• Scorpion	80	80	1975	
Total	**~470**	**~400**		
Future procurement				
• Leclerc	438			390 MBTs, 46 recovery vehicles and 2 training vehicles

APCs/AFVs

Model	Quantity	In service	Since	Notes
APCs				
• ACV AESV	61	61	1999	Also listed under Logistics and Engineering Equipment
• AMX-VCI	10	10	1978	
• Engesa EE-11 Urutu	30	30	1985	
• Saracen	30	0	1977	
• VAB	20	20	1980	
• VCR	+	+		
• M-3 (Panhard)	300	300	1977	
• Fahd	100	100		
• AT-105 Saxon	20	20		Possibly with police
• Terrier	+	+	2001	Delivery in progress
Subtotal	~ 580	~ 550		
IFVs				
• AMX-10P	20	20	1980	
• BMP-3	400	400	1980	
Subtotal	420	420		
Reconnaissance				
• AML-60/90	105	105	1980	
• Engessa EE-9 Cascavel	100	100		
• Ferret	60	0		
• ACV AAOV	75	75	1999	
• Saladin	70	0		
• VBC-90	+	+		
Subtotal	~410	~280		
Total	**~1,410**	**~1,250**		
Future procurement				
• Terrier	+			Delivery in progress

Artillery

Model	Quantity	In service	Since	Notes
Self-propelled guns and howitzers				
• 155mm Mk F3 (AMX-13)	20	20	1976	
• 155mm G-6	78	78		
• 155mm M109 A3	85	85	1995	
Subtotal	183	183		

Artillery *(continued)*

Model	Quantity	In service	Since	Notes
Towed guns and howitzers				
• 130mm Type 59	30	30		
• 105mm L-118 light gun	81	81		
• 105mm M102	50	50		
• 105mm M56	18	18		
Subtotal	179	179		
Mortars, under 160mm				
• 120mm	12	12		
MRLs				
• 122mm Firos-25/30	48	25		
Total	**422**	**399**		
Future procurement				
• 227mm MLRS				

Logistics and Engineering Equipment

Matenin automatic mine layers, Aardvark Mk 3 flail, Leclerc ARVs (46), ACV AESVs (53), ACV ARVs (8)

Anti-Tank Missiles

Model	Launchers	Missiles	Since	Notes
• BGM-71B TOW	24	+	1983	
• HOT	50	+		
• MILAN	230	+		
Total	**~300**	+		

Anti-Tank Guns

Model	Quantity	In service	Since	Notes
• 120mm BAT L-4 recoilless rifle	*	*		
• 84mm Carl Gustav M-2 light recoilless rifle	250	250		

Air Force

Order-of-Battle

Category	Quantity	In service	Notes
• Combat	66	54	
• Transport	36	33	
• Helicopters	103	91	

Combat Aircraft

Model	Quantity	In service	Since	Notes
Advanced multi-role				
• Mirage 2000-5	36	36	1989	8 listed also under reconnaissance
Obsolete				
• Mirage V-AD/RAD/ DAD	18	18	1974	5 listed also under reconnaissance
• Mirage III	12	0		
Subtotal	30	18		
Total	**66**	**54**		
Future procurement				
• Mirage 2000-9	30			
• F-16 Block 60	80			

Transport Aircraft

Model	Quantity	In service	Since	Notes
• BAe 125	1	1		
• Beech King Air 350	2	2		
• Boeing 707	2	2	1976	
• Boeing 737	1	1	1976	
• Boeing 747	3	3	1985	
• BN-2 Islander	1	1	1983	
• C-130H Hercules/L-100-30	6	6	1975/1981	
• CASA C-212	4	4	1982	Employed in EW role
• DHC-4 Caribou	3	0		Possibly phased out
• CN-235	7	7	1993	Some in maritime patrol role
• G-222	1	1		Number unconfirmed
• IL-76	4	4	1994	On lease
• Mystère-Falcon 20	1	1		
Total	**36**	**33**		

Training and Liaison Aircraft

Model	Quantity	In service	Since	Notes
Jet trainers				
• Aermacchi MB-326 KD/LD	8	8	1974	
• Aermacchi MB-339	5	5	1984	
• Hawk Mk 102	26	18	1993	
• Hawk Mk 61/63	22	15	1983/1984	
Subtotal	61	46		
Piston/Turbo-prop				
• Cessna 182 Skylane	1	1		
• Pilatus PC-7	23	23	1982	
• G-115T (Grob)	12	12	1997	
• SF-260 WD	6	6	1983	
Subtotal	42	42		
Total	**103**	**88**		
Future procurement				
• G-115T (Grob)	12			Option for additional 12
• Alpha jet	30			

Helicopters

Model	Quantity	In service	Since	Notes
Attack				
• AH-64A Apache	20	20	1993	
• SA-342K Gazelle	12	10	1980	
• Alouette III	7	7		
Subtotal	39	37		
Medium transport				
• AB-205/Bell 205	8	6	1969	
• AB-212	3	3	1977	
• AB-214	4	4	1981	
• AB-412	5	2	1994	Possibly with police
• SA-330 Puma/IAR-330	11	11	1972	
Subtotal	31	26		
Light transport				
• A-109	3	3	1995	Possibly with police
• Bell 206 JetRanger	10	5	1984	
• BO-105	6	6	1992	
Subtotal	19	14		

Helicopters *(continued)*

Model	Quantity	In service	Since	Notes
Naval combat				
• AS-332/532 Super Puma/Cougar	7	7	1982	
• AS-565 Panther	7	7	1998	
Subtotal	14	14		
Total	**103**	**91**		
Future procurement				
• AS-350B	14			

Miscellaneous Aircraft

Model	Quantity	In service	Since	Notes
Reconnaissance				
• Mirage 2000-5	8	8		Also listed under Combat Aircraft
• Mirage V	5	5		Also listed under Combat Aircraft
AEW aircraft				
• C-130 EW				Also listed under Transport Aircraft
• CASA C-212				Also listed under Transport Aircraft
Maritime surveillance aircraft				
• CN-235	5	5		Also listed under Transport Aircraft
Target drones				
• TTL BTT-3 Banshee	+	+		
UAVs and mini-UAVs				
• Beech MQM-107A	20	20		
• Nibbio	+	+		
Future procurement				
• C-295	4			For Maritime Patrol missions
• SAT 800 Falco				
• al-Shabah UAV	30			

Advanced Armament

Air-to-air missiles
AIM-9L Sidewinder, R-550 Magic (108)
Air-to-ground missiles
AS-11, AS-12, AS-15TT (56), AS-30L, AM-39 Exocet, al-Hakim (PGM-1/2/3) (1,750)
Bombs
BAP-100 anti-runway
Future procurement
AIM-120 (491), Black Shahin, Harpoon, ASRAAM, Pave Way, AIM-9M (267), AGM-88 HARM (163), AGM-84 (52), AGM-65D/G (1,163), Mica EM, Mica IR, JDAMs guided bombs (500)

Note: Numbers in parentheses refer to quantity of units purchased, not to current inventory levels.

Air Force Infrastructure

Aircraft shelters
For combat aircraft at Abu Dhabi and Jabil (Jebel) Ali
Military airfields : 7
Abu Dhabi (international), al-Dhafra (Sharja), Bateen (Abu Dhabi), Dubai (international), Fujaira, Sharja, Mindhat

Air Defense Forces

Surface-to-Air Missiles

Model	Batteries	Launchers	Since	Notes
Heavy missiles				
• MIM-23B improved HAWK	5		1989	
Medium missiles				
• Crotale	3		1978	
• Rapier	3		1976	
Total	**6**			
Light missiles				
• RBS-70		13	1980	
• Mistral		100	1993	
• Javelin		+		
• Tigercat		+		Probably phased out
Total		**~115**		

Surface-to-Air Missiles *(continued)*

Model	Batteries	Launchers	Since	Notes
Shoulder-launched missiles				
• Blowpipe		~20	1992	Probably phased out
• FIM-92A Stinger		+		
• SA-7 (Grail)		+		
• SA-14 (Gremlin)		+		
• SA-16 (Gimlet)		10	1992	
Total		**~30**		
Future procurement				
• Pantzyr-S1				

Other Air Defense Systems

Model	Quantity	In service	Since	Notes
Air defense systems (missiles, radars, and guns)				
• Skyguard AD system	7	7		
Short-range guns				
• 30mm M-3 VDA SP	+	+		
• 20mm GCF-BM2 SP	+	+	1986	
Radars				
• AN/TPS-70	3	3		
• Watchman	+	+		

Navy

Combat Vessels

Type	Quantity	Length (m.)/ displacement (t.)	Notes/ armament
Missile frigates			
• Abu Dhabi (Kortenaer class)	2	130.5/3,050	2xhelicopters 8xHarpoon SSMs 4x324mm torpedoes 8xSea Sparrow SAM 1x76mm gun 1x30mm gun 2x20mm guns

Combat Vessels *(continued)*

Type	Quantity	Length (m.)/ displacement (t.)	Notes/ armament
Missile corvettes			
• Muray-Jib (Lürssen 62)	2	63/630	1xAlouette helicopter 8xExocet MM40 SSMs 8xCrotale Navale SAM 1x76mm gun 1x30mm Goalkeeper
MFPBs			
• Ban-Yas (Lürssen TNC-45)	6	44.9/260	4xExocet MM40 SSMs 1x76mm gun
• Mubarraz class (Lürssen)	2	44.9/260	4xExocet MM40 SSMs 1x6 Mistral SAM 1x76mm gun 2x20mm gun
Subtotal	8		
Total	**12**		
Future procurement			
• Oliver Hazard Perry missile frigates	2		From US Drawdown

Patrol Craft

Type	Quantity	Length (m.)/ displacement (t.)	Notes/ armament
• Ardhana (Vosper Thornycroft type)	6	33.5/110	2x30mm guns 1x20mm gun
• Camcraft	5	23.4/70	2x20mm guns with Coast Guard
• Camcraft	16	19.8/50	1x20mm gun with Coast Guard
• Watercraft	6	13.7/25	
• Boghammar	3	13m	With police
• Baglietto GC-23	6	24/50.7	1x20mm gun with Coast Guard
• Baglietto	3	18.1/22	With Coast Guard
• Al-Shaali/Arctic 28	20	8.5/4	
• Harbor patrol craft	35	6.6-10m	With Coast Guard
• Protector patrol craft	2	33/180	1x20mm gun 2x12.7mm MGs
• Dhafeer/Spear	10	9-12m	With police
Total	**112**		

Landing Craft

Type	Quantity	Length (m.)/ displacement (t.)	Notes/ armament
• Al-Feyi (Siong Huat LSL)	3	50/650	
• LCM	1	40/100	
• LCT	2		
• Serana class	2	26.3/105	45 tons or 100 troops
Total	8		
Future procurement			
LCT	2		

Auxiliary Vessels

Type	Quantity	Length (m.)/ displacement (t.)	Notes/ armament
• Arun pilot craft	2		
• Coastal tug	1	35.0/795	
• Diving tender	1	31.4/100	
• Diving tender	2		Coast Guard

Coastal Defense

Type	Quantity	Notes
• MM-40 Exocet	+	Unconfirmed

Naval Infrastructure

Naval bases (including Coast Guard): 11

Ajman, Dalma (Abu Dhabi), Fujaira, Mina Jabil (Jebel) Ali (Dubai), Mina Khalid (Sharja), Mina Khor Fakkan (Sharja), Mina Rashid (Dubai), Mina Saqr (Ras al-Khaima), Mina Sultan (Sharja), Taweela, Mina Zayd (Abu Dhabi)

Ship maintenance and repair facilities

Dubai wharf for maintenance and repair of merchant and naval vessels, 2 dry-docks available, ship building facility in Mussafah to be enlarged

21. YEMEN

General Data

Official Name of the State: Republic of Yemen
Head of State: President Ali Abdallah Salih
Prime Minister: Abd al-Qadir Ba Jamal
Minister of Defense: Brigadier General Abdallah Ali Alaywa
Chief of General Staff: Brigadier General Abdallah Ali Alaywah
Commander of the Air Force: Colonel Muhammad Salih al-Ahmar
Commander of the Navy: Admiral Abdallah al-Mujawar

Area: 527,970 sq. km.
Population: 18,300,000

Demography

Ethnic groups		
Arabs	16,781,000	91.7%
Afro-Arabs	1,153,000	6.3%
Others	366,000	2.0%
Religious Groups		
Sunni Muslims	11,346,000	62.0%
Shi'ite Zaydi Muslims	6,588,000	36.0%
Shi'ite Ismaili Muslims	92,000	0.5%
Others	274,000	1.5%

Economic Data

		1996	1997	1998	1999	2000
GDP (current price)	$ bn	5.5	6.6	5.9	6.7	8.7
GDP per capita	$	346	400	345	378	475
Real GDP growth	%	4.4	5.4	3.8	3.8	6.5
Consumer price index	%	30.0	5.4	8.0	8.0	10.9
External debt	$ bn	6.4	3.9	4.1	4.4	4.4
Balance of payments						
• Exports fob	$ bn	2.26	2.27	1.50	2.46	4.04
• Imports fob	$ bn	2.29	2.41	2.23	2.44	3.04
• Current account balance (including services and income)	$ bn	0.11	0.06	-0.25	0.17	0.85

Economic Data *(continued)*

		1996	1997	1998	1999	2000
Government expenditure						
• Total expenditure	$ bn	3.0	2.27	1.88	1.89	2.42
• Defense expenditure	$ bn	0.85	0.98	0.89	0.87	NA
• Real change in defense expenditure	%	-3.75	16.19	-9.96	-1.58	NA
• Defense expenditure/ GDP	%	15.38	14.89	15	13	NA
Population	m	15.9	16.5	17.1	17.7	18.3
Official exchange rate	YR:$1	94.16	129.28	135.88	155.72	161.73

Sources: EIU Quarterly Report, EIU Country Profile, IMF International Financial Statistical Yearbook, SIPRI Yearbook

Arms Procurement and Security Assistance Received

Country	Type	Details
Czech Republic	• Arms transfers	L-39C jet trainers, T-54/55 MBTs
Moldova	• Arms transfers	MRLs
Poland	• Arms transfers	T-55 MBTs (suspended), trucks
Russia	• Arms transfers	T-72 MBTs
	• Maintenance of equipment	SS-21 missiles
US	• Arms transfers	Spare parts for American-made systems

Arms Sales and Security Assistance Extended

Country	Type	Details
Iraq	• Facilities	Refuge to a small number of Iraqi aircraft (unconfirmed)
Sudan	• Arms transfers	T-55 MBTs (from Poland)

Weapons of Mass Destruction

NBC Capabilities

Nuclear capability

No known nuclear activity. Signatory to the NPT.

Chemical weapons and protective equipment

No known CW activities. Signed and ratified the CWC.

Biological weapons

No known BW activities. Party to the BWC.

Ballistic Missiles

Model	Launchers	Missiles	Since	Notes
• SS-1 (Scud B)	6			
• SS-21 (Scarab)	4		1988	
Total	**10**			

Note: Serviceability of missiles and launchers unknown.

Armed Forces

Note: All figures are rough estimates, due to 1994 civil war.

Major Changes: The Yemenite army received T-72 MBTs from Russia, and some 100 upgraded T-55 MBTs from the Czech Republic. No other major change was recorded.

Order-of-Battle

Year	1996	1997	1999	2000	2001
General data					
• Personnel (regular)	~65,000	~65,000	~65,000	~65,000	~65,000
• SSM launchers	10	10	10	10	10
Ground Forces					
• Number of brigades	30	33	33	33	33
• Tanks	1,040	575	575	605	~715
		(1,040)	(1,040)	(1,070)	(~1,180)
• APCs/AFVs	1,320	480	~480	~480	~480
		(1,165)	(~1,170)	(~1,200)	(~1,200)
• Artillery (including MRLs)	1,020	~670	~670	~670	~670
		(~1,020)	(~990)*	(~1,000)	(~1,000)
Air Force					
• Combat aircraft	166	~55(~150)	~50(~150)	~50(~150)	~55(~180)
• Transport aircraft	23	18(23)	18(23)	18(23)	20(30)
• Helicopters	67	27(67)	27(67)	26(66)	26(70)
Air Defense Forces					
• Heavy SAM batteries	25	25	25	25	25
• Medium SAM batteries	+	+	+	+	+
• Light SAM launchers	+	120*	120	120	120
Navy					
• Combat vessels	13	11	11	10	10
• Patrol craft	7	7	3	9	9

Note: Beginning with 1997, data refers to quantities in active service. The number in parentheses refers to the total inventory.

* Due to change in estimate.

Personnel

	Regular	Reserves	Total
Ground Forces	~60,000	200,000	~260,000
Air Force	3,000		3,000
Navy	2,000		2,000
Total	**~65,000**	**200,000**	**~265,000**
Paramilitary			
• Central Security Force	50,000		50,000

Note: The military forces are a combination of personnel from the former Yemen Arab Republic and the People's Democratic Republic of Yemen; no information regarding reorganization is available.

Ground Forces

Formations

	Independent Brigades/ Groups	Independent Battations
Armored	7	
Mechanized	5	
Infantry*	18	
Artillery	4	
SSM	1	
Air Defense		2
Commando/Paratroops	1	
Special Forces	1	
Central Guards	1	
Total	**38**	**2**

* Many infantry brigades are undermanned or retain only skeleton formations

Tanks

Model	Quantity	In service	Since	Notes
MBTs				
High quality				
• T-72	39	39	2000	
Medium and low quality				
• T-62	200	75	1979	
• M60 A1	140	50	1979	
• T-54/55	800	550	1971/1999	
Subtotal	1,140	675		
Total	**~1,180**	**~715**		

APCs/AFVs

Model	Quantity	In service	Since	Notes
APCs				
• al-Walid	+	+	1977	
• BTR-152	+	+	1977	
• BTR-40/50/60	650	180	1977	
• M113 A1	76	70	1979	Including several derivatives
Subtotal	~750	~250		
IFVs				
• BMP-1/2	150	100		
Reconnaissance				
• AML-90/AML-60	125	80	1975	
• BRDM-2	100	50		
• Ferret	10	*	1974	Possibly phased out
• Saladin	60	*	1974	Possibly phased out
Subtotal	295	130		
Total	**~1,200**	**~480**		

Artillery

Model	Quantity	In service	Since	Notes
Self-propelled guns and howitzers				
• 122mm M-1974	+	+		
• 100mm SU-100	30	0		Possibly phased out
Subtotal	~50	+		
Towed guns and howitzers				
• 155mm M114	12	12	1980	
• 152mm D-20	10	+		
• 130mm M-46	75	60	1976	
• 122mm D-30	150	130	1977	
• 122mm M-1938	100	40	1975	
• 122mm M-1931/7	30	30		
• 105mm M101	30	25		
Subtotal	407	~300		
Mortars, over 160mm				
• 160mm	100	100		
Mortars, under 160mm				
• 120mm	100	100	1978	
• 107mm	12	12		
Subtotal	112	112		

Artillery *(continued)*

Model	Quantity	In service	Since	Notes
MRLs				
• 240mm BM-24	35	+	1991	Unconfirmed
• 140mm BM-14	14	+	1986	
• 132mm BM-13	15	+		
• 122mm BM-21	280	150	1980	
Subtotal	344	~150		
Rockets				
• Frog-7	12	12		
Total	**~1,000**	**~670**		

Anti-Tank Missiles

Model	Launchers	Missiles	Since	Notes
• AT-3 (Sagger)	+	+		
• BGM-71A TOW	12	+	1979	
• M47 Dragon	24	+	1982	

Anti-Tank Guns

Model	Quantity	In service	Since	Notes
• 107mm B-11 recoilless rifle	+	+		
• 100mm M-1955 field/AT	20	+		
• 85mm M-1945/ D-44 field/AT	100	90		
• 82mm recoilless rifle	+	+		
• 76mm M-1942	100	70		
• 75mm recoilless rifle	+	+	1975	
• 57mm	+	+		

Air Force

Order-of-Battle

Category	Quantity	In service	Notes
• Combat	~180	~55	Some in storage
• Transport	30	20	
• Helicopters	70	26	

Combat Aircraft

Model	Quantity	In service	Since	Notes
Interceptors				
• MiG-29 (Fulcrum)	12	8	1995	
Multi-role				
• F-5E/B	9	9	1980	
Ground attack				
• MiG 23 BN	25	0	1980	
• Su-20/22 (Fitter C)	48	15	1980	
Subtotal	73	15		
Obsolete				
• MiG-21 (Fishbed)	82	21	1979	
• MiG-17 (Fresco)/ MiG-15 (Faggot/Midget)	+	+		In training role, some not serviceable
Total	**~180**	**~55**		

Transport Aircraft

Model	Quantity	In service	Since	Notes
• An-12	3	2		
• An-24/An-26 (Coke/Curl)	15	10	1984/1985	
• C-130H Hercules	2	2	1979	
• IL-14 (Crate)	8	4		
• Short Skyvan Srs. 3	2	2		
Total	**30**	**20**		

Training and Liaison Aircraft

Model	Quantity	In service	Since	Notes
Jet trainers				
• L-39C	12	12	1999	

Helicopters

Model	Quantity	In service	Since	Notes
Attack				
• Mi-24 (Hind)	15	6	1980	
Medium transport				
• AB-212	6	3	1980	
• AB-204	2	2		
• AB-205	2	2	1976	
• Mi-8/Mi-17 (Hip)	39	9	1974	
Subtotal	49	16		

Helicopters *(continued)*

Model	Quantity	In service	Since	Notes
Light transport				
• Bell 206 JetRanger	6	4	1980	
Total	**70**	**26**		

Advanced Armament

Air-to-air missiles

AA-2 (Atoll)

Air-to-ground missiles

AT-2 (Swatter)

Air Force Infrastructure

Military airfields: **15**

Aden (Khormaksar), al-Anad, Ataq, Bayhan, Ghor Ubyad, al-Hudaydah, Ir-Fadhl, Kamaran Island, Lawdar, al-Mukalla, Nugaissa, al-Qasab, al Riyan (Rayane), San'a, Socotra.

Air Defense Forces

Surface-to-Air Missiles

Model	Batteries	Launchers	Since	Notes
Heavy missiles				
• SA-2 (Guideline)	+			
• SA-3	+		1980	
Total	**25**			
Medium missiles				
• SA-6	+			
Light missiles				
• SA-9 (Gaskin)		120	1979	
Shoulder-launched missiles				
• SA-7 (Grail)		100-200	1975	

Other Air Defense Systems

Model	Quantity	In service	Since	Notes
Short-range guns				
• 57mm ZSU 57x2 SP	+	+	1978	
• 57mm S-60	150	100	1974	
• 37mm M-1939	150	150	1974	
• 23mm ZSU 23x4 SP (Gun Dish)	40	+	1978	
• 23mm ZU 23x2	30	30	1976	
• 20mm M163 Vulcan SP	20	20	1979	
• 20mm M167 Vulcan	52	20	1979	
Total	**~440**	**~330**		

Navy

Combat Vessels

Type	Quantity	Length (m.)/ displacement (t.)	Notes/ armament
Missile corvettes			
• Tarantul-I (Type 1241)	1	56.1/385	4xSSN-2C SSMs 4xSA-N-5 SAMs 1x76mm gun 2x30mm guns possibly not operational
MFPBs			
• Huang-Feng	3	38.6/171	4xYJ-1 (C-801) SSMs 4x25mm guns
Mine warfare vessels			
• Yevgenia class (Type 1258)	5	24.6/90	2x25mm guns
• Natya class (Type 266ME)	1	61/804	Acoustic and magnetic sweeps 4x30mm guns 4x25mm guns 2xRBU 1200 ASW mortars 10 mines
Subtotal	6		
Total	**10**		

Patrol Craft

Type	Quantity	Length (m.)/ displacement (t.)	Notes/ armament
• Baklan (CMN)	6	15.5/12	2x12.7mm MGs
• Broadsword class (customs)	1	32/90.5	2x25mm guns 2x14.5mm MGs 2x12.7mm MGs
• Zhuk class (Type 1400M)	2	24/39	4x14.5mm MGs
Total	**9**		

Landing Craft

Type	Quantity	Length (m.)/ displacement (t.)	Notes/ armament
• Ondatra LCU (Type 1176)	2	24/145	1 tank
• Ropucha LST (Type 775)	1	112.5/4,080	10 tanks and 190 troops 4xSA-N-5 SAMs 4x57mm guns 2x122mm MRLs 92 mines
• T-4 LCM/LCU	1	19.9/93	
Total	**4**		
Future procurement			
• Deba class (Type 716)		37.2/176	50 troops 2x23mm gun

Auxiliary Vessels

Type	Quantity	Length (m.)/ displacement (t.)	Notes/ armament
• Toplivo class	2	53.7/1,029	500 tons

Coastal Defense

Type	Quantity	Notes
• SS-N-2 Styx	8	

Naval Infrastructure

Naval bases: **6**

Aden, al-Hudaydah; anchorage at Kamaran Island (unconfirmed); al-Mukalla, Perim Island, Socotra

Ship maintenance and repair facilities

National Dockyards, Aden; 4,500-ton floating dock and 1,500-ton slipway

Tables and Charts

The Middle East Military Balance at a glance

	Personnel			Ground Forces			
	Regular	Reserves	Total	Tanks	Fighting Vehicles	Artillery	Ballistic Missile Launchers
Eastern Mediterranean							
Egypt	450,000	254,000	704,000	~3,000	~3,400	~3,530	24
Israel	186,500	445,000	631,500	3,930	8,040	1,348	12
Jordan	94,200	60,000	154,200	~920	~1,500	838	
Lebanon	51,400		51,400	280	1,235	~330	
Palestinian Authority	45,000		45,000		~40		
Syria	380,000	132,500	512,500	3,700	~5,000	~2,600	44
Turkey	610,000	398,000	1,008,000	2,600	5,460	~4,350	28
Subtotal	**1,817,100**	**1,289,500**	**3,106,600**	**~14,430**	**~24,675**	**~12,996**	**108**
The Gulf							
Bahrain	7,400		7,400	180	277	48	9
Iran	~520,000	350,000	~870,000	~1,700	~1,570	~2,700	~40
Iraq	432,500	650,000	1,082,500	~2,000	~2,000	~2,100	5
Kuwait	19,500	24,000	43,500	318	~530	~100	
Oman	34,000		34,000	151	~225	148	
Qatar	11,800		11,800	44	~260	56	
Saudi Arabia	171,500	20,000	191,500	750	~4,500	~410	12
UAE	46,500		46,500	~400	~1,250	399	6
Subtotal	**~1,243,200**	**1,044,000**	**~2,287,200**	**~5,543**	**~10,612**	**~5,961**	**71**
North Africa and others							
Algeria	127,000	150,000	277,000	860	2,080	900	
Libya	76,000		76,000	~650	~2,750	~2,320	80
Morocco	145,500	150,000	295,500	588	1,120	1,060	
Sudan	103,000		103,000	~350	~560	~760	
Tunisia	35,500		35,500	139	316	205	
Yemen	~65,000	200,000	~265,000	715	~480	~670	10
Subtotal	**~552,000**	**500,000**	**~1,052,000**	**~3,302**	**~7,306**	**~5,915**	**90**

The Middle East Military Balance at a glance *(continued)*

	Air Force			Air Defense			Navy		
	Combat Aircraft	Transport Aircraft	Helicopters	Heavy Batteries	Medium Batteries	Light Launchers	Sub-marines	Combat Vessels	Patrol Craft
Eastern Mediterranean									
Egypt	481	44	~225	109	44	105	4	64	104
Israel	533	64	287	22		~70	6	20	32
Jordan	91	12	74	14	50	50			13
Lebanon			16						32
Palestinian Authority			2						13
Syria	490	23	285	108	64	55		14	8
Turkey	~445	90	407	24		86	14	78	103
Subtotal	**~2,040**	**233**	**1,296**	**277**	**158**	**366**	**24**	**176**	**305**
The Gulf									
Bahrain	34	2	39	1	2	40		11	21
Iran	209	105	325	29		95	6	29	~110
Iraq	~200	10	360	60	10	130			
Kuwait	40	5	23	12				10	69
Oman	29	41	41			58		9	22
Qatar	18	7	30			51		7	26
Saudi Arabia	~360	42	214	25	21			24	74
UAE	54	33	91	5	6	~115		12	112
Subtotal	**944**	**245**	**1,123**	**132**	**39**	**489**	**6**	**102**	**434**
North Africa and others									
Algeria	184	41	133	11	18	78	2	26	16
Libya	~360	85	127	30	10	55		24	
Morocco	59	41	121			37		13	52
Sudan	~35	24	57	20					18
Tunisia	18	9	51			83		9	37
Yemen	~55	20	26	25		120		10	9
Subtotal	**711**	**220**	**515**	**86**	**28**	**373**	**2**	**82**	**132**

The Eastern Mediterranean Military Forces

Personnel (In Thousands)

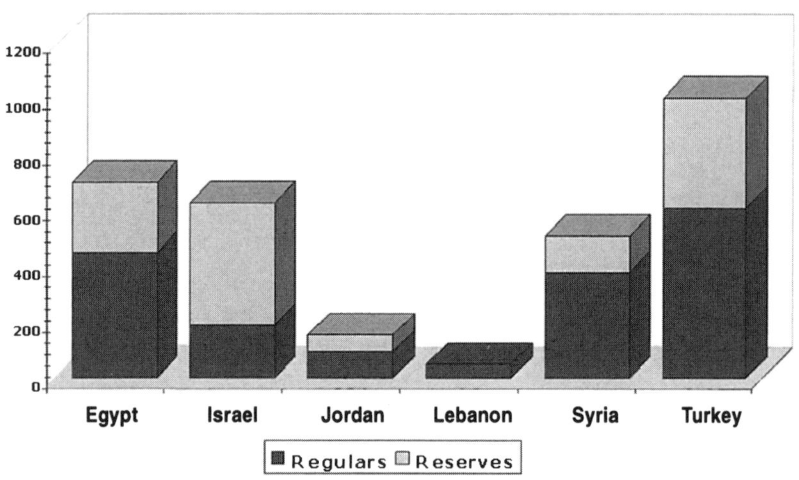

Tanks

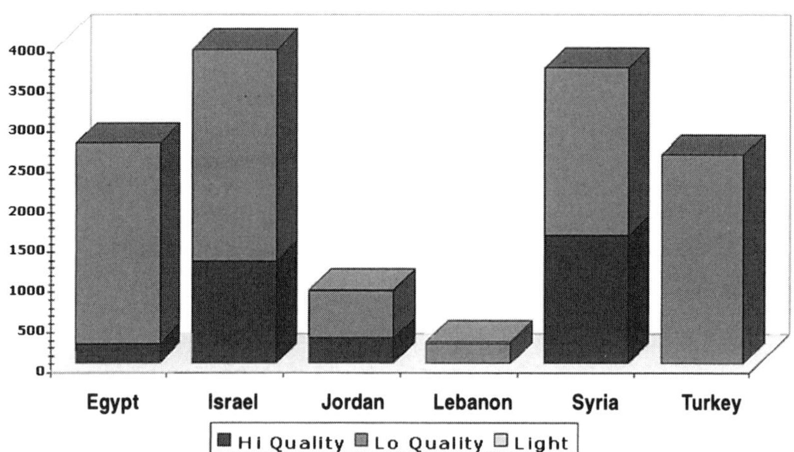

The Eastern Mediterranean Military Forces *(continued)*

AFVs

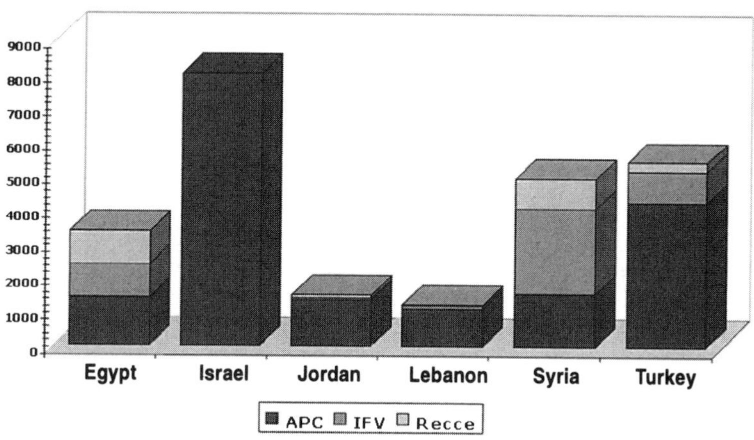

Artillery

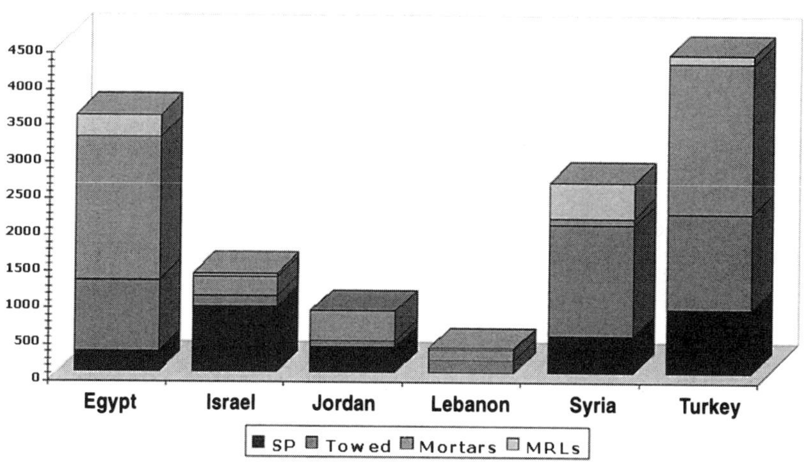

The Eastern Mediterranean Military Forces *(continued)*

Air Defense

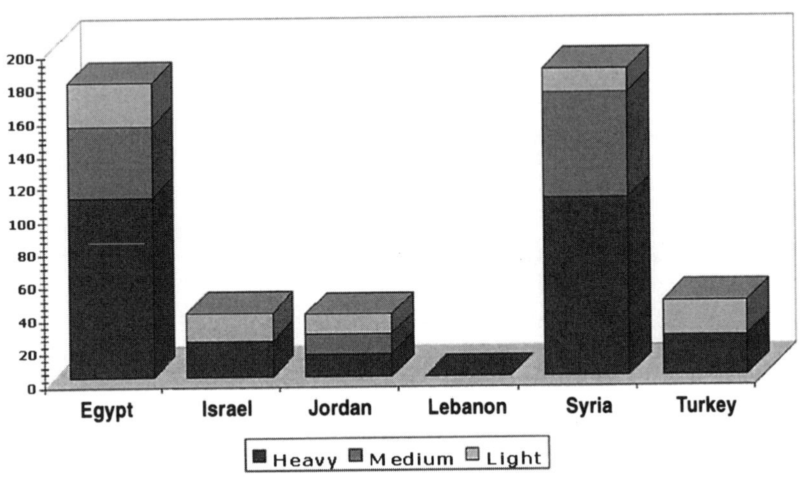

Combat Aircraft

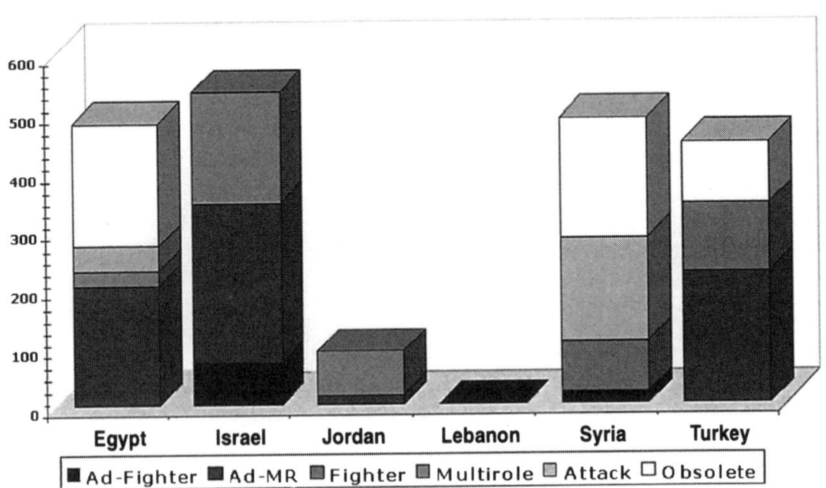

The Eastern Mediterranean Military Forces *(continued)*

Helicopters

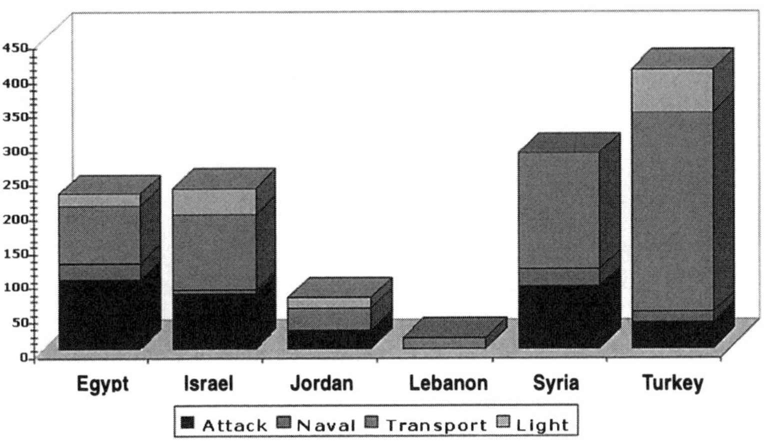

Combat Naval Vessels

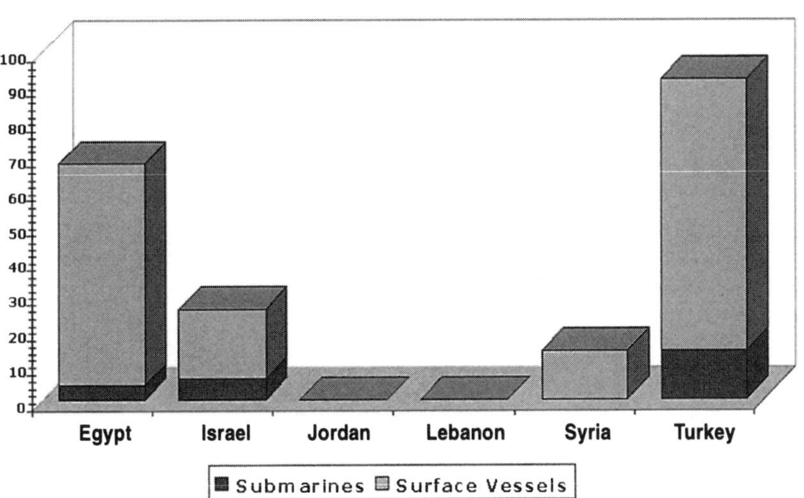

The Persian Gulf Military Forces

Personnel (In Thousands)

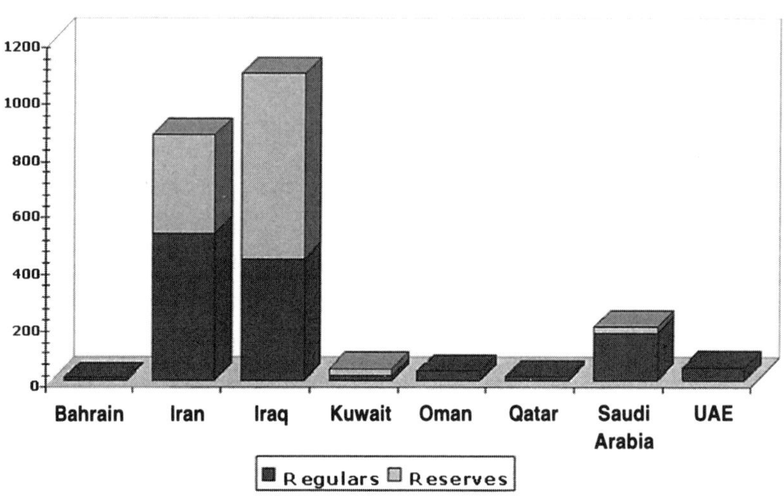

Tanks

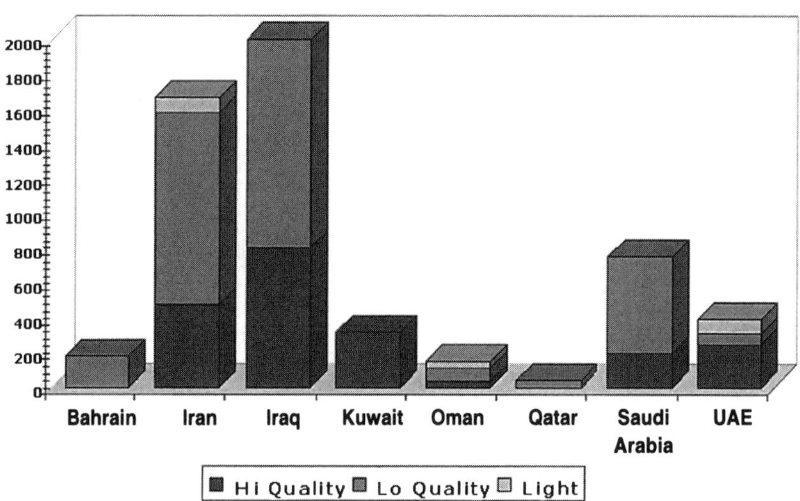

The Persian Gulf Military Forces *(continued)*

AFVs

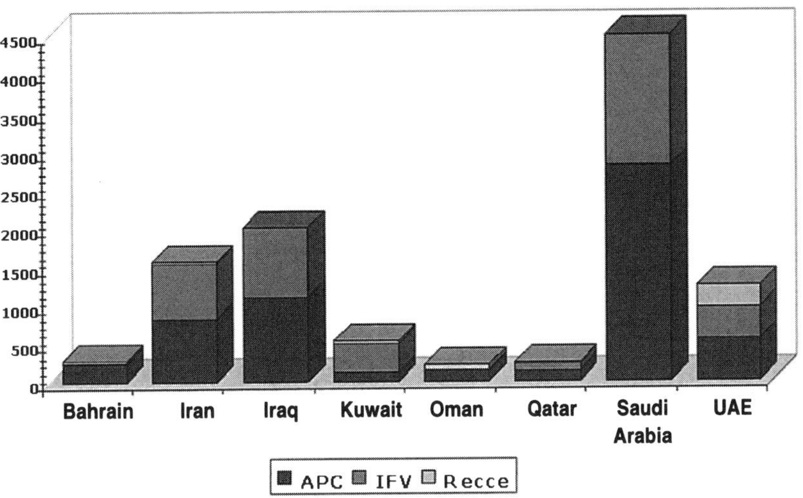

Artillery

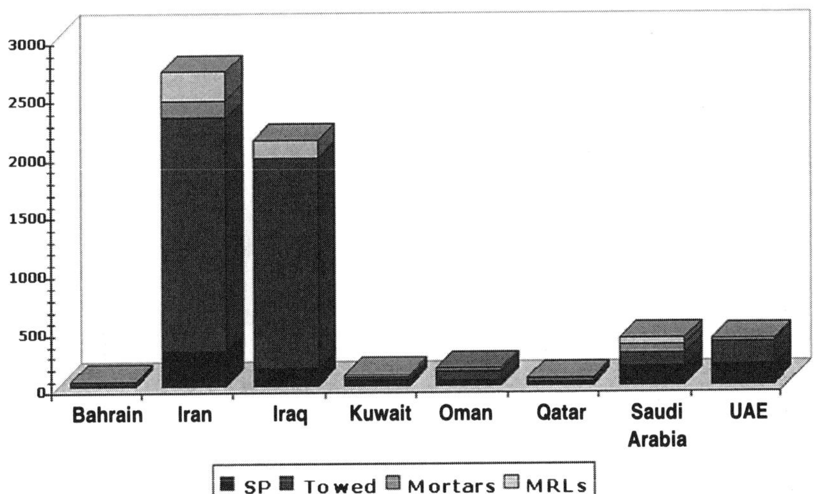

The Persian Gulf Military Forces *(continued)*

Air Defense

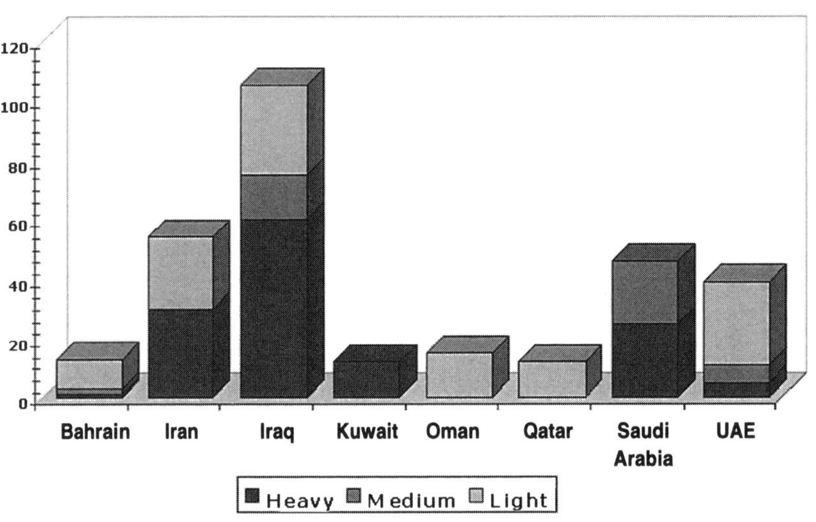

Combat Aircraft

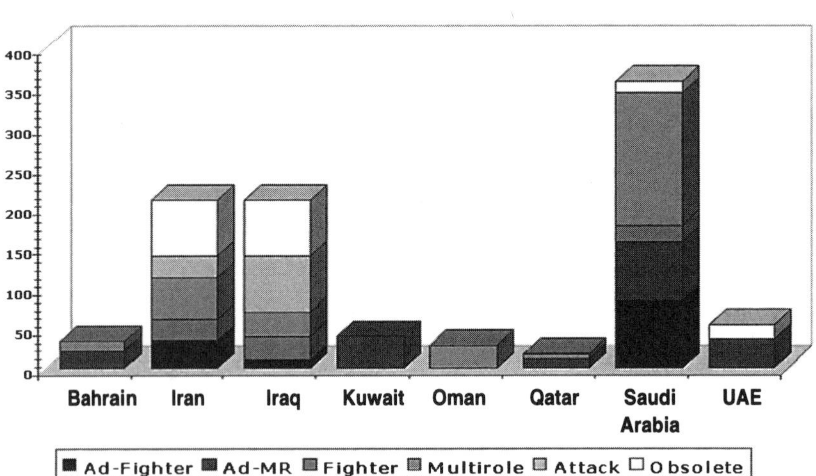

The Persian Gulf Military Forces *(continued)*

Helicopters

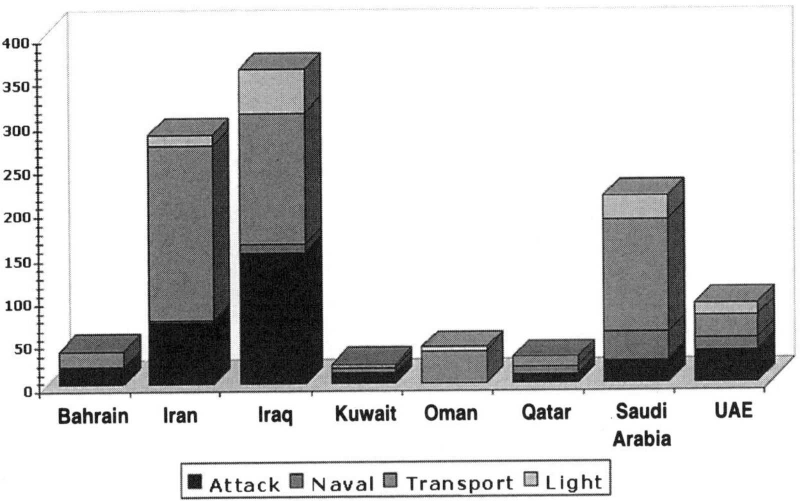

Combat Naval Vessels

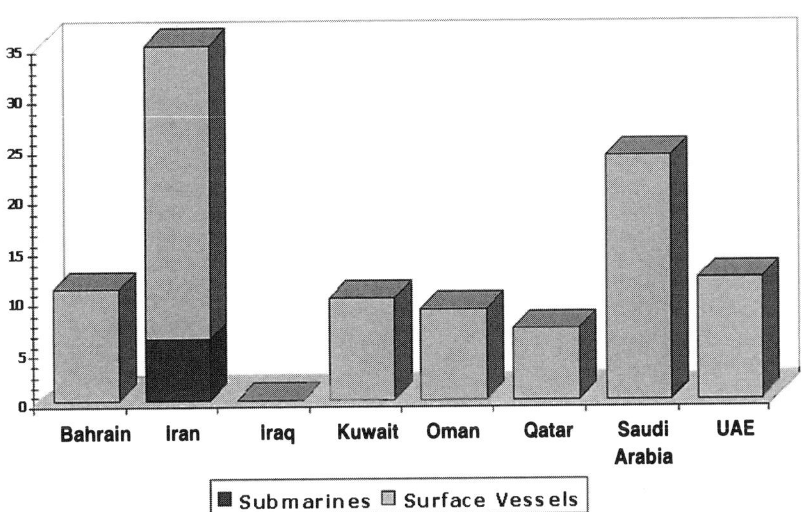

The North African Military Forces

Personnel (In Thousands)

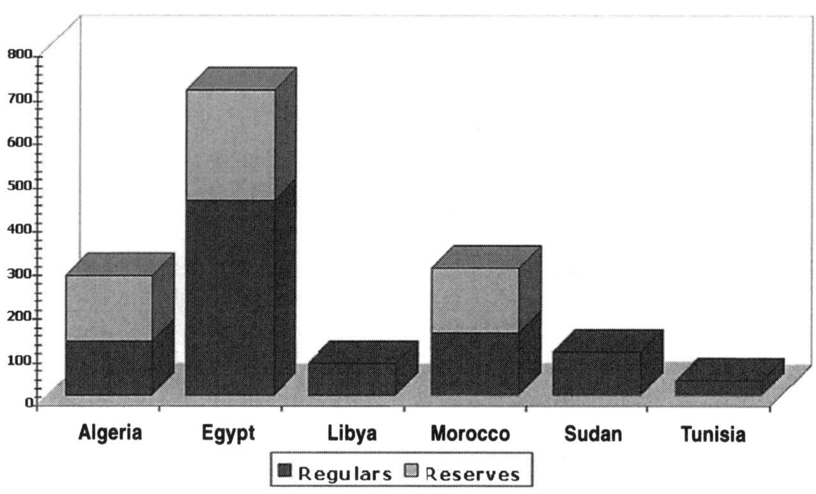

Tanks

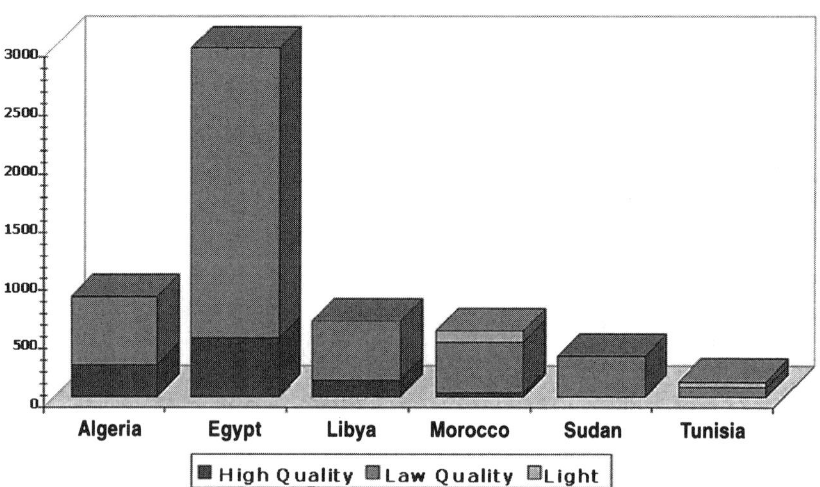

The North African Military Forces *(continued)*

AFVs

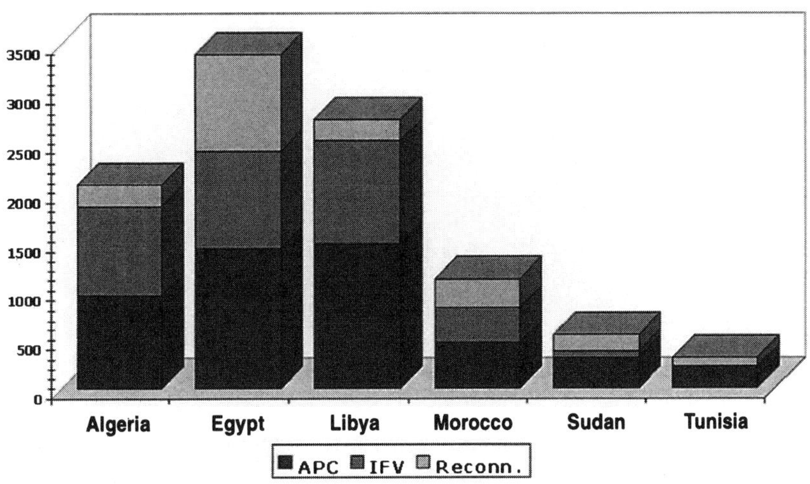

Artillery

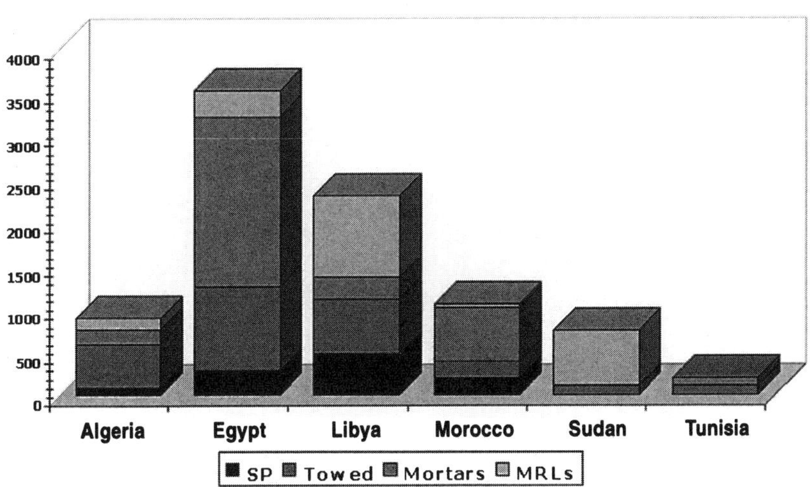

The North African Military Forces *(continued)*

Air Defense

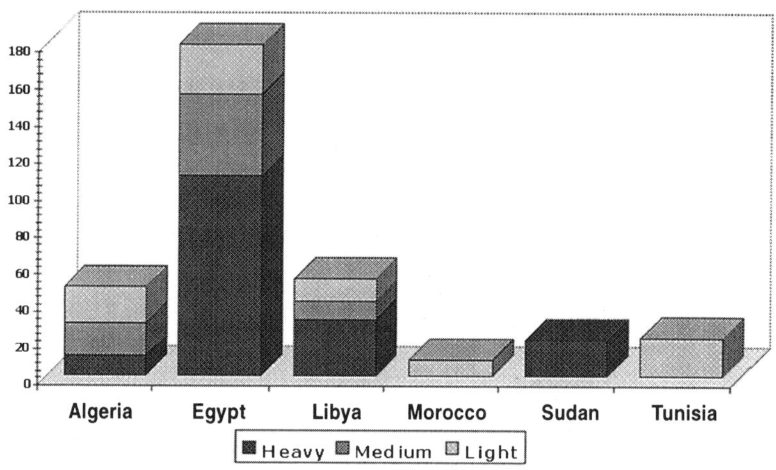

Combat Aircraft

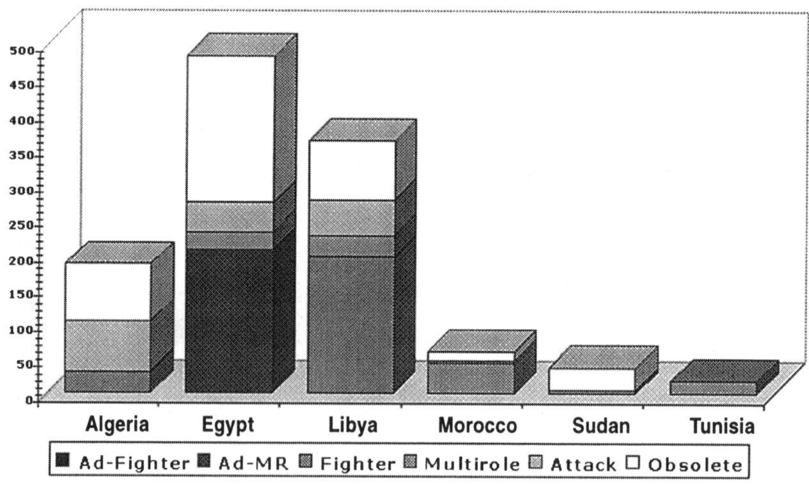

The North African Military Forces *(continued)*

Helicopters

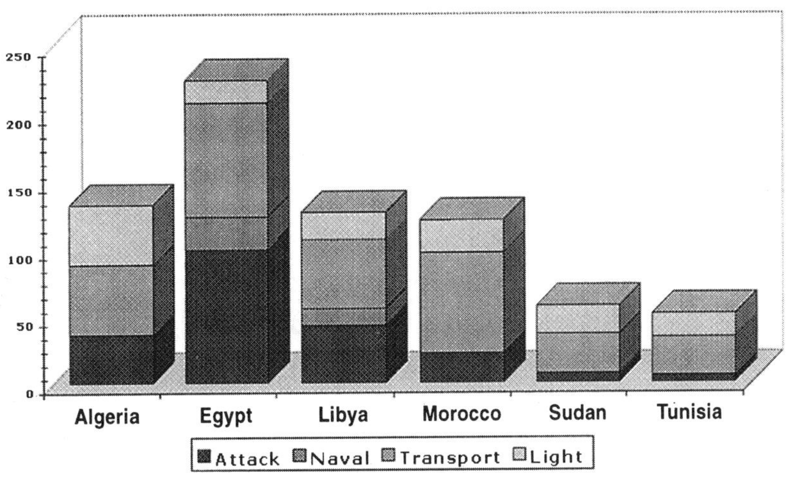

Combat Naval Vessels

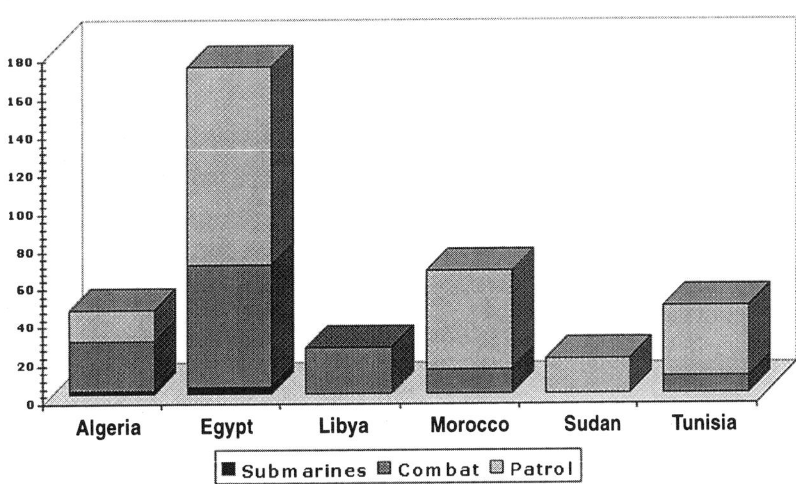

GLOSSARY OF WEAPONS SYSTEMS

GROUND FORCES EQUIPMENT

Armor

Tanks

	Crew	Combat weight/ power-to-weight ratio (hp/t)	Gun	Ammunition	Max. op. range (km)	Country of origin	Notes
MBTs							
High quality							
Challenger 1 Al-Hussein	4	62/19.35	120mm L11A5	64 Shells	450 road 250 cross country	UK	Incorporating Chobham armor and IFCS
Challenger 2	4	62.5/19.2	120mm L30	50 shells	450 road 250 cross country	UK	
Challenger 2E	4	62/24.2	120mm L30	50 shells	550 road 350 cross country	UK	
Khalid	4	58/20.68	120mm L11A5	64 shells		Jordan	Improved Chieftain Mk 5 with Chobham armor
Leclerc	3	54.5/27.52	120mm	40 shells	550	France	
Leopard A1/A3	4	42.4/20.75	105mm L7A3	60 shells	600 road 450 cross country	Germany	

Tanks *(continued)*

	Crew	Combat weight/ power-to-weight ratio (hp/t)	Gun	Ammunition	Max. op. range (km)	Country of origin	Notes
M1A1	4	57.15/26.24	105mm	40 shells	465	US	The Egyptian version is fitted with a 120mm gun
M1A2	4	54.54/27	120mm	55 shells	500	US	
M-84-120	3	48/25	120mm	42 shells		Ukraine	ERA, FCS, LWS
Merkava Mk I	4	60/15	105mm	62 shells	400	Israel	
Merkava Mk II	4	61/15	105mm, 60mm mortar	62 shells	400	Israel	
Merkava Mk III	4	61/19.67	120mm MG251	50 shells	500	Israel	Knight III FCS, LWS
Sabra Mk I	4	56/17.85	120mm MG251	42 shells	450	Israel	Upgraded M-60A3 with Knight III FCS, passive armor
Sabra Mk II	4	59/20.33	120mm MG251 60mm mortar	40 shells	450	Israel	Upgraded M-60A3 with Knight III FCS, hybrid passive reactive armor
T-72	3	44.5/18.9	125mm 2A46	45 shells 6 Svir ATGM	480	Russia	Arena LWS
Zulfikar		40/25	125mm			Iran	FCS, Arena LWS

Tanks *(continued)*

	Crew	Combat weight/ power-to-weight ratio (hp/t)	Gun	Ammunition	Max. op. range (km)	Country of origin	Notes
Medium and low quality							
AMX-30	4	37/20	105mm	47 shells	450	France	
Centurion	4	51.8/12.54	105mm	64 shells	190	UK	Upgraded version
Chieftain Mk 5	4	55/13.63	120mm L11A5	64 shells	400-500 road 200-300 cross country	UK	
Chieftain Mk 3	4	54.1/13.49	120mm	53 shells	400-500 road 200-300 cross country	UK	
Falcon AB9 C4	3		120mm L50	24 shells		Jordan	Upgraded Tariq MBT, including day/night FCS, Avimo LWS, automatic loader
M47	5	46.17/17.54	90mm	71 shells	130	US	
M47M	4	46.8/16.1	90mm	79 shells	600	US	
M48A1	4	47.173/17.17	90mm M41	60 shells	113	US	
M48A5	4	48.98/15.89	105mm M68	54 shells	500	US	
M60 A1	4	52.61/14.24	105mm M68	63 shells	500	US	

Tanks *(continued)*

	Crew	Combat weight/ power-to-weight ratio (hp/t)	Gun	Ammunition	Max. op. range (km)	Country of origin	Notes
M60 A3	4	52.61/14.24	105mm M68	63 shells	480	US	
M60 AB9 B1	4		120mm L50			Jordan	Upgraded M60, including integrated day/night IFCS, Avimo LWS
Magach-7	4	53.6/16.97	105mm M68	63 shells	480	Israel	Upgraded M60, including passive armor and FCS
OF-40 Mk 2	4	45.5/18.24	105mm	57 shells	600	Italy	
Qayd Ard	4	55/13.63	120mm L11A5	64 shells	400-500 road 200-300 cross country	Oman	Improved Chieftain Mk 5
PT-76	3	14.6/16.4	76.2mm	40 shells	400	Russia	
Shot Kal	4	51.8/12.54	105mm	72 shells	190	Israel	Upgraded Centurion
SK-105	3	17.7/18.1	105mm 105G1	41 shells	500	Austria	
T-54	4	36/14.44	100mm D-10	35 shells	510	Russia	
T-55	4	36.5/16.3	100mm D-10 T2S	43 shells	460	Russia	
T-62	4	40/14.5	115mm 2A20	40 shells	450 road 320 cross country	Russia	

Tanks *(continued)*

	Crew	Combat weight/ power-to-weight ratio (hp/t)	Gun	Ammunition	Max. op. range (km)	Country of origin	Notes
Tariq	4	51.8/12.54	105mm	64 shells	190	Jordan	Upgraded Centurion
Type 59	4	36/14.44	100mm	34 shells	420—440	PRC	Chinese T-54
Type 69	4	36.5/15.9	100mm	34 shells		PRC	Chinese T-62
T-55/Type-69	3		125mm				Iraqi upgrade of T-55
Type 72Z/Safir-74		36/21.66	105mm	50 Shells		Iran	Upgrade of T-55 incorporates Fontana EFCS-3 and ERA
Vickers Mk 1	4	38.6/16.8	105mm L7	44 shells	480	UK	
Light tanks							
AMX-13	3	15/16.6	90mm	32 shells	350-400	France	There are versions with 75mm and 105mm guns
Scorpion	3	8/23.5	76mm	40 shells	750 road	UK	Alvis Scorpion reconnaissance vehicle

Armored Personnel Carriers

Type	Crew	Configuration	Combat weight / power-to-weight ratio (hp/ton)	Country of origin	Notes
Achzarit	3+7	Tracked		Israel	Based on T-55 MBT hull
ACV-AAPC	13	Tracked	12.94/23.16	Turkey	
AT-105	2+8	4x4	11.66/14.06	UK	

Armored Personnel Carriers *(continued)*

Type	Crew	Configuration	Combat weight / power-to-weight ratio (hp/ton)	Country of origin	Notes
BMR-600	2+10	6x6	14/22	Spain	
Boragh	12	Tracked	13/25.4	Iran	Iranian version of BMP-1, Arena LWS
BTR-152	2+17	6x6	9/12.29	Russia	
BTR-40	2+8	4x4	5.3/15	Russia	
BTR-50	2+20	Tracked	14.2/16.9	Russia	
BTR-60PA	2+16	8x8	10/18.03	Russia	
BTR-80	3+7	8x8	13.6/19.11	Russia	
Casspir Mk 3	2+10	4x4	12.6/13.5	South Africa	Used for internal security
Cobra	11	4x4	6/31	Turkey	
Dragoon	12	4x4	12.7/23.6	USA	
Engesa EE-11	13	6x6	14/18.6	Brazil	
al-Fahd	2+10	4x4	10.9/15.4	Egypt	
al-Fahd 240	2+10	4x4	10.9/22	Egypt	
al-Fahd	2+12	8x8		Saudi Arabia	Also known as AD-40-8-1
FIAT OtoBreda 6614	1+10	4x4	8.5/18.82	Italy	
FUG-70/ PSZH-IV	3+6	Wheeled	7.6/13.15	Hungary	
GKN-Defence Piranha	15	8x8	12.3/24.4	UK	

Armored Personnel Carriers *(continued)*

Type	Crew	Configuration	Combat weight / power-to-weight ratio (hp/ton)	Country of origin	Notes
M113 A1	2+11	Tracked	11.07/19.27	US	
M113 A2	2+11	Tracked	11.25/18.51	US	
M125 A1	6	Tracked	11.26/19.09	US	
M-2 halftrack	10	Halftrack	8.89/14.39	US	
M-3 halftrack	13	Halftrack	8.89/14.39	US	
M-3 Panhard	2+10	4x4	6.1/14.75	France	
M-60P	3+10	Tracked	11/12.73	Slovenia	
MT-LB	2+11	Tracked	11.9/20.16	Russia	
Nagmachon	8	Tracked		Israel	Based on Centurion MBT chassis with reactive armor
Nagmashot	8	Tracked	55/13.64	Israel	Based on Centurion MBT chassis
Nakpadon		Tracked	55/16.36	Israel	Based on Centurion MBT chassis with reactive armor
Nyala RG-12	8	4x4	9.4/18	South Africa	Used for internal security
OT-62B	2+18	Tracked	15/20	Czech Republic/Poland	Czech/Polish BTR-50
OT-64C(1) SKOT-2A	2+10	8x8	14.5/12.41	Czech Republic/Poland	
Peninsula Shield	9	6x6	16/22.8	Saudi Arabia	See also Armored Reconn. Vehicles

Armored Personnel Carriers *(continued)*

Type	Crew	Configuration	Combat weight / power-to-weight ratio (hp/ton)	Country of origin	Notes
RBY	2+6	4x4	4/30	Israel	
S-55	2+6	4x4	3.6/31.2	UK	
S600	9	4x4	12.5/17.1	UK	
Saracen FV603 (C)	2+10	6x6	10.17/15.73	UK	
Spartan	3+4	Tracked	8.17/23.25	UK	
Terrier	8	4x4		Germany	
Tiger (AB17)	2+6	4x4	4.44	Jordan	
UR-416	2+8	4x4	7.6/16.5	Germany	
VAB-VTT	2+10	4x4	13/16.92	France	
VAB-VTT	2+10	6x6	14.2/16.54	France	
VCR	3+9	6x6	7.9/18.35	France	
al-Walid	2+8	4x4		Egypt	
YW-531	2+13	Tracked	12.6/25.39	PRC	

Infantry Fighting Vehicles

Type	Crew	Configuration	Combat weight / power-to-weight ratio (hp/ton)	Armament	Country of origin
ACV-NG	3+8	Tracked	18/19.44	1x30mm Bushmaster II gun	Turkey
ACV-AIFV	13	Tracked	13.68/21.92	1x25mm gun	Turkey

Infantry Fighting Vehicles *(continued)*

Type	Crew	Configuration	Combat weight / power-to-weight ratio (hp/ton)	Armament	Country of origin
AMX-10P	3+8	Tracked	14.5/17.93	1x20mm gun	France
AMX-VCI	3+10	Tracked	15/16.67	1x20mm gun	France
BMD-1	3+4	Tracked	7.5/32	1x73mm 2A28 gun 1xAT-3 (Sagger) ATGM	Russia
BMP-1	3+8	Tracked	13.5/22.22	1x73mm 2A28 gun 1xAT-3 (Sagger) ATGM	Russia
BMP-2	3+7	Tracked	14.3/20.30	1x30mm 2A42 gun 1xAT-5 (Spandrel) or AT-4 (Spigot) ATGM	Russia
BMP-3	3+7	Tracked	18.7/26.73	1x100mm 2A70 gun 1x30mm 2A72 gun	Russia
BTR-94 Guardian	8	8x8	16.4/19.75	1x30mm KBA-3 gun 1x30mm AGS-17 grenade launcher AT-5 (9M113) ATGM or 1x 23mm ZU 23x2 gun	Ukraine
Condor	2+12	4x4	12.4/13.54	1x20mm gun	Germany
Desert Warrior	3+7	Tracked	25.7/21.4	1x25mm gun 2xTOW ATGM launchers	UK
Engesa EE-11	3+5	6x6	14/18.6	1x90mm gun	Brazil
al-Fahd 240-30	2+10	4x4	12.5/19.2	1x30mm 2A42 gun 1xAT-5 (Spandrel) ATGM	Egypt

Infantry Fighting Vehicles *(continued)*

Type	Crew	Configuration	Combat weight / power-to-weight ratio (hp/ton)	Armament	Country of origin
Goliath AB13	3+7	Tracked	30.1/23.25	2x30mm gun, 30mm AGS-17 grenade launcher, smoke grenade system	Jordan
M2 Bradley IFV	3+6	Tracked	22.94/20.38	1x25mm gun 2xTOW ATGM launcher	US
M3 Bradley CFV	3+2	Tracked	22.44/20.51	1x25mm gun 2xTOW ATGM launcher	US
Pandur	2+8	6x6	13.5/19.25	1x30mm gun	Austria
Piranha LAV-25	3+6	8x8	12.79/21.49	1x25mm gun	Canada
RN-94	2+11	6x6	13/18.46	1x25mm gun	Turkey/Romania
Ratel 20	11	6x6	18.5/15.24	1x20mm gun	South Africa
Ratel 90	10	6x6	19/14.84	1x90mm gun	South Africa
Temsah AB14	2+10	Tracked	46.9/16	1x20mm M621 gun	Jordan
V-150	3+2	4x4	9.88/20.42	1x20mm gun	US
V-150 S	3+2	4x4	10.88/22.96	1x20mm gun	US
V-300	3+9	6x6	14.96/18.94	25mm or 20mm gun	US
VAB-VCI	2+10	4x4	13/16.92	1x20mm gun	France
VAB-VCI	2+10	6x6	14.2/15.49	1x20mm gun	France
YPR-765	3+7	Tracked	13.68/19.29	1x25mm gun	Netherlands

Armored Reconnaissance Vehicles

Type	Crew	Configuration	Combat weight / power-to-weight ratio (hp/ton)	Armament	Country of origin	Notes
ACV-AAOV		Tracked	12.94/23.16	MORS reconnaissance system	Turkey	Including ground surveillance radar, FLIR, TV camera
ACV-ATV		Tracked		TOW ATGMs	Turkey	
Aigis (AB2)	6-8	4x4	5.45/42.2	Helio SWARM	UK	Reconnaissance systems
Akrep (Scorpion)	4	4x4	3.6/37		Turkey	
AML-60	3	4x4	5.5/16.36	60mm mortar	France	
AML-90	3	4x4	5.5/16.36	1x90mm gun	France	
AMX-10RC	4	6x6	15.88/16.45	1x105mm gun	France	
Black Iris AB3	3	4x4		TOW ATGMs or 106mm recoilless gun	Jordan	
BRDM-1	5	4x4	5.6 /16.07		Russia	
BRDM-2	4	4x4	7/20	14.5mm KPVT MG or 1x23mm gun; 1xAT-3 (Sagger) ATGM	Russia	
Cobra	4	4x4	6/31	1x25mm gun	Turkey	See Armored Personnel Carriers

Armored Reconnaissance Vehicles *(continued)*

Type	Crew	Configuration	Combat weight / power-to-weight ratio (hp/ton)	Armament	Country of origin	Notes
Defender 110 AB5	8	4x4		12.7mm MG, smoke grenade launchers	Jordan	
EBR-75	4	8x8	13.5/14.81	1x75mm gun	France	
Engesa EE-9	3	6x6	13.4/15.82	1x90mm gun	Brazil	
al-Fahd	3	8x8		Various turrets can be fitted, up to a three-man model with a 105mm gun	Saudi Arabia	Also known as AD-40 8-2
Ferret	2	4x4	4.4/29.35	2xVigilance ATGMs	UK	
Ferret Mk 1/2	3	4x4	4.37/29.51		UK	
FIAT OtoBreda 6616	3	4x4	8/20.2	1x20mm cannon	Italy	
Fox	3	4x4	6.12/30.04		UK	
M-3 (Panhard)		4x4	6.1/14.75	HOT ATGM	France	Also listed under Armored Personnel Carriers
M901 ITV	4	Tracked	11.8/18	TOW ATGM	US	
Pandur		6x6		1x90mm LCTS Mk.8	Austria	

Armored Reconnaissance Vehicles *(continued)*

Type	Crew	Configuration	Combat weight / power-to-weight ratio (hp/ton)	Armament	Country of origin	Notes
Peninsula Shield	3	6x6	18.5/22.8	1x90mm gun	Saudi Arabia	Also listed under Armored Personnel Carriers
Piranha LAV-AG		8x8		1x90mm	Canada LCTS Mk.8	
Saladin	3	6x6	11.6/14.66		UK	
Scimitar	3	Tracked	7.8/24.5	1x30mm gun	UK	
VBC-90	3	6x6	13.5/16	1x90mm gun	France	
VBL	3	4x4	3.6/29.7		France	
VCR /TH		6x6		HOT ATGM	France	

Artillery

Artillery-Guns, Howitzers and Mortars

Caliber	Designation	Type	Range (km)	Country of origin	Notes
240mm	M-240	Towed mortar	9.7	Russia	
210mm	al-Faw	SP gun	57	Iraq	With assistance from Belgium and UK
203mm	M110 A1	SP howitzer	16.8	US	
203mm	M115	Towed howitzer	16.8	US	

Artillery-Guns, Howitzers and Mortars *(continued)*

Caliber	Designation	Type	Range (km)	Country of origin	Notes
180mm	S-23	Towed gun	32	Russia	
175mm	M107	SP gun	32.7	US	
170mm	M-1978 (Koksan)	SP gun	40	North Korea	
160mm	M-43/53	Towed mortar	5.1	Russia	
160mm	M-66	SP mortar	9.3	Israel	
155mm	FH-70	Towed howitzer	24	Germany	
155mm	FH2000	Towed howitzer	40	Turkey	Variant of Singaporean 155mm gun
155mm	G-5	Towed howitzer	30	South Africa	
155mm	G-6	SP howitzer	30	South Africa	
155mm	GCT (AuF1)	SP howitzer	23.5	France	
155mm	GH 52 APU	Towed howitzer	27	Finland	
155mm	GHN-45	Towed howitzer	17.8	Austria	
155mm	K9 Thunder	SP howitzer	30	South Korea	On board FCS, night vision equipment
155mm	L-33 (Sherman /Soltam)	SP howitzer	21	Israel	Gun-Israel; chassis obsolete US-made tanks
155mm	M109 A1/A2/A6	SP howitzer	21	US	
155mm	M109 Doher	SP howitzer		Israel	Upgrading of M-109
155mm	M114 A2	Towed howitzer	14.6	US	
155mm	M-1950	Towed howitzer	17.5	France	
155mm	M198 A1	Towed howitzer	18.1	US	

Artillery-Guns, Howitzers and Mortars *(continued)*

Caliber	Designation	Type	Range (km)	Country of origin	Notes
155mm	M-41	Towed gun	30	Iraq/Austria	Combination of the 130mm gun and Austrian 155mm tubes
155mm	M44	SP howitzer	14.6	US	
155mm	M-50 (Sherman)	SP howitzer	17.5	Israel	Gun-France; chassis-US
155mm	M52T/M44T	SP howitzer	18/30	Turkey	Upgrading of former US M52 and M44 tanks
155mm	M59 (Long Tom)	Towed gun	22	US	
155mm	M-71	Towed gun	24	Israel	
155mm	Majnoon	SP howitzer	30.2	Iraq	With assistance from Belgian company
155mm	Mk F-3 (AMX)	SP howitzer	18	France	
155mm	Palmaria	SP howitzer	24	Italy	
155mm	PLZ-45	SP howitzer	39	PRC	
155mm	Slammer	SP gun		Israel	Based on Merkava chassis
155mm	SPGW	SP gun		Israel	FCS and GPS navigation
155mm	SP2000	SP howitzer	30	Turkey	
155mm	Thunder-2	SP gun		Iran	
155mm	ZTS Zuzana	SP gun		Slovak Republic	
152mm	D-20	Towed howitzer	18	Russia	
152mm	ZTS DANA	SP howitzer	20	Slovak Republic	

Artillery-Guns, Howitzers and Mortars *(continued)*

Caliber	Designation	Type	Range (km)	Country of origin	Notes
152mm	M-1937 (ML-20)	Towed howitzer	17.25	Russia	
152mm	M-1943 (D-1)	Towed howitzer	12.4	Russia	
152mm	M-1976 2A36	Towed howitzer	27	Russia	
152mm	M-1973 (2S3)	SP howitzer	18	Russia	
130mm	M-46	Towed gun	27.1	Russia	
130mm	Type 59	Towed gun	27.4	PRC	Copy of Soviet 130mm M-46, the same designation is also used for a Chinese MBT
122mm	D-30	Towed howitzer	16	Russia	
122mm	D-74	Towed gun	24	Russia	
122mm	ISU	SP gun	16	Russia	
122mm	M-1931/37	Towed gun	20.8	Russia	
122mm	M-1938 (M-30)	Towed howitzer	11.8	Russia	
122mm	M-1974 (2S1)	SP howitzer	15.3	Russia	
122mm	Saddam	Towed howitzer	16	Iraq/Russia	Russian 122mm D-30, produced in Iraq, with assistance from Yugoslavia
122mm	SP122	SP howitzer	15.4	Russia/Egypt	Russian-licensed D-30 based on US M109 chassis
122mm	Thunder-1	SP gun		Iran	Based on Russian 122mm D-30

Artillery-Guns, Howitzers and Mortars *(continued)*

Caliber	Designation	Type	Range (km)	Country of origin	Notes
120mm		SP mortar	11.5	Iraq	Mounted on Russian-made MT-LB carrier
120mm	Brandt	SP mortar		France/ Canada	Mounted on LAV chassis
120mm	Brandt M-50/M-60	Towed mortar	6.6	France	
120mm	M-43	Towed mortar	5.7	Russia	
120mm	M-65	Towed mortar	6.3	Israel	Also available as SP, mounted on U.S. made M-2 halftrack
120mm	RT	Towed mortar	13	France	
120mm	TDA	SP rifled mortar	13	France	Mounted on Mowag Piranha 8x8 APC
107mm	M30	SP/ towed mortar	5.6	US	Mounted on M106 A2 carrier, a derivative of M-113 APC
105mm	L-118	Towed light gun	17.2	UK	
105mm	M101 A1	Towed howitzer	11.3	US	
105mm	M102 A1	Towed howitzer	11.5	US	
105mm	M108	SP howitzer	11.5	US	
105mm	M52	SP howitzer	11.3	US	
105mm	M-56	Towed pack howitzer	10.6	Italy	
105mm	Mk 61	SP howitzer	15	France	
100mm	M-1955	Towed field/AT gun	21	Russia	

Artillery-Guns, Howitzers and Mortars *(continued)*

Caliber	Designation	Type	Range (km)	Country of origin	Notes
100mm	SU-100	SP gun		Russia	
87mm	25lb.	Towed howitzer	12.2	UK	
85mm	M-1945/D-44	Towed field/AT gun	15.8	Russia	
76mm	M-1942 (ZIS-3)	Towed divisional gun	13.3	Russia	

Artillery/Mortar-Locating Radars

Designation	Detection range (km)	Frequency band	Country of origin
AN/TPQ-37	50	I/J-band	US
AN/TPQ-36	24	I/J-band	US
AN/PPS-15A	3	J-band	US
ARS 2000			Turkey
Cymbeline	30	I-band	UK
RATAC-S	30	I-band	Germany
Rasit	50	I-band	France
Shilem			Israel

Artillery Ammunition Carriers

Designation	Configuration	Country of origin	Notes
M-992	Tracked	US	
MT-LB	Tracked	Russia	Also serves as prime mover for towed artillery and APC

Surface-to-Surface Missiles

Designation	Range (km)/ CEP	Propulsion	Payload (kg)	Country of origin	Notes
Condor 2/Vector	800	Two stage, solid/liquid	450	Egypt/Iraq	Operational status unconfirmed
CSS-2 (East Wind)	2,700/~4 km	Single stage, liquid	2,045	PRC	
CSS-8 (M-7)	150	Single stage, liquid	190	PRC	This is derived from HQ-2 SAM for export
GHAURI-I	1,300-1,500	Single stage, liquid	750	Pakistan	Possibly based on the No Dong
GHAURI-II	2,000-2,300		1,000	Pakistan	
al-Hussein	~600/~4 km	Single stage, liquid	300	Iraq	Extended range Scuds
Jericho I	450	Two stage, solid	500	Israel	According to foreign publications
Jericho II	800	Two stage, solid	500	Israel	According to foreign publications
Jericho II B	1,500	Two stage, solid	1,000	Israel	According to foreign publications
M-9	600/600m	Solid	500	PRC	
M-11	250/250m	Solid	500	PRC	
MGM-52C Lance	75/150m	Liquid	225	US	
MGM-140 ATACMS	135	Solid	450	US	
No-Dong	1,000	Liquid	1,000	North Korea	
Shehab-3	1,300/3-4 km	Liquid	1,000	Iran	Possibly based on No Dong
Shehab-4	2,000			Iran	
Scud B (SS-1, R-17 or 9K72)	280/1 km	Single stage, liquid	800-1,000	Russia	
Scud C	550/2-3 km	Single stage, liquid	500-700	North Korea	Upgrading of Russian SS-1 Scud B
Scud D	600/2-3 km	Single stage, solid	350-450	Syria/North Korea	Extended-range Scud C

Surface-to-Surface Missiles *(continued)*

Designation	Range (km)/ CEP	Propulsion	Payload (kg)	Country of origin	Notes
SS-21 (Scarab, OTR-21 or Tochka)	70/150m	Single stage, solid	120	Russia	
Shaheen	750	Single stage, solid	1,000	Pakistan	Possibly based on Chinese M-9
al-Samoud	150	Single stage, liquid	300	Iraq	Formally developed within the restrictions of the UNSC resolutions, but probably exceeds the limitations considerably
Taepo Dong 1	1,700-2,200	Two stage, liquid	700-1,000	North Korea	
Taepo Dong 2	4,000-6,000	Three stage, liquid	700-1,000	North Korea	
Tamuz 1	2,000	Two stage, liquid		Iraq	Not operational

Surface-to-Surface Strategic Rockets

Caliber	Designation	Number of rails/tubes	Range (km)	Payload (kg)	Country of origin	Notes
610mm	Zelzal 2	1	200	600	Iran	
550mm	Laith 90	1	90	450	Iraq	Extended range version of the Russian FROG-7
540mm	FROG-7 (Luna-M or 9K52)	1	70	450	Russia	
400mm	Ababil-100	4	100		Iraq	Improved version of Yugoslavia's 262mm LRSV M-87
355mm	Nazeat	1	90	150	Iran	
333mm	Fadjr 5	4	75	175	Iran	

Surface-to-Surface Strategic Rockets *(continued)*

Caliber	Designation	Number of rails/tubes	Range (km)	Payload (kg)	Country of origin	Notes
320mm	WS-1	4	80	150	Iran	
300mm	Sajeel 60	4	60		Iraq	Copy of Brazilian 300mm SS-60
300mm	Smerch (BM 9A52-2)	12	70-90	100	Russia	
300mm	SS-60	4	60		Brazil	
260mm	Toros-260	4	100	144	Turkey	
230mm	Oghab	3	80	70	Iran	Improved version of Chinese Type 83 273mm rocket
230mm	Toros-230	8	65	121	Turkey	
210mm	Saqr-80	1	80	200	Egypt	Launched from FROG-7 launcher

Multiple Rocket Launchers

Caliber	Designation	Number of rails/tubes	Range (km)	Country of origin	Notes
350mm	Kachlilit	4	40	Israel	Anti-radar missile
333mm	Shahin 2	2	20	Iran	
290mm	MAR 290	4	25	Israel	
262mm	Ababil-50	12	50	Iraq	Copy or production under license of Yugoslavia's 262mm LRSV M-87
240mm	Fadjr 3	12	43	Iran	
240mm	BM-24	12	10.2	Russia	

Multiple Rocket Launchers *(continued)*

Caliber	Designation	Number of rails/tubes	Range (km)	Country of origin	Notes
227mm	MLRS	12	30	US	
180mm	Sajeel 40	16	35	Iraq	Copy of Brazilian 180mm SS-40
180mm	SS-40 Astros II	16	35	Brazil	
160mm	Keres/LAR-160	18	25	Israel	Anti-radar missile; a derivative of US RGM-66D
140mm	BM-14-16	16	9.8	Russia	
140mm	RPU-14	16	9.8	Russia	
140mm	Teruel	40	18.2	Spain	
132mm	BM-13-16	16	9	Russia	
130mm	M-51 (RM-130)	32	8.2	Romania/Russia	
130mm	M-51	32	8.2	Czech Republic	
130mm	Type 63	19	10.4	PRC	
128mm	M-63	32	8.5	Yugoslavia	
127mm	Sajeel 30	32	30	Iraq	Copy of Brazilian 127mm SS-30
127mm	SS-30 Astros II	32	30	Brazil	
122mm	Azrash	40	21.5	Iran	
122mm	BM-11	30		North Korea	Variant of Soviet BM-21
122mm	BM-21	40	20.8	Russia	
122mm	Firos-25	40	25	Italy	
122mm	Hadid	40	20.4	Iran	
122mm	Nur	40	18	Iran	
122mm	RM-70	40	20.4	Czech Republic	Similar to Russian BM-21
122mm	Saqr 10 and Saqr 18		18	Egypt	

Multiple Rocket Launchers *(continued)*

Caliber	Designation	Number of rails/tubes	Range (km)	Country of origin	Notes
122mm	Saqr 30	30	22.5	Egypt	
122mm	Saqr 36	30	20.4	Egypt	
122mm	TR-122	40	30	Turkey	
120mm	Qassam-2	1	6-8	PA	
107mm		12	8	Iraq	Copy of 107mm from PRC or RM-11 from North Korea
107mm	RM-11		8.1	North Korea	
107mm	Type 63	12	8.5	PRC	
90mm	Qassam-1	1	4-5	PA	

Engineering and Anti-Tank Equipment

Anti-Tank Guns

Caliber	Designation and Type	Country of origin	Notes
120mm	BAT L-4 recoilless rifle	UK	
107mm	B-11 recoilless rifle	Russia	
106mm	M40 A1C/A2 recoilless rifle	US /Israel	
100mm	M-1944 BS-3 field/AT gun	Russia	
100mm	M-1955 field/AT gun	Russia	Also listed under Guns and Howitzers

Anti-Tank Guns *(continued)*

Caliber	Designation and Type	Country of origin	Notes
100mm	T-12 field/AT gun	Russia	
90mm	Light recoilless gun	Belgium	Used on AFVs
85mm	M-1945/D-44 field/AT gun	Russia	Also listed under Guns and Howitzers
84mm	Carl Gustav light recoilless rifle	Sweden	
82mm	B-10 recoilless rifle	Russia	
76mm	M-1942 (ZIS-3) field/AT gun	Russia	Also listed under Guns and Howitzers
75mm	M20 recoilless rifle	US	
57mm	AT gun	Czech Republic	

Anti-Tank Guided Missiles

Designation	Range (m)	Guidance	Country of origin	Notes
AT-1 (Snapper)	2,300	Wire	Russia	
AT-2 (Swatter)	2,500	Radio	Russia	
AT-3 (Sagger)	3,000	Wire	Russia	
AT-4 (Spigot)	2,500	Wire	Russia	
AT-5 (Spandrel)	3,600	Wire	Russia	
AT-6 (Spiral)	5,000	Radio	Russia	
AT-10 (Stabber)	4,000	Laser	Russia	BMP-3 laser-guided projectile
AT-11 (Svir-9K120)	5,000	Laser	Russia	T-72 laser-guided projectile
AT-14 (Kornet)	5,500	Laser	Russia	
Dandy (NT-D)	6,000	TV/IIR	Israel	
Dragon I/II	1,000	Wire	US	

Anti-Tank Guided Missiles *(continued)*

Designation	Range (m)	Guidance	Country of origin	Notes
Dragon II+/III (Superdragon)	2,000	Wire	US	
Eryx	600	Wire	France/Canada	
I-Raad	3,000	Wire	Iran	Licensed production of Russian AT-3
Gill (NT-G)	2,500	CCD/IIR	Israel	
Hellfire	8,000	Laser	US	
HOT	4,000	Wire	France/Germany	
Lahat		Laser	Israel	Merkava/M60 laser-guided projectile
Mapats	5,000	Laser	Israel	
MILAN	2,000	Wire	France/Germany	
Nimrod	26,000	Laser	Israel	Land-based variant of Nimrod AGM.
SS-11	3,000	Wire	France	
SS-12	5,000	Wire	France	Can be employed as ATGM or as anti-ship missile launched from ground, helicopter, or ship
Spike (NT-S)	4,000	Fiber optics/IIR	Israel	
Swingfire	4,000	Wire	UK/Egypt	
Toophan	3,850	Wire	Iran	Variant of TOW
TOW (BGM 71A / C /D)	3,750	Wire	US	
TOW IIA (BGM-71E)	3,750	Wire	US	Tandem warhead
TOW IIB (BGM-71F)	3,750	Wire	US	Tandem warhead programmed for top attack
Towsan-1	4,000	Wire	Iran	Licensed production of Russian AT-5
TRIGAT	2,000	Laser	France	

Engineering Equipment

Designation	Country of Origin	Notes
Aardvark Mk2/Mk3 flail	UK	Anti-mine vehicle
ACV-AESV	Turkey	Engineering combat vehicle
Bar mine-lying system	UK	
BLG-60	Germany/Poland	Bridging tank
EWK pontoon bridge (Faltschwimmbrucke)	Germany	
Fuchs (Fox)	France	NBC reconnaissance vehicle
FWMP	Israel	Full-width mine ploughs
Gilois motorized bridge	France	Bridge and ferry system
GSP	Russia	Heavy amphibious self propelled ferry
M60 AVLB	US	Bridging tank
M69 A1	US	Bridging tank
M123 Viper	US	Minefield-crossing system
M728	US	Engineering combat vehicle based on M60 tank chassis
Matenin SA	France	Automatic mine layers
MT-55	Russia	Bridging tank
MTU-55	Russia	Bridging tank
MTU-67	Russia	Bridging tank
Pelë	Israel	Combat vehicle tele-operation kit
PMP pontoon bridge	Russia	Heavy folding pontoon bridge
Pomins II	Israel	Portable (infantry) mine neutralization system
PRP motorized bridge	Russia	
Puma	Israel	Combat vehicle carrying a squad of combat engineers and some equipment (an improvement of Centurion chassis)
TAB	Israel	tactical assault bridge

Engineering Equipment *(continued)*

Designation	Country of Origin	Notes
TLB	Israel	trailer-launched bridge
TPP, pontoon bridge	Russia	Can be used as a pontoon bridge or a raft
TWMP	Israel	tread-width mine ploughs
UDK-1	UK	bridge

Recovery Vehicles

Designation	Type	Combat weight (ton)	Lifting/towing capability	Country of origin	Notes
ACV	Armored recovery vehicle	13.6	Crane and winch	Turkey	
Leclerc	Armored recovery vehicle	54	Crane maximum capacity of 30 tons; main winch pull capacity of 35 tons.	France	
Challenger	Armored recovery vehicle	62	Winch-52 tons capacity-direct pull; crane lift-6.5 tons-max	UK	
M47 AB1	Armored recovery vehicle	42	6.5 ton capacity crane; 28 ton capacity winch; bulldozer blade	Jordan	Based on M47 MBT
M47/M48	Armored recovery vehicle	48.5	22 ton capacity crane; 35 ton capacity winch; dozer blade	Germany	
M88 A1	Armored recovery vehicle	50.8	Up to 22 tons when using a stabilizing blade; 2 winches: max. capacity of 40.8 ton	US	Based on the M48 MBT

Recovery Vehicles *(continued)*

Designation	Type	Combat weight (ton)	Lifting/towing capability	Country of origin	Notes
M578	Light armored recovery vehicle	24.3	Crane lift capability-6.7 tons, 2 winches with max. capacity of 27 ton	US	Hull is similar to that of the 175mm M107 and 203mm M110 SPGs
Samson	Armored recovery vehicle	8.74	Heavy duty winch, max. capacity of 12 ton	UK	
SK-105 Greif	Armored recovery vehicle	19.8	Crane max. capacity 6 ton; 20 ton winch	Austria	
T-55	Armored recovery vehicle	34	Lifting capability of between 10 to 20 tons	Russia	Additional models were developed by the Czech Republic, Poland and Germany
T-62	Armored recovery vehicle	38		Russia	

AIR DEFENSE EQUIPMENT

Anti-Aircraft Guns

Caliber	Designation	SP, tracked or wheeled (where relevant)	Country of origin	Notes
57mm	S-60		Russia	
57mm	ZSU 57x2	SP, tracked	Russia	
40mm	Bofors L-60		Sweden	
40mm	Bofors L-70		Sweden	
40mm	M42 (twin 40mm)	SP, tracked	US	
37mm	M-1939		Russia	
35mm	Contraves Skyguard		Switzerland	Also listed under Air Defense Systems
35mm	Gepard	SP	Germany	
35mm	Oerlikon-Buhrle 35x2 GDF-002		Switzerland	May be part of 35mm Skyguard system
30mm	AMX DCA 30 2x30mm	SP, tracked	France	
30mm	M-3 30x2	SP	France	
30mm	M-53/59 30x2	SP, wheeled	Czech Republic	
30mm	Oerlikon		Switzerland	
30mm	Wildcat 30x2	SP, wheeled	Germany	
23mm	ZSU 23x4	SP, tracked	Russia	Russian designation: Shilka
23mm	ZU 23x2		Russia	
20mm	TCM-20x2	SP	Israel	Mounting of French gun on US-made M-3 halftrack
20mm	Oerlikon GAI		Switzerland	
20mm	M163 A1 Vulcan	SP	US	

Anti-Aircraft Guns *(continued)*

Caliber	Designation	SP, tracked or wheeled (where relevant)	Country of origin	Notes
20mm	M167 Vulcan		US	
20mm	20x2	SP	France	Mounted on Panhard VCR 6x6
20mm	M-55 A4 20x3		Slovenia	
20mm	VDAA 2x20mm	SP	France	Mounted on VAB 6x6, M3 VDA 4x4

Air Defense Systems

Caliber	Designation	Missiles	Country of origin	Notes
35mm	Skyguard (Contraves Skyguard) 2x35	Aspide or RIM-7M Sparrow	Italy	Gun-Switzerland, SAM Italy, or US; chassis and radar-Italy or Austria; Egyptian designation: Amoun
30mm	Pantzyr-S1 (96K6)	12x9M335 (SA-19)	Russia	Including surveillance and fire-control radars
23mm	Sinai 23 23x2	4xSA-7	Egypt	Gun and SAM-Russia or Egypt; chassis-US
20mm	Mahbet	Stinger	Israel	Based on M-163 Vulcan
12.7mm	Zipkin	Stinger	Turkey	Based on Land Rover chassis, passive tracking system

Air Defense Missiles

Model	Range (km)	Guidance	Configuration	Country of origin
Heavy missiles				
Aspide	15	Semi-active radar	Towed	Italy
HAWK	35	Semi-active radar	Towed	US
Improved HAWK (MIM-23B)	40	Semi-active radar	Towed	US
HQ-2J	34	Command	Towed	PRC
Nike Hercules	155	Command	Towed	US
Patriot (MIM-104)	160	Command, semi-active radar	Trucked	US
S-300 MV (SA-10)	70	Command, active radar	Trucked	Russia
S-300 PMU (SA-12)	150	Command, active radar	Trucked	Russia
SA-2	35	Command	Towed	Russia
SA-3	22	Command	Towed	Russia
SA-5	250	Command, active radar	Static	Russia
Sayyad-1 (SA-2)	~30	Command	Towed	Iran
Sparrow	20	Semi-active radar	Towed	Swiss/US
Medium missiles				
ADAMS	12	Command	SP	Israel
Crotale	9	Command	SP	France
Crotale NG	11	Command, IR, optical	SP	France
HUMRAAM (AIM-120)	15	Command	SP	US
Roland I/II	6.3	Command	SP	France
SA-6 (Kub)	24	Semi-active radar	Trucked	Russia
SA-8 (Osa romb)	9.9	Command	SP	Russia
SA-11	28	Semi-active radar	SP	Russia
Shahine I/II	8-11	Command, IR, optical	SP	France

Air Defense Missiles *(continued)*

Model	Range (km)	Guidance	Configuration	Country of origin
Tor-M1 9M331 (SA-15)	12	Command, optical	SP	Russia
Tula 9M311/9M335 (SA-19)	8/12	Command, optical, laser	SP	Russia
Ya-Zahra (Crotale)	8.6	Command, optical, IR	Trucked	Iran
Light missiles				
ADATS	8	Laser	SP	Switzerland
Atiligan	5	Optical, IR	SP	Turkey
Avenger	4.5	IR	SP	US
Chaparral (MIM-72A)	8	Active, IR	SP	US
Mistral	6	Optical, IR	Portable	France
Rapier	7	Command, optical command	Towed	UK
RBS-70	6	Laser	Portable	Sweden
SA-9	8	Optical, IR	SP	Russia
SA-13 (Strella 10)	5	Optical, IR	SP	Russia
Tigercat	5.5	Optical command	Towed	UK
Shoulder-launched missiles				
Ain al-Saqer	4.4	Optical, IR	Portable	Egypt
Blowpipe	3.5	Optical command	Portable	UK
HN-5	4	Optical, IR	Portable	PRC
Javelin	5	Optical command	Portable	UK
Misagh-1	5	Optical, IR	Portable	Iran
Redeye (MIM-43A)	5.5	Optical, IR	Portable	US
SA-7 (Strella)	3.5	Optical, IR	Portable	Russia
SA-14 (Strella 3)	6	Optical, IR	Portable	Russia
SA-16 (Igla-1)	5	Optical, IR	Portable	Russia

Air Defense Missiles *(continued)*

Model	Range (km)	Guidance	Configuration	Country of origin
SA-18 (Igla)	5.2	Optical,IR	Portable	Russia
Starburst	4	Laser	Portable	UK
Stinger (FIM-92A)	4.5	Optical, IR	Portable	US

AIR FORCE EQUIPMENT

Fighter Aircraft

Model	Radius of action (km)	Radar	Air-to-air missiles	Air-to-ground missiles	Navigation and fire-control instrumentation	Country of origin
Interceptors						
F-14		AVG-12 (315 km)	Sparrow, Phoenix		IR seeker	US
F-15C /D		APG-63 look-down and shoot-down capability	Sidewinder, Sparrow, AMRAAM		ATLIS II laser pod	US
MiG-23 MF/ML	1,150 (AA) 700 (AG)	High Lark look-down (85km)	AA-7 (R-23), AA-8 (R-60)		IR seeker	Russia
MiG-25	1,130	Fox Fire (85km) limited look-down and shoot-down	AA-6, AA-7 (R-23), AA-8 (R-60)		ECCM pods	Russia

Fighter Aircraft *(continued)*

Model	Radius of action (km)	Radar	Air-to-air missiles	Air-to-ground missiles	Navigation and fire-control instrumentation	Country of origin
MiG-29		RLS RP-29 Slot Back (100km) look-down and shoot-down	AA-8 (R-60), AA-10 (R-27), AA-11 (R-73)		IR seeker	Russia
Tornado ADV Mk 3	740	Foxhunter multi-mode , ground mapping (185 km)	Sky Flash, Sidewinder		Internal ECM/ECCM, TI FL radar	UK, Germany
Advanced multi-role						
F-15I/S	1,270	APG-70 look-down and shoot-down capability	Sidewinder, Sparrow, AMRAAM	Maverick, Paveway, Popeye	FLIR, LANTIRN targeting pod, SAR	US
F-16 A/B	925	APG-66 (74 km) Look-down/ shoot-down capability	Sidewinder, AMRAAM	Maverick, HARM/ Shrike	FLIR, ALQ-119/131 ECM, Pave-Penny laser pod	US
F-16 C/D	925	APG-68V air-to-air/ air-to-ground	Sidewinder AMRAAM, Sparrow, Python 4	Maverick Paveway, HARM/ Shrike, Harpoon, Popeye II	FLIR ALQ-131/187 ECM, Pave Penny laser pod, LANTIRN, Orphus (reconn.), Atils laser pod, ELM-2060 SAR pod	US

Fighter Aircraft *(continued)*

Model	Radius of action (km)	Radar	Air-to-air missiles	Air-to-ground missiles	Navigation and fire-control instrumentation	Country of origin
F-16 I (Block 60)	2,100	ABR air-to-air/ air-to-ground/ ground following	Sidewinder AMRAAM, Sparrow, Python 4	Maverick Paveway, HARM/ Shrike, Harpoon, Popeye II	Integral FLIR, targeting system, SAR and ECM /EW	US
F-18 C /D		APG-65 air-to-air/ air-to-ground	Sidewinder, AMRAAM, Sparrow	Maverick, Paveway, HARM/ Shrike, Harpoon	AAS-38 FLIR, ALQ-126/165 ECM, ASQ-173 laser pod	US
Mirage 2000	1,200 (hi-lo-hi), 925 (lo-lo-lo)	RDM/RDY multi-mode (100 km)	R 530/550 Magic, Mica	ARMAT, Exocet, AS-30L, laser-guided bombs	Atlis laser pod, SLAR, reconn. pods, ECM pods, Astac ELINT pod	France
Phantom 2000		APG-76	Python 3, Sidewinder	Griffin, Popeye, Paveway, Maverick, GBU-15	INS, WDNS weapons and nav. computer, internal ECM, SAR	Israel
Multi-role						
F-4E		APQ-72	Sparrow III, Sidewinder	Bullpop, Maverick, Standard/Shrike, Paveway, GBU-15, C-801	ASQ-19 navigation package, AJB-3 bombing system laser pod	US
F-5 E/F	222 (lo-lo-lo), 890 (hi-lo-hi)	APQ-159 (37km)	Sidewinder	Paveway	Laser pod	US
Hawk 200	945 (hi-lo-hi)	APG-66H multi-mode	Sky Flash, Sidewinder	Sea Eagle, Maverick	HUDWAC weapons computer, FLIR, reconn. pod	UK

Fighter Aircraft *(continued)*

Model	Radius of action (km)	Radar	Air-to-air missiles	Air-to-ground missiles	Navigation and fire-control instrumentation	Country of origin
Jaguar	1,400 (hi-lo-hi), 917 (lo-lo-lo)	Agave	R550 Magic, Sidewinder	AS 37	HUD/WAC weapons computer, reconn. pod, TV night sensors	UK
Mirage F1	425 (hi-lo-hi)	Cyrano IV, Doppler nav. radar	R530/550 Magic, Sidewinder	ARMAT, Exocet, AS-30L, laser-guided bombs	Nav/bombing computer, Atlis laser pod, SLAR, reconn. pods, ECM pods	France
Tornado IDS Mk 1	1,390 (hi-lo-lo-hi)	TI FL radar, Decca Doppler terrain-following radar	Sidewinder	AS-30L, Maverick, Paveway, Sea Eagle, munitions dispenser	Digital attack/nav. system, Ferranti laser pod, internal ECM	UK, Germany
Obsolete						
A-5/Q-5	400 (lo-lo-lo), 600 (hi-lo-hi)	High Fix	PL-2, PL-7, Sidewinder, R550 Magic	C-802, Durandal, Snakeye	ECM	PRC
F-5 A/B	350		Sidewinder			US
F-6	685	Izumrud	PL-2, PL-5			PRC
F-7	600 (hi-lo-hi), 370 (lo-lo-lo)	Ranging radar	PL-2, PL-5, PL-7, R550 Magic		HUDWAC weapons computer	PRC
MiG-21 MF/BIS	740 (hi-lo-hi)	Jay Bird (20km)	AA-2 C/D (K-13)			Russia
Mirage III-E	1,200	Cyrano II	R530 Magic	AS-30 IR/com	Nav./bombing computer	France

Fighter Aircraft *(continued)*

Model	Radius of action (km)	Radar	Air-to-air missiles	Air-to-ground missiles	Navigation and fire-control instrumentation	Country of origin
Mirage V	1,300 (hi-lo-hi) 650 (lo-lo-lo)	Agave	R530/550 Magic Sidewinder	AS-30 IR/com	Laser range finder, refuel pod	France
Ground attack						
MiG-23BN	700	Doppler nav. radar	AA-8 (R-60)	AS-7	Laser range finder	Russia
OV-10	367	Doppler nav. radar	Sidewinder	Paveway	TV/laser designation pod	US
Su-20/22	2,300 (hi-hi-hi) 1,400 (lo-lo-lo)	SRD-5M ranging radar	AA-8 (R-60)	AS-7, AS-9, AS-10	ASP-5ND fire control system, laser pod, reconn. Pod, ECM pod	Russia
Su-24	322 (lo-lo-lo) 950 (lo-lo-hi) 1,050 (hi-lo-hi)	PNS-24M terrain-following/ nav. System	AA-8 (R-60) AA-11 (R-73)	AS-9,AS-10, AS-11, AS-12, AS-14 KAB-500/1500Kr	Kaira-24 laser/TV guidance system, laser pod, internal ECM	Russia
Su-25	400 (lo-lo-lo) 630 (hi-hi-hi)	Kinzhal ground radar, Doppler nav. System	AA-8 (R-60)	AS-10, AS-11, AS-14, laser-guided bombs	Voskhod nav./attack system, internal TV/ laser guidance system, internal ECM, IIR pod	Russia
Bombers						
Tu-16	3,150			AS-5, AS-6		Russia
Tu-22	2,200 (hi-hi-hi) 1,500 (lo-lo-lo)	Down Beat nav. radar		AS-4		Russia

Helicopters

Model	Number of passengers	External payload (kg)	Max range (km)	Armament	Avionics	Country of origin
Light transport						
300C	1+2	408	370			US
500D	6		482 (S/L); 531 (5,000 ft)			US
530F	6	907	371 (S/L); 429 (5,000 ft)		FLIR	US
AS-350 Ecureuil	6	907	720	Machine guns, 20mm guns, rockets		France
Bell 206B	3-4		645			US
Bell 406 (OH-58B) Kiowa	2+2		556		Doppler nav. system, night vision	US
BK-117	7		500		Laser-1 Doppler nav. system	Japan
BO-105	1+4		575 (S/L) 657 (5,000 ft)		Doppler nav. system,	Germany
Mi-2	8	800	440			Russia
SA-315 Lama	1+4	1,135	515			France
SA-318C Alouette II	1+4	600	300			France
SA-319 Alouette III	6	750	290			France
UH-12	1+2	454	346			US

Helicopters *(continued)*

Model	Number of passengers	External payload (kg)	Max range (km)	Armament	Avionics	Country of origin
Medium transport						
AS-61/SH-3D	31	3,630	582		Doppler nav. system	US
AS-330 Puma	16	3,200	572	Machine guns, 20mm gun, rockets	Doppler nav. radar, Decca nav. system, rolling map	France
AS-332 Super Puma/AS-532 Cougar	21-25	4,500	870	Machine guns, 20mm gun, rockets	Doppler nav. radar, Decca nav. system, rolling map	France
AS-365 Dauphin II	10	1,600	250		Digital nav. system	France
Bell 204	7-8	1,360	615	Machine guns, rocket launchers		US
UH-1H (Bell 205, 212)	11-14	1,760	511	Machine guns, rocket launchers		US
Bell 214	18		678			Italy
Bell 412	14	1,814	656 (S/L) 804 (5,000 ft)		Doppler nav. radar	Italy
KV-107	26		175		Doppler nav. radar	Japan
MD 600N	8	1,225	620 (S/L) 703 (5,000 ft)			US
Mi-4	2+14	1,600	250	Machine guns, rockets		Russia
Mi-8/17	24	3,000	500	Machine guns, rockets, bombs	Doppler nav. radar	Russia

Helicopters *(continued)*

Model	Number of passengers	External payload (kg)	Max range (km)	Armament	Avionics	Country of origin
S-61R/HH-3E	25	3,620	748			US
S-70A Blackhawk	11	3,630	600	Machine guns	Doppler nav. radar, night vision, ALQ-144 ECM	US
SA-321 Super Ferlon	27	4,500	630		Doppler radar, INS	France
Westland Commando	28	2,720	445		Doppler nav. radar	UK
Heavy transport						
CH-47D Chinook	44	12,700	185		Doppler nav. radar	US
CH-53D	64	14,515	413			US
Mi-6	70	8,000	620	Machine guns, rockets		Russia
Ground attack						
500MD	2		389 (S/L) 428 (5,000 ft)	TOW missiles, Stinger missiles	TV/FLIR targeting system	US
A-109A Mk II	7	907	550	Machine guns, rocket launchers, TOW missiles	Doppler nav. radar, TV targeting system	Italy
AH-1 G/J/P Cobra	2	574	507	TOW missiles Mini-gun	Optical targeting system	US
AH-1W/Z King Cobra	2		635	20mm gun, TOW missiles, Hellfire missiles	Optical targeting system, laser designator	US

Helicopters *(continued)*

Model	Number of passengers	External payload (kg)	Max range (km)	Armament	Avionics	Country of origin
AH-64A Apache	2	771	482	30mm gun, Hellfire missiles, rockets, Stinger missiles	Doppler nav. System, ALQ-136/144 ECM, TV/FLIR targeting system, laser designator	US
AH-64D Apache Longbow	2	771	482	30mm gun, Hellfire missiles, AAMs	AGP-78 AA/AG mission radar, TADS day/night targeting system, ESM, ECM	US
BO-105	1+4		575 (S/L), 657 (5,000 ft)	HOT missiles, TOW missiles	Doppler nav. system, optical targeting system	Germany
Mi-24	8		450	AT-2 missiles, machine guns, rockets, bombs	Doppler nav. system, optical targeting system, internal ECM	Russia
OH-58D Kiowa Warrior (Bell 406)			556	Machine guns, TOW missiles, Stinger missiles	Doppler nav system, TV/IIR targeting system, laser designator, night vision system	US
SA-319 Alouette III	6	750	290	Machine guns, 20mm gun, AS-11 /12 missiles	Optical targeting system	France
SA-342 Gazelle	1+4	700	670	AS-12 missiles, HOT missiles, rockets, machine guns	Optical targeting system, laser designator (342 L)	France

Helicopters *(continued)*

Model	Number of passengers	External payload (kg)	Max range (km)	Armament	Avionics	Country of origin
Naval combat						
AS-61/SH-3D		3,630	582	Torpedoes, depth charges	Doppler ASW, nav. system, APS-707 radar, AQS-13/18 sonar	US
AS-332 Super Puma/AS-532 Cougar		4,500	870	Exocet missiles, AS-15TT missiles, torpedoes	Doppler nav. radar, Decca nav. system, RDR 1400/1500 search radar or Varan ASW radar, Sonar, magnetic sweep, Sonobuoys	France
AS-365 Dauphin II		1,600	250	AS-15TT, torpedoes	Agrion 15 plan position radar or Omera ORB 32 search radar, Croyzet magnetic sweep, HS 12 sonar, digital nav. system	France
Bell 204		1,360	615	Torpedoes	Sonar	US
Bell 212		1,760	511	Torpedoes	Doppler ASW nav. system, AQS-13 B/F sonar	US
Bell 412		1,814	656 (S/L) 804 (5,000 ft)	25mm cannon, Sea Skua missiles	Doppler radar, TV/FLIR targeting system, ALQ-144 ECM	Italy
Kamov 28			200	Torpedoes, depth charges	Doppler nav. radar, radar, magnetic sweep, OKA-2 sonar, sonobuoys	Russia

Helicopters *(continued)*

Model	Number of passengers	External payload (kg)	Max range (km)	Armament	Avionics	Country of origin
Mi-14 PL			1,135	Torpedoes, depth charges	Doppler nav. radar, 12M radar, magnetic sweep, OKA-2 sonar, sonobuoys	Russia
S-70B Seahawk	3	3,600	600	Penguin Mk. 2 ASM or Hellfire II ASM	APS-143 search radar, AQS-18 and HLARS sonars, FLIR	US
SA-321 Super Frelon		4,500	630	Torpedoes	Doppler radar or Sylphe ASW radar, INS, sonar	France
SH-2G Seasprite	4	1,814	885	Torpedoes	LN-66HP radar, magnetic and acoustic sweeps, 15 sonobuoys, FLIR	US
Super Lynx 300	10	1,360	600	Torpedoes, depth charges Sea Skua/ Penguin Mk.2 ASMs	Seaspray Mk 3000 radar, AQS-18/ HS-312 sonar, dipping sonar, AFCS, FLIR	UK
Westland Sea King Mk 47			1,230	Torpedoes, depth charges	AD 580 Doppler nav. system, AW 391 radar, AQS-13B Plessey sonar, sonobuoys	UK

Training Aircraft

Model	Range (km)	External weight (kg)	Armament	Avionics	Country of origin
Jet engines					
Alpha Jet	555	2,500	30mm gun, rockets, bombs, Magic AAM	Weapon aiming computer, camera reconn. pod	France , Germany
Azarakhsh		4,400			Iran
BAC 167	900	1,360	Machine guns, bombs, rockets		UK
C-101	964	2,250	30mm gun, rockets, bombs	INS, optical sight, laser designator, reconn. pod, ECM pod	Spain
Cessna 318/T-37B	1,400		Machine gun, rockets, bombs	INS, computing gunsight/ camera reconn. pod	US
CM 170 Fuga Magister	910	500	Machine guns, rockets	Gyro gunsight	France
G2-A Galeb		700	Machine guns, bombs, rockets	Fixed gunsight	Yugoslavia
Hawk Mk 60	998	3,084	30mm gun, rockets, bombs, Magic/Sidewinder AAM, Maverick AGM, Sea Eagle AGM	INS, gunsight/camera, camera reconn. pod	UK
Hawk Mk 100	998	3,084	30mm gun, rockets, bombs, Magic/Sidewinder AAM, Maverick AGM, Sea Eagle AGM	INS, gunsight/camera, HUDWAC weapon system, FLIR, camera reconn. pod, ECM pod	UK

Training Aircraft *(continued)*

Model	Range (km)	External weight (kg)	Armament	Avionics	Country of origin
K-8	1,400	388	20mm gun, PL-7 AAMs, rockets. Bombs	INS, air data computer, gunsight/camera	PRC
L-29 Delfin	397		Machine guns, rockets, bombs	Gyro gunsight/camera	Czech Republic
L-39 Albatros		1,100	23mm gun, rockets, bombs, IR missiles	Camera reconn. pod, gyro gunsight	Czech Republic
L-59	1,210	1,700	23mm gun, bombs, rockets	HUD mission computer	Czech Republic
MB 326	648	1,814	Machine guns, rockets, bombs, AS-12 AGM	INS, fixed/gyro gunsight/ camera, camera reconn. pod	Italy
MB 339	593	1,815	30mm guns, bombs, rockets, Magic/Sidewinder AAM	INS, fixed/gyro gunsight, camera reconn. pod, ECM pod	Italy
T-33			Machine gun		US
T-38 Talon				INS	US
Piston/Turbo-prop					
AS-202 Bravo	965				Switzerland
BAe SA-3-120 Bulldog	1,000	290	Machine guns, bombs		UK
Bonanza F 33C	1,326				US
CAP 10	1,000				France
Cessna 150	909				US
Cessna 172/T-41	963			INS	US
Cessna 180/185	1,100			INS	US
Cessna 182	1,380			INS	US

Training Aircraft *(continued)*

Model	Range (km)	External weight (kg)	Armament	Avionics	Country of origin
Cessna U-206	1,045		Minigun, bombs		US
EMB-312	1,844	625	Machine gun, rockets, bombs	Fixed gunsight	Brazil
G-115E	1,050				Germany
MBB 223 Flamingo	500				Germany, Spain
MFI-17 Safari	800				Sweden
Mushshak		300	Machine guns, rockets, Bantam AGM		India
PA-18 Piper Cub	735	22			US
PC-6	1,050				Switzerland
PC-7/9	1,200			Computer nav. system (PC-9)	Switzerland
S 208M	1,200			INS	Italy
SA 202 Bravo	1,100	270		INS	Italy
SF 260 Warrior	556	300	Machine guns, bombs, rockets	Camera reconn. pod	US
Sierra 200	1,270				US
T-34C	555	544	Machine guns, rockets, bombs, Walleye AGM		US
TB 20 /21 /200	1,170				France
Zlin 142	525				Czech Republic

Transport Aircraft

Model	Passengers	Range (km)	Payload (kg)	Country of origin
Airbus A340	295	12,416	47,127	France
An-12	90	Max. load: 3,600, max. fuel: 5,700	20,000	Russia
An-24	44-50	Max. load: 550, max. fuel: 2,400	5,500	Russia
An-26	40	Max. load: 1,100, max. fuel: 2,550	5,500	Russia
An-74TK	20	Max. load: 1,350, max. fuel: 4,300	10,000	Ukraine
An-140 (Iran-140)	52	2,500	6,000	Ukraine/Iran
Arava	20	Max. load: 486, max. fuel: 1,400	2,350	Israel
BAe 125/HS 125	8/12	3,120	857	UK
BN-2B Islander	10	Max. load: 672, max. fuel: 2,027	1,200	UK
Boeing 707	181	4,235	24,950	US
Boeing 727	145	4,390	18,144	US
Boeing 737	130	4,180	17,223	US
Boeing 747-200	452	10,562		US
Boeing 747-200F		8,060	109,315	US
C-130B/E/H	92	Max. load: 3,790, max. fuel: 7,876	19,356	US
C-140 Jetstar	10	Max. load: 3,410, max. fuel: 3,595	1,327	US
C-160	93	Max. load: 1,853, max. fuel: 5,095	16,000	Germany
CASA C-212	16	Max. load: 720, max. fuel: 1,920	2,000	Spain
Challenger 604	22	7,550	2,435	Canada
Citation III	11	4,815		US
CN-235	48	4,350	6,000	Spain
CN-295	70	Max. load: 1,348, max. fuel: 4,537	7,500	Spain
Commander 690	8	2,116		Britain
DC-3 Dakota	38	1,853	2,500	US

Transport Aircraft *(continued)*

Model	Passengers	Range (km)	Payload (kg)	Country of origin
DC-8	189	11,410	30,240	US
DC-9	105	3,100	12,743	US
DC-10	380	7,400	43,300	US
DHC-4	32	Max. load: 390, max. fuel: 2,100	3,965	Canada
DHC-5	41	Max. load: 815, max. fuel: 3,490	6,280	Canada
Dornier Do 228	15/20	1,740	2,200	Germany
Dove	11	620	670	Canada
EMB 110P	18	2,000	1,681	Brazil
Falcon 10	7	3,370	603	France
Falcon 20	8/14	3,540	1,380	France
Falcon 50	8	6,480	1,570	France
Falcon 900	8	7,229	2,185	France
Fokker F-27	44	2,213	6,438	Netherlands
G222L	53	Max. load: 1,890, max. fuel: 5,100	9,000	Italy
Gulfstream II/III	19	7,590	907	US
Gulfstream V	19	12,038	2,948	US
IL-14	18	2,600	5,300	Russia
IL-76	120	6,700	48,000	Russia
IL-78 Tanker		2,500	60,000 fuel	Russia
Jetstream 31	20	1,760	1,200	UK
KC-130 Tanker		1,850	23,587 fuel	US
KC-135 Tanker		4,630	92,210 fuel	US
King Air B100/ B200/200T	8/14	2,456		US

Transport Aircraft *(continued)*

Model	Passengers	Range (km)	Payload (kg)	Country of origin
L-100-30	128	Max. load: 2,585, max. fuel: 10,000	23,679	US
L-1011-500	246	Max. load: 9,900, max. fuel: 11,286	42,000	US
L-410 UVP	15	Max. load: 390, max. fuel: 1,140	1,310	Czech Republic
Learjet 25	8	2,650		US
Maule MX-7	4	845	317	US
Piper Navajo	6	1,800		US
Skyvan Srs 3M	22	Max. load: 386, max. fuel: 1,075	2,358	UK
Tu-124	44	Max. load: 1,220, max. fuel: 3,500	6,000	Russia
Tu-134	80	Max. load: 2,400, max. fuel: 3,500	8,165	Russia
VC-140 Jetstar	11-15	Max. load: 3,410, max. fuel: 3,595	1,330	US
Yak-40	27	Max. load: 1,000, max. fuel: 1,480	2,300	Russia

Miscellaneous Aircraft

Model	Crew	Mission	Systems	Endurance (h)	Range (km)	In service	Country of origin
Adnan-1/2	8-10	AEW	Tiger TRS-2100 radar, ESM		5,000	Iraq	Iraq
ATR 72MP	6	Maritime surveillance	Radar, FLIR, AM-39 Exocet, MU90 torpedoes		2,200	UAE	France/Italy
Beechcraft 1900C	6	Maritime surveillance	Liton APS-504 radar, SLAM -MR, Singer S-3075 ESM		2,900	Egypt	US
Beechcraft 1900C	2	EW	ECM, comm. Relay, USD-9 Guardrail		2,900	Egypt	US
BN-2T Maritime Defender	4	Maritime surveillance	Bendix RDR-1400 radar, torpedoes		800	Morocco, Oman	UK

Miscellaneous Aircraft *(continued)*

Model	Crew	Mission	Systems	Endurance (h)	Range (km)	In service	Country of origin
Boeing 707 AEW		AEW	Phalcon radar, ECM, ESM			Israel	Israel
Boeing 707 EW		EW	Elta EL-8300 SIGINT system, ESM	6		Israel	Israel
C-130		EW	COMINT, ELINT, EW systems			Israel	Israel
C-130H MP		Maritime surveillance	Search radar, IRDS, SLAR-PI, TV sensor	16	3,300	Egypt, Morocco	US
Casa C-212	4	ASW/ Maritime surveillance	APS-128 radar, ESM, MAD, sonobouys, torpedoes		1,700	Sudan	UK
CN 235 MP	5	Maritime surveillance	Liton APS-504 radar, ALR-85 ESM, FLIR-2000HP, torpedoes		1,500	Turkey	Spain/ Indonesia
CN 235 MPA	6	Maritime surveillance	Thomson-CSF Ocean Master 100 radar, AMASCOS 300 with FLIR and ESM systems	8	1,400	UAE , Tunisia	Spain/ Indonesia
E-2C Hawkeye	5	AEW	APS-138 /139 radar (480 km), ALR-73 passive detection	6	2,500	Egypt, Israel	US
E-3A Sentry	20	AWACS	APY-1 radar, ECM, ESM, CC-1 mission computer	12		Saudi Arabia	US
Fokker F-27 MP	6	Maritime surveillance	Liton APS-504 radar	12	5,000	Algeria	Netherlands

Miscellaneous Aircraft *(continued)*

Model	Crew	Mission	Systems	Endurance (h)	Range (km)	In service	Country of origin
Mystère-Falcon 20F	6	EW	ELINT, SIGINT and ECM systems		4,400	Morocco	France
P-3C Orion	10	ASW/ Maritime surveillance	APS-115 radar, ARR-72 sonar, ASQ-114 mission computer, magnetic and maritime anomaly detectors, sonobuoys, ESM, mines and torpedoes		3,800	Iran	US
Sea Scan 1124N	8	Maritime surveillance	Liton APS-504 radar	8	2,800	Israel	Israel
Super King Air 200CT	2	EW	ECM, comm. Relay, USD-9 Guardrail			Israel	US
Super King Air B-200T	8	Maritime surveillance	Search radar, FLIR, Seehawk ESM, sonobuoys	6.5	3,300	Algeria	US

UAVs and Mini-UAVs

Model	Length (m)	Wing span (m)	Endurance (h)	Range (km)	Payload (kg)	Payload type	Country of origin
Ababil-S	2.8	3.3	3	150		TV	Iran
Ababil-T				50-150		Strike drone	Iran
AQM-37	3.8	1	2.3	185		Target drone	US
Banshee BTT 342	2.9	2.46	1.5			Target drone	US

UAVs and Mini-UAVs *(continued)*

Model	Length (m)	Wing span (m)	Endurance (h)	Range (km)	Payload (kg)	Payload type	Country of origin
BQM-34	6.87	3.87				Target drone	US
BQM-74C Chukar II	3.87	1.68	1.7	450		Target drone	US
Bravo				80	20	TV, FLIR	Pakistan
Camcopter	2.7	3.1	6	10	25	TV	Austria
CL-89	2.5	0.9		135	20	TV, IR	Canada
Falco	3.5	2.7	1	150	20	Target drone	UAE
Foucade	1.6	1.8	0.5	5	3	TV	France
Gnat 750	5.4	10.5	40			TV, FLIR	US
Harpy			7	550		Strike drone	Israel
Hermes 1500	8.4	10	24			TV, SAR/MTI	Israel
Hermes 450S	6	10	20		150	TV, SAR/MTI	Israel
Heron/ Mahatz/ Eagle 1	8.4	16.4	50	1,400	250	TV,IIR,SAR/MTI, laser designator	Israel
Hunter	6.9	8.7	12	140		TV, FLIR, laser designator	Israel
Mastiff	3.3	4.3	6	200	30	TV, FLIR, ECM, laser designator	Israel
Mirach 100	3.9	1.8	1.1		30	Target drone	Italy
Mohajer II			2	50		TV, EW	Iran
Mohajer III (Dorna)			3	100		TV, EW	Iran
Mohajer IV (Hodhod)			3	150		TV, IR, EW	Iran
MQM-107	5.5	3	2.5			Target drone	US
Nibbio	5.1	5.6	10	200	55	TV, ECM	UAE

UAVs and Mini-UAVs *(continued)*

Model	Length (m)	Wing span (m)	Endurance (h)	Range (km)	Payload (kg)	Payload type	Country of origin
Pioneer	4.2	5	6.5	210		TV, FLIR	US
Ranger	5	6.2	5	150		TV, IR, ESM, laser designator	Israel
al-Shabah		3.13	1.5	70		Target drone	UAE
Saeqeh I/II				50		Target drone	Iran
Scarab 324	6	3.3				TV	US
Scout	3.7	3.6	7	100	30	TV, IIR, laser designator	Israel
Searcher	5	7.1	12			TV, FLIR	Israel
Searcher II	6.4	9.4	16	260		TV, FLIR, IIR, SAR/MTI	Israel
Seeker			9	200	40	TV, IIR	South Africa
Shmel (Yak-61)	2.7	3.2	2			TV, IR	Russia
Shaspar				250	50	TV, FLIR, laser designator	Pakistan
Skyeye R4E-50	4	7.2	12	430		TV, IR, FLIR, EW, IRLS	US
Teledyne Ryan model 124 Firebee	7	3.9	1.25	1,200		Target drone	US

Advanced Armament

Air-to-Air missiles

Type	Guidance	Range (km)	Counter measures	Country of origin
AA-2C/D	Semi-active radar/IR	8/3		Russia
AA-6	Semi-active radar/IR	30		Russia
AA-7	Semi-active radar/IR	25/15	IRCM	Russia
AA-8	IR	3-5		Russia
AA-10	Semi-active radar/IR	50/40	IRCM	Russia
AA-11	IR	30	Improved IRCM	Russia
AIM-120 AMRAAM	Active radar	50		US
Derby	Active radar	60	ECCM	Israel
Mica	Active radar/IIR	60	Enhanced IRCM	France
Phoenix	Active radar	150	ECCM	US
PL-2	IR	3		PRC
PL-5	IR	3		PRC
PL-7	IR	3		PRC
Python-3	IR	5	IRCM	Israel
Python-4	IR	8	IRCM	Israel
R530	Semi-active radar/IR	15/3		France
Super 530F/D	Semi-active radar	30/40	Improved ECCM	France
R 550 Magic II	IR	5	Improved IRCM	France
Red Top	IR		IRCM	UK
Shafrir 2	IR	3		Israel
Sidewinder	IR	8	Improved IRCM	US
Sky Flash	Semi-active radar	40	Improved ECCM	UK
Sparrow	Semi-active radar	45	Improved ECCM	US

Air-to-Surface Missiles

Type	Purpose	Guidance	Range (km)	Country of origin
AS-4	ALCM/ARM	Passive radar homing	400	Russia
AS 6	ALCM	Internal/passive radar	400	Russia
Black Shahine/ APACHE	ALCM	INS, GPS, IIR	400	France
ALARM	ARM	Passive radar homing	45	UK
ARMAT	ARM	Passive radar homing	90	France
AS-9	ARM	Passive radar homing	90	Russia
AS-11	ARM	Passive radar homing	50	Russia
AS-12	ARM	Passive radar homing	35	Russia
HARM	ARM	Passive radar homing	25	US
Shrike	ARM	Passive radar homing	12	US
Standard	ARM	Passive radar homing	55	US
AM 39 Exocet	ASM	Active radar	50	France
AS 15TT	ASM	Radar command	15	France
AS-5	ASM	Active radar	180	Russia
C-801	ASM	Active radar	40	PRC
C-802/ Fajr-a-dayra	ASM	Active radar	130	PRC
Gabriel	ASM	Active radar	35	Israel
Harpoon	ASM	Active radar	120	US
Penguin	ASM	IR30	Norway	
Sea Eagle	ASM	Active radar	110	UK

Air-to-Air missiles *(continued)*

Type	Guidance	Range (km)	Counter measures	Country of origin
Sea Skua	ASM	Semi-active radar	18	UK
AS-11	ATGM	Manual wire	3	France
AS-12	ATGM	Manual wire	5	France
AT-2	ATGM	Radio command	4	Russia
AT-6	ATGM	Radio command	5	Russia
Hellfire	ATGM	Laser/IIR	8	US
HOT	ATGM	Auto-Wire	4	France
TOW	ATGM	Auto-wire	4	US
Nimrod	ATGM	laser	22	Israel
NT-D (Dandy)	ATGM	laser/IIR	6	Israel
Trigat 3LR	ATGM	IIR	4.5	France
AS 7	AGM	Radio command	5	Russia
AS 10	AGM	Laser	10	Russia
AS 14	AGM	Laser/TV	12	Russia
AS 30	AGM	Radio command/laser	10	France
Bullpop	AGM	Radio command	10	US
Durandal	AGM	Internal navigation	7	France
Excalibur	AGM	Internal navigation	10	France
GBU-15	AGM	TV/IIR-guided bombs	80	US
Griffin	AGM	Laser-guided bombs	10	Israel
JDAM	AGM	INS/GPS-guided bombs	25	US
KAB-500Kr	AGM	Laser-guided bombs		Russia
KAB-1500Kr	AGM	Laser-guided bombs		Russia
Lizard	AGM	Laser-guided bombs		Israel

Air-to-Air missiles *(continued)*

Type	Guidance	Range (km)	Counter measures	Country of origin
AGM-65 Maverick	AGM	TV/IIR/Laser	8/25/20	US
Opher	AGM	IR-guided bombs		Israel
Paveway GBU-10/ 12/16	AGM	Laser-guided bombs	7	US
PGM 1/2/3	AGM	Laser/IR	20	UK
AGM-142 A/B/E Popeye	AGM	TV/IIR	80	Israel
Pyramid	AGM	TV-guided bombs		Israel
RAM	AGM	Runway penetration bomb		Israel
Sattar-1/2	AGM	Laser	20/30	Iran
Skipper	AGM	Laser-guided bombs	7	US
Spice	AGM	TV-guided bombs	45	Israel
UAB-500	AGM	Laser-guided bombs		Russia
Walleye	AGM	TV-guided bombs	20	US

Optical Systems

Type	Mission	Systems description	Country of origin
Atlis	Target acquisition	TV, laser designator	France
EL-2055	Reconnaissance pod	Lightweight SAR/MTI for UAVs	Israel
EL-2060P TACL-SAR	Reconnaissance pod	Long range SAR/MTI	Israel
Hawkeye	Target acquisition	TV, FLIR, laser designator	US
Iris	Target acquisition	FLIR	US
Lantirn/Sharpshooter	Target acquisition/ navigation	TV, FLIR, laser, terrain-following radar	US

Optical Systems *(continued)*

Type	Mission	Systems description	Country of origin
Litening I/II	Target acquisition/navigation	TV, FLIR, laser, CCD	Israel
Lorops	Reconnaissance pod	TV, IIR, oblique cameras	Israel
Pave Penny	Target acquisition	Laser designator and tracer	US
Tiald	Target acquisition	IIR, laser designator	UK

NAVY EQUIPMENT

Sea-to-Sea missiles

Type	Guidance	Range (km)	Payload (kg)	Warhead	Country of origin
Barak 1	Command to line of sight	12	22	HE fragmentation	Israel
C-801/YJ-1	Inertial and active radar	40	165	HE	PRC
C-802/YJ-2/ Tondar	Inertial and active radar	120	165	HE	PRC
FL-10	Inertial and active radar	30-40		HE	Iran
Gabriel Mk 2/3	Internal and semi-active radar	35	180	HE SAP	Israel
Hai Ying II/SY-1	Internal with active radar, IR	95	513	HE	PRC
Harpoon	Internal and active radar	130	222	HE blast penetration	US
Kh-35 (Uran-E/3M24E)	Internal and active radar, IR	130	145	HE fragmentation	Russia

Sea-to-Sea missiles *(continued)*

Type	Guidance	Range (km)	Payload (kg)	Warhead	Country of origin
MM 40 Exocet	Inertial with active radar	70	165	HE fragmentation	France
Otomat Mk 1	Inertial, command and active radar	60	210	HE SAP	International
Penguin Mk 2	Inertial and passive IR	30	120	HE SAP	Norway
Sea Killer II	Command	25	70	HE SAP	Italy
Sea Skua SL	Semi-active radar	15	30	HE SAP	UK
SS-12M	Wire-guided	5.5	30	HE	France
SS-N-2A /B Styx	Internal with active radar, IR	35/40	350/450	HE	Russia
SS-N-12	Internal, command and active radar	550	1,000	HE	Russia
Standard SM-1	Command and semi-active radar	40	115	HE fragmentation	US
Yakhont (SS-NX-26)	Active/passive radar	300		HE	Russia

Sea-to-Air missiles

Type	Guidance	Range (km)	Country of origin	Notes
Aspide Mk1	Semi-active radar	15	Italy	Based on the US AIM-7 Sparrow
Bora	Optical, IR	5	Turkey	Based on Stinger SAMs and 12.7mm
gun				
Crotale-NG	Command	11	France	Naval version of Crotale
Mistral	Optical, IR	6	France	
SA-N-4	Semi-active radar	14.8	Russia	Naval version of the SA-8
SA-N-5	IR homing	10	Russia	Naval version of the SA-7
Sea Sparrow	Semi-active radar	15	US	
Standard RIM-66A/C		Semi-active radar	40/70	US

Coastal Defense

Type	Guidance	Range (km)	Payload (kg)	Warhead	Country of origin
C-802	Inertial and active radar	120	165	HE	PRC
Hai Ying II (Silkworm)	Autopilot with active radar or IR	95	513	HE	PRC
Otomat Mk 1	Inertial, command and active radar	60	210	HE	International
SS-N-22 (Sunburn/Moskit)	Inertial with updates and active/passive radar	150	300	HE	Russia
SSC-1B (Sepal)	Inertial with commands and IR or active radar	300	1,000	HE	Russia
SSC-3/SS-N-2A/B (Styx)	Autopilot with active radar or IR	80	513	HE	Russia
Yakhont (SS-NX-26)	Active/passive radar	300		HE	Russia

ABBREVIATIONS

a/c	aircraft
AA	air-to-air/Anti-aircraft
AAG	anti-aircraft gun
AAM	air-to-air missile
AD	air defense
AEW	airborne early warning
AFB	air force base
AFCS	advanced fire control system
AFV	armored fighting vehicle
AGM	air-to-ground missile
ALCM	air-launched cruise missile
APC	armored personnel carrier
APFSDS	armour piercing fin stabilized discarding sabot
armd.	armored
ARM	Anti-radiation missile
ARV	armored recovery vehicle
AS	air-to-surface
ASM	anti-ship missile
ASW	anti-submarine warfare
AT	anti-tank
ATGM	anti-tank guided missile
aty.	artillery
AWACS	airborne warning and control system
batt.	battalion
bn	billion
BW	biological warfare
BWC	Biological Weapon Convention
CAS	close air support
CBU	cluster bomb unit
cif	cost insurance and freight
CW	chemical warfare / Chemical Weapons
CWC	Chemical Weapon Convention
dwt	deadweight tons
ECCM	electronic counter-countermeasures
ECM	electronic countermeasures
ELINT	electronic intelligence gathering

ABBREVIATIONS *(CONTINUED)*

ERA	explosive reactive armor
ESM	electronic support measures
EW	electronic warfare
FCS	fire control system
FLIR	forward looking infra-red
FMS	foreign military sales
fob	free on board
ft	feet
GBU	glide bomb unit
GCC	Gulf Cooperation Council
GDP	gross domestic product
h	hours
HAWK	homing all the way killer
HE	high explosive
HEAT	high explosive anti tank
HUD	heads up display (in combat aircraft)
IFCS	Integrated fire control system
IFV	infantry fighting vehicle
IIR	imaging infra-red
Inf.	Infantry
IR	infra-red
IRCM	infra-red counter measures
IRLS	infra-red linescan
ITV	improved tow vehicle
KDP	Kurdistan Democratic Party
KFOR	Kosovo Force (NATO)
kg	kilogram
km	kilometer
kw	kilowatt
Laser	light amplification by stimulated emission of radiation
LCM	landing craft, mechanized
LCT	landing craft, tank
LCU	landing craft, utility
LCVP	landing craft, vehicle/personnel
LSM	landing ship, mechanized
LST	landing ship, tank
LWS	laser warning system
m	million / meter
max	maximum
MBT	main battle tank
Mech.	mechanized

ABBREVIATIONS *(CONTINUED)*

MFPB	missile fast patrol boat
MG	machine gun
Mk	mark
MLRS	multiple-launch rocket system
mm	millimeter
MRL	multiple-rocket launcher
MTI	moving target indication radar
Mw	megawatt
NATO	North Atlantic Treaty Organization
Nav	navigation
NPT	Non-Proliferation Treaty
op	operational
OWS	over-head weapons station
PGM	precision-guided munition
PKK	Kurdish Workers' Party
PLO	Palestine Liberation Organization
PRC	People's Republic of China
PUK	People's Union of Kurdistan
R&D	research and development
reconn.	reconnaissance
SAM	surface-to-air missile
SAP	semi-armor piercing
SAR	search and rescue / synthetic aperture radar
SIGINT	signal intelligence
SLAR	sideways-looking airborne radar
SP	self-propelled
sq	square
SSM	surface-to-surface missile
SWARM	stabilized weapons and reconnaissance mount
TAB	towed assault bridge
TEL	transport erector launcher
TIPH	Temporary International Presence in Hebron
TLB	trailer launched bridge
TOW	tube-launched optically-tracked wire-guided
TV	television
TWMP	track-width mine plough
UAE	United Arab Emirates
UAV	unmanned aerial vehicle
UFO	unidentified flying object
UK	United Kingdom
UN	United Nations

ABBREVIATIONS *(CONTINUED)*

UNDOF	United Nations Disengagement Observer Force (Golan Heights)
UNAMSIL	United Nations Armed Mission in Sierra Leone
UNIFIL	United Nations Interim force in Lebanon
UNIKOM	United Nations Iraq-Kuwait Observation Mission
UNMEE	United Nations Mission in Ethiopia and Eritrea
UNMIBH	United Nations Mission in Bosnia and Herzegovina
UNMOVIC	United Nations Monitoring, Verification and Inspection Commission (in Iraq)
UNOMIG	United Nations Observer Mission In Georgia
UNSC	United Nations Security Council
UNSCOM	United Nations Special Commission (in Iraq)
UNTSO	United Nations Truce Supervision Organization
US	United States of America
WAC	weapon aiming computer

Contributors

Shlomo Brom

Brig. Gen. (res.) Shlomo Brom joined the Jaffee Center as a Senior Research Associate in late 1998. From 1970 to 1987, he held several posts in the Israeli Air Force, and served as Defense Attaché at the Israeli Embassy in the Republic of South Africa from 1988 to 1990. From 1990 to 1998, he served as Deputy Chief and then Chief of the Strategic Planning Division of the Israel Defense Forces. Brom also edited the qualitative section of the *Middle East Military Balance, 1999-2000.*

Yiftah Shapir

Yiftah Shapir joined the Jaffee Center in 1993 as an associate of the Center's Project on Security and Arms Control in the Middle East, where he followed proliferation of weapons of mass destruction (WMD) in the Middle East. Since 1996, he has been responsible for the quantitative section of *The Middle East Military Balance*. Before joining the center, Shapir served as an officer in the Israeli Air Force. He holds a B.Sc. degree in physics and chemistry from the Hebrew University of Jerusalem, and an MBA from the Recanati School of Business Administration at Tel Aviv University.

BCSIA Studies in International Security
Published by The MIT Press

Sean M. Lynn-Jones and Steven E. Miller, series editors
Karen Motley, executive editor
Belfer Center for Science and International Affairs (BCSIA)
John F. Kennedy School of Government, Harvard University

Allison, Graham T., Owen R. Coté, Jr., Richard A. Falkenrath, and Steven E. Miller, *Avoiding Nuclear Anarchy: Containing the Threat of Loose Russian Nuclear Weapons and Fissile Material* (1996)

Allison, Graham T., and Kalypso Nicolaïdis, eds., *The Greek Paradox: Promise vs. Performance* (1996)

Arbatov, Alexei, Abram Chayes, Antonia Handler Chayes, and Lara Olson, eds., *Managing Conflict in the Former Soviet Union: Russian and American Perspectives* (1997)

Bennett, Andrew, *Condemned to Repetition? The Rise, Fall, and Reprise of Soviet-Russian Military Interventionism, 1973–1996* (1999)

Blackwill, Robert D., and Michael Stürmer, eds., *Allies Divided: Transatlantic Policies for the Greater Middle East* (1997)

Blackwill, Robert D., and Paul Dibb, eds., *America's Asian Allies* (2000)

Brom, Shlomo, and Yiftah Shapir, eds.,*The Middle East Military Balance 1999–2000* (1999)

Brom, Shlomo, and Yiftah Shapir, eds.,*The Middle East Military Balance 2001–2002* (2002)

Brown, Michael E., ed., *The International Dimensions of Internal Conflict* (1996)

Brown, Michael E., and Sumit Ganguly, eds., *Government Policies and Ethnic Relations in Asia and the Pacific* (1997)

Carter, Ashton B., and John P. White, eds., *Keeping the Edge: Managing Defense for the Future* (2001)

Elman, Colin, and Miriam Fendius Elman, eds., *Bridges and Boundaries: Historians, Political Scientists, and the Study of International Relations* (2001)

Elman, Miriam Fendius, ed., *Paths to Peace: Is Democracy the Answer?* (1997)

Falkenrath, Richard A., *Shaping Europe's Military Order: The Origins and Consequences of the CFE Treaty* (1994)

Falkenrath; Richard A., Robert D. Newman, and Bradley A. Thayer, *America's Achilles' Heel: Nuclear, Biological, and Chemical Terrorism and Covert Attack* (1998)

Feaver, Peter D., and Richard H. Kohn, eds., *Soldiers and Civilians: The Civil-Military Gap and American National Security* (2001)

Feldman, Shai, *Nuclear Weapons and Arms Control in the Middle East* (1996)

Feldman, Shai, and Yiftah Shapir, eds.,*The Middle East Military Balance 2000–2001* (2001)

Forsberg, Randall, ed., *The Arms Production Dilemma: Contraction and Restraint in the World Combat Aircraft Industry* (1994)

Hagerty, Devin T., *The Consequences of Nuclear Proliferation: Lessons from South Asia* (1998)

Heymann, Philip B., *Terrorism and America: A Commonsense Strategy for a Democratic Society* (1998)

Kokoshin, Andrei A., *Soviet Strategic Thought, 1917–91* (1998)

Lederberg, Joshua, *Biological Weapons: Limiting the Threat* (1999)

Shields, John M., and William C. Potter, eds., *Dismantling the Cold War: U.S. and NIS Perspectives on the Nunn-Lugar Cooperative Threat Reduction Program* (1997)

Tucker, Jonathan B., ed., *Toxic Terror: Assessing Terrorist Use of Chemical and Biological Weapons* (2000)

Utgoff, Victor A., ed., *The Coming Crisis: Nuclear Proliferation, U.S. Interests, and World Order* (2000)

Williams, Cindy, ed., *Holding the Line: U.S. Defense Alternatives for the Early 21st Century* (2001)

The Robert and Renée Belfer Center for Science and International Affairs

Graham Allison, Director
John F. Kennedy School of Government
Harvard University
79 JFK Street
Cambridge, MA 02138

Tel: (617) 495-1400; Fax: (617) 495-8963; E-mail: bcsia_ksg@harvard.edu
http://www.ksg.harvard.edu/bcsia

The Belfer Center for Science and International Affairs (BCSIA) is the hub of research, teaching, and training in international security affairs, environmental and resource issues, science and technology policy, human rights, and conflict studies at Harvard's John F. Kennedy School of Government. The Center's mission is to provide leadership in advancing policy-relevant knowledge about the most important challenges of international security and other critical issues where science, technology, and international affairs intersect.

BCSIA's leadership begins with the recognition of science and technology as driving forces transforming international affairs. The Center integrates insights of social scientists, natural scientists, technologists, and practitioners with experience in government, diplomacy, the military, and business to address these challenges. The Center pursues its mission in five complementary research programs:

- The International Security Program (ISP) addresses the most pressing threats to U.S. national interests and international security.

- The Environment and Natural Resources Program (ENRP) is the locus of Harvard's interdisciplinary research on resource and environmental problems and policy responses.

- The Science, Technology, and Public Policy Program (STPP) analyzes ways in which science and technology policy influence international security, resources, environment, and development, and such cross-cutting issues as technological innovation and information infrastructure.

- The Strengthening Democratic Institutions Project (SDI) catalyzes support for three great transformations in Russia, Ukraine, and the other former Soviet republics--to sustainable democracies, free market economies, and cooperative international relations.

- The WPF Program on Intrastate Conflict, Conflict Prevention, and Conflict Resolution analyzes the causes of ethnic, religious, and other conflicts, and seeks to identify practical ways to prevent and limit such conflicts.

The heart of the Center is its resident research community of more than 140 scholars: Harvard faculty, analysts, practitioners, and each year a new, interdisciplinary group of research fellows. BCSIA sponsors frequent seminars, workshops, and conferences, maintains a substantial specialized library, and publishes books, monographs, and discussion papers.

The Center's International Security Program, directed by Steven E. Miller, publishes the BCSIA Studies in International Security, and sponsors and edits the quarterly journal *International Security*.

The Center is supported by an endowment established with funds from Robert and Renée Belfer, the Ford Foundation and Harvard University, by foundation grants, by individual gifts, and by occasional government contracts.